T0315131

THE IDEA OF A MORAL ECONOMY

Gerard of Siena on Usury, Restitution, and Prescription

Giotto di Bondone, *The Last Judgment* (detail), Arena Chapel, Padua

The Idea of a Moral Economy

Gerard of Siena on Usury, Restitution, and Prescription

LAWRIN ARMSTRONG

UNIVERSITY OF TORONTO PRESS
Toronto Buffalo London

© University of Toronto Press 2016
Toronto Buffalo London
www.utppublishing.com

ISBN 978-1-4426-4322-2

Library and Archives Canada Cataloguing in Publication

Gerardus, de Senis, –1336?, author
The idea of a moral economy : Gerard of Siena on usury, restitution, and prescription /
[edited and translated by] Lawrin Armstrong.

(Toronto studies in medieval law)
Includes the Latin text and English translations of: Quaestio de usura; Tractatus de
restitution; and Quaestio de praescriptione.
Includes bibliographical references and index.
Includes text in English and Latin.
ISBN 978-1-4426-4322-2 (bound)

1. Gerardus, de Senis, –1336? Quaestio de usura.   2. Gerardus, de Senis, –1336?
Tractatus de restitution.   3. Gerardus, de Senis, –1336? Quaestio de praescriptione.
4. Usury – Early works to 1800.   5. Restitution – Early works to 1800.   6. Prescription
(Law) – Early works to 1800.   7. Economics – Moral and ethical aspects – Early works
to 1800.   8. Natural law – Early works to 1800.   9. Law, Medieval.   10. Philosophy,
Medieval.   11. Theology – History – Middle Ages, 600–1500.   I. Armstrong, Lawrin
D. (Lawrin David), editor, translator   II. Gerardus, de Senis, –1336? Works.   Selec-
tions.   III. Gerardus, de Senis, –1336?   Works.   Selections.   English.   IV. Title.
V. Series: Toronto studies in medieval law

HB79.G47 2016   330.109′02   C2015-907224-7

This book has been published with the help of a grant from the Federation for the
Humanities and Social Sciences, through the Awards to Scholarly Publications Program,
using funds provided by the Social Sciences and Humanities Research Council of
Canada.

University of Toronto Press gratefully acknowledges the financial assistance of the
Centre for Medieval Studies, University of Toronto in the publication of this book.

University of Toronto Press acknowledges the financial assistance to its publishing
program of the Canada Council for the Arts and the Ontario Arts Council, an agency
of the Government of Ontario.

Zum Andenken an

ERWIN WILL
1924–1999

und

MARIANNE WILL (GEB. RITTER)
1933–2014

Saepe etiam cupidis argentum inmane coruscat
Accenditque animos auri fallentis amore
Delusos fugiens uano phantasmate tactus.

To the avaricious, he often appears as a glittering heap of silver
and inflames their minds with lust for false gold,
but touched, he flees such fools like an empty fantasy.

Avitus, *De spiritalis historiae gestis* 2. 66–8.

E perché l'usuriere altra via tene,
   per sé natura e per la sua seguace
   dispregia, poi ch'in altro pon la spene.

But the usurer contrives a third way yet,
   And in herself and her follower, Art,
   Scorns Nature, for his hope is elsewhere set.

Dante, *Inferno* 11.109–11 (trans. D.L. Sayers)

Mit der Entwicklung des zinstragenden Kapitals und des Kreditsystems
scheint sich alles Kapital zu verdoppeln und stellenweis zu verdreifachen
durch die verschiedne Weise, worin dasselbe Kapital oder auch nur dieselbe
Schuldforderung in verschiednen Händen unter verschiednen Formen
erscheint. Der größte Teil dieses 'Geldkapitals' ist rein fiktiv ... In diesen
Tatsachen, daß sogar eine Akkumulation von Schulden als Akkumulation von
Kapital erscheinen kann, zeigt sich die Vollendung der Verdrehung, die im
Kreditsystem stattfindet.

With the development of interest-bearing capital and the credit system, all
capital seems to be duplicated, and at some points triplicated by the various
ways in which the same capital, or even the same claim, appears in various
hands in different guises. The greater part of this 'money capital' is purely
fictitious ... In the way that even an accumulation of debts can appear as an
accumulation of capital, we see the distortion involved in the credit system
reach its culmination.

Marx, *Das Kapital, Volume 3*, 29–30 (trans. D. Fernbach)

Contents

Preface and Acknowledgments

Few would deny that the crisis precipitated by the collapse of Lehman Brothers in 2008, which, as I write, shows every sign of entering a fresh circuit of instability, is a crisis of what Marx called 'fictitious capital,' or credit. Confronted by stagnating markets, themselves the product of the defeat of organized labour and static or declining real wages since the late 1970s, capital has increasingly bypassed production in favour of financial speculation – above all, speculation in asset values – to maintain profits. The result has been a massive expansion of debt – a recent calculation puts total private and public debt at 212 per cent of global GDP, an increase of 38 per cent since 2008 – a series of destructive devaluations, and the dramatic enrichment of a tiny global oligarchy. The social and political consequences are clear: mass unemployment, political instability, and skewed wealth distributions, not just between the developed and developing worlds, but within the advanced economies themselves, which have witnessed levels of material inequality unknown since the Great Depression.

The crisis has inspired several Marxist and neo-Keynesian critiques of the neoliberal program responsible for the débâcle of 2008. These have been matched by renewed attention to pre-capitalist traditions of moral economy among historians, anthropologists, sociologists, and non-orthodox economists seeking to imagine an economic order dedicated to the common good rather than to private profit and limitless growth. This book, though begun before the crisis, is conceived as a modest contribution to the latter literature. It offers an edition and translation of three questions disputed in Paris in 1330 by the Augustinian friar and master of theology Gerard of Siena on the topics of usury, the restitution of usurious profits, and prescription (a mode of acquiring ownership of real property). Together they offer a particularly lucid example of scholastic ideas

about the nature and purpose of economic activity and as such, I hope, can help us to situate our present predicament in a longer historical and moral perspective than the one offered by contemporary economics. Although Gerard was a theologian, he framed his questions largely in legal terms or in response to commonly held legal opinions. Moreover, his views on usury and prescription were taken up and popularized by the most famous canonist of his day, Giovanni d'Andrea, so it seems appropriate that this edition appears as the third volume of the Toronto Studies in Medieval Law series.

The research for this project was funded by a fellowship from the Social Sciences and Humanities Research Council Institutional Grant Fund of the University of Toronto and by a Director's research stipend from the Faculty of Arts and Science in 2007–8, whose support is acknowledged with thanks. I wish to record my thanks to the Universitätsbibliothek, Leipzig, and the Biblioteca Angelica, Rome, for permission to consult the manuscripts on which this edition is based, and to the personnel of both libraries for their kind assistance. I am also grateful to the Bodleian Library and the Österreichische Nationalbibliothek for supplying copies of manuscripts and early printed editions in their collections. Julius Kirshner of the University of Chicago kindly read an early typescript and saved me from many errors; Martin Pickavé of the University of Toronto helped me identify citations from Aristotle and explained several philosophical terms; and the anonymous referees retained by the University of Toronto Press offered many useful suggestions. I am particularly indebted to Giulio Silano of St Michael's College and the University of Toronto for permission to quote from his forthcoming translation of Gratian's *Decretum*. Thanks are due as well to Shami Ghosh, currently a Mellon fellow of the Pontifical Institute of Mediaeval Studies, for the many hours we have spent over the past eight years discussing problems in economic history and the relationship between scholarship and political action. I wish to thank Suzanne Rancourt of the University of Toronto Press for her encouragement of the TSML series and Barbara Porter and Judy Williams of the University of Toronto Press for their splendid copyediting. Finally, I am grateful to my wife Johanna Will-Armstrong for her encouragement in the completion of this long overdue book.

Bielefeld
25 March 2015

THE IDEA OF A MORAL ECONOMY

Introduction

On the feast of the Annunciation (25 March), 1303, a chapel in honour of Santa Maria della Carità was dedicated in Padua.[1] Adjoining the new palace constructed on the site of a Roman arena by Enrico Scrovegni, one of the city's richest citizens, the 'Arena' chapel, as it is commonly known, was designed both as a mausoleum for the Scrovegni and as a venue for civic celebrations of the Annunciation. Enrico spared no effort or expense in the adornment of his oratory: he retained the leading artists of his day, the sculptor Giovanni Pisano and the painter Giotto di Bondone, to decorate the interior, and in March 1304 he obtained from Benedict XI a generous dispensation of a year and forty days for those who visited the chapel on the four great Marian feasts of the Nativity of the Virgin (8 September), the Annunciation, the Purification (2 February), and the Assumption (15 August).

There can be little doubt that the Arena chapel was also intended as an expiatory offering for sin: Enrico's father, Reginaldo, famously consigned to hell by Dante, had been the among the most successful and notorious usurers of the Veneto, and until 1300, when the Jubilee seems to have induced a change of heart, Enrico himself numbered among the region's leading moneylenders.[2] This interpretation of Enrico's motives is confirmed not only by Giotto's Last Judgment on the west wall, which prominently

---

1 For the details that follow, I am indebted to the superb study of the Arena chapel by Derbes and Sandona, *Usurer's Heart*, especially 1–43, which offers rich evidence on the civic and biographical significance of the chapel, and 44–83 on the juxtaposition of usury and charity.

2 *Inferno* 17.64–75.

features the donor and his confessor presenting the chapel to the Virgin, but by the elaborate fresco cycle illustrating episodes from the life of the Virgin and of Christ that occupies the remaining walls. The cycle contains many iconographic peculiarities – most notably the inclusion of several rare or unprecedented narratives – and eccentric juxtapositions, such as the pact of Judas and the Visitation opposite one another on the chancel arch. As Anne Derbes and Mark Sandona have recently argued, however, this and several other unexpected oppositions illustrate the contradictions between 'usury and charity, sterility and fertility, unnatural generation and supernatural generation,' themes that echo the unanimous verdict of contemporary moralists on usury.[3] According to Dante, for example, the usurer is to be condemned because he

> Contrives a third way yet,
>> And in herself and her follower, Art,
>> Scorns Nature, for his hope is elsewhere set.[4]

Indeed, in an opposition reminiscent of Giotto, the poet pairs the damned moneylenders, who render fruitful what is naturally sterile (coin), with the sodomites, whose sin consists in rendering sterile what is naturally fruitful (the sex act), in the seventh circle of Hell, where they endure a perpetual rain of fire.[5] The idea that usury was a perversion of nature did not, of course, originate with Dante or Giotto: Aristotle condemned the breeding of coins from coins in the *Politics*, remarking that 'of all modes of getting wealth this is the most unnatural.'[6]

The Philosopher's authority was invoked by most scholastic commentators of the later twelfth and thirteenth century, such as Thomas Aquinas, from whom Dante almost certainly took the idea. The reformulation of the argument by a contemporary of Dante and Giotto, the Augustinian hermit and master of theology Gerard of Siena (✝ ca. 1336), who maintained that the unnaturalness of usury consisted in causing 'a natural thing to transcend its nature and an artificial thing to transcend the skill that made it,' enjoyed particular prestige in the fourteenth and fifteenth century, es-

---

3 Derbes and Sandona, *Usurer's Heart*, 83.
4 *Inferno* 11.109–11 (trans. Sayers).
5 A similar preoccupation is reflected in the grotesque tortures of sexual transgressors in Giotto's Last Judgment; for a detailed interpretation linking sexual and commercial sin, see Derbes and Sandona, *Usurer's Heart*, 65–70.
6 *Politics* 1.10.1258b (trans. Jowett in *Basic Works of Aristotle*, 1141).

pecially after it was adopted by Giovanni d'Andrea (Iohannes Andreae), the pre-eminent canonist of the day, in a disputed question included in his own *Quaestiones mercuriales* (*Wednesday Questions*) on the title *De regulis iuris* (*On the rules of law*) of the *Liber sextus*.[7] Contemporaries acknowledged – and modern scholars agree – that Gerard's was the most elegant and persuasive version of the natural law argument against usury, and one that largely held the field until it was undermined by debates in the early sixteenth century about the so-called triple contract, which implicitly attributed fertility to commercial capital.[8]

Gerard's *Questio de usura* remains his most enduring contribution to scholastic economics, but two additional questions he disputed at the same time on the restitution of usury and the acquisition of real property by prescription merit attention in their own right. Giovanni d'Andrea considered the *Questio de prescriptione* sufficiently acute to incorporate it, along with an extensive critique, into his own *quaestio* on the rule *Possessor non praescribit* of the *Liber sextus*; and the *Tractatus de restitutione* presents a particularly lucid and rigorous formulation of the scholastic doctrine on the restitution of usury. Modern scholarship, however, has overlooked two additional themes of Gerard's trilogy that explain why the questions were disputed as a group and treated as such in the only surviving manuscript that contains all three. The first is the problem of the conflict of laws: together, the questions constitute a threefold, interlocking treatise on the contradictions between canon and Roman law on each of the topics considered.[9] The second concerns the nature of ownership (*dominium*), a matter that was the subject of intense controversy in the early fourteenth century because of debates about apostolic poverty and Fran-

---

7 To the extent that Gerard's argument has often been attributed to the more famous canonist in the modern scholarship; see, for example, Noonan, *Scholastic Analysis*, 67, and, most recently, Tierney, *Liberty and Law*, 142–56. The correct attribution was established as long ago as 1984 by Langholm, *Aristotelian Analysis*, 30–1; and idem, *Economics in the Medieval Schools*, 550, 556–7.

8 On Gerard's argument, see also Langholm, *Aristotelian Analysis*, 75–90; idem, *Economics in the Medieval Schools*, 549–60; and Armstrong, 'Law, Ethics and Economy,' 47–56. On the triple contract, see Noonan, *Scholastic Analysis*, 202–29. It is not impossible that Gerard was familiar with Giotto's cycle: the Arena chapel virtually abutted the church of the *Eremitani* of Padua, who formally complained to the bishop in 1305 about its extravagance; Derbes and Sandona, *Usurer's Heart*, 2.

9 For a review of the contradictions between medieval canonistic and Romanist opinion on usury in particular, see McLaughlin, 'Teaching of the Canonists,' 1:84–98.

ciscan *usus pauper* (poor use).[10] Both usury and prescription in bad faith represented illegitimate modes of acquiring ownership par excellence.

Gerard of Siena

We know very little about the life and career of Gerard of Siena.[11] As the toponym indicates, he was Sienese, possibly patrician by birth, and joined the Augustinian hermits, perhaps in the first decade of the fourteenth century. Gerard's familiarity with the canons and *leges* suggests that he might have studied law, perhaps in Bologna, the biggest Italian centre for legal studies, before entering the order and proceeding to Paris, where he 'read' (that is, lectured on) the *Sentences* of Peter Lombard as a bachelor in 1319–21.[12] He incepted as Master of Theology in 1329 or 1330, and the university cartulary records that he presided as regent master in the latter year.[13] Gerard's commentary on the first two books of the *Sentences* was highly esteemed in the fifteenth century and survives in thirty manuscripts; his *Quodlibet* appears to have been less widely diffused and is represented by only two manuscripts.[14] Gerard returned to Italy soon after he was licensed, participating in the general chapter of his order in Venice in 1332 and lecturing in Bologna and Siena before his death around 1336.[15]

The Questions

Gerard's authorship of the *Questio de usura*, the *Tractatus de restitutione*, and the *Questio de prescriptione* is not in doubt, but the manuscript tradition raises questions about the genre to which they should be assigned: should we classify them as examples of curricular disputed questions, as a series of short, thematically related treatises, or as extra-curricular

---

10 On the whole subject, see most recently the valuable study by Robinson, *William of Ockham's Early Theory of Property Rights*.

11 For the scant details, see Schulte, *Geschichte*, 2:204–5; Glorieux, *La littérature quodlibétique*, 2:97; Zumkeller, 'Die Augustinerschule,' 208–9; Langholm, *Economics in the Medieval Schools*, 549; Schabel and Courtenay, 'Augustinian *Quodlibeta*,' 557–8; and Courtenay, 'Sentences Commentary,' 247–52.

12 Ibid., 249–50. On the typical stages of a mendicant academic career and the difficulties with estimating the age of friars on the basis of the date of inception, see Courtenay, 'Instructional Programme.'

13 Denifle and Châtelain, eds, *Chartularium Universitatis Parisiensis*, 2:339 (no. 904).

14 Schabel and Courtenay, 'Augustinian *Quodlibeta*,' 557–8.

15 Courtenay, 'Sentences Commentary,' 251.

quodlibetal questions?[16] As a group, they survive in a single manuscript preserved in the Biblioteca Angelica, Rome, cod. 625, where they were copied together after a selection of questions from Gerard's quodlibet; they are not included in the only other extant copy of the quodlibet, Munich, Bayerische Staatsbibliothek, Clm 26309. The length (five folios each) and complexity of the questions (two are divided into five, one into six articles or sub-questions) set them apart from the quodlibetals, which are considerably shorter (usually about a folio) and less elaborate. It appears, moreover, that at least two questions circulated as free-standing texts: a longer recension of the *Questio de usura* is preserved in a miscellany of theological and canonistic material in MS 894 of the Universitätsbibliothek, Leipzig; and extracts from both the *Questio de usura* and the *Tractatus de restitutione* are contained in a manuscript in the Österreichische Nationalbibliothek (Vindob. 4151). Finally, although the copyist of the Rome manuscript entitles the second question *tractatus* (at fols 209ra and 214ra), he also describes it in an earlier rubric as a *quaestio* (fol. 208vb; see below), thus leaving open the question of genre.

The topics, all of which are framed in terms of law rather than theology – and it is notable that some 80 per cent of Gerard's authorities are legal – are typically quodlibetal, and the Leipzig version of the *Questio de usura* contains an appendix rebutting a series of arguments and cases of exactly the kind one would expect to be aired in the opening stages of a quodlibetal session. Nor is length alone grounds for excluding the questions from Gerard's quodlibet, since other fourteenth-century examples of the genre were often quite as long.[17] More to the point, however, the Rome manuscript states clearly that the questions derive from Gerard's quodlibet: not only does the copyist note at both the incipit (fol. 209ra)[18] and the explicit (fol. 225ra)[19] of the trilogy that Gerard disputed the questions at Paris, the venue for his quodlibet of 1330, but also at fol. 208v, immediately following quodlibetal 14, he remarks in a rather garbled passage that

> It was said earlier that two quodlibetals were held by this master with special attention to mutual human acts insofar as they touch on the just or the unjust.

16 The problems are clearly summarized by Schabel and Courtenay, 'Augustinian *Quodlibeta*,' 560–1. On quodlibetal disputations, see below, 10–11.

17 Hamesse, 'Theological *Quaestiones Quodlibetales*,' 31.

18 'Incipit questio de usura cum .v. articulis infrascriptis, et cum quodam tractatu addito de restitucione usurarum continente .4. alios articulos, determinata Parisius a fratre Gerardo de Senis in sacra theologia magistro fratrum heremitarum ordinis sancti Augustini.'

19 See below, 20/114–15.

Because by such mutual acts one person can conclude a usurious contract with another, it was first asked whether a usurious contract is permissible by any law; second, whether a usurer can be absolved of the obligation incurred by usury without restitution or in some other way. These two questions, as well as another two that follow on prescription, I have included here in the quodlibet, but I have placed them together, along with certain other, related questions; and if someone wants to have them without the preceding questions, he can.[20]

The questions that begin at fol. 209ra of the Rome manuscript are each introduced by a preamble that outlines the principal problem and the structure of the question, followed by five articles (six in the *Questio de prescriptione*). In the Leipzig manuscript, the fifth article of the *Questio de usura* is followed by an appendix – promised in the preamble to both manuscripts but omitted from the Rome copy – in which Gerard responds to various arguments that appear to contradict his conclusions. The resulting twenty subdivisions treat the following topics (drawn from the incipits of each section in the Rome manuscript):[21]

Questio de usura

1. Vtrum contractus usurarius sit permissibilis in aliquo iure. (*Whether a usurious contract is permissible by any law.*)
2. Art. 1: Quid est usura et in quibus rebus commictitur? (*What is usury and in what things is it committed?*)
3. Art. 2: Vtrum contractus usurarius ex natura rei viciosus et malicia convolutus. (*Whether a usurious contract is by its very nature wicked and bound up with vice.*)

---

20 'Vlterius dicebatur superius quod isto magistro in speciali ad actus humanos que [*pro* qui] sunt ad alterum secundum quod in eis racio iusti vel iniusti fiebant due quidditates [*pro* quodlibetales?]. Nam quia per tales actus ad alterum potest habere unus homo contractum usurarium cum aliquo homine, idcirco querebatur primo utrum contractus usurarius sit permissibilis aliquo iure; secundo utrum usurarius possit absolvi ab obligacione usurarum sine restitucione vel per aliquam aliam viam. Has duas conclusiones [*pro* questiones] necnon et alias duas sequentes de prospectione [*pro* prescriptione] sic incorporeum [*pro* incorporavi] hic quemlibet [*pro* quodlibet?], quia vero ordinavi eas per se cum quibusdam aliis questionibus annexis, et si quis eas voluit habere sine precedentibus questionibus eas possit habere' (fol. 208vb).
21 I retain the orthography of the manuscript, thus 'commictitur' for 'commititur,' 'viciosus' for 'vitiosus,' etc.

4. Art. 3: Vtrum iura debeant permictere contractum usurarium propter aliquod bonum quod inde oriatur vel propter aliquod malum quod inde vitetur. (*Whether the laws should permit a usurious contract on account of some good that might follow or to avoid an evil that might thereby be avoided.*)

5. Art. 4: Vtrum in aliquo casu de facto usurarius contractus sit concessus vel permissus a iure. (*Whether a usurious contract is allowed or tolerated by the law in any specific case.*)

6. Art. 5: Vtrum ius civile possit iure canonico obviare vel utrum dicta iura habeant ad se invicem tantam concordiam quod quidquid est contra unum necessario sit contra alterum ac per consequens utrum contractus usurarius eo ipso quod prohibitus est in iure canonico sit prohibitus eciam in iure civili. (*Whether civil law can oppose canon law or whether the two laws are in such mutual accord that whatever is contrary to one is necessarily contrary to the other, and consequently whether, by the very fact that canon law prohibits usurious contracts, civil law prohibits them as well.*)

7. Solutio rationum ad oppositum. (*Solution of arguments to the contrary.*) [In the Leipzig manuscript only].

Tractatus de restitutione

8. Hic incipit tractatus de restitucione usurarum et quorumcumque male ablatorum. (*Here begins the treatise on the restitution of usury and other things wickedly appropriated.*)

9. Art. 1: Vtrum usurarius acquirat aliquod dominium in usura per quod videatur non teneri ad restitucionem. (*Whether a usurer acquires such ownership by means of usury that he might appear free of the obligation to make restitution.*)

10. Art. 2: Vtrum restitucio usurarum requirat aliquam formam cum aliquibus circumstanciis servatam. (*Whether it is necessary to observe some form in the restitution of usury that takes into account the relevant circumstances.*)

11. Art. 3: Vtrum usurarius non reddendo usuras nec aliquam caucionem pro eis reddendis faciendo possit liberari ab earum obligacione per viam remissionis vel per aliquam aliam viam. (*Whether a usurer, without making restitution or posting a pledge to make restitution, can be freed of this obligation either by remission or in some other way.*)

12. Art. 4: Vtrum usurarius teneatur restituere non solum usuram extortam sed etiam totum illud quod per eam lucratus est. (*Whether a usu-*

rer is obliged to restore not only the usury he extorted but also all the profits he gained by means of it.)

13. Art. 5: Vtrum usurarius in restituendo debeat servare aliquem ordinem, ita quod prius restituat uni quam alteri. (*Whether a usurer should observe some order in making restitution such that he makes restitution to one in preference to another.*)

Questio de prescriptione

14. Incipit questio de prescripcione cum VI articulis. (*Here begins the question on prescription in six articles.*)
15. Art. 1: Quid sit prescripcio? (*What is prescription?*)
16. Art. 2: Vtrum prescripcio sit contra ius nature. (*Whether prescription is contrary to natural law.*)
17. Art. 3: Vtrum prescripcio iuris canonici debuit esse alia et distincta a prescripcione iuris civilis. (*Whether prescription in canon law should be different and distinct from prescription in civil law.*)
18. Art. 4: Vtrum in prescripcione acquiratur dominium. (*Whether ownership is acquired by means of prescription.*)
19. Art. 5: Vtrum prescribens mala fide debeat censeri cum raptore vel cum fure sive in qua alia specie peccati sit locandus. (*Whether a prescriber in bad faith should be classified with the thief or robber, or classified with some other species of sinner.*)
20. Art. 6: Vtrum mala fides adveniens prescripcione completa tollat prescripcionem et utrum obliget prescribentem ad restitucionem secundum iura canonica quemadmodum mala fides preveniens. (*Whether bad faith emerging after prescription is complete breaks it and whether it obliges the prescriber to make restitution in accordance with canon law, just like a prescriber in bad faith.*)

The rubric at fol. 208vb of the Rome manuscript refers to *two* questions on prescription: it appears that this is because Gerard himself regarded article 6 of the *Questio de prescriptione* as an additional question beyond the scope of the principal inquiry, which was whether prescription is contrary to natural law.

It seems therefore most likely that the questions on usury, restitution, and prescription do indeed represent part of Gerard's quodlibet but that we have them in a revised and considerably augmented form prepared for publication by the university stationer, perhaps as a free-standing trilogy. Such definitive redactions, known as *ordinationes*, were the product of a

process that began in the quodlibetal sessions themselves.[22] Held twice a year – in Advent and Lent – the disputes were presided over by masters of theology and open to the entire university and to the public. In contrast to formal, intramural debates tied to the curriculum (*disputationes* or *quaestiones disputatae*), masters were not obliged to preside over the lively and often unpredictable quodlibetal sessions, during which, as the name suggests, any question 'whatsoever' (*quodlibet*) might be put from the floor. Nevertheless, for the masters who chose to preside, quodlibetal disputations provided an opportunity to parade their erudition and dialectical virtuosity.

During the first session, the master's bachelor assistants supplied provisonal responses to the questions in the form of arguments for and against the various propositions. Minutes (*reportationes*) of the arguments, objections, and refutations were recorded by the bachelors or a university scribe. After two or three days, a second session, the *determinatio*, was held, when, on the basis of the notes taken by his assistants, the master summarized the arguments in support or refutation of the propositions raised in the opening session and offered his own definitive resolution of each question. In the case of Gerard's questions on usury and restitution, traces of the initial oral debate survive in the master's replies to the arguments of the *opponentes* at the end of each. Often a long period separated the second quodlibetal session and the master's redaction of a definitive text, in which he might elaborate on any of the points raised in the oral sessions, enrich his exposition with additional authorities, and purge the text of the oral and ad hoc features of the original disputations.

Economics, Theology, and Law

Economics understood as an autonomous discipline that 'studies human behaviour as a relationship between ends and scarce means which have alternative uses' did not exist in the Middle Ages; it was an invention of the late eighteenth and nineteenth century.[23] Scholastic thinkers nevertheless reflected extensively on matters that we would describe as 'economic' in a variety of genres, such as Gerard's quodlibetal questions, but also in

---

22 For what follows, I am indebted to Hamesse, 'Theological *Quaestiones Quodlibetales*,' 30–8.

23 The definition is from Robbins, *An Essay*, 16. For a broader definition of economics, see the elegant and amusing introduction to the whole subject by Chang, *Economics*.

thematic treatises, in *summae* compiled for the use of confessors, in sermons, and in commentaries on Aristotle, on Peter Lombard, and on the systematic compilations of law, namely, the *Corpus iuris civilis* of Justinian, Gratian's *Decretum*, and the medieval collections of papal law.[24] Scholastic economic analysis was sometimes directly prompted by developments in the 'commercial revolution' of the twelfth and thirteenth century – as treatises on money, exchange, and debasement by Henry of Ghent, John Buridan, and Nicholas Oresme attest – but analysis arising from lectures and debates in the schools tended to be prescriptive and normative rather than descriptive, explanatory, or predictive.[25] The reason for this is clear, if insufficiently acknowledged in the modern literature. In all pre-capitalist societies, economic relations were dependent upon and subordinated to social and political relations; they were, as the economic historian and anthropologist Karl Polanyi observed, socially and politically 'embedded.'[26] The economic was not conceived as a distinct analytical category or the economy as a sphere of human activity independent of – much less at odds with – the social and the political, as it usually is, for example, in neoliberal economics. For medieval thinkers this meant that markets, exchange, trade, credit, debt, ownership, public finance, and many other matters that we would categorize as economic and subject to their own laws of motion were understood as subordinate to justice, charity, and the common good and therefore pre-eminently amenable to analysis by lawyers, philosophers, and theologians.[27]

The observations of the canonist Sinibaldo dei Fieschi (later Pope Innocent IV) in his commentary on the *Decretals* explaining the usury prohibition in terms of justice and social order illustrate this point:

> Usury is generally prohibited because if it were allowed, all manner of evils would result, above all the abandonment by farmers of their holdings, save when they had no other choice. The result of this would be such dearth that the poor would die of starvation; for even if they had access to workable land

---

24 The most recent synthesis of philosophical and theological opinion is Langholm, *Economics in the Medieval Schools*. On the quodlibetal literature in particular, see the survey of Ceccarelli, '"Whatever" Economics.'

25 On this, see, in particular, Langholm, 'The Medieval Schoolmen,' esp. 439–43.

26 Polanyi, *Great Transformation*, esp. 45–80. For a lucid discussion of Polanyi's thought in the light of the current scholarship and the crisis of 2008, see Dale, *Karl Polanyi*, 188–206.

27 On public finance in particular, see the classic studies of Kirshner, especially his synthetic essay, 'Reading Bernardino's Sermon.'

they would be unable to obtain the livestock and tools they need to farm, since they have no money of their own and the rich would prefer to lend at usury with its higher and more secure returns than to invest their money in less profitable and riskier ventures like farming. The result would be to drive the price of food beyond the means of the poor, from which would arise great danger to the faithful ... Again, it is scarcely ever the case that anyone who pays usury for very long avoids being reduced to poverty, which is a dangerous condition unless it is embraced as a gift of God ... And so it is clear that practically every evil follows from usury, and for this reason it is condemned in both the Old Testament and the New.[28]

Despite Innocent's bland assertion that usury is universally condemned, the two laws – and even theology and canon law – were not always in perfect accord on this and other economic matters.[29] Indeed, a theme that frames each of Gerard's questions is the contradiction between Roman and canon law and, to a lesser extent, between theology and canon law, on usury, restitution, and prescription. Civil law not only tolerated usury, but granted usurers legal title to their profits; moreover, it permitted a measure of bad faith in prescription, which the canons strictly forbade. Theology and canon law also differed on modes of restitution and the degree of good faith required for successful prescription. The analytical tension in each of Gerard's questions is supplied by the status of both the canons and the *leges* as *auctoritates* which, in accordance with the norms of scholastic reasoning, could not be rejected but only interpreted. Thus, although Gerard freely contested the opinions of the *moderni*, particularly the canonists, his main interpretative strategy in each question was to qualify the sense in which Roman law permitted canonically or morally prohibited activities in such a way that the contradiction between the two sources of law evaporated. In my remarks on each question I shall emphasize this dimension of the argument.

Usury

The main question asked by the *Questio de usura* is whether a usurious

---

28 Innocent IV, *In quinque libros Decretalium commentaria*, ad X 5.19 rubr. (Venice, 1570; repr. Frankfurt am Main 2008, fol. 615rb–va).

29 See Armstrong, 'Law, Ethics and Economy' for a fuller discussion of the conflict between theology and canon law with reference to Gerard's *quaestio* on usury.

contract is permissible by any law.[30] The answer is never in doubt for, as Gerard observes at the beginning of article 2, 'it must be said that the conclusion of this article does not appear to be in doubt because the common view, which accords both with the truth and with the opinion of everyone who has considered this matter, is that a usurious contract is by its very nature wicked and bound up with vice' and therefore necessarily prohibited by law. Nevertheless, as Gerard also notes, 'it is not altogether easy to assign a reason for this.' Four observations in particular inspire doubt and structure the question as a whole. The first is the apparent dissonance between the two laws on usury; the second the fact that evils such as usury are arguably tolerable in view of a greater good; the third that canon law in practice allows certain exceptions to the prohibition; and the fourth that it is unclear which of the two laws takes precedence in the event of a conflict.

Gerard's account of the nature and contractual locus of usury (article 1) is conventional: usury is any pre-agreed charge for a loan of things that are measured, weighed, or counted.[31] The definition derives from the Roman law definition of a loan (*mutuum*) of a natural fungible, such as wine, oil, or grain, or an artificial one, such as coin, whose use involved its consumption (or, in the case of coin, its alienation).[32] Roman law classified *mutuum* as a gratuitous agreement, although it permitted a supplementary contract called *stipulatio* by which the borrower agreed to pay interest. The latter, however, was forbidden by the ecclesiastical authorities from the fourth century onward on the basis of the dominical precept at Luke 6.35 to 'lend (*mutuum date*), expecting nothing in return.'

Article 2 elaborates on these basic postulates, demonstrating that usury is 'by the very nature of the thing wicked and bound up with vice.' Gerard

---

30 On the novelty of Gerard's contribution to usury analysis, see also the discussions in Langholm, *Aristotelian Analysis*, 75–90; idem, *Economics in the Medieval Schools*, 549–60; and Armstrong, 'Law, Ethics and Economy,' 46–53.

31 The literature on the medieval usury prohibition is vast. For a comprehensive bibliography, see Barile, 'Credito, usura, prestito a interesse.' Fundamental studies are Noonan, *Scholastic Analysis*; McLaughlin, 'Teaching of the Canonists'; Langholm, *Aristotelian Analysis*; and idem, *Economics in the Medieval Schools*. Significant recent studies include Le Goff, *Your Money or Your Life*; Spicciani, *Capitale e interesse*; and Barile, 'Il dibattito sul prestito a interesse.'

32 Inst. 3.14.pr.: 'Mutui autem obligatio in his rebus consistit, quae pondere numero mensurave constant, veluti vino oleo frumento pecunia numerata aere argento auro.' See also the parallel definition at Dig. 12.1.2.1. The gratuitous loan of a non-fungible was called *commodatum* (Inst. 3.14.2; Dig. 13.6.5.3–5, 8, 9).

notes that, in Roman law, ownership of a *mutuum* is understood to pass to the borrower, who is not obliged to repay the substance of the thing lent but rather its equivalent in terms of quantity and quality. Because the debtor becomes owner of the principal, it is unjust to charge him for the use of what has become his property. A variation of this analysis was proposed by Thomas Aquinas, who observed that it is impossible to separate the ownership of a fungible from its use, since its proper use consists precisely in its consumption. The usurer, however, sells a fungible and its use separately and so illegitimately sells something that does not exist or sells the same thing twice.[33]

Gerard considers both arguments flawed. With respect to the juridical case, he notes that even if ownership of the *substance* of a lent fungible passes to the borrower, it can be maintained that the creditor retains ownership of its economic *value* and that this is the source of his profit rather than the substance. The theological argument is similarly defective because the distinction between the use and ownership of a fungible is purely conceptual; in practice they are necessarily identical, for 'insofar as the creditor transfers the thing itself, he also transfers its use, and vice versa, and therefore he does not separate the one from the other, as this argument supposes.'

Gerard's correction of both Thomas and the jurists has been aptly described by Odd Langholm as a theory of the 'auto-valuation of fungibles.'[34] Beginning with the Roman law definition of a fungible as something that can be 'counted, weighed, or measured,' Gerard proceeds to argue that natural and artificial fungibles derive from their measure, weight, or number a determinate value that remains constant so long as the measure, weight, or number itself remains intact. If the value of such things seems to fluctuate, it is not because of any change in their intrinsic value fixed by number, weight, or measure, but because of changes in the value of the things for which they may be exchanged. A litre of wine is therefore always worth a litre of wine of the same quality, but in terms of something else, for example, coin or goats, it might, say, for reasons of scarcity, be worth more in February than in October. Natural and artificial non-fungibles – for example, farms, boats, vineyards, houses, or donkeys – derive their value from external and contingent circumstances, such as

---

33 Thomas Aquinas, *Summa theologiae*, 2ª 2ªᵉ, q.78 art.1, in *Opera omnia*, vol. 9 (Rome, 1897), 155b.
34 Langholm, *Economics in the Medieval Schools*, 557.

time, condition, and location. For this reason, they are not directly comparable and cannot be the subject of a *mutuum*. Such variables, however, do not influence the value of fungibles: in terms of number, weight, and measure a fungible is never worth more than itself; 100 grams of tobacco are always worth 100 grams of tobacco of the same quality, not 150 grams; ten florins are always worth ten florins, not twelve. By demanding in return more than the principal of the loan, the usurer violates the intrinsic or natural value of a fungible fixed by nature or skill (in Dante's phrase, 'Nature's follower, Art') in terms of number, measure, or weight.

The analysis also provides a corrective to the juristic argument from ownership. Because fungibles have a naturally determinate value in terms of number, weight, or measure, they are necessarily sterile:

> That a usurious contract causes a thing that does not bear fruit to generate a profit is clear, because it has been established in the foregoing argument that lendable things [i.e., fungibles], in which usury is committed, have a determinate value assigned to them by nature or skill, and as a result cannot increase in this respect. By the same token, they cannot bear fruit, because a thing that bears fruit always increases in value along with the fruit, for it is of greater value when it is with fruit than when it is without. Therefore, inasmuch as a usurious contract causes things that have a determinate value – and as a result do not bear fruit – to increase in value and thus generate a profit, it follows that it causes a thing that does not bear fruit to generate a profit, which is completely unnatural and wicked.

Consequently, although ownership of the value of the principal may indeed vest in the creditor – only ownership of the substance passes to the debtor – to demand an increment in the form of interest violates the intrinsically sterile nature of a fungible.

In light of this argument, it is clear that usury cannot be approved by any law because it represents a violation of natural law, which in turn is the foundation of all positive law, canon and civil. But can usury be tolerated to avoid an even greater evil, since, all things considered, usury is a bilateral agreement that benefits both parties? The simple answer to this question, which is the subject of article 3, is 'no' because, in a sense, there is no evil greater than usury. In Gerard's estimate, the usurer is guilty of four offences that particularly compound his crime: first, he 'rashly treats God with contempt; second, he openly treats nature with contempt; third, he wickedly holds scripture in contempt; and fourth, he habitually treats the laws with contempt.' Why, then, does Roman law permit usury? Ge-

rard responds by distinguishing three senses in which law may be said to 'permit' something: the law may waive the penalty for an act without approving it; it may, in a more positive sense, remove some obstacle to the performance of an act; or it may actively aid and abet an act. Roman law permits usury only in the first sense by declining to impose penalties on the usurer and so cannot be said to contradict canon or natural law. The distinction also underlies article 5, where Gerard asks whether one of the two laws takes precedence in the event of a conflict. Noting that the usury prohibition is rooted in natural law, he reiterates that civil law simply waives the penalty for usury without attempting to impede the canonical prohibition or to abet usury in opposition to the canons. In the event of a flat contradiction, canon law would necessarily take precedence and the civil law would be void.[35] According to Gerard, the disharmony between the two laws on this point may be explained by their objectives: civil law exists to promote civic peace and the common good – to use Augustine's terminology, the 'city of man' – which is best served by tolerating credit markets, however morally flawed; canon law, by contrast, looks to salvation – the 'city of God' – which is attained through the virtue of charity (*caritas*), and is therefore intolerant of acts that are prohibited by nature.

In article 4 Gerard dispenses summarily (and conventionally) with the objection that canon law permits exceptions to the usury ban – notably the privilege enjoyed by a son-in-law to retain the income on a pledge for an unpaid dowry, and that of clerics to withhold the revenues of an ecclesiastical possession unjustly detained by a layman – by observing that neither case involves a loan and therefore that neither involves usury.[36]

The final section of the *Questio de usura* provides a vivid impression of the jumble of arguments and counter-arguments that might be advanced in the initial quodlibetal session, and from which the master distilled his considered opinion in the *determinatio* and the final *ordinatio*. For example: usury is not contrary to charity because it serves the utility of both contracting parties; a usurer should be free to profit from his private property; usury should be allowed because it promotes trade and subvenes the poor; if usury were not permitted, the poor would be denied credit and perish of starvation; because civil law is sacrosanct, usury, which civil law permits, is also sacrosanct; a loan is a good, therefore so is usury, which

---

35 For the wider context, see McLaughlin, 'Teaching of the Canonists,' 1:91–5.
36 On this, see ibid., 1:131–6.

is the cause of a loan. Two arguments in particular shed light on the real economic practices that lay behind the questions proposed in quodlibetal sessions but which tend to be obscured by the abstract formulations of the *ordinatio*. The eleventh and sixteenth arguments describe competition in services: in the first a miller offers a farmer a discount in return for his business; in the second, a loan. Are the transactions usurious? If so, to whom is restitution due?

Restitution

It was an axiom of scholastic economic thought that usury is an act of usurpation and therefore a violation of justice, which – in contrast to mere avarice or uncharitable acts – can be rectified only by restitution and not simply by repentance.[37] Gerard accordingly dedicates the first article of his question on restitution to establishing that the usurer does not and cannot acquire ownership of his usurious profits. The issue is significant because in contrast to theft and robbery – two other forms of usurpation to which usury was often assimilated – usury is a consensual contract by which the debtor is willingly usurped. Gerard draws on the conclusions of the *Questio de usura* to show that usury cannot confer ownership for four reasons. First, because usury violates natural law, the contract is illegitimate and therefore cannot serve as a medium for the transfer of ownership. Second, no contract that effects usurpation is legitimate. Third, ownership of a non-existent thing cannot be transferred: since profit on a loan derives from something that is sterile by nature, it is not really a profit and in effect does not exist. Finally, the debtor's consent to pay usury can only be described as conditional at best: confronted by two evils, he chooses the lesser, that is, to accept a loan at interest in preference to enduring want.[38] Echoing the argument of the *Questio de usura*, Gerard maintains that if a usurer can be said to 'own' his profits, it is only in the sense that the civil law does not compel him to restore them and denies the debtor an action for recovery. But such ownership is merely apparent, a legal fiction that cannot alter the fundamentally illicit character of the contract.

Article 2 elaborates on the injustice of usury by contrasting it with theft and robbery. In Gerard's view, usury is more heinous than either because

---

37 On this, see Noonan, *Scholastic Analysis*, 30–1.

38 For an extended meditation on the theme of qualified volition and its traces in modern critiques of neoclassical economics, see Langholm, *Legacy of Scholasticism*.

'it is uniquely hateful to God, to the Church, to nature, to fortune, and to the human race.' The usurer mocks God by openly and indiscriminately usurping the property of others; thieves and robbers, by contrast, must choose their time and place with care. The usurer deceives the Church by hiding behind the legal fiction that his profits are really his property, thus evading legal punishment. He perverts nature by abusing the nature of fungibles, which are naturally sterile, and he thwarts fortune by profiting without risk, neither of which can be said of the thief or the robber. Finally, the usurer offends humanity because he exploits his neighbour with a greater degree of impunity than the robber or thief, neither of whom can pretend that his usurpation is willed by his victim. The injustice of usury, then, is such that it can be rectified only by complete and unconditional restitution.

With regard to the act of restitution itself, a particular point of contention between theologians and canonists was whether a debtor could forgive his creditor the obligation to make restitution of usurious profit. Hostiensis and the ordinary gloss to the *Liber sextus* (by Giovanni d'Andrea) maintained that verbal remission without physical restitution was sufficient to absolve the usurer, though the canonist Dino of Mugello insisted that the usurer must at least have the sum at hand and be on the point of making restitution, a point acknowledged by Giovanni in a subsequent annotation to his own gloss. Gerard dedicates article 3 – the key to the entire *quaestio* – to demolishing the arguments of the jurists on purely logical grounds by an exegesis of 'remission,' 'satisfaction,' 'payment,' 'transfer of ownership,' 'gift,' and 'renunciation,' terms the canonists routinely employed in elaborating their position. The most notable characteristic of the article is Gerard's deployment of a canonical authority to undermine in turn each Roman law tag invoked by the jurists to define their terms. So, for example, if 'satisfaction' means 'whatever is acceptable to the creditor' (Dig. 13.7.9.3) – and here we must understand 'creditor,' in a significant semantic inversion, to be the original borrower to whom restitution is now due – we can respond with Gratian (quoting Augustine) that 'satisfaction is not made unless the cause of sin is excised.' With regard to restitution this means that the original borrower must be put in real possession of his usurped property. Gerard's key text is a passage from Augustine's letters included in Gratian and in the title *On the rules of law* in the *Liber sextus*: 'sin is not remitted unless the stolen good is returned' (VI *de reg. iur.* 4, *Peccatum*). Unless restitution – or its equivalent in the form of a guaranteed pledge – is real, Gerard concludes, the usurer cannot be absolved of his offences against God, nature, the Church, fortune, and humanity.

Is the usurer obliged to restore not only his usurious gains but also any secondary profits he earned by means of them? Gerard's response in article 4 echoes Thomas Aquinas in arguing that he is not: since the usurer's profit is the product of his own labour and ingenuity, it properly remains his own.[39] Indeed, if this were not the case it could be argued that a profit accruing to the borrower from the principal of the loan was owed to the usurer, which would be absurd. This holds true, however, only if the usurious profit takes the form of a fungible, which cannot by nature bear fruit; if – as Thomas also observes – the profit from the loan is a non-fungible, such as a vineyard or a field, which by nature bears fruit, he is obliged to restore both the thing itself and any profits he obtained from it, because he possesses it by usurpation.

The last article considers the order of priority a usurer should observe in making restitution. Gerard maintains that the usurer is first obliged to pay his contractual debts before making restitution of any usury he has extorted, even if this means he lacks the means to repay the victims of his usury. Similarly, he must make restitution to those from whom he has stolen or robbed before those he has usured. If his resources permit him to satisfy those from whom he has extorted usury, the poor should be compensated first because they suffer proportionately greater harm by delayed restitution, but if resources do not permit complete satisfaction, then all should be compensated on a prorated basis. Similarly, those usured most recently should be the last to be repaid, but if resources do not extend to the full satisfaction of all claims, all should be paid on a prorated basis.

Prescription

For classical Roman law, ownership (*dominium*) was, in the words of a modern authority, 'the ultimate right to a thing, the right which had no right behind it.'[40] In principle, *dominium* also embraced the use, enjoyment, and disposition of a thing, and to this extent implied possession, though in practice possession, or something very like it – and along with it, use and enjoyment – might vest in another, such as a usufructuary.[41] This, of course, was often the case in the Middle Ages, when real property

---

39 Cf. Thomas Aquinas, *Summa theologiae*, 2ª 2ᵃᵉ, q.78 art.3, in *Opera omnia*, vol. 9, 165b.
40 Buckland, *A Textbook*, 189. For what follows, I draw on the succinct and useful discussion by Kuehn with reference to the scholarship in 'Conflicting Conceptions of Property,' 108–11.
41 Nicholas, *Introduction to Roman Law*, 110–12.

was more often than not held by someone other than the owner under a long-term lease or as a fief. Acknowledging the objective reality of possession, use, and enjoyment, medieval Romanists and canonists distinguished between *dominium directum* ('original' or 'absolute ownership') and *dominium utile* (literally, 'useful ownership'), which acceded to a possessor over time. Sometimes conceived as parallel or subordinate to *dominium directum*, *dominium utile* was even regarded by some jurists as the only real form of ownership.[42]

The tension between the two emerged clearly in prescription (*praescriptio*), a mode of acquiring ownership of real property by uncontested possession and use over a determinate, usually lengthy, period of time, such as twenty or thirty years. The limitation of prescription to real property was introduced by Justinian, who restricted usucapion (*usucapio*), a similar institution that had existed since the Twelve Tables, to moveables. Prescription was subject, particularly in canon law, to a number of restrictions, most notably 'good faith,' that is, the prescriber's (*praescribens*) honest belief, even if mistaken, that he was not usurping the title of another. Civil law was content to define good faith as the absence of any intention to violate another's right, but canon law insisted on a higher standard of subjective innocence and regarded any bad faith that emerged while prescription ran as voiding its effects. Successful prescription conferred on the prescriber a defence (*exceptio*) against recovery by the original owner and extinguished the latter's title, which acceded to the prescriber. Jurists, however, were reluctant to concede that the successful prescriber obtained *dominium directum*, which, like other *iura personalia*, they understood to inhere in the owner's personality, and generally admitted him only to *dominium utile*. Although Gerard's leading question is whether prescription is contrary to natural law, much of his discussion in fact turns on the nature of *dominium, directum* or *utile*.

Gerard dedicates article 1 to redefining prescription. He rejects the definition of the ordinary gloss to the *Decretum* – 'prescription is a defence that takes its substance from time' – as inadequate because, as it stands, it implies that prescription draws its efficacy from nature in the form of time rather than from law or convention. Gerard's own definition – 'pre-

---

42 See Kuehn, 'Conflicting Conceptions of Property,' 109, n. 48. Because the translations 'original' or 'absolute ownership' and 'useful ownership' do not fully capture the sense of the Latin, I leave the terms untranslated in my discussion. In the facing-page translation below, I have, however, rendered the terms as 'absolute' and 'useful ownership.'

scription is a certain right that derives its fitness from time, draws its force from the authority of law, imposes a penalty on the negligent, and places a limit on lawsuits' – clarifies the relationship between prescription and time by indicating that time simply supplies a convenient measure of negligence. The efficient cause of prescription, then, is not time as such, but law, and its final cause or objective is twofold, namely, to penalize owners who neglect or abandon their property by establishing the possessor's title and, as a consequence, to place a limit on quarrels and lawsuits over ownership.

On the face of it, prescription appears to be a violation of natural right because, as the ordinary glosses to both the *Digest* and the *Decretum* note, it contradicts the natural law rule that no one should be enriched at the expense of another. But the abolition of prescription and usucapion would violate another rule of natural equity that places the common good before that of the individual because the negligent would go unpunished and their negligence would give rise to disputes and litigation. Article 2, which responds to Gerard's leading question, is a lengthy disquisition on the way in which positive law explicates and specifies natural law principles. In brief, the function of natural law is abstract and generalizing: it indicates a wrong in a way that anyone can acknowledge ('Do not kill,' 'Do not steal,' etc.). By contrast, though based on the same principles, positive law must apply them to a multitude of specific cases such that knowledge of the equitable in any given circumstance is the preserve of specialists, such as lawyers and judges. Moreover, although the application of any particular rule of natural law to a concrete case might involve the prima facie denial of another, in the final analysis it will be seen to accord with the intentions of natural equity. Gerard offers a conventional example that derived ultimately from Plato:

> By natural law it is right to return a deposit ... But this rule must be understood and observed in such a way that it does not contradict other rules of natural law. For example, if a madman seeks to recover a sword he has placed in deposit, and it is returned to him, and with it he kills a man, two natural law rules are violated, one of which says that we must not kill, and consequently that no assistance should be offered to a killer. But he who returns the deposited sword in this case offers assistance to a killer. There is also a natural law rule that says that the public good must be preserved, and consequently that peace among men should not be disturbed in any way. But he who returns the deposited sword in this case disturbs the common peace or at least provides an occasion for disturbance. Therefore, the first rule should

not be observed in a literal sense but according to its real meaning, such that it is understood that a deposit should always be returned except in cases where the circumstances involve vice, and then a supervening rule of natural law prohibits its return, as in the case under discussion. For the supervening rule of natural law that prohibits killing and giving assistance to a killer decrees that a deposited sword should not be returned to a madman. Nor does this involve any contravention of natural law, but rather natural law is more seriously violated if the sword is returned to the madman.[43]

Prescription, then, cannot be said to represent a violation of natural equity because positive law (of which prescription is an institution) and natural law ultimately share the same principles. Moreover, prescription has a reasonable cause in natural law terms – namely, to prevent real property from falling into desuetude – and it therefore serves the common good by punishing the negligent and curbing disputes.

Should canonical prescription differ from civil law prescription? As I noted earlier, the standard of good faith demanded by canon law was higher than that required by Roman law. In article 3 Gerard resolves the dissonance by applying the distinctions he proposed in the *Questio de usura* regarding the modes of permission and the objectives of the two laws. If Roman law tolerates a measure of bad faith in prescription, he argues, this is because its objective is civic harmony, which is best achieved by limiting disputes and litigation, but Roman law in no way abets or advances the wicked intention of the prescriber in bad faith. Canon law, by contrast, insists on good faith at every stage of the process because it attends to the internal dispositions of the prescriber, which, for purposes of salvation, must conform to the ethic of reciprocity. In the final analysis, then, the two laws are complementary rather than contradictory, for what one omits, the other punishes or corrects.

On the question of whether the successful prescriber acquires *dominium directum* or simply *dominium utile*, Gerard rejects both of the common juristic opinions: the first that prescription confers only *dominium utile* and the second that it confers both (article 4). In Gerard's view, the jurists err in conceiving of *dominium directum* and *utile* as two distinct forms of ownership, when they are actually two modes of enjoying the same ownership. The conceptual distinction arises from the fact that *dominium directum*

---

43 Cf. *Republic* 331c–332b; and Thomas Aquinas, *Sententia libri Ethicorum*, lib. 5, lectio 12, 1134 b24, in *Opera omnia*, vol 47.2 (Rome, 1969), 306.

derives immediately from natural law – as in the case of *res nullius* ('the property of no one'), which becomes the property of the first occupant – but *dominium utile* from the mechanisms of positive law. In Gerard's view, he who acquires a thing by prescription necessarily obtains both *dominium directum* and *utile*, since these do not somehow represent partial or incomplete ways of using a thing. But viewed from the perspective of the mode of acquisition, prescription, as an institution of positive law, confers only useful ownership, because *dominium directum*, which 'inheres in our very bones,' alone arises directly from the law of nature.

Should the prescriber in bad faith be classified with the thief or robber with respect to intention (article 5)? The brief answer is 'no,' because the constitutive sin of prescription in bad faith is not the usurpation but rather the illicit detention of another's property. This is clear when we consider that Roman law punishes theft and robbery but not prescription in bad faith, because the prescriber in bad faith does not undermine the common good in the way that the thief or robber does; indeed, he performs a service to the commonwealth by punishing those who neglect their property. With respect to conscience, however, the prescriber in bad faith is rightly classified with the thief and the robber, and can purge himself morally only by restitution.

Article 6 extends this conclusion to the case of one who learns only after he has successfully prescribed that his title was bad. The case – which Gerard concedes is rare – was a particular point of contention between theologians and canonists. The canonists generally maintained that the prescriber's title was unaffected by the new information: provided he acted in good faith during the period of prescription, his ownership was secure. Hostiensis' remarks in the *Summa aurea* reflect not only the juristic consensus opinion, but the lawyers' evaluation of theological opinion:

> What if, after prescription, [the prescriber] becomes aware that he possesses the property of another, say he learned for certain that the property he prescribed belonged to Martin: should he return it to Martin? The theologians say that he should ... but the masters of the canons commonly say the opposite because, according to both laws [canon and Roman], once prescription is complete he who prescribed is secure ... It seems to me that on this question the conscience of the theologians is too angelic ... Therefore, if somebody who has legitimately prescribed thinks that he sins mortally by retaining the thing prescribed, I do not consider him a theologian so much as a fraud, for he fears what is above suspicion ... Nevertheless, if he cannot compose his

conscience, he should obey it and return the thing, for otherwise he places himself at risk.[44]

In keeping with the theological *opinio communis*, Gerard insists that the prescriber in this case is obliged to make restitution for three reasons. First because prescription is void if it violates the intention of the law, which is framed to reward good faith. Second because good faith represents the foundation of canonical prescription, which is destroyed by emergent bad faith. And finally because that which is mistaken is corrected by the truth: emergent bad faith shows that the prescription was in error and therefore necessarily overturns it. Gerard concludes therefore that the prescriber in this case is bound in the forum of conscience, if not in law, to make restitution.

The Idea of a Moral Economy

As I remarked earlier, Gerard's theses on usury and prescription enjoyed posthumous fame through the medium of Giovanni d'Andrea's *Quaestiones mercuriales*: if Giovanni considered Gerard 'too obstinate in his opinion' on prescription,[45] he nevertheless endorsed his account of usury with few reservations.[46] In this he was followed by most subsequent authorities on usury: Giovanni Calderini, Lorenzo Ridolfi, and Bernardino of Siena, for example, all adopted Gerard's analysis with Giovanni d'Andrea's qualifications; indeed, Ridolfi characterized the argument as both 'useful and elegant.'[47] More generally, Gerard's 'hard line' prefigured a rigorist position on usury and related issues among theologians of his order in the later fourteenth century and beyond to the Reformation.[48]

---

44 Hostiensis, *Summa aurea*, X 2.26, *de praescriptione rerum immobilium*, n. 3 (Lyons, 1537; repr. Frankfurt am Main, 2009, fol. 116ra–b).

45 Giovanni d'Andrea, *In titulum de regulis iuris novella commentaria*, ad VI *de reg. iur.* 2, *Possessor non praescribit*, n. 41 (Venice, 1581; repr. Turin, 1963, fol. 61va).

46 Ibid., ad VI *de reg. iur.* 4, *Peccatum* (fols 62ra–66ra). For a discussion, see Armstrong, 'Law, Ethics and Economy,' 53–6.

47 Armstrong, *Usury and Public Debt*, 144. For Calderini, see Armstrong, 'Law, Ethics and Economy,' 55, n. 47.

48 Julius Kirshner and I are preparing a study of what we provisionally describe as 'Augustinian economics' in the writings of Gregory of Rimini, Guido of Bellosguardo, and John Klenkock. Luther, himself an Augustinian hermit, shared the views of his predecessors on usury; for representative texts, see Kerridge, *Usury, Interest and the Reformation*. The formulation 'Augustinian economics' is intended as a riposte to

More significantly, the legacy of scholastic economics, with its emphasis on justice, charity, and the common good – on a 'moral economy' in which human needs take precedence over profit – continued to find expression in traditions of social analysis and codes of behaviour that emphasized reciprocity and solidarity.[49] For example, the intense and (to modern eyes) absurdly detailed regulation of markets and economic relations generally under the *ancien régime* was designed to protect consumers of essential commodities, such as grain and other foodstuffs, from the machinations of merchants.[50] In England on the very eve of the industrial revolution, essentially medieval notions of moral economy, particularly in times of dearth, continued to animate riots and protests provoked by market manipulation and artificially inflated food prices.[51] If Karl Marx was indeed, as Tawney once famously described him, 'the last of the Schoolmen,' it was not simply because of the labour theory of value, which had analogues in scholastic economics.[52] Marx's account of surplus value, by which capital acquires 'the occult ability to add value to itself,' to bring 'forth living offspring, or at least lay golden eggs,' is fundamentally Aristotelian;[53] and he quotes with approval the Philosopher's analysis of usury in the *Politics* in his own discussion of 'usurers' capital,' in which 'money is exchanged for more money, a form incompatible with the nature of money.'[54] In the third volume of *Capital*, he elaborates in a discussion of 'fictitious' or 'interest-bearing capital' – the modern form of usurers' capital – which is 'always the mother of every insane form, so that debts, for example, can appear as commodities in the mind of the banker.'[55] Indeed, as Marx

---

Giacomo Todeschini's identification of a scholastic discourse that paved the way for a 'market economy,' which he describes as 'Franciscan economics'; see most recently *Richezza francescana*. For a critique of Todeschini and his school, see Barile, 'Il dibattito sul prestito a interesse.'

49 This has never ceased to be true of Islam; for a recent review of Sharia-compliant banking, see Harding, 'The Money That Prays' and 'Islam and the Armies of Mammon.' It is notable that no Sharia-compliant banks failed in the crisis of 2008. The expression 'moral economy' was introduced into the scholarship by Thompson, 'Moral Economy.'

50 For an elegant discussion, see Harcourt, *Illusion of Free Markets*.

51 Thompson, 'Moral Economy.' For a recent examination of the theme with a focus on late medieval England, see Davis, *Medieval Market Morality*. I am grateful to Shami Ghosh for this reference. On this topic, see, most recently, Fontaine, *The Moral Economy*.

52 Tawney, *Religion and the Rise of Capitalism*, 36. On the vexed question of medieval theories of value, see Langholm, *Economics in the Medieval Schools*, 190–1, 412, 482–3, 579–83; and idem, *Legacy of Scholasticism*, 87.

53 Marx, *Capital, Volume 1*, 255.

54 Ibid., 267.

55 Marx, *Capital, Volume 3*, 596.

observes, 'with the development of interest-bearing capital and the credit system, all capital seems to be duplicated, and at some points triplicated, by the various ways in which the same capital, or even the same claim, appears in various hands in different guises. The greater part of this "money capital" is purely fictitious.'[56]

Similarly, Karl Polanyi considered the distinctive feature of the modern self-regulating market economy to be the transformation of land, labour, and money into – as he termed them – 'fictitious commodities.' They are fictitious because none of them – the natural environment (land), human activity (labour), or the medium of exchange (money) – is really a commodity, that is, something produced for sale on a market. Their commodification is nevertheless a necessary step in the subordination of the social to the economic that characterizes modern capitalism.[57]

There is considerable evidence that the usury prohibition in particular – usually dismissed by historians working within the assumptions of neoclassical economics as an irrational constraint on self-interest and therefore a dead letter – continued to exercise an often decisive influence on economic behaviour up to and, indeed, beyond the Reformation.[58] For instance, in Thomas Mann's family epic, Thomas, the fourth-generation head of the Lübeck wholesale grain firm of Buddenbrooks, is approached by his sister in spring 1868 on behalf of an aristocratic landowner who has incurred urgent gambling debts of 35,000 marks. The proposition is that Buddenbrooks buy the farmer's corn crop 'in the blade,' in other words, that he advance the required sum immediately in return for a crop that would command a higher market price at harvest in July. Buddenbrooks' reaction is testimony to the residual force of medieval economic ethics in modern, Lutheran Prussia:

> Can't you understand that you are asking me to do something discreditable, to engage in underhanded manoeuvres? Why should I go fishing in troubled waters? Why should I fleece this poor landowner? Why should I take advan-

---

56 Ibid., 601. For a lucid discussion of these passages, see Harvey, *Limits to Capital*, 260–70; and more generally, the essay of Kunkel with reference to the current crisis in *Utopia or Bust*, 23–50.

57 Polanyi, *Great Transformation*, 75–80.

58 As I have argued for fifteenth-century Florence; see 'Usury, Conscience, and Public Debt,' 175, 181–4; see also the bibliography in nn. 37–42. For the opinions of the Protestant reformers generally, see Kerridge, *Usury, Interest and the Reformation*. Schüssler attempts to salvage a modified version of neoclassical *homo economicus* in response to my arguments in 'Business Morality at the Dawn of Modernity.'

tage of his necessity to do him out of a year's harvest at a usurious profit to myself? … In short, he has made a mistake in his calculations about me and the character of my firm. I have my own traditions. We have been a business a hundred years without touching that sort of transaction, and I have no idea of beginning at this late day.[59]

What we would describe as a 'futures' contract medieval theorists called *emptio ad terminum* and condemned as usury because the discount is equivalent to interest on a loan. It is a measure of the moral gulf that separates us from nineteenth-century Germany, let alone medieval Europe, that agricultural producers now routinely sell futures for crops on commodity markets as a hedge against price swings.[60]

It is in bridging this gulf that the study of scholastic economics (and of pre-modern interpretations of economic matters generally) can be of assistance. As David Harvey, Pierre Bourdieu, Wolfgang Streeck, Colin Crouch, and many others have argued, among the most corrosive developments of the past forty years has been the saturation of public discourse by a neoliberal theory and rhetoric of unregulated markets to the degree that neoliberalism has come to represent a kind of 'common sense' that justifies the colonization of ever wider sectors of social and political life by capital, with the catastrophic consequences we have experienced since 2008.[61] David Graeber's anthropological study of debt over five millennia,

---

59 Mann, *Buddenbrooks*, 358–9. Buddenbrooks nevertheless succumbs to the proposal, with disastrous consequences for his firm.
60 See, however, Harcourt, *Illusion of Free Markets*, 179–90, on the Chicago Board of Trade's efforts to ban futures markets in grain in the early twentieth century precisely because of their distorting effect on spot markets.
61 For authoritative analyses of the crisis itself, see Duménil and Lévy, *Crisis of Neoliberalism*; Streeck, *Buying Time*, 'Markets versus Voters?' and 'Markets and Peoples.' Krugman offers a centrist, mildly Keynsian, account in *End This Depression Now*. On the broader ideological and political context, see Harvey, *Brief History of Neoliberalism*; Bourdieu, *La misère du monde* and *Acts of Resistance*; Crouch, *Strange Non-Death of Neoliberalism*; Kunkel, *Utopia or Bust*; and Harvey, *Seventeen Contradictions*. For the reflections of a moral philosopher, see Sandel, *What Money Can't Buy*. Mirowski, *Never Let a Serious Crisis Go to Waste*, argues that the collapse of 2008 has further entrenched neoliberal economics as the prevailing orthodoxy. Arrighi, *Long Twentieth*

itself provoked by the crisis and informed by Graeber's experience of the mass 'Occupy' movement, illustrates how attention to pre-modern and pre-capitalist conceptions of economic relations can undermine the notion that the markets of neoliberal theory are either natural or inevitable.[62] Indeed, few historians, sociologists, or anthropologists would maintain that capitalism is anything but historically contingent: it had a beginning and must be brought to an end because, by any measure, social, political, or environmental, it is unsustainable. The question is not whether capitalism will end, but simply when (in time or too late?) and how (peacefully or violently?).[63]

What, in broad strokes, would a modern economics in the spirit of the scholastics and the tradition of moral economy I have been describing look like? It would first of all insist that people have social and political rights that are exempt from market laws and the imperatives of private property – for instance, rights to food, housing, education, health care, and a clean environment – and the freedom to organize collectively to enforce these rights, a view most recently and forcibly expressed by Pope Francis in his 'Apostolic Exhortation' of November 2013 and his recent encyclical on the environment.[64] More specifically, it would propose an economic order that was not dependent on credit and increasingly 'insane forms' of fictitious capital to subsidize unlimited consumption and growth, especially in the rich countries that have benefited most from lib-

---

Century and *Adam Smith in Beijing*, argues that intense financialization at the expense of production of the kind we have witnessed characterizes the terminal stage of a historical cycle of capitalist accumulation.

62 Graeber, *Debt*. See also Lazzarato, *Making of Indebted Man*. Harcourt, *Illusion of Free Markets*, is a useful corrective to the idea that neoliberal markets are in any meaningful sense free or unregulated. Markets are always regulated; the only question is in whose interest are they regulated.

63 The literature on the origins of capitalism is vast; a good place to begin is still Weber, *Protestant Ethic*; but see more recently Aston and Philpin, eds, *Brenner Debate*; Braudel, *Civilization and Capitalism*; and Arrighi, *Long Twentieth Century*. Economists and economic historians working within the assumptions of mainstream economics regard capitalism as an immanent characteristic of all societies; see, for example, the recent *Cambridge History of Capitalism*, vol. 1: *The Rise of Capitalism: From Ancient Origins to 1848*, ed. Neal and Williamson, which traces the origins of capitalism to Mesopotamia. Needless to say, such a procedure robs the term of any analytical value whatsoever.

64 Francis (Jorge Mario Borgoglio), *Evangelii Gaudium* (24 November 2013), ch. 2, para. 53–60 and the encyclical letter *Laudato si* of 24 May 2015. See also the intervention by the German constitutional judge and legal philosopher Ernst-Wolfgang Böckenförde, 'Woran der Kapitalismus krankt.'

eralization and globalization.[65] Indeed, it would question the whole idea
of perpetual, exponential growth as the goal of economic activity and propose a 'steady-state,' zero-growth order.[66] It would, moreover, insist on
the repudiation of illegitimate or 'odious' debt, not only in developing
countries – where loans by the International Monetary Fund and World
Bank under punitive terms must be forgiven – but also in contexts like that
of Greece, where an unsustainable public debt is the product of a flawed
social compromise in the wake of a military dictatorship that left elites
essentially tax-free.[67] An economics in the spirit of the scholastics would
condemn the increasingly grotesque disparities of wealth revealed by recent studies, such as that of Thomas Piketty and his collaborators. Excess
wealth should, as Piketty suggests, be confiscated and redistributed, ide-
ally on a global scale, to ensure an equitable share of the social product
for all, itself the precondition for the creation of a society characterized
by justice and solidarity, in which the slogan 'from each according to his
ability, to each according to his needs' might finally be realized.[68] Finally,
a scholastic economics for today would demand a halt to capital's progres-
sive enclosure of the environment, a genuine 'commons' in the traditional
sense, the degradation of which cannot be written off simply as a 'negative
externality' in cost calculations, as it is in conventional economics.[69]

These are deductions from the principles implicit in scholastic economics, which admittedly cannot provide us with detailed prescriptions for
the organization of an advanced economy. But the study of the tradition
of moral economy that descends from the scholastics can help us call into
question the notion of an economy based fundamentally on debt and
speculation, and the whole idea of an economic order that subordinates

---

65 See, for example, the critique of unrestricted free trade by Reinert, *How Rich Countries
    Got Rich*, notable for its long historical perspective and appeal to traditions of thought
    other than those of classical or neoclassical economics.
66 See in particular Harvey, *Seventeen Contradictions*, 222–45, 296; and Rubin, *End of
    Growth*.
67 On the whole issue, particularly the recent case of Ecuador, see Chesnais, *Les dettes
    illégitimes*. Graeber, *Debt*, 390–1, proposes jubilees in the tradition of the ancient Near
    East in which the indebtedness of individuals and communities would be periodically
    wiped clean.
68 Marx, *Critique of the Gotha Programme*, 89. For proposals to regulate global wealth,
    see Piketty, *Capital*, 471–539. For a long historical perspective on contemporary oligar-
    chy, see Winters, *Oligarchy*.
69 See Harvey, *Seventeen Contradictions*, 246–62, 296–7; and Klein, *This
    Changes Everything*.

humanity and nature to the profit of a tiny minority. The stakes are very high: they are nothing less than the possibility of a truly democratic polity, the dignity of human labour, and the integrity of the environment on which we all depend for our existence. Happily, as Sartre once observed, 'the field of the possible is much vaster than the dominant classes' – and their apologists in the economics departments, the business schools, government, and the media – 'have accustomed us to believing.'[70]

Manuscripts and Printed Texts Used in This Edition

L: Leipzig, Universitätsbibliothek, 894 is a paper manuscript of the fifteenth century containing 175 leaves measuring 290 × 200 mm. Leaves are arranged as follows: 1 (unfoliated) + 170 (foliated 1–170) + 4 (unfoliated). The manuscript is a miscellany of canonistic and theological material in several hands: (1) Giovanni Calderini, *Tabula auctoritatum et sententiarum bibliae cum concordantiis decretorum et decretalium* (fols 1r–64v); (2) Gerard of Siena, *Questio de usura* (fols 65r–74r); (3) *Summa abbreviata contra manicheos et hereticos passagios et alios* (fols 74v–79r); fols 79v–83v are blank; (4) two tractates *de anno iubilaeo* and *de remissione plenaria peccatorum in auctoritate apostolica* (fols 84r–105v); (5) Henricus de Oyta, *Tractatus de contractibus* (fols 105v–131v); (6) two fragments of questions on Peter Lombard's *Sentences*, book 1, distinctions 2–5 and book 2, distinctions 1–21 (fols 132r–170v). (1) and (2) are written in the same *cursiva libraria* hand.[71] The written space of this section is lightly ruled in ink and measures 240 × 148 mm. It is divided into two columns, each measuring 240 × 64 mm, with an average of 44 lines per column. The title, capitals, and paragraph marks are red; initials are often overstroked and citations sometimes underlined in red. The manuscript originally belonged to the Dominican convent of Leipzig, which was dissolved and absorbed by the university in 1543. For a full description of the codex and its contents, see Rudolf Helssig, *Katalog der lateinischen und deutschen Handschriften der Universitäts-Bibliothek zu Leipzig*, vol. 3: *Die juristischen Handschriften* (Leipzig, 1905), 19–20.

---

70 Sartre in an interview of 1969 with Rossana Rossanda of *Il Manifesto*, quoted by Pavone, *A Civil War*, 5, n. 2.
71 I use Lieftinck's nomenclature as adapted by Derolez, *Palaeography of Gothic Manuscript Books*.

R: Rome, Biblioteca Angelica, 625 is a parchment manuscript from the first half of the fourteenth century containing 225 leaves that measure 345 × 248 mm.[72] It is composed of two manuscripts, each in a different hand, that were bound together at some stage. The first part (fols 1r–157r) contains Gerard's commentary on the second book of the *Sentences*; the second, James of Pamiers' *Quodlibet* (incorrectly attributed to Gerard, fols 158r–185v) and eleven authentic quodlibetal questions of Gerard (fols 185v–208v), to which are appended the three additional questions on usury, restitution, and prescription (fols 209r–225r).[73] The copyist indicates at fol. 208vb that he has added the last separately from the other quodlibetal questions for those who might find them of interest. The written space of the second part is ruled in pencil and measures 235 × 164 mm. It is divided into two columns each measuring 235 × 74 mm., with 58 lines per column. Titles and rubrics are red; paragraph marks and capitals also contain blue. The hand is a *textualis currens*, possibly French. According to a note on fol. 1r, the manuscript originally belonged to the Augustinian convent of St John the Evangelist, Rimini, and was presented to the Biblioteca Angelica in 1638 by Angelo Vanci.[74] For additional details of the codex, see Enrico Narducci, *Catalogus codicum manuscriptorum praeter graecos et orientales in Bibliotheca Angelica*, vol. 1 (Rome, 1893), 259b–260a.

W: Vienna, Österreichische Nationalbibliothek, Vindob. 4151 is a miscellany of theological, philosophical, canonical, and historical texts dating from the first half of the fifteenth century. It contains summaries of or extracts from the first two articles of the *Questio de usura* (fol. 202ra–b) and of the *Tractatus de restitutione* (fols 202rb–204ra) in a *cursiva currens* hand. I consulted this text in a photocopy. For a complete list of the manuscript's contents, see *Tabulae codicum manu scriptorum praeter graecos et orientales in Bibliotheca Palatina Vindobonensi asservatorum*, vol. 3: *Cod. 3501–Cod. 5000* (Vienna, 1869; repr. Graz, 1965), 153–4.

---

72 According to Narducci's catalogue; but Courtenay, 'Sentences Commentary,' 255, n. 30, considers it 'probably 15th cent.' without giving any particular reason for this assertion. I have spent much time with the manuscript and am inclined to agree with Narducci.

73 On the quodlibetal material in *R*, see Schabel and Courtenay, 'Augustinian *Quodlibeta*,' 557–61; for a list of the questions contained in James of Pamiers' *Quodlibet*, see 564–6.

74 'Est conventus sancti Ioannis evangelistae de Arim. ad usum f. sanctis <*sic*>Arim.' Added in a second hand: 'Sed a magistro Angelo Vancio Ariminensi Romam missum pro bibliotheca sancti patris nostri Augustini 1638.'

I have also made use of the following printed editions:

C: Gerard of Siena. *Tractatus de usuris et de praescriptionibus*. Ed. Angelo Vancio. Cesena, 1630.

V: Giovanni d'Andrea. *In sextum Decretalium commentaria et in titulum de regulis iuris novella commentaria*. Venice, 1581; repr. Turin, 1963.

Editorial Practices

Manuscript witnesses to Gerard's economic questions are scarce, possibly because, as I noted earlier, his theses on usury and prescription were adopted and popularized by the more renowned canonist Giovanni d'Andrea. The three questions survive as a group only in *R*. The Leipzig manuscript (*L*) contains the *Questio de usura*, but lacks the other two questions. Vienna (*W*) contains extracts from the first two articles of the *Questio de usura* and about a quarter of the *Tractatus de restitutione*. I have been unable to locate any other copies of Gerard's economic questions.

In view of the paucity of manuscript evidence, it has not been possible to establish the relationship between the witnesses and therefore to prepare a critical edition in the traditional sense. What is offered here is a corrected base text edition, in which each question is based on a single witness with corrections from the other witnesses.

Although it was copied as much as a century after *R*, *L* is an independent and, in some respects, superior witness to the *Questio de usura* because it includes a sixth section, promised in the preamble to the *quaestio* but omitted from *R*, in which Gerard responds to sixteen arguments advanced in the course of the disputation in support of the contention that usury is permissible in law. *R* and *L* are marred by a comparable measure of scribal errors and omissions, but I have decided to edit the *Questio de usura* entirely from *L*, both because it presents a fuller version of the text and also because it has never been published in any form, whereas *R* is reflected in the 1630 Cesena edition of Angelo Vancio. I have, however, resorted to *R* and *C* to supply *homoeoteleuta* and omissions in *L*, and (along with *W* for the first two articles) as the basis of most emendations. Because there are no other manuscript witnesses to the sixth section, I have depended on Giovanni d'Andrea's almost verbatim report of it as printed in the Venice 1581 edition of his *Quaestiones mercuriales* (*V*) as a source of emendations and corrections.

As the only complete copy of the *Tractatus de restitutione* and the *Questio de prescriptione*, *R* necessarily forms the basis of this part of the edition.

I have depended principally on Vancio's edition (*C*) and the extracts in *W* to supply missing words and phrases and as the basis of most emendations in the *Tractatus de restitutione*; for the *Questio de prescriptione*, I have depended on *C* and referred selectively to *V* where the texts of *R* and *C* are particularly corrupt. Like most early modern editors, Vancio does not state what manuscripts he used in compiling his edition, but a note on the first folio of *R* indicates that he had access to the manuscript and it certainly formed the basis of his edition. A collation of *C* against *R* nevertheless suggests that Vancio might have had before him at least one other exemplar, because he was able to supply several *homoeoteleuta* in *R*. *C* therefore represents an additional though not entirely satisfactory witness because it is not always clear which of *C*'s variants reflect the manuscript tradition and which the product of conjectural emendation by Vancio himself. Consequently, wherever possible, I have preferred the excerpts in the Vienna manuscript (*W*) as a source of corrections to the *Tractatus de restitutione*.

Because the edition is based on such a slim manuscript foundation, I have decided to reproduce the orthography of the two base-text manuscripts with two exceptions: I have transcribed the *i*-longa that occurs at the end of words and in Roman numerals as *i* <*I*>; and I have regularized both scribes' inconsistent handling of *u* and *v*, transcribing *u* <*V*> when it stands for a vowel and *v* <*V*> a consonant. Common features of both witnesses that I have reproduced include *e* for the diphthongs *ae* and *oe,* and the frequent use of *y* or dotted *y* (*ÿ*) – the latter principally in *R* – for *i.* I have also reproduced both manuscripts' fairly consistent rendering of assibilated *-ti* as *-ci,* although this sometimes results in forms, such as *dacio* (*datio*) and *exaccio* (*exactio*), that are not immediately recognizable. The scribe of *R* also frequently writes *ct* for *tt*; for example, *commicto* for *committo* and *remicto* for *remitto*. Other unfamiliar spellings include the doubled consonants of *tollero* (*tolero*), *auttentica* (*authentica*), *Pollitica* (*Politica*), *equippollere* (*equipollere*), *apperire* (*aperire*), *aufferre* (*auferre*), and *transsit* (*transit*); the *mp* combination in *idemptitas* (*identitas*) and *dampnum* (*damnum*); and the forms *inquid* (*inquit*), *relinquid* (*relinquit*), *actenus* (*hactenus*), and *superhabundare* (*superabundare*). Cardinal numbers have been transcribed as they appear in the manuscripts in their Roman or Arabic forms, but, with the exception of citations of the legal compilations, the Bible, and patristic texts, I have chosen to read ordinals as abbreviated words and therefore spell them out. All abbreviations have been silently resolved and in such a way as to conform to the scribes' prevailing usage.

I have noted scribal deletions and expunctuations in the relevant base texts in the textual apparatus, but I have not indicated where the scribe of

L inverts the order of two or more words with the signs " ", or the places in *R* where the scribe fills out a short line with a stray letter. I have also noted the corrections that appear in *R* in a second hand, most of which I have accepted. The *apparatus criticus* notes all other significant variants in *R*, *C*, *W*, and *V* (in the *Questio de usura*), and in *C*, *W*, or *V* (where appropriate) for the remaining questions.

Punctuation, capitalization, and paragraph divisions are editorial and reflect modern English usage. Angle brackets < > signal an editorial addition. The sections consecutively numbered 1–20 reflect the natural divisions of the texts but are an editorial convenience.

Titles of biblical, patristic, and philosophical texts are italicized. In accordance with the prevailing convention among editors of medieval legal texts, I have left the sigla and titles of the canon and Roman law collections in their abbreviated forms, but have italicized titles and lemmata in order to distinguish them from the surrounding text and to prevent confusion. Legal sigla occurring in the text are listed below in the table of abbreviations along with the modern sigla that are used in the notes. Note that legal citations were understood to be in the ablative case, in the sense of 'at' or 'in' unless they were dependent on a previous ablative, when they were read as genitives. Modern citations proceed from the largest to the smallest unit of text. Dig. 12.1.2.2, for example, means Digest of Justinian, book 12, title 1 (*de rebus creditis*), *lex* 2, paragraph 2.

References to the *Corpus iuris canonici* are to the critical edition of Emil Friedberg (Leipzig, 1879; repr. Graz, 1959) and, to the *Corpus iuris civilis*, that of Theodor Mommsen et al. (Berlin, 1915–28). Where the arrangement of the medieval vulgate edition of the text differs from the critical edition, the citation includes the medieval numbering in brackets thus: Dig. 50.17.206(207).

Note on the Translation

Scholastic texts are characterized by a high degree of formulaic repetition and syntactical looseness, both probably the result of the origin of such material in lectures and disputations. I have not attempted to disguise the first feature in the translation, although it sometimes makes for dull reading; and it must be confessed that Gerard is unusually repetitive and long-winded, even by scholastic standards. I have tried to make the sense of the text as clear as possible, even if this means sometimes departing from Gerard's choice of mood, tense, or voice, or his use of highly technical jargon and sometimes tortured syntax. My objective has been to provide a

translation that reads as naturally as possible in English without falsifying the character or intention of the Latin.

Translations of texts from the *Decretum* of Gratian are from Giulio Silano's forthcoming translation. I have adapted translations of the *Digest* from *The Digest of Justinian*, ed. and trans. Alan Watson et al., 4 vols. (Philadelphia, 1985). Otherwise translations are my own.

Abbreviations

Auth.	*Authenticum*
C.	*causa*
CCSL	Corpus Christianorum, Series Latina
CSEL	Corpus Scriptorum Ecclesiasticorum Latinorum
c.	*capitulum*
coll.	*collatio*
cap.	*capitulum*
D.	*distinctio*
d.	*distinctio* (in the Latin text)
di.	*distinctio* (in the Latin text)
ff.	*Digesta Iustiniani* (in the Latin text)
Decretum Grat.	*Decretum Gratiani*
Dig.	*Digesta Iustiniani*
extra	*Decretales Gregorii IX* (in the Latin text)
gl. ord.	*glossa ordinaria*
Inst.	*Institutiones Iustiniani*
l.	*lex* (in the Latin text)
lib.	*liber*
Nov.	*Novella constitutio Iustiniani*
PL	Patrologia Latina
pr.	*principium*
q.	*quaestio*
rubr.	*rubrica*
v.	*verbo*
VI	*Liber sextus decretalium Bonifacii VIII*
X	*Decretales Gregorii IX*

Questio de usura

A Question on Usury

<1> <Questio de usura>

L.65r Materia de usura disputata per fratrem Gerhardum de Senis ordinis fratrum heremitarum Augustini.

Queritur utrum contractus usurarius sit permissibilis in aliquo iure. Et
5 videtur quod sic quia unusquisque licite potest accipere quod sibi voluntarie est donatum. Sed illud quod recipit fenerator per contractum est sibi voluntarie donatum, ergo potest illud licite accipere, et per consequens contractus usurarius erit licitus et de iure permissibilis. Maior patet; minor probatur quia dacio usurarum est per voluntarium pactum.

10 Ad oppositum est quia rapina nullo modo est permissibilis; sed usura rapina est, ergo et cetera. Maior patet; minor probatur per Ambrosium in libro *de bono mortis* et habetur 14. q. 4.: 'si quis usuram acceperit, rapinam facit.'

Respondeo: in ista questione sic proceditur, quod primo ponuntur om
15 nes vie ex quibus potest oriri dubitacio in ista questione; secundo proceditur ad solucionem eius.

Quantum ad primum sciendum quod ex quatuor viis potest dubitacio in ista questione oriri. Prima via est quia videmus quod quedam sunt peccata solum quia prohibita, non quod ex natura sua habeant maliciam convolu
20 tam, sicut utique fuit peccatum primorum parentum. Nam esus ligni vetiti non fuit peccatum quia ex natura rei fuit viciosus sive malicia convolutus

---

1/2–3 Materia ... Augustini : Incipit questio de usura cum .v. articulis infrascriptis, et cum quodam tractatu addito de restitucione usurarum continente .4. alios articulos, determinata Parisius a fratre Gerardo de Senis in sacra theologia magistro fratrum heremitarum ordinis sancto Augustini. *R*   1/2–119 Materia ... tenendus : *om. W*   1/4 Queritur : *om. RC*   1/4 Et : *om. C*   1/5 accipere : recipere *RC*   1/6 illud ... sibi : lucrum proveniens ex usura est *RC*   1/7 donatum : ipsi usurario *add. RC*   1/7 illud : ipsum *RC*   1/7 accipere : recipere *RC*   1/7 et : ac *RC*   1/10 Ad oppositum : In contrarium *C*   1/10 modo : iure *RC*   1/11 per : dominum *add. C*   1/11–12 in libro : *om. C*   1/12 habetur : refertur *C*   1/12 acceperit : accipit *RC*   1/14 proceditur : procedam *RC*   1/14–15 quod ... vie : quia primo ponam omnes illas vias *RC*   1/15 ista : dicta *RC*   1/15–16 secundo proceditur : secundo vero procedam *RC*   1/17 sciendum : est *add. C*   1/18 ista : hac *C*   1/19 quod : quia *RC*   1/19 ex : malicia sua *add. et del. L*   1/19 sua : rei *RC*   1/20 Nam : ille *add. RC*   1/21 rei : non *interlin. al. man. L*   1/21 fuit^2 : fuerit *RC*

1/11–13 Ambrose, *De bono mortis*, 12.56, in CSEL 32, ed. K. Schenkl (Vienna, 1897), p. 752; quoted in Decretum Grat. C.14 q.4 c.10.

A Question on Usury

1. *A question on usury disputed by Brother Gerard of Siena of the order of the hermit brothers of Augustine.*

The question is whether a usurious contract is permissible by any law. And it seems that it is because one may accept licitly something that is given voluntarily. Now, whatever a usurer receives by contract is given to him voluntarily, therefore he may licitly accept it, and consequently a usurious contract is licit and permitted by law. The major premiss is clear. The minor premiss is evident because usury is paid as a result of a voluntary agreement.

On the contrary, it is a fact that robbery is never permissible; but usury is a form of robbery, therefore et cetera. The major premiss is clear. The minor premiss is proved by Ambrose in his book *Death as a Good* and quoted at C.14 q.4 c.10: 'if anyone accepts usury, he commits robbery.'

I reply that we shall proceed first by laying out the all the ways in which doubt might arise in this matter, and second by providing a solution to the question.

With respect to the first it must be understood that there are four ways in which doubt might arise in this matter. The first is that we see that certain things are sins simply because they are forbidden, not because they are by their very nature bound up with vice, and such was the sin of Adam and Eve. For eating of the forbidden tree was not a sin because it was by

sed solum quia prohibitus, teste beato Gregorio 35. *moralium*, ubi sic ait:
'non in paradiso mala arbor extitit quam dominus homini ne contingeret
interdixit, sed ut melius per obedientie meritum homo bene conditus cres-
25 ceret dignum fuit ut hunc eciam a bono prohiberet quatenus tanto verius
hoc esset virtus quod ageret quanto et a bono cessans actori suo se subdi-
tum humilius exhiberet.' Sunt ergo quedam peccata solum quia prohibita. Quedam vero sunt alia peccata, non quia prohibita, ymmo econtrario,
utpote quia ideo sunt prohibita quia peccata. Ideo autem sunt peccata quia
30 ex natura rei habent maliciam convolutam, secundum quem modum actus
transgressionis mandatorum decalogi ideo est prohibitus quia est peccatum, et ideo peccatum quia ex natura rei viciosus et malicia convolutus.
Talis namque actus ex natura rei contrariatur virtuti et ex natura rei habet
a Deo avertere et deordinare ac per consequens ex natura rei est viciosus
35 et malicia convolutus.

Ex quibus omnibus apparet quod ista est una via ex qua potest oriri
dubitacio in presenti questione. Nam potest racionabiliter dubitari utrum
contractus usurarius sit peccatum solum quia prohibitus vel quia ex natura
rei malicia convolutus. Nam si esset peccatum solum quia prohibitus, non
40 videretur inconveniens ipsum esse permissibilem in aliquo iure. Et ista via
sumit robur ex omnibus argumentis que probant quod contractus usurarius non sit viciosus ex natura rei. Qualia possunt fieri multa apparencia
argumenta.

1/22 prohibitus *RC* : prohibitum *L*   1/22 beato : domino *C*   1/22 35 : libro *add. RC*
1/23 non : autem *add. RC*   1/23 dominus : Deus *RC*   1/23 homini ne : e communi
et *corr. al. man. R*   1/24 bene : *om. R*   1/25 fuit : fuerat *RC*   1/25–6 quatenus …
hoc : aut tanto verius ipsa *R*   1/26 et : etiam *R*   1/26 actori : auctori *C*   1/27 humilius : humilibus *R*   1/27 quedam : *om. C*   1/27 peccata : que ideo sunt peccata *add.*
RC   1/28 ymmo : magis *add. RC*   1/28 econtrario : e converso *C*   1/29 quia¹ : ideo
autem *add. et del. R*   1/29 Ideo² : Imo *C*   1/30 ex natura rei : *om. C*   1/31 est¹ : *om. R*
1/31 est² : *om. RC*   1/34 est : *om. RC*   1/36 apparet : statim *add. RC*   1/37 dubitari
RC : *om. L*   1/38–9 vel … prohibitus : et tunc *RC*   1/40 permissibilem : permissibile *C*
1/40 Et : ideo *add. R*   1/41 robur *RC* : *vac. L*   1/41 omnibus : illis *add. RC*   1/42 sit :
esset *RC*   1/42–3 Qualia … argumenta : sicut utique possent fieri multa et apparencia
argumenta *RC*   1/43 argumenta *RC* : *om. L*

1/22–7 Gregory the Great, *Moralia in Iob*, 35.14, in CCSL 143B, ed. M. Adriaen (Turnhout, 1985), pp. 1793–4; quoted in Decretum Grat. C.11 q.3 c.99.

its very nature wicked and bound up with vice, but only because it was prohibited, as the blessed Gregory observes in chapter 35 of his *Moralia*, where he says that 'the tree in paradise which God forbade man to touch was not evil; but in order that man, who had been well created, might better increase by the merit of obedience, it was right that he should prohibit him even what is good so that what he did might be the more truly virtuous the more humbly he showed himself subject to his maker by abstaining from a good.' Therefore, some things are sins simply because they are forbidden. But certain other things are not sins because they are prohibited, but are rather prohibited because they are sins: they are sins because by their very nature they are bound up with vice. And in this way an act that violates the decalogue is forbidden because it is a sin, and it is a sin because by nature it is wicked and bound up with vice. For such an act is by nature contrary to virtue and by nature must turn one away from God and lead one astray, and as a result by nature it is wicked and bound up with vice.

From these observations it is clear that one way in which doubt might arise in the present question is because it may reasonably be asked whether a usurious contract is sinful simply because it is prohibited or because by its very nature it is bound up with vice. For if it is a sin solely because it is prohibited, it does not seem inappropriate that it be permitted under some law. And this position is reinforced by all the arguments that demonstrate that a usurious contract is not wicked by its very nature. And several such obvious arguments may be adduced.

Secunda via eciam est quia videmus quedam peccata permitti et tole-
45 rari vel quia propter eorum permissionem aliquod bonum sequitur vel
quia si non permittuntur maius inde malum et periculum oritur, sicud
possunt haberi exempla de utroque. Videmus enim quod ecclesia tollerat
ritus Iudeorum, ymmo concedit eis expressam licenciam de observancia
sui ritus, sicud patet in decretis 45. d. c. *Qui sincera*, ubi Gregorius lo-
50 quens de Iudeis sic ait: 'omnes ferias festivitatesque suas sicud actenus
tam ipsi quam parentes eorum per longa colentes retro tempora tenuerunt
liberam habeant observandi celebrandique licenciam.' Et tamen constat
quod illius ritus observancia magnum est peccatum in tantum eciam quod
ydolatrie comparatur, sicud patet in glosa super illo Gallatarum 5., 'nolite
55 iterum iugo servitutis contineri,' ubi dicitur quod 'non est levior hec legis
servitus|^{L65v} quam ydolatrie.' Tolleratur ergo ab ecclesia et a iure cano-
nico Iudeorum infidelitas et sui ritus observancia permittitur, quantumcumque sit grave peccatum, propter bonum quod inde oritur. Nam quia
Iudei inter nos tollerantur et sui ritus observancia coram oculis nostris
60 agitur, idcirco nostre fidei veritas in eorum libris velata et in eorum ritu
figurata lucide demonstratur ac per consequens ex eorum libris et eorum
ritu nostre fidei testimonium roboratur. Et ista est intencio beati Augustini 18. *de civitate Dei* c. 45, ubi dicit quod 'nobis sufficiunt' prophetie
pro nostre fidei confirmacione, 'que de inimicorum nostrorum codici-
65 bus proferuntur quos cognoscimus propter hoc testimonium quod no-

---

1/44 eciam est : ex qua potest oriri dubitacio in dicta questione *RC*   1/45 sequitur :
inde oritur *RC*   1/46 permittuntur : permicterentur *RC*   1/47 possunt : possum
RC   1/47 haberi exempla : habere exemplum *RC*   1/48 ymmo : primo *RC*   1/50 omnes : Deus *R*   1/51 tam : *ex* quod *corr. al. man. R*   1/52 habeant : observsanciam *add. et*
del. L   1/52 observandi ... licentiam : *non liq. R*   1/53 ritus : vel *add. RC*   1/53 tantum : esset *add. et del. L*   1/54 in : per *RC*   1/54 illo : verbo *add. RC*   1/54 Gallatarum : ad Galatas *RC*   1/55 servitutis : servitus *add. et exp. R*   1/55 ubi dicitur : dicit
enim ibi glossa *RC*   1/56 iure : *ex* iule *del. et corr. al. man. marg. R*   1/59 ritus : tollerantur *add. et expunc. R*   1/60 libris : observ- *add. et del. L*   1/60 ritu : ritu *add. et*
expunc. R   1/61 demonstratur : demonstrat *R*   1/62 beati : divi patris *C*   1/63 45 : 46
C   1/63 quod : *om. C*   1/63 nobis : quod ille *add. R* : quidem illae *C*   1/63 sufficiunt :
scilicet *add. RC*   1/63 prophetie : supple *add. RC*   1/65 cognoscimus : agnoscimus *RC*

1/49–52 Decretum Grat. D.45 c.3.   1/54–6 *Gal* 5.1; gl. ord. ad *Gal* 5.1, gl. interlineata
super v. *Servitutis* (ed. *Biblia sacra cum glossa ordinaria*, Paris, 1590, vol. 6, cols. 509–
10).   1/62–74 Augustine, *De civitate Dei* 18.46, in CSEL 40, ed. E. Hoffmann (Vienna,
1900), pp. 344–5.

A second way in which doubt might arise is that we see certain sins permitted or tolerated either because some good follows from allowing them or because a greater evil or danger emerges if they are not permitted; and examples of both may be adduced. We see, for example, that the Church tolerates the rites of the Jews, indeed grants them explicit permission to observe their rites, as is clear in D.45 c.3, where Gregory, speaking of the Jews, says 'let them have free permission to keep and celebrate all their festivities and feast days, in the same way as both they and their ancestors for a long time have kept them.' And nevertheless it is the case that the observance of such rites is a great sin insofar as it approximates idolatry, as is clear in the gloss to Galatians 5.1, 'do not submit again to the yoke of slavery,' where it is said that 'servitude to this law is no lighter than to idolatry.' Therefore the infidelity of the Jews is tolerated by the Church and by canon law – and the observance of their rites allowed – even though it is a great sin, on account of the good that arises thereby. For inasmuch as the Jews are tolerated in our midst and their rites observed before our eyes, the truth of our faith which is hidden in their books and prefigured in their rites is revealed, and as a result the witness of our faith is confirmed by their own books and rites. And this is the intention of the blessed Augustine in book 18, chapter 45 of the *City of God*, where he says that those prophecies 'suffice us' for the confirmation of our faith 'which are quoted from the books of our enemies, for we know that it is because of this witness, which our enemies

bis inviti perhibent eosdem codices habendo atque servando per omnes
gentes ipsos esse dispersos.' Et quibusdam interpositis statim subiungit
quomodo propter illud testimonium debent tollerari inter nos ipsi et eorum ritus, pro cuius dicti probacione allegat illud psalmiste 'Deus ostendit
70 mihi super inimicos meos ne occidas eos ne quando obliviscantur populi
mei.' Quod sic exponit: quod 'Deus demonstravit ecclesie inimicis Iudeis
graciam misericordie sue, quoniam "delictum eorum salus est gentibus,"
et ideo non eos occidit,' scilicet ecclesia, 'ne obliti,' scilicet Christiani, 'legem Dei ad hoc, de quo agimus, testimonium nil valerent,' scilicet Iudei.
75 Apparet ergo quomodo aliquod malum a iure divino et a iure canonico
permittitur propter aliquod bonum quod inde oritur.

Vlterius dico quod malum minus quandoque permittitur propter
malum maius quod inde sequeretur si non permitteretur. Sicud utique de
hoc habemus exemplum a beato Gregorio in decretis d. 4. c. *Denique*,
80 ubi Augustino Anglorum episcopo de observanciis ieiunii sic scribit: 'de
ipsa die dominica hesitamus quidnam dicendum sit, cum omnes laÿci
sive seculares illa die plus solito et ceteris diebus acuracius cibos carnium
appetant et nisi quadam aviditate usque ad medias noctes se ingurgitent
non aliter se huius sancti temporis observacionem suscipere putant, quod
85 utique non racioni sed voluptati, ymmo cuidam cecitati mentis asscriben-
dum est, unde nec a tali consuetudine averti possunt, et ideo cum venia
suo ingenio relinquendi sunt ne forte peiores fiant, si a tali consuetudine
prohibeantur.' Apparet ergo hic manifeste quod malum fuit a iure permissum propter maius malum quod inde fuisset sequutum si non fuisset
90 permissum.

1/66 inviti *R* : inimici *L* : invite *C*   1/66 atque : ac *R*   1/67 gentes : etiam *add. C*
1/67 dispersos : diversos *R*   1/68 illud : eundem *R* : idem *C*   1/69 illud : verbum *add.*
RC   1/70 super *RC* : *om. L*   1/70 inimicos *RC* : inimici *L*   1/71 Quod ... exponit : Dicit ergo beatus Augustinus prefata verba exponens *RC*   1/71 ecclesie : in eius
add. C   1/73 scilicet[1] : *marg. L*   1/74 scilicet Iudei *RC* : *om. L*   1/75–6 aliquod ...
propter *RC* : *om. per hom. L*   1/77 minus : *add. marg. al. man. R*   1/78 si non : sive
R   1/79 Gregorio : quod ponitur *add. RC*   1/80 ubi : scribens namque Gregorius
RC   1/80 observanciis : observantia *RC*   1/80 sic scribit : ita dicit *RC*   1/81 ipsa :
vero *add. RC*   1/81 hesitamus *RC* : hesitatus *L*   1/82 sive : et *RC*   1/82 plus : populo
R   1/82 et : *om. C*   1/82 acuracius : a curatis *R*   1/83 quadam : nova *add. RC*   1/83 se :
hec autem *add. et exp. R*   1/87 fiant : existant *C*   1/88 hic : hoc *C*   1/89 maius : *om. C*

1/69–71 *Ps* 58.12.   1/72 *Rom* 11.11.   1/79–88 Decretum Grat. D.4 c.6.

supply to us by possessing and preserving the same books, that they have been scattered among all the nations.' And a bit further on he adds that on account of that witness they and their rites should be tolerated among us, adducing by way of support the saying of the psalmist: 'God has shown me concerning my enemies that you are not to slay them, lest my people forget.' He explains the passage thus: 'God showed the Church the grace of his mercy in her enemies the Jews, since "their sin is the salvation of the gentiles" and therefore she' – that is, the Church – 'did not kill them, lest they' – that is, the Christians – 'forgetting the law of God on this point with which we are concerned, they' – that is, the Jews – 'should bear no witness.' It is clear, then, how an evil may be permitted by divine and canon law on account of a good that arises from it.

Moreover, I say that a lesser evil is sometimes permitted because a greater evil would ensue if it were not. We have an example of this from the blessed Gregory in D.4 c.6, where he writes thus to Augustine, the bishop of the English, about the keeping of fasts: 'Concerning the Lord's day itself, we are perplexed as to what is to be said because all lay and worldly people, on that day more than on others, desire more greatly to feed on meat. They can think of no other way to keep this sacred time than by so gorging themselves, with extraordinary greed, until the middle of the night. This must surely be ascribed not to reason, but to immoderate desire, or even to some blindness of the mind, nor can they be turned away from such a custom. And so, they are to be mercifully left to their devices, lest they become worse if they are forbidden to follow such a custom.' Here, then, it is clear that an evil has been permitted on account of a greater evil that would follow if it were not.

Applicando ergo istam viam ad propositum quantum ad utramque partem, dico quod ex ista via merito potest fieri dubitacio in presenti questione, nam si malum potest permitti propter bonum quod inde sequitur vel propter maius malum quod inde vitatur, videtur quod contractus usura-
95   rius sit utroque modo permissibilis a iure, tum quia magnum bonum inde sequitur, ut cum fiat in favorem utriusque partis, tum eciam quia magna mala inde vitantur, sicud posset probari per plura argumenta. Et ex hoc apparet quod ista via sumeretur ex omnibus argumentis que probant quod contractus usurarius sit utilis rei publice et utrique parti contrahendo, et
100   ex illis que probant quod sit causa vitandi multa mala.
          Tercia via eciam est quia videmus de facto quod ius civile et canonicum concedunt quod in aliquo casu non tenetur quis ad restitucionem si recipiat ultra sortem, utpote cum socer assignat genero pro numerata dote aliquam possessionem in pignore, fructus qui percipientur de dicta posses-
105   sione non computabuntur in sortem, sicut patet ff. *de doli excepcione* l. *Pater*; sicud eciam patet *extra, de usuris* c. *Salubriter.* Si ergo gener in tali casu potest recipere ultra sortem de concessione utriusque iuris, cum tamen talis receptio ex suo modo et ex sua forma sit usuraria, videtur quod contractus usurarius quantum ex sua forma sit permissibilis in utroque iure,
110   et ista via posset roborari per illam specialem excepcionem quam facit ius |^L66r^ canonicum concedens quod clericus posset redimere possessionem ecclesie ab alieno male vel violenter detentam nec tamen fructus sibi computabuntur in sortem, sicut patet *extra* eodem titulo c. i. et c. *Conquestus.*

1/92 fieri : oriri *RC*   1/96 sequitur : sequi videtur *R* : ut *om. RC*   1/96 fiat : fuit *R* 1/98 sumeretur : fuit robur *R* : sumit robur *C*   1/98 omnibus : illis *add. RC*   1/98 probant : possent probare *RC*   1/99 et² : etiam *add. RC*   1/100 probant : possunt probare *RC*   1/100 vitandi : et *add. R*   1/100 mala : et plura talia argumenta fuerant inducta in argumento ad questionem *add. R* : et plura talia argumenta possent duci in arguendo ad quaestionem *add. C*   1/101 eciam : ex qua potest oriri dubitacio in ista questione *RC*   1/103 ultra : suam *add. et corr. ex* servi *al. man. R* : suam *add. C*   1/103 pro : non *add. C*   1/104 pignore : pignus *C*   1/104 de : ex *C*   1/105 ff. : de dode. *add. et del. L*   1/106 usuris *C* : usurariis *LR*   1/109 quantum : est *add. C*   1/109 sua : ista *RC*   1/110 roborari : colorari *C*   1/110 exceptionem : concessionem *RC* 1/111 posset : possit *R* : potest *C*   1/112 ab alieno : a layico *RC*   1/113 titulo : *om. C*

1/105–6 Dig. 44.4.17.1.   1/106 X 5.19.16.   1/113 X 5.19.1 and 8.

Applying both elements of this reasoning to the point under consideration, I say that doubt may well arise in the present question, for if an evil may be permitted because of a good that follows or to avoid an even greater evil, it seems that a usurious contract is permissible by law either because a great good follows from a contract designed to benefit both parties, or because many evils are thereby avoided, which may be proven by several arguments. And it is clear that this reasoning is reinforced by arguments that show that a usurious contract is beneficial to the commonwealth and to the contracting parties, and by those that show that many evils are thereby avoided.

A third way in which doubt may arise is that we see that in practice civil and canon law allow that in certain cases one is not obliged to restore something received beyond the principal, as, for example, when a father-in-law grants his son-in-law a pledge in place of an agreed dowry, the fruits derived from the pledge are not counted against the principal, as is clear in Dig. 44.4.17.1 and X 5.19.16. If in this case a son-in-law is permitted to accept something beyond the principal by the indulgence of Roman and canon law – although such profit is usurious in both manner and form – it seems that a usurious contract – at least so far as form is concerned – is permissible under both laws. And this observation is reinforced by a special exception of canon law, which allows a cleric to redeem an ecclesiastical possession detained by another through fraud or force by not counting the revenues against the principal, as is clear in X 5.19.1 and 8.

Quarta via eciam est quia dubium est utrum ius civile possit iuri cano-
115   nico obviare, sicud ponitur in decretis di. 10. c. *Lege imperatorum*. Nam si
ponatur quod sic, poterit contractus usurarius esse permissibilis iure civili
quamvis non sit permissibilis iure canonico.

Hiis ergo premissis, procedendum est ad questionem, ad cuius facilio-
rem solucionem talis ordo videtur esse in ea tenendus. Quia primo declara-
120   bitur quid sit usura et in quibus rebus committi valeat. Secundo inquiretur
utrum contractus usurarius sit ex natura rei viciosus et malicia convolutus,
ut per hoc tollatur illa via que ingerebat dubium primo loco. Tercio inquiretur utrum iura deceant concedere contractum usurarium propter aliquod
bonum quod inde oriatur vel propter malum quod inde vitetur, ut per hoc
125   tollatur illa via que ingerebat dubium secundo loco. Quarto inquiretur
utrum iura concedant vel concedere valeant usuram in aliquo casu, ut per
hoc tollatur illa via que ingerebat dubium tercio loco. Quinto inquiretur
utrum ius civile possit iuri canonico obviare vel utrum dicta iura habeant
ad invicem tantam concordiam quod quidquid est contra unum necessario
130   sit contra alterum, ac per consequens utrum contractus usurarius eo ipso
quod prohibitus est in iure canonico necessario sit prohibitus in iure civili.
Sexto solventur argumenta aliqua que inducuntur ad questionem.

\<2\>   \<Articulus primus\>

Primo ergo videndum quid sit usura et in quibus rebus committi valeat.
Vbi sciendum quod due descripciones inveniuntur de usura que videntur satis racionabiles quia ex natura rei sunt sumpte, quarum una talis est:

1/114 eciam est : ex qua potest oriri dubium in presenti questione *RC*   1/114 possit :
e posset *corr. L*; in *add. et del. L*   1/114 iuri *RC* : iure *L*   1/115 10 *scripsi* : 19 *L* : V
RC   1/116 permissibilis : in *add. RC*   1/119 esse : *om. RC*   1/119–20 Quia primo de-
clarabitur : est ergo primo videndum *W*   1/120 sit : est *RC*   1/120 et: secundo *W*
1/120 rebus : usura *add. W*   1/120 committi : commititur *W*   1/120–2/2 valeat …
valeat : *om. W*   1/123 deceant : debeant *C*   1/123 aliquod : quod *R*   1/124 oriatur
RC : oritur *L*   1/124 vel : aut *C*   1/124 propter : maius *add. C*   1/124 inde : *om.*
C   1/124 vitetur : videtur *R* : sine tali concessione sequeretur vel oriretur *C*   1/124 ut :
vel *R*   1/125 inquiretur : inquiritur *C*   1/127 dubium : in *add. R*   1/128 iuri *RC* : iure
L   1/129 tantam : certam *C*   1/130 alterum : aliud *C*   1/132 aliqua : et dubia *RC*
1/132 inducuntur : fuerant inducta *RC*   2/2 Primo ergo : Est ergo primo *RC*   2/2 sit :
est *RC*   2/3 Vbi : Et quantum ad primum est *W*   2/3 de usura *RCW* : usure *L*   2/4 sumpte : desumptae *C*

1/115 Decretum Grat. D.10 c.1.

A fourth way in which doubt may arise is because it is unclear whether civil law can obstruct canon law, as is noted in D.10 c.1. For if it is argued that it can, a usurious contract might be permissible in civil law even if it is not in canon law.

In the light of these observations, let us now proceed to the question proper; and it seems good that we observe the following order in reaching a solution. First, we shall explain what usury is and in what things it may be committed. Second, we shall ask whether a usurious contract is by its very nature wicked and bound up with vice, so that we can dispose of the first source of doubt. Third, we shall ask whether it is fitting that the laws permit a usurious contract because of some good that might follow or in order to avoid some evil, so that we may respond to the second source of doubt. Fourth, we shall ask whether the laws permit or may permit usury in any case, by way of response to the third source of doubt. Fifth, we shall ask whether civil law can obstruct canon law or whether the two laws are in such harmony that whatever is contrary to one is contrary to the other, and as a result we shall see whether a usurious contract by the very fact that it has been prohibited by canon law is necessarily prohibited by civil law. Sixth, any other arguments proposed in the disputation will be resolved.

2. Article 1

It is necessary first to understand what usury is and in what things it may be committed. In this regard, you should know that there are two definitions of usury that appear reasonable because they derive from the nature

5   'usura est lucrum ex mutuo pacto debitum vel exactum.' In qua descripcione duo tanguntur que videntur esse de racione usure, scilicet unum
materiale et alterum formale. Materiale quidem in usura est ipsum mutuum, quia usura non gignitur materialiter nisi de mutuo. Racio autem huius
designabitur infra in sequenti articulo.

10   Formale vero in usura est ipsa exaccio sive obligacio in pactum deducta, quia ubi nullum est pactum et nulla obligacio ibi mutuans non potest
ultra sortem aliquid petere; si ultra sortem sibi aliquid offeratur, potest
illud tamquam gratis oblatum recipere. Ideo autem dico 'tamquam gratis
oblatum' quia illa donacio vel oblacio presumitur esse grata et libens quam
15   non prevenit peticio sive obligans paccio et per consequens illius oblati
licita est recepcio, nam possumus licite recipere que tamen prohibemur
petere, sicud patet per illud decretum quod habetur 1 q. 2 *Sicud episco-*
pum, ubi dicitur quod pro ingressu ecclesie non licet pecuniam exigere sed
spontanee oblatam licet recipere. Cuius racio redditur ibidem auctoritate
20   Gregorii dicentis quod 'oblacio nullam culpam vel maculam ingerit que
non ex ambientis peticione precessit.' Et de hoc possumus habere simile
argumentum ibidem in precedenti decreto, quod incipit *Quam pio* et 18. d.
De eulogiis et 13. q. 2. *Questa est nobis*, ex quibus omnibus colligitur quod
formale in usura sit ipsa paccio vel exaccio lucri ex pacto obligante, ex
25   quo eciam ulterius apparet quod descripcio habita de usura sit bona, quia
comprehendit totum quod est de racione usure. Comprehendit enim illud

---

2/5 pacto : deductum sive *add. C*   2/6 videntur : viduntur *C*   2/7 quidem : siquidem
RCW   2/8–9 Racio ... articulo : *om. W*   2/9 designabitur : assignabitur *RC*   2/10 usura : usuris *W*   2/10 exaccio *RC* : accio *L* : lucri ex pacto *add. RCW*   2/11–30 quia ...
Datur : *om. W*   2/11 ibi *RC* : et *L*   2/12 petere : et ideo *add. RC*   2/12 ultra sortem[2] :
om. RC   2/13 autem : iam *R*   2/14 oblatum : ultra sortem *add. RC*   2/14 quia : *om. R*
2/14 oblacio *RC* : obligacio *L*   2/14 libens : libera *RC*   2/16 prohibemur : prohibentur
RC   2/17 2 : capitulo *add. RC*   2/18 sed *RC* : *om. L*   2/19 recipere : suscipere *RC*
2/20 quod : quia *C* : est *add. R*   2/20 culpam : culpe *RC*   2/20 vel : *om. RC*   2/21 ambientis *RC* : ambigentis *L*   2/21 precessit : processit *RC*   2/22 pio *RC* : pie *L*
2/24 paccio : peticio *RC*   2/25 habita : prehabita *RC*   2/25 sit bona : est probabilis
RC   2/26 enim : namque *RC*

2/5 Innocent IV, *In quinque libros Decretalium commentaria*, ad X 5.19.1, n.1 (ed. Venice,
1570, repr. Frankfurt am Main, 2008, p. 616a).   2/8–9 Vid. inf. 3/213–55.   2/17–19 Decretum Grat. C.1 q.2 c.4.   2/19–21 Decretum Grat. C.1 q.2 c.4.1.   2/22–3 Decretum Grat.
C.1 q.2 c.2 ; D.18 c.8; C.13 q.2 c.12.

of the thing itself. The first is this: 'usury is profit from a loan owed or exacted on the basis of an agreement.' This definition touches on two elements – the one material and the other formal – that seem to belong to the definition of usury. The material element of usury is the loan itself, since usury arises only in a loan; and the reason for this will be explained in the following article.

The formal element of usury is an exaction or obligation expressed in an agreement, for where there is no agreement, there is no obligation, and the lender may not seek anything beyond the principal, though if something is offered to him beyond the principal he may accept it freely as a gift. I say 'freely as a gift' because a donation or gift, which is not the result of a request or a binding agreement, is presumed to be free and willing. Consequently, it is licit to accept such a gift, because we may licitly accept things that we are prohibited from seeking, as is clear in the decree cited at C.1 q.2 c.4, where it is said that one may not demand money to enter a church but one may accept a free-will offering. The reason for this is explained on the authority of Gregory, who says that 'an offering that does not arise from the request of the recipient is free of the stain of guilt.' And on this point we can advance analogous arguments in the preceding decree, namely, C.1 q.2 c.2, and in D.18 c.8 and C.13 q.2 c.12. From all of these we may conclude that the formal dimension of usury consists in an agreement or in the exaction of profit on the basis of a binding agreement. Moreover, it is clear that this definition of usury is good because it

quod est materiale in eo quod dicit 'usura sit lucrum ex mutuo.' Comprehendit quod est in ea formale per hoc quod dicit quod est lucrum pacto
debitum vel exactum.

30   Datur alia descripcio de usura, que talis est: 'usura est quidquid sorti accedit,' et ponitur in decretis 14 q. 3 *Plerique*. Ista tamen descripcio
non videtur completa nisi aliquid aliud ibi addatur, et ideo Goffredus dicit
quod debet addi 'ex pacto vel intentione precedente,' quia ex sola intentione et spe lucri videtur committi vicium usure, secundum quod ipse di-
35 cit et habetur *extra, de usuris* c. *Consuluit*. Hec autem descripcio si |^L66v
compleatur isto modo incidit in idem cum prima, quia comprehendit illud
quod est materiale et formale in usura sicud et prima, nam per hoc quod
dicitur quod 'usura est quidquid accedit sorti' comprehenditur illud quod
est in ea materiale. Illud enim quod sorti accedit non est aliud quam ipsum
40 lucrum; sors vero cui accedit non est aliud quam ipsum mutuum. Idem
est ergo dicere 'usura est quidquid sorti accedit' acsi diceretur 'usura est
lucrum accedens mutuo,' quasi genitum et proveniens materialiter ex mutuo. Per hoc vero quod ibi additur, 'ex pacto vel ex intencione precedente,'
comprehenditur in dicta descripcione illud quod est formale in usura, nam
45 dicebatur superius quod formale est in usura ipsa exaccio lucri ex pacto
obligante.

2/27 eo : ea per hoc *RC*   2/27 dicit : *om. RC*   2/27 usura sit : usura est *R* : est *C*   2/27–
8 Comprehendit : vero illud *add. R* : vero *add. C*   2/28 per : quod *add. R*   2/29 debitum : debita *R* : ductum *C*   2/29 exactum : exactio *R*   2/30 Datur : insuper *add.*
RC   2/30 alia : vero *add. W*   2/31 decretis : 19 *add. et del. L*   2/31 3 : capitulo *add.*
C   2/32 ibi *RCW* : forte *L*   2/32 Goffredus : Godofredus *RC* : Ganfredus *W*   2/33 debet : debent *R* : illi *add. RC* : ibi *W*   2/33 vel : ex *add. RC*   2/33 precedente *RCW* : precedenti *L*   2/33–5 quia … *Consuluit* : *om. W*   2/34 usure : usurarum *RC*   2/36 isto *RCW* :
hoc *L*   2/36 illud : istud *W*   2/38 comprehenditur : comprehendit *RCW*   2/40 vero :
autem *C*   2/40 Idem : Quid *W*   2/41 diceretur : diceret *W*   2/41 est² : mutuum accedens
lucro *add. et del. L* : quidquid … est³ *RC* : *om. per hom. L*   2/42–3 quasi … mutuo *RC* :
om. per hom. L   2/43 quod : dicitur et *add. C*   2/44 illud : id *RC* : istud *W*

2/30–1 Decretum Grat. C.14 q.3 c.3.   2/33–5 X 5.19.10; Gottofredo da Trani, *Summa*
super titulis Decretalium, X 5.19 *de usuris*, n.1 (ed. Lyons, 1519, repr. Darmstadt, 1968,
p. 438b).   2/45–6 Vid. sup. 2/10–29.

comprehends the entire character of usury: on the one hand, the material dimension, because it defines usury as 'profit on a loan'; on the other, the formal dimension, because it defines usury as 'profit owed or exacted on the basis of an agreement.'

Another common definition of usury, found at C.14 q.3 c.3, goes like this: 'usury is anything that accrues to the principal.' But this definition seems incomplete unless something is added to it, and therefore Gotto-fredo da Trani says that the phrase 'because of an agreement or a prior intention' should be added because it appears that the vice of usury is committed only on the basis of intention or in the hope of profit, as Got-tofredo himself observes, and as is noted in X 5.19.10. Now if the defini-tion is expanded thus, it amounts to the same thing as the first definition because it comprehends both the material and formal elements of usury. To say that 'usury is anything that accrues to the principal' expresses the material element of usury, because what accrues to the principal is nothing other than profit, and the principal to which it accrues is nothing other than the loan itself. Therefore to say that 'usury is anything that accrues to the principal' is equivalent to saying that 'usury is profit accruing to a loan,' profit that, as it were, is born of, and proceeds materially from, a loan. The additional phrase, 'from an agreement or a prior intention,' expresses the formal element of usury, for, as the first definition stated, the formal element of usury consists precisely in the exaction of profit on the basis of a binding obligation.

Occurrit tamen dubium de eo quod dictum est statim supra, utrum sola intencio sive sola spes lucri constituat hominem usurarium non interveniente ibi aliquo pacto obligante. Ad hoc autem videntur communiter re-
50   spondere omnes iurisperiti quod ubi est sola intencio et sola spes lucri principalis causa mutui, ibi ex sola intencione et ex sola spe lucri constituitur homo usurarius et tenetur ad restitucionem in foro penitentiali coram Deo. Et confirmatur per illam decretalem superius habitam, que ponitur *extra, de usuris*, c. *Consuluit*, ubi dominus papa vult quod illi qui spe lu-
55   cri mutuaverunt ita quod alias non mutuassent iudicandi sint in iudicio animarum ad restituendum accepta. Que quidem opinio videtur fundari super sentencia salvatoris nostri dicentis Luce 6: 'mutuum date nichil inde sperantes' et super auctoritatibus sanctorum Augustini, Ambrosii, et Ieronomi et ponuntur 14 q. 3. Et videntur omnes in hoc concordare, scilicet
60   quod ubi mutuans expectat aliquid ultra illud quod dedit debitori usuram committit et per consequens ad restitucionem tenetur.

Sed salva reverencia, hec opinio videtur irracionabilis propter tria. Primo quia, sicud patuit superius, formale in usura est exaccio ex pacto obligante et ideo ubi non est exaccio lucri ex pacto obligante vel aliquod ei
65   equipollens, ibi non potest esse usura ad restitucionem obligans, quamvis possit esse usura vicians. Illi ergo qui tenent istam opinionem nullo modo possunt salvare primam descripcionem de usura, que dicebat quod usura est lucrum ex mutuo pacto debitum vel exactum.

Vlterius secundo apparet idem per simile quod videmus de furto. Nam

---

2/47–117 Occurit ... exaccionem : *om.* W   2/47 tamen : mihi *RC*   2/47 supra : scilicet *RC*   2/48 non : si *R* : sine *C*   2/50 omnes : *om. RC*   2/50 lucri : et *add. L*   2/51 causa *RC* : *om. L*   2/51 ibi *RC* : *om. L*   2/51 et : *om. R*   2/51 ex² : *om. C*   2/52 penitentiali : spirituali *RC*   2/52 coram : Deo *add. et del. L*   2/53 habitam : citatam *C*   2/53 ponitur : habetur *C*   2/54 c. Consuluit : *om. RC*   2/55 iudicandi : inducendi *RC*   2/57 date : dantes *R*   2/58 Ambrosii : q *add. et del. L*   2/59 et¹ : qui *R* : quae *C*   2/60 expectat *RC* : ex pacto *L*   2/60 illud : id *C*   2/60 debitori : *om. RC*   2/62 salva : horum *add. C*   2/62 opinio : non *add. RC*   2/62 videtur : est *C*   2/62 irracionabilis : racionabilis *RC*   2/62 propter tria *RC* : propterea *L*   2/64 aliquod : aliquid *RC*   2/65 quamvis : ibi *add. RC*   2/66 istam : illam *RC*   2/67 salvare : illam *add. RC*   2/68 ex : de *RC*   2/68 debitum : deductum *RC*   2/69 secundo : *om. C*   2/69 idem : hoc eodem *R* : hoc ratione *C*   2/69 simile *RC* : similem *L*

2/47 Vid. sup. 2/10–35.   2/53–6 X 5.19.10; vid. sup. 2/35.   2/57–8 *Lc* 6.35.   2/58–9 Decretum Grat. C.14 q.3 c.1, 2, 3.

But a doubt arises with respect to what has just been said, and that is whether the intention to profit or the hope of profit alone renders someone a usurer, even in the absence of a binding obligation. It seems that on this point the jurists are agreed that when an intention to profit or hope of profit is the principal motive for extending a loan, then this intention or hope alone renders the lender a usurer and he is bound before God to make restitution in the context of penance. This is confirmed by the decretal we cited earlier, namely X 5.19.10, where the pope wills that those who would not have extended a loan unless they could expect a profit be compelled in penance to make restitution of what they have received from their debtors. And this opinion is clearly based on the opinion of our saviour, who says in Luke 6: 'lend, expecting nothing in return,' and on the authority of the saints Augustine, Ambrose, and Jerome cited at C.14 q.3 c.1–3. It appears that everyone is agreed on this point, namely, that when a creditor anticipates something beyond what he has lent to his debtor, he commits usury and is consequently obliged to make restitution.

But with due respect, this opinion appears contrary to reason on three counts. First, as is clear from what was said above, the formal dimension of usury is an exaction on the basis of a binding agreement; therefore, where there is no exaction of profit on the basis of a binding agreement or something equivalent to it, there can be no usury subject to restitution, although the vice of usury itself might be present in the transaction. Those, then, who maintain this opinion cannot sustain the first definition, which says that usury is profit owed or exacted on the basis of an agreement.

Second, the same might be said with reference to theft. For if some-

70   si aliquis gratis et liberaliter in dono recipiat quod furari intendebat et af-
      fectabat, quamvis sit fur in corde, non tamen in opere ita quod teneatur ad
      restitucionem. Igitur si quis furari intendit ex mutuo quod concedit et ta-
      men a suo debitore nihil exigit nec ipsum quasi per pactum compellit, sed
      gratis et liberaliter ab eo recipit aliquid, quamvis sit usurarius mente, non
75   tamen est censendus usurarius in opere ita quod teneatur ad restitucionem.

      Tercio patet hoc idem quia tota racio quare usurarius tenetur ad restitu-
      cionem est quod illud quod recipit ultra sortem non fuit ei gratis et libe-
      raliter donatum sed cum quadam exaccione et pacto indebite usurpatum.
      Sed ubi est sola spes lucri et sola intencio corrupta ex parte recipientis,
80   dummodo illa non sit nota debitori, quidquid debitor donat, gratis et li-
      bere donat, et per consequens non est ibi indebite usurpatum et ideo ipse
      recipiens, quamvis fuerit in intencione depravatus, non videtur teneri ad
      restitucionem; nec obstat illa decretalis que superius inducebatur pro illa
      opinione.
85   Ad cuius evidenciam distinguendum est de usura mentali que fit exac-
      tione et pacto, nam duplex est usura talis. Vna est in qua intencio mu-
      tuantis depravata innotescit ipsi debitori, et talis usura non solum vicians
      ipsam mentem sed eciam est obligans ad restitucionem, quia quamvis ta-
      lis usura fit sine exaccione et pacto explicato, est tamen cum exaccione et
90   pacto implicite intellecto. Propter quod possumus dicere quod talis usura
      mentalis equipollet illi usure que fit cum exaccione et pacto explicito, nam
      sicud pactum explicitum facit quod illud lucrum quod accedit sorti non
      sit gratuite nec libere donatum, ita eciam hoc idem facit pactum implicite
      et ideo utrobique tenetur quis ad restitucionem illius lucri. De tali ergo

---

2/71 corde : mente *RC*   2/71 non : est censendus fur *add. RC*   2/72 Igitur : Ergo a
simili *RC*   2/72 furari *RC* : feurari *L*   2/72 intendit *RC* : capit *L*   2/73 nihil *RC* :
non *L*   2/73 quasi : *om. RC*   2/73 per : aliquod *add. RC*   2/74 usurarius : in *add.*
RC   2/76 hoc idem : hec racio *R* : hoc ratione *C*   2/77 quod : quia *RC*   2/77 illud :
id *C*   2/78 indebite usurpatum *RC* : indebito usurpapivo *L*   2/80 debitori : ipsi *add.*
RC   2/81 non : nihil *RC*   2/82 in : *om. RC*   2/83–6 nec obstat … et pacto *RC* : *om.*
L   2/86 Vna : quidem *add. RC*   2/86 est[1] : *om. RC*   2/87 solum : est *add. RC*
2/88 quamvis : licet *C*   2/89 explicato : explicito *RC*   2/93 gratuite : gratuitum *RC*
2/93 idem : *om. C*   2/93 implicite : implicitum *RC*   2/94 restitucionem : restituendum
RC   2/94 illius lucri : talem lucrum *RC*

2/83 X 5.19.10; vid. sup. 2/53–6.

body freely accepts as a gift something that he previously intended and attempted to steal, although he is a thief by intention, he cannot in practice be obliged to make restitution. Therefore, if somebody intends theft by means of a loan that he advances but does not demand a profit from his debtor or bind him with an agreement, but rather freely receives something from him, although he is a usurer in intention, he cannot be condemned as a usurer in practice such that he is obliged to make restitution.

Third, it is clear that the very reason a usurer is obliged to make restitution is that what he receives beyond the principal is not freely given but rather usurped by means of an exaction and owed by an agreement. But when a creditor hopes for a profit and his intention alone is corrupt, provided this is unknown to the debtor, whatever the debtor gives he gives freely, and consequently we cannot say that it was unjustly usurped. And although the creditor's intention is corrupt, it does not seem that he is obliged to make restitution, notwithstanding the decretal cited above in support of this opinion.

To clarify this point it is necessary to make some distinctions with regard to mental usury, which in reality expresses itself by means of an exaction and an agreement, for such usury is twofold. In one form, the debtor is aware of the corrupt intention of the lender, and usury of this kind not only corrupts the mind of the lender but must also be restored because, although such usury is committed without an explicit exaction or agreement, it is nevertheless made with an implicit exaction and agreement. And for this reason, we can say that such mental usury is equivalent to usury committed by means of an explicit exaction and agreement. For just as an explicit agreement has the effect that the profit that accrues to the prin-

95　usura mentali intellexit dominus papa quando dixit quod illi qui ex sola
intencione nullo interveniente pacto erant usurarii sunt inducendi ad restitucionem in iudicio animarum.

Alia vero est usura mentalis in qua intencio depravata mutuantis nullo
modo fit nota ipsi debitori, et talis usura est solum vicians ipsam inten-
100　cionem sed non est obligans ad restitucionem, quia in tali usura nulla est
exaccio et nullum pactum explicitum vel implicitum |$^{\text{L67r}}$ quod impedi-
re posset liberam et gratuitam donacionem illius lucri quod sorti accedit;
stante autem libera et gratuita donacione ipsius dantis, non tenetur reci-
piens ad restitucionem. Et ita patet quomodo potest exponi decretalis vel
105　auctoritates que faciebant pro illa opinione. Patet eciam ex dictis quid est
usura et quomodo duplex est usura, quarum una simplex mentalis et est
solum vicians et non obligans ad restitucionem eo quod fiat sine omni
exaccione et sine omni pacto explicito vel implicito; alia vero est vicians et
obligans ad restitucionem eo quod fiat cum exaccione et pacto explicito vel
110　implicite intellecto. Propter quod subdividitur: quia si fiat cum exactione
et pacto implicito, sic est usura mentalis; si vero cum exaccione et pacto
explicito, sic est usura vocalis contractus.

Apparet ulterius ex dictis quod duo sunt de racione usure, qualiter-
cumque accipiatur, quorum unum est materiale, utpote quod sit lucrum
115　proveniens et genitum materialiter de ipso mutuo; alterum vero formale,
utpote quod gignatur ex mutuo tali modo, scilicet per pravam intencionem
vel per pactum et exaccionem.
Sed si queratur ulterius in quibus rebus usura committitur, quia videtur

2/96 erant : erunt *RC*　2/99–100 intencionem : mentem *RC*　2/101 et : *om. RC*
2/101 nullum : est *add. RC*　2/102 posset : valeat *RC*　2/102 donacionem : dationem *C*
2/102 quod : quia *R*　2/103 donacione : datione *C*　2/104 vel : et *RC*　2/105 faciebant
RC : faciebat *L*　2/105–6 est usura *RC* : usuras *L*　2/106 simplex : simpliciter est *RC*
2/110 implicite : implicito *RC*　2/110–11 Propter ... implicito *RC* : *om. L*　2/111 sic :
om. C　2/113 ulterius : eciam *add. RC*　2/115 vero : est *add. RC*　2/116 gignatur
RC : gignitur *L*　2/116 ex : de *RC*　2/116 scilicet : vel *add. RC*　2/116 per : solam
add. RC　2/116 intencionem : acceptacionem *RC*　2/118–19 Sed si ... quod : Quantum ad secundum, usura *W*　2/118 in *RC* : ex *L*　2/118 committitur : commictatur
RC　2/118 quia : eciam *add. RC*　2/118 videtur : *om. RC*

cipal is not given gratuitously or freely, so also this implicit agreement; and therefore the lender is doubly obliged to restore such profit. It was, therefore, of such mental usury that the pope spoke when he said that those who lend with the sole intention of profit, even without an explicit agreement, are to be considered usurers and obliged to make restitution in the sacrament of penance.

But there is another kind of mental usury in which the corrupt intention of the creditor is completely unknown to the debtor, and such usury simply corrupts the intention but does not involve an obligation to make restitution, because in this case there is no exaction nor any explicit or implicit agreement that might invalidate a free and gratuitous gift of profit in addition to the principal. If the debtor's gift is truly free and gratuitous, the creditor is not obliged to make restitution. And so it is clear how the said decretal and other authorities that support this view may be expounded. It is also clear from what I have said how usury is twofold: there is mental usury, which is simply corrupt but does not impose an obligation to make restitution because there is no explicit or implicit exaction or agreement; and there is usury which both is corrupt and imposes an obligation to make restitution insofar as there is an explicit or implicit exaction or agreement. And for this reason usury may be subdivided into two forms: if usury is contracted with an implicit exaction or agreement, it is 'mental' usury; if it is contracted with an explicit exaction or agreement, it is 'oral' usury.

Moreover, from what I have said it is clear that there are two dimensions to usury, however it is received, of which one is material, inasmuch as it is a profit that arises from, and is born of, a loan, the other formal, since it is born of a loan in a certain way, that is, through a perverse intention or by means of an agreement and exaction.

If you ask further in what sorts of things usury is committed – because

120 hoc ad istum articulum pertinere, videtur dicendum esse quod committitur in hiis rebus circa quas consistit mutuum, ut concorditer omnes dicunt. Res autem circa quas consistit mutuum sunt in triplici genere, quia quedam sunt res que mutuantur sub certo numero, sicut pecunia; quedam sub certo pondere, sicud aurum vel argentum; quedam sub certa mensura, sicut granum, vinum, oleum, et similia. Et ideo solum in hiis tribus generi-
125 bus rerum usura committitur.

Intelligendum tamen quod Goffredus obiciens contra Raymundum dicit quod usura potest committi eciam in aliis rebus, nam si pro pecunia mutuata recipiam inde equum vel predium sive vestem vel quidquid tale ultra sortem, usura est, sicud patet 14 q. 3 *Plerique.* Hec tamen obieccio
130 leviter potest tolli quia distinccio debet fieri inter usuram que ab usurario exigitur et rem illam in qua dicta usura committitur, nam ista que ab usurario exigitur proprie loquendo est illud lucrum quod exigitur ultra sortem sive ultra mutuum; res vero illa in qua dicta usura committitur est ipsum mutuum de quo, ut dictum est, lucrum gignitur. Quamvis ergo quelibet
135 res possit accedere feneratori tanquam lucrum usurarium, dictum tamen lucrum non gignitur nisi solum de illis tribus in quibus, ut dictum est, usura committitur.

Occurrunt tamen contra dicta quedam dubia et sunt duo. Primum est

---

2/119 esse : est *RC*   2/120–1 ut concorditer omnes dicunt : *om. C*   2/120–1 ut concorditer ... mutuum : *om. per hom. RW*   2/121 sunt : autem *add. W*   2/121 triplici *RC* : duplici *L*   2/121 triplici : differentia sive *add. C*   2/122 sicut pecunia : *om. W*   2/122 quedam[2] : vero sunt que mutuantur *add. RCW*   2/123 sub[1] : *om. R*   2/123 vel : et *RC*   2/123 quedam : vero sunt res que mutuantur *add. RCW*   2/126 Goffredus : Gottofredus *R* : Godofredus *C*   2/127 pro *RC* : *om. L*   2/128 vestem : vestera *R*   2/128 vel quidquid : et quid *RC*   2/129 sortem : accipiatur *add. RC*   2/130 distinccio : potest *add. et exp. R*   2/131 ista : usura *RC*   2/134 ut : *om. RC*   2/134 est : *om. RC*   2/135 usurarium : usurarum *RC*   2/136 solum de : de solis *RC*   2/136–7 in quibus ... committitur : earum rerum generibus, propter quod bene dictum est quod usura in solis tribus commicitur *RC* : illis *post* solis *add. C*   2/138 tamen : dicta *add. R*   2/138 quedam ... duo : duo dubia *RC*

2/121–4 Cf. Inst. 3.14.pr.   2/126–9 Gottofredo da Trani, *Summa*, X 5.19 *de usuris*, n.3 (ed. cit. p. 439b–440a); Raymond of Penyafort, *Summa de poenitentia et matrimonio cum glossis Ioannis de Friburgo* (*recte* Guillelmi Redonensis), 2.7 *de usuris*, n.1 (ed. Rome, 1603, repr. Farnborough, 1967, p. 227b).   2/129 Decretum Grat. C.14 q.3 c.3.   2/129–37 Cf. Hostiensis (Henricus de Segusio), *Summa aurea*, X 5.19 *de usuris*, n.1 (Lyons, 1537, repr. Frankfurt am Main, 2009, fol. 249rb–va).

this seems to pertain to this article – it should be said that it is committed in the things in which a loan consists, as everyone agrees. Now the things in which a loan consists are of three kinds: there are things that are lent according to number, such as money; things that are lent according to weight, such as gold and silver; and things that are lent according measure, such as grain, wine, oil, and similar things. Usury is committed only in these three classes of things.

You should know that Gottofredo da Trani, objecting to this formulation in Raymond of Penyafort, says that usury can be committed in other things as well, for if in exchange for money lent I should receive a horse or a farm or clothing or any such thing beyond the principal, it is usury, as is clear in C.14 q.3 c.3. But this objection is easily disposed of, because a distinction must be made between the usury which is exacted by a usurer and the thing in which the usury is committed, for what is exacted by a usurer is properly speaking the profit that is extracted beyond the principal of the loan. But the thing in which usury is committed is the loan itself, from which, as I have said, a profit is generated. Therefore, although anything could accede to the creditor as usurious profit, the said profit can only be generated, as I have said, from the three classes of things in which usury is committed.

Nevertheless, two questions arise from the things just said. The first

quare mutuum consistit solum circa tria dicta genera rerum. Secundum
140   dubium est quare usura committitur solum in illis rebus circa quas consistit mutuum.

Ad primum dico quod in mutuo non tenetur debitor restituere rem mutuatam sub ydemptitate substancie, quia hoc est impossibile, sed tenetur
eam restituere sub certitudine eiusdem valoris sive equalis valoris si debeat
145   salvari vera iusticia inter mutuantem et illum cui fit mutuum. Certitudo
autem equalis valoris non invenitur ex natura rei nisi in illis rebus quarum valor pensatur ex numero, pondere, vel mensura, quapropter racio
mutui debet consistere solum in illis tribus que ad habendam sui valoris
certitudinem possunt numerari, ponderari, vel mensurari. Et ita patet quid
150   dicendum sit ad primum dubium. Quid vero dicendum sit ad secundum
patebit in sequenti articulo.

<3>   <Articulus secundus>

Hiis ergo visis, secundo videndum utrum contractus usurarius sit ex natura rei viciosus et malicia convolutus. Dicendum quod conclusio quantum
ad istum articulum non videtur dubia, quia creditur secundum veritatem
5   et secundum intencionem omnium qui de ista materia aliquid sentiunt fore
dicendum quod contractus usurarius ex natura rei sit viciosus et malicia
convolutus, quod patet ex tribus.

Primo videmus quod ipse Aristoteles nulla lege scripta artatus vel edoc-
tus sed sola racione naturali deductus lucrum usurarium est detestatus,

---

2/140 est : *om. C*   2/140 solum : tantum *C*   2/142 in *RC* : *om. L*   2/142 rem : debitam
add. et del. L   2/143 hoc : sepius *add. RC*   2/144 eam : *om. RC*   2/145 Certitudo :
Rectitudo *RC*   2/147 numero : vel ex *add. RC*   2/147 vel : ex *add. RC*   2/148 solum
in illis tribus : in solis illis rebus *RC*   2/149 certitudinem : possunt *add. et del. L per
ditt.*   2/149 numerari : et *add. R* : vel *add. C*   1/149 mensurari : usurari *R*   2/150 dicendum[1] : dictum *RC*   2/150 secundum : dubium *add. RC*   2/151 sequenti : capitulo *add. et
exp. R* : secundo *C*   2/151 articulo : Viso ergo quantum ad istum articulum quid est usura
et in quibus rebus commictatur, restat videre secundo quantum ad sequentem articulum :
add. RC   3/2 Hiis … videndum : *om. RC*   3/2–3 ex natura rei : *om. C*   3/3 Dicendum quod : *om. RC*   3/3 conclusio : convolutus ergo etiam *R*   3/4 videtur : mihi *add.
RC*   3/4 creditur : credo *RC*   3/5 fore : forte *R*   3/8 Primo : quia *add. RC*   3/9 deductus : deducitur *R*   3/9 usurarium : usurarum *RC*

is why a loan consists only in the three aforesaid classes of things. The second is why usury is committed only in those things of which a loan consists.

To the first question I reply that in a loan the debtor is not bound to restore the identical substance of the thing borrowed because this is impossible, but he is obliged to restore a thing of precisely the same or equal value, if true justice between lender and borrower is to be maintained. But precision in the calculation of value does not exist in nature except in things whose value is conceived in terms of number, weight, or measure, and therefore the index of a loan is that it consists only in those three kinds of things whose value can be calculated precisely by counting, weighing, or measuring them. And so it is clear what the response to the first question is. The response to the second will be made clear in the next article.

3. Article 2

In the light of the foregoing, it is necessary to consider second whether a usurious contract is by its very nature wicked and bound up with vice. It must be said that the conclusion of this article does not appear to be in doubt, because the common view, which accords both with the truth and with the opinion of everyone who has considered the matter, is that a usurious contract is by its very nature wicked and bound up with vice, which is evident for three reasons.

First, we see that Aristotle, who was neither bound nor informed by any written law but guided by natural reason alone, execrated usurious profit,

10   sicud patet primo *Polliticorum*, quod non fecisset nisi contractus usurarius
fuisset ex natura rei viciosus et malicia convolutus.

Secundo patet hoc idem quia certum est quod rapina ex natura rei est
viciosa et malicia convoluta. Qui autem accipit usuram facit rapinam, ut
patet 14 q. 4 *Si quis usuram*. Quapropter relinquitur quod contractus usu-
15   rarius ex natura rei sit viciosus et malicia convolutus.

Tercio patet hoc idem quia illud quod est prohibitum non solum in lege
Mosaÿca sed eciam in lege evangelica ex natura rei videtur esse viciosum et
malicia convolutum. Sed contractus usurarius est prohibitus non solum in
lege Mosaÿca sed evangelica, ergo ex natura rei est viciosus et malicia con-
20   volutus. Maior patet quia videmus quod illa que in lege Mosaÿca fuerunt
prohibita et tamen ex natura rei |L67v non fuerunt viciosa, postea in lege
evangelica fuerunt concessa. Minor eciam apparet per textum utriusque
legis et habetur *extra, de usuris* c. *Super eo*, ubi dominus papa Alexander
dicit quod 'cum usurarum crimen utriusque testamenti pagina detestetur,
25   super hoc dispensacionem aliquam posse fieri non videmus.'

Dico ergo quod conclusio huius articuli non videtur esse dubia, quia
omnino videtur esse dicendum quod contractus usurarius ex natura rei sit
viciosus et malicia convolutus. Assignare autem de hoc causam per quam
evidencius demonstretur quod contractus usurarius habet ex natura rei vi-
30   ciositatem et maliciam convolutam non puto omnino facile eo quod raciones aliorum que super hoc ponuntur videntur penitus dubie, quod patet si
per eas discurratur.

3/11 fuisset : esset *C*   3/11 malicia : maliciis *R*   3/12 certum : rectum *R* : manifestum
C   3/13 facit : usuram *add. et del. R*   3/14 14 : VIIII *R*   3/14 4 : cap. *add. C*   3/14 Si
quis usuram : *om. R* : Si quis *C*   3/17 Mosaÿca : Moysi *C*   3/19 sed : eciam in lege
add. RC   3/21 fuerunt : erant *RC*   3/21 viciosa : et *add. R*   3/22 fuerunt : sunt
RC   3/22 textum : testum *R*   3/23 legis : scilicet Mosaÿce et evangelice *add. RC*   3/23–
5 ubi dominus ... super hoc : *om. per hom. R* : his verbis, super hoc *C*   3/26 ergo : *om.*
RC   3/26 huius : istius *RC*   3/26 esse : *om. C*   3/26 quia : sed *RC*   3/27 esse : *om.*
RC   3/28 autem : tamen *RC*   3/29 evidencius : evidenter *RC*   3/29 quod : dictus *add.*
RC   3/29 usurarius : *om. RC*   3/31 videntur : mihi *add. RC*   3/32 discurratur : discur-
ramus *RC*

3/10 Aristotle, *Politica* 1.10.1258a20–b8 (*Politica, Libri I–II.11: Translatio imperfecta interprete Guillelmo de Moerbeka(?)*, ed. Pierre Michaud-Quantin, Aristoteles Latinus 29.1,
Bruges and Paris, 1961, p. 18).   3/14 Decretum Grat. C.14 q.4 c.10.   3/16–17 Cf. *Dt*
23.19–20; *Ez* 18.8–9; *Ez* 18.17.   3/17 *Lc* 6.35.   3/21–2 Cf. *Act* 10.1–6.   3/23–5 X 5.19.4.

as is clear in book 1 of the *Politics*, which he would not have done if a usurious contract were not by its very nature wicked and bound up with vice.

Second, this conclusion is obvious because it is certain that robbery is by its very nature wicked and bound up with vice. But he who accepts usury commits robbery, as is clear in C.14 q.4 c.10; therefore it follows that a usurious contract is by its very nature wicked and bound up with vice.

Third, this conclusion is obvious because that which is prohibited not only in the Mosaic law but also in the law of the Gospels appears by its very nature to be wicked and bound up with vice. Now a usurious contract is prohibited not only in the Mosaic law but also in that of the Gospels, therefore it is by its very nature wicked and bound up with vice. The major premiss is clear because we see that those things that had been prohibited in the law of Moses but were not by their very nature wicked were later permitted in the law of the gospels. The minor premiss is evident from the very words of each law and confirmed in X 5.19.4, where the lord pope Alexander says that 'since the crime of usury is execrated by the text of both laws, we do not see how any relaxation can be granted in this matter.'

I say, then, that the conclusion of this article is not in doubt, since it appears completely beyond question that a usurious contract is by its very nature wicked and bound up with vice. But I do not think it altogether easy to assign a clear reason for this, since the arguments advanced by others on this matter appear wholly questionable, which will become clear as we review them in turn.

Vna enim racio quam videtur tangere Goffredus et quam tenent communiter iuriste et ponitur in glosa 14 q. 3 est ista. Dicunt enim quod in
35   contractu usurario acquirit usurarius lucrum quod non est suum, exigit
enim lucrum de ipso mutuo quod transsit in dominium ipsius debitoris,
quia mutuum est 'quod de meo fit tuum,' ut patet ff. *de rebus credi. si certum petatur* l. *Mutuum § Appellata est.* Posset ergo ex hiis dictis talis racio
formari: ille contractus ex natura rei est viciosus et malicia convolutus in
40   quo aliquis exigit lucrum de re non sua. Sed in usura est hoc, ut ex dictis
patet, ergo ex natura rei est viciosus et malicia convolutus.

Hec autem racio, quamvis videatur valde pulchra et apparens, tamen
videtur valde dubia quia licet maior proposicio sit manifesta, minor tamen omnino videtur falsa. Cum enim dicitur quod fenerator exigit lucrum
45   de re non sua, potest dici immediate quod est falsum, quia pecunia quam
mutuat, quamvis transseat in dominium debitoris quantum ad ydemptitatem substancie, quia debitor non tenetur restituere eandem pecuniam
secundum substanciam, remanet tamen dicta pecunia in dominio feneratoris quantum ad idemptitatem et equalitatem valoris. Et hoc ipsum vi-
50   detur sufficere, quia ipse fenerator non exigit lucrum de pecunia quam
mutuat in quantum talis substancia est, secundum quem modum ad eum
non pertinet nec potest eam repetere, sed exigit magis de ea in quantum
tanti valoris est, secundum quem modum ad eum pertinet, quia remanet in
suo dominio, et semper potest eam licite expetere. Quapropter dicta racio

---

3/33 tangere : tenere *RC*   3/34 quod : con *add. et del. R*   3/35 lucrum : de eo *add.*
RC   3/36 quod : mutuavit *add. L* : quidem mutuum *add. RC*   3/37 mutuum : non
add. L   3/37 meo : non *add. L*   3/37–8 si certum petatur *C* : ei fecit pe. *L* : et fec. pe.
R   3/38 Appellata : Applicata *RC*   3/38 hiis : istis *RC*   3/40 Sed ... hoc : Sed contractus
usurarius est talis quia in eo ipse fenerator exigit lucrum de re non sua *RC*   3/42 valde : valida *RC*   3/42 apparens : mihi *add. RC*   3/43 quia : et *add. R*   3/44 omnino *RC* : non *L*   3/44 quod *RC* : *om. L*   3/45 pecunia *RC* : pecuniam *L*   3/49 et[1] :
sive *RC*   3/49 equalitatem *RC* : qualitatem *L*   3/49 ipsum : *om. RC*   3/50 ipse :
idem *RC*   3/51 est *RC* : *om. L*   3/52 magis : lucrum *RC*   3/54 expetere : repetere
RC   3/54 racio : vel *add. RC*

3/33–8 Gottofredo da Trani, *Summa*, X 5.19 *de usuris* n.1 (ed. cit. p. 439a–b). Cf. Hostiensis, *Summa aurea*, X 5.19 *de usuris*, n.1 (ed. cit. fol. 249va); gl. ord. ad Decretum Grat. C.14
q.3 c.1, v. *Plus quam* (ed. Lyons, 1560, col. 1032).   3/37–8 Dig. 12.1.2.2. Cf. Inst. 3.14.
pr.   3/40 Vid. sup. 3/34–8.

One argument, which Gottofredo da Trani seems to endorse and which jurists commonly advance, is found in the gloss to C.14 q.3 c.1 and runs as follows: in a usurious contract the usurer obtains a profit that does not belong to him because he extracts a profit from the loan itself, which has passed into the ownership of the debtor, as is clear from Dig. 12.1.2.2, where it says that in a loan 'what is mine becomes yours.' On this basis, the following argument may be constructed: a contract in which someone extracts a profit from something that he does not own is by its very nature wicked and bound up with malice. This is what happens in usury, as is clear from what has been said; therefore usury is by its very nature wicked and bound up with malice.

Although this argument seems very elegant and clear, it is nevertheless highly questionable because although the major premiss is clear, the minor appears to be false. For when it is said that a usurer extracts a profit from something he does not own, one can immediately object that this is false because even if the money he lends becomes the property of the debtor so far as the substance of the money is concerned – because the debtor is not obliged to restore the very same coins he borrowed – nevertheless, the money remains the property of the usurer with regard to its value. And this seems an adequate response because a usurer does not extract profit from the money he lends with respect to its substance – for in this regard the money does not belong to him nor can he demand its return – but rather he extracts profit from it insofar as it is of a certain value, and this value does belong to him because it remains his property and he can

55 omnino non valet vel si debet aliquid valere, oportet eam corrigere, sicud
inferius corrigetur.

Intelligendum tamen quod illi qui utuntur tali racione prefata videntur
eam confirmare, quia dicunt quod pecunia mutuata transit in debitorem
cum suo periculo et ideo iniustum videtur quod de ea gravetur amplius ul-
60 tra sortem. Ex quibus verbis posset formari una alia racio ad propositum,
que talis esset: ille contractus ex natura rei est viciosus et malicia convolutus in quo altera pars gravatur ultra id quod debet; sed in contractu usurario ipse debitor ultra id quod debet gravatur, ut patet per verba prehabita,
ergo talis contractus ex natura rei est viciosus et malicia convolutus. Sed
65 nec ista racio sive confirmacio videtur valere propter duo. Primo quia videmus sepe quod non solum res mutuata sed eciam res commodata manet
apud illum cui commodatur in suo periculo, sicud patet in equo commo-
dato, qui quidem manet in periculo illius cui commodatur; sicut eciam patet in pecunia commodata ad ostentacionem, que eciam manet in periculo
70 illius cui commodatur; et tamen hoc non obstante conceditur quod licite
exigitur lucrum de rebus commodatis.

Vlterius secundo non videtur valere dicta confirmacio quia posset aliquis dicere quod ille qui accipit pecuniam in mutuo potest licite gravari
de ea quantum ad duo, scilicet quantum ad periculum et quantum ad red-
75 dendum lucrum, et hoc propter aliam et aliam causam, utpote gravabitur
de periculo in quantum efficitur conservator pecunie quantum ad suum
profectum; gravabitur vero de lucro in quantum mutuans potest ab eo
exigere beneficium pro servicio impenso. Vbi autem diverse sunt cause
gravaminis, potest quis gravari diversis gravaminibus, nec hoc erit contra
80 equitatem iusticie.

3/57 tali : *om. RC*   3/58 confirmare : per hoc *add. RC*   3/60 verbis : vero *R* : nihi-
lominus *C*   3/61 esset : est *C*   3/65 sive : seu *C*   3/65 confirmacio *RC* : convolucio
L   3/68–9 qui quidem … commodata *RC* : *om. per hom. L*   3/71 exigitur : exigatur
C   3/73 in : *om. RC*   3/75 et aliam : *om. RC*   3/76 quantum : *om. RC*   3/76 suum :
beneficium seu *add. C*   3/77 profectum : perfectum *R*   3/77 vero : etiam *C*   3/78 servicio *RC* : lucro *L* : sibi *add. RC*   3/79 gravari : in *add. RC*   3/79 contra *RC* : *om. L*

3/55–6 Vid. inf. 3/242–51.   3/63 Vid. sup. 3/57–60.

always demand its repayment. Therefore this argument is completely invalid, or rather, if it is to be rendered valid, it needs to be corrected, as it shall be below.

It should also be noted that those who deploy this argument appear to reinforce it by maintaining that lent money passes to the debtor along with the risk and therefore it appears unjust that he should be burdened beyond the repayment of the principal. On these grounds a second argument may be devised with respect to the question, which runs like this: a contract in which one party is bound to repay more than the principal is by its nature wicked and bound up with vice. Now in a usurious contract the debtor is obliged to repay more than he owes, as is clear from what I just said, therefore the contract is by nature wicked and bound up with vice. But this argument does not seem to hold for two reasons. First, because we know from experience that risk passes to the borrower not only in loans of fungibles but in loans of non-fungible things, as is clear in the loan of a horse, where risk passes to the borrower, and even in a loan of coins for purposes of display rather than consumption, where risk also passes to the borrower. Despite this, it is generally conceded that one may licitly extract a profit from the loan of a non-fungible.

Moreover, this second argument seems to fail because one could say that he who receives money in a loan can be obliged licitly in two respects: first with respect to risk and second with regard to rendering a profit, and this for two reasons; first, because he is obliged with respect to risk so far as he manages the money for his own profit; and second, because he is also obliged to provide a profit to the lender, since the latter can demand of him a favour on account of the service he has rendered him by lending. When obligations arise from various causes, one may be variously obliged, and this does not appear contrary to equity.

Inducitur insuper alia racio a theologis que videtur probare quod contractus usurarius sit viciosus et malicia convolutus ex natura rei. Dicunt enim quod in dicto contractu venditur usus rei cuius usus est ipsa consumpcio, et ubi sic est ibi non potest res seorsum computari et separari
85   a suo usu nec econverso, et ideo eadem concessione qua conceditur res conceditur et usus rei et econverso. Quicumque autem vellet separatim vendere usum rei sine re tali cuius usus est ipsa consumpcio ageret viciose et contra naturam; sed fenerator vendit separatim usum rei quam |^L68r mutuat ab ipsa re cuius usus est ipsa consumpcio, ergo agit viciose et contra
90   naturam. Maior patet, ymmo probatur, quia exigit lucrum de usu pecunie quam mutuavit, non obstante quod eam semper solidam in eadem quantitate requirit.

Ista eciam racio videtur dubia quia posset aliquis dicere quod fenerator non vendit usum rei quam mutuat sine ipsa re, immo simul vendit utrum-
95   que, quia alienat a se non solum usum rei sed eciam ipsam rem quantum ad substanciam; et ideo quantum ad hoc idem iudicium videtur de utroque, quia eo modo quo transfert ipsam rem, transfert et ipsum usum et econverso, quapropter non separat unum a reliquo sicud supposuit dicta racio. Vnde videtur quod prefata racio non valeat vel quod eam corrigere
100   oporteat.

Consuevit insuper induci alia racio ad propositum, que videtur esse tac-

---

3/82 et malicia convolutus : *om. RC*   3/83 enim : *om. R*   3/83 usus : illius *add.*
RC   3/84 et ubi sic est : quod est viciosum et contra naturam, nam ubi usus rei est
eius consumpcio *RC* : et *pro* est *R*   3/84 non : potest *add. et del. per ditt.* L   3/84 et² :
vel *RC*   3/85 et : *om. C*   3/85–6 res conceditur et : *om. R* : res intelligitur concedi et
C   3/86 autem : ergo *RC*   3/87 ipsa : sua *RC*   3/88 separatim *RC* : *om.* L   3/90 patet
ymmo : *om. RC*   3/91 mutuavit : mutuat *RC*   3/91 solidam : salvam *RC*   3/92 requirit : requirat *RC*   3/93 Ista : Secunda *RC*   3/93 videtur : mihi *add. RC*   3/93 quia *RC* :
om. L   3/95 a se : anime (!) *R* : omnino *C*   3/96 iudicium : videtur *add. et del. per ditt.*
L   3/97 et¹ : eciam *RC*   3/98 supposuit : supponit *RC*   3/99 Vnde : *om. RC*   3/99 videtur : ergo vel *add. RC*   3/99 valeat : valet *RC*   3/101 racio *RC* : *om.* L   3/101–2 esse
tacta : trahi *RC*

3/81–92 Cf. Thomas Aquinas, *Summa theologiae*, 2ª 2ᵃᵉ, q.78 art.1, in *Opera omnia*, vol.
9 (Rome, 1897), p. 155b.   3/101–7 Aristotle, *Politica* 1.10.1258a38–b8 (ed. cit. p. 18). Cf.
Thomas Aquinas, *Summa theologiae*, 2ª 2ᵃᵉ, q.78 art.1, ad 3, in *Opera omnia*, vol. 9 (ed. cit.),
p. 156; idem, *Sententia libri Politicorum*, lib. 1, cap. 8, in *Opera omnia* 48 (Rome, 1971), p.
A107; Decretum Grat. D.88 c.11 palea *Eiiciens*.

A third argument, which is advanced by the theologians, seems to demonstrate that a usurious contract is wicked and bound up with vice by nature, for, as they argue, a usurer sells the use of a thing whose use is its consumption by means of this contract. In such a case, the thing cannot be considered in isolation or separately from its use and vice versa, and therefore, by the very act of lending, both the thing and its use are transferred and vice versa. Whoever wishes to sell the use of a thing whose use is its consumption without the thing itself acts wickedly and contrary to nature. Now a usurer sells the use of a thing whose use is its consumption independently of the thing itself, therefore he behaves wickedly and contrary to nature. The major premiss is clear, indeed proven, because the usurer extracts profit from the use of the money he has lent, notwithstanding the fact that he also requires the complete repayment of the same quantity of principal.

This argument also seems doubtful because one could argue that a usurer does not sell the use of the thing he lends without the thing itself; rather he sells both together, since he alienates not only the use of the thing but the thing itself so far as its substance is concerned, and therefore in this respect it appears that both elements are to be considered the same. For insofar as he transfers the thing itself, he also transfers its use, and vice versa, and therefore he does not separate the one from the other, as this argument supposes. Therefore it seems that the foregoing argument does not hold and that it stands in need of correction.

It is customary to advance another argument in relation to this ques-

ta a Philosopho I *Polliticorum*, cuius racionis fundamentum stat in hoc:
quia contra naturam videtur esse quod artificialia habeant partum et gene-
racionem per quam se multiplicent. In contractu vero usurario denarius,
105 qui est quid artificiale, parit denarium et seipsum multiplicat isto modo,
ergo ex natura rei hic contractus est contra naturam et per consequens
viciosus. Sed nec ista racio videtur valere propter duo. Primo quia usura
committitur non solum in artificialibus sed eciam in naturalibus, utpote in
vino et oleo et similibus, et per consequens dicta racio non potest applicari
110 tantum ad illa. Secundo quia videmus quod domus est quoddam artificiale
et tamen usque ad certum tempus potest quis per unam domum lucrari
aliam domum equivalentem, et sic domus pareret domum.

Consueverunt insuper induci due raciones alie que videntur omnino fri-
vole, quarum prima est quia dicunt quidam quod ideo licet accipere pen-
115 sionem et fructum alicuius rei de usu, quia res illa deterioratur per usum
suum. Nunc autem pecunia non deterioratur per usum suum, ergo non
licet de eius usu accipere aliquam pecuniariam pensionem vel fructum. Ista
racio, si quis bene considerat, est digna derisione, quia videmus quod domus illa de cuius usu accipimus pensionem vel fructum sepe melioratur
120 per inhabitacionem.
Alia racio que consuevit induci ad idem est talis; dixerunt enim qui-

---

3/102 Philosopho : in *add. RC*   3/102 hoc : scilicet *add. R*   3/103 contra : vi *add.
et del. L*   3/104 vero : autem *RC*   3/105 isto : primo *R* : predicto *C*   3/106 hic : talis *RC*   3/107 usura *RC* : *om. L*   3/110 tantum *RC* : *om. L*   3/110 quoddam : quid
RC   3/111 tamen : *om. C*   3/111 potest : posset *RC*   3/111 lucrari : unam *add.
R*   3/113 alie : ad istud propositum *add. RC*   3/116 suum[1] : *om. RC*   3/116 Nunc ...
suum : *om. R* : sed res circa quas usura commicitur eius generis existunt quarum usus
est ipsa rerum consumpcio *C*   3/116 non[2] : habet *add. R*   3/117 pecuniariam : *om.
RC*   3/117 vel : aliquem *add. RC*   3/117 Ista : tamen *add. RC*   3/118 considerat : consi-
deret *RC*   3/118 digna : *om. R*   3/118–19 domus illa ... sepe : res ille de quarum (quorum
C) usu accipimus pensionem et fructum sepe meliorantur per usum, sicut patet de domo
que *RC*

3/113–17 Cf. Bonaventure, *Commentaria in quatuor libros sententiarum*, lib. 3, distinctio
37, dubium 7, in *Opera omnia*, vol. 3 (Quaracchi, 1887), p. 836a.   3/121–3 Decretum Grat.
D.88 c.11 palea *Eiiciens*. Cf. William of Auxerre, *Summa aurea*, lib. 3, tractatus 48, cap. 3,
q. 2, ed. Jean Ribaillier, Spicilegium Bonaventurianum 18B (Paris and Rome, 1986), vol. 2,
p. 831; Bonaventure, *Collationes de decem praeceptis*, collatio 6, cap. 19, in *Opera omnia*,
vol. 5 (Quaracchi, 1891), p. 528b; Innocent IV, *Commentaria*, ad X 5.19.6, n.2 (ed. cit. fol.
517va).

tion, which Aristotle touches on in book 1 of the *Politics* and which basically consists in the following: it seems contrary to nature that artificial things should give birth and possess the power of generation such that they multiply themselves. Now in a usurious contract, coin, which is an artificial thing, begets further coins and so multiplies itself; therefore, this contract is by its very nature contrary to nature and as a result wicked. But this argument also appears invalid for two reasons. First, because usury is committed not only in artificial things but also in natural things, such as wine and oil and such things, and consequently the argument cannot be restricted simply to artificial things. Second, we know that a house is an artificial thing, and nevertheless one may profit from a house to the value of a second, and thus a house begets a house.

Two further, utterly frivolous, arguments are often advanced. The first is that it is permissible to receive a payment or profit for the use of a thing that deteriorates through use. But because money does not deteriorate through use, it is not permissible to receive any payment or profit on money. If you think about it, this argument is laughable, because we know that a house for which we receive a payment or profit is often improved by habitation.

The second argument is as follows. Some say that a usurious contract is

dam quod contractus usurarius est viciosus quia in eo venditur tempus, quod omnibus est commune. Sed nec ista racio potest stare; ymmo omnino videtur frivola quia multi sunt liciti contractus in quibus interponitur
125 duracio temporis et tamen propter hoc non dicitur quod vendatur in eis tempus, ergo a simili nec in isto contractu. Propter que omnia videtur aliter probanda dicta conclusio.

Dico ergo quod contractus usurarius ex natura rei est viciosus et malicia convolutus propter quatuor. Primo quia facit rem naturalem supervalere
130 sue nature et rem artificialem supervalere sue arti, quod maxime est contra naturam. Secundo quia facit quod res que non generat fructum generet lucrum, quod est contra naturam, ut patebit. Tercio quia facit quod illa que habent omnino eundem valorem, unum eorum excrescat in valore per alterum. Quarto quia facit quod res mutuata trahatur per abusum ad aliquid
135 ad quod non est ordinata nec principaliter nec consequenter, quod maxime est viciosum et contra naturam.

Dico ergo quod contractus usurarius est viciosus et malicia convolutus quia facit rem naturalem supervalere sue nature et rem artificialem supervalere sue arti, quod maxime est contra naturam. Ad cuius evidenciam est
140 intelligendum quod illarum rerum in quibus committitur usura quedam sunt artificiales, sicud denarii, qui mutuantur sub certo pondere vel sub certo numero; quedam vero sunt naturales, sicud aurum, argentum, et similia, que mutuantur sub certo pondere, vel, sicud vinum, oleum, et granum, que mutuantur sub certa mensura. Contractus vero usurarius facit quod
145 dicte res naturales supervaleant sue nature et quod prefate res artificiales supervaleant sue arti. Et quod ita sit apparet, quia videmus quod natura dedit prefatis rebus naturalibus determinatum et taxatum valorem, cuius

---

3/124 in *RC* : *om. L*   3/125 duracio : dilatio *RC*   3/126 videtur : videretur *C*
3/131 que *RC* : *om. L*   3/131 fructum : et *add. L*   3/133–4 alterum : quod est contra naturam *add. RC*   3/134 aliquid : aliud *add. RC*   3/137 ergo : primo *add. RC*   3/137 convolutus : ex natura rei *add. RC*   3/141–2 pondere vel sub certo : *om. RC*   3/142 aurum : vel *add. RC*   3/142–3 et similia : *om. RC*   3/143 et *RC* : *om. L*   3/144 vero : ergo
RC   3/146 quia videmus : *om. C*   3/146 arti : *ex* arte *corr. L*   3/146 videmus : enim *add.
R*   3/147 taxatum : *ex* pertaxatum *corr. L*

3/123–6 Cf. Giles of Rome, *Quodlibeta*, quodlibet 5, q. 24 (Louvain, 1646, repr. Frankfurt am Main, 1966), p. 338a.

wicked because it sells time, which is common to all. Now this argument cannot be sustained, indeed, it is completely worthless, because there are many licit contracts that involve a lapse of time, but we do not assert that they sell time; neither, therefore, should we in the case of this contract. It appears, therefore, that all of these objections undermine the conclusion that usury is by its very nature wicked and bound up with vice.

I say therefore that a usurious contract is by its very nature wicked and bound up with vice for four reasons. First, because it causes a natural thing to transcend its nature and an artificial thing to transcend the skill that made it, which is completely contrary to nature. Second, because, as will be made clear, it causes a thing that does not bear fruit to do so, which is contrary to nature. Third, because it causes one of two things that share an identical value to increase in value by means of the other. Fourth, because it causes a lent thing to be used abusively for a purpose for which it was neither primarily nor secondarily intended, which is completely wicked and unnatural.

I say, then, that a usurious contract is wicked and bound up with vice because it causes a natural thing to transcend its nature and an artificial thing to transcend the skill that made it, which is completely contrary to nature. By way of demonstration, it must be understood that of the things in which usury is committed, some are artificial, such as coins, which are lent according to a determinate number, and others are natural, such as gold, silver, and so on, which are lent according to a determinate weight, or, like wine, oil, and grain, according to a determinate measure. Now a usurious contract causes natural things to transcend their nature and artificial things to transcend the skill that made them. That this is so is clear, for we know that nature has given natural things a fixed and de-

signum est quia dedit eis naturam talem secundum quam potest certitudinaliter cognosci earum valor, ut in illis rebus que consueverunt ponderari,
150   sicud aurum et argentum, quibus dedit Deus talem naturam quod earum
valor in sua specie pensatur ex suo pondere, ita quod quamdiu remanent
sub eodem pondere remanent sub eodem valore; et quecumque habent
eandem naturam habent communiter ponderari. Idcirco ab intrinsico sue
nature potest certitudinaliter cognosci eorum valor, |^{L68v} nec augentur nec
155   minuuntur in suo valore quamdiu non distrahuntur in suo pondere; et si
videantur augeri vel minui, hoc non est propter aliquod augmentum vel
minucionem valoris qui sit in eis sed per augmentum et minucionem nostre indigencie sive eciam propter augmentum vel minucionem valoris in
aliis rebus in quas commutantur. Et sicud de rebus que consueverunt pon-
160   derari, in suo modo sic dico de aliis rebus que consueverunt mensurari,
sicut vinum, granum, oleum, et consimilia; habent enim tales res a Deo et a
natura determinatum et taxatum valorem in sua specie, quia dedit eis talem
naturam secundum quam earum valor taxatur sive pensatur ex sola men-
suracione ita quod quamdiu manent in eadem mensura manent in eodem
165   valore. Et quia habent naturam secundum quam congruit eis mensurari,
idcirco ab intrinseco sue nature potest certitudinaliter cognosci earum valor, nec augentur nec minuuntur in suo valore, nisi eo modo quo dicebatur
de rebus que possunt ponderari.

Hoc autem quod dictum est de prefatis rebus non potest dici de rebus
170   aliis naturalibus, quecumque sint ille, nam alie res naturales non se habent

---

3/148 est : *om. RC*   3/149 earum *scripsi* : eorum *RCL*   3/149 ut in : nam *RC*   3/150 et :
vel *RC*   3/150 quibus : *om. RC*   3/150 dedit *RC* : det *L*   3/150 earum *RC* : eorum
L   3/151 suo : solo *RC*   3/151 remanent : manent *RC*   3/152 remanent : manent
RC   3/152–3 et quecumque … ponderari : quod quia habent naturam secundum quam
congruit eis ponderari *RC*   3/155 pondere *RC* : *om. L*   3/155 si : vero *R* : si vero
C   3/156 videantur : videamus *C* : aliquando eas *add. RC*   3/156 vel^2 : detrimentum *add. R*   3/157 qui : quod *RC*   3/157 per : propter *RC*   3/158 sive : i *add. et*
del. L   3/158 vel : et *RC*   3/158 minucionem : diminucionem *R*   3/158 valoris *RC* :
om. L   3/159 sicud : dico *add. RC*   3/159–60 ponderari : ita *add. C*   3/160 sic : *om.*
RC   3/160 de : illis *add. RC*   3/160 consueverunt : consueverant *R*   3/161 granum : et
add. R   3/161 consimilia : similia *RC*   3/162 valorem : valore *R*   3/162 quia *RC* : que
L   3/162 dedit : Deus *add. RC*   3/163 quam *RC* : quod *L*   3/163 earum *RC* : eorum
L   3/163 taxatur sive : *om. RC*   3/163 sola : secunda *R* : sua *C*   3/165 valore : Et quia
add. et del. per ditt. L   3/167 nec^2 : vel *RC*   3/167 dicebatur *RC* : docebatur *L*   3/168 de
rebus : de rebus *add. per ditt. R*   3/170 naturalibus : *om. RC*   3/170 se : *om. RC*

terminate value, the evidence of which is that it has given them a nature such that their value can be known with certainty, as in the case of things we are accustomed to weigh, such as gold and silver, to which God has given a nature such that their value may be measured by their weight: so long as their weight remains constant, their value also remains constant. And things that have the same nature are weighed in exactly the same way; and therefore according to their very nature their value can be known with certainty, nor can their value rise or fall provided the weight remains constant. And if their value seems to rise or fall, this is not because of some change in the value of the things themselves, but because of a change in our need of them or a change in the value of the things for which they may be exchanged. And I maintain that things which we are accustomed to measure, such as wine, grain, oil, and so on, are the same in their own way as things that are weighed. For God and nature have given such things a fixed and determinate value inasmuch as they have given them a nature such that their value may be estimated and conceived by measure: so long as the measure remains constant, their value remains constant. And because their nature is such that they are measurable, according to their very nature their value can be known with certainty, nor can their value rise or fall except in the ways we mentioned with regard to things that are weighed.

What has just been said about measurable and weighable things cannot be said of other natural things of any kind, since other natural things

in sua natura ad unum aliquod determinate, ex quo possit earum valor
pensari et certitudinaliter cognosci; immo est impossibile certitudinaliter
cognoscere aliarum valorem, quia earum valor non potest pensari aliquo
intrinseco ex necessitate sed ex diversis causis extrinsecis et contingenti-
175 bus; verbi gratia, valor istius vinee vel valor istius agri quandoque pensatur
ex loco, quandoque ex tempore, quandoque ex condicionibus persona-
rum, quandoque ex diversis aliis circumstantiis que possunt multipliciter
variari. Et sicud dico in vinea vel in agro, ita et in quibuscumque aliis rebus
naturalibus que non ponderantur vel mensurantur. Hoc autem totum ideo
180 fit quia Deus et natura non determinavit nec taxavit talibus rebus valorem earum; ymmo voluit earum valorem variari penes augmentum valoris
in aliis et diminucionem secundum diversas circumstancias extrinsecas et
contingentes. Et ideo hec applicando ad propositum, dico quod contractus
usurarius facit illas res naturales que ponderantur et mensurantur super-
185 valere sue nature sive suo valori quem habent a Deo et a natura taxatum et
determinatum secundum certum pondus et secundum certam mensuram;
nam per dictum contractum exigit fenerator ultra pondus et ultra mensuram rei mutuate, et per consequens facit quod dicte res transcendant
in valore suum pondus et suam mensuram, quod est viciosum et contra
190 naturam, quia Deus et natura prestituit tali rei mutuate valorem suum secundum pondus quo ponderatur vel mensuram qua mensuratur.

Vlterius dicebatur quod usura non solum committitur in rebus naturalibus que ponderantur et mensurantur sed eciam in rebus artificialibus
que numerantur, sicud pecunia. Nam sicud valor rerum naturalium que
195 ponderantur et mensurantur pensatur ex pondere vel mensura, sic valor
rerum artificialium que numerantur, ut pecunia, pensatur ex numero. Na-

---

3/171 sua : sui *RC*   3/171 ad : *om. RC*   3/171 determinate : determinare *RC* : in sua
natura *add. et del. L*   3/172 immo : omnino *add. RC*   3/173 cognoscere *RC* : cognosci *L*   3/173 aliarum : quarum rerum *R* : earum rerum *C*   3/173 valorem *RC* : *om.*
L   3/173 earum : rerum *add. C*   3/173 potest pensari : pensatur ex *RC*   3/174 ex
necessitate : et necessario *RC*   3/174 extrinsecis *RC* : intrinsecis *L*   3/174–5 contingen-
tibus : ut *add. RC*   3/175 vel *R* : et *C* : *om. L*   3/175 valor² : *om. RC*   3/178 et² : etiam
C   3/180 fit : contingit *RC*   3/181 earum *RC* : eorum *L*   3/181 earum *RC* : eorum
L   3/181 augmentum : argumentum *R*   3/181–2 valoris in aliis *RC* : *om. L*   3/182 cir-
cumstancias : et *add. RC*   3/182 et² : id est *RC*   3/183 hec : hoc *RC*   3/184 mensurantur : numerantur *RC*   3/185 sive *RC* : non *L*   3/185 valori *RC* : valore *L*   3/185 a Deo
et : *om. RC*   3/188 facit : faciunt *C*   3/190 suum : *om. RC*   3/190–1 secundum : iuxta
RC : suum *add. RC*   3/191 vel : iuxta suam *add. RC*   3/192 committitur : committebatur
C   3/193 in : *om. R*   3/195 vel : ex *add. RC*   3/195 sic : eciam *add. RC*   3/196 numero
RC : pecunia *L*

are not such that their value can be conceived determinately or known with certainty; indeed, it is impossible to know their value with certainty because their value is not conceived in terms of some intrinsic quality, but on account of external and contingent factors, as, for example, the value of this or that vineyard or field is sometimes dependent on location, sometimes on the season, sometimes on the status of the owner, or various other circumstances that might be enumerated at length. And what I say of a vineyard or a field is true of all other natural things that are not weighed or measured. And this is so because neither God nor nature has assigned them a determinate value, but rather their value is intended to fluctuate in relation to various external and contingent circumstances. With regard to our question, then, I maintain that a usurious contract causes natural things that are weighed or measured to transcend the nature or the value, fixed and determined by weight and measure, that they have been assigned by God or nature. For by means of this contract the usurer extracts something beyond the weight and measure of the thing lent, and consequently causes such things to transcend their value with respect to weight and measure, which is wicked and unnatural, because God and nature have assigned their value in accordance with the weight by which they are weighed and the measure by which they are measured.

It was said, moreover, that usury is not only committed in natural things that are weighed and measured but also in artificial things that are counted, such as money. For just as the value of natural things that are weighed and measured must be conceived with regard to their weight and measure, so too is the value of artificial things that are counted, such as money,

tura namque prefatis rebus naturalibus ponderatis et mensuratis prestituit
valorem iuxta suum pondus vel suam mensuram, sic eciam ars suo modo
prestituit denariis artificialiter adinventis valorem iuxta eorum numeracio-
200   nem. Quapropter sicut contractus usurarius est viciosus et contra naturam
ex eo quod facit prefatas res naturales transcendere suum valorem quem
habent sibi a natura prestitutum secundum certum pondus et secundum
certam mensuram, sic eciam in artificialibus, utpote in denariis, erit viciosus ex eo quod facit eas transcendere suum valorem quem habent sibi
205   prestitutum ab arte. Quapropter bene dicebatur quod contractus usurarius
faciebat rem naturalem supervalere sue nature et rem artificialem sue arti.

Posset ergo ex toto isto processu formari talis racio: ille contractus ex
natura rei est viciosus et malicia convolutus qui facit rem naturalem transcendere suum valorem sibi prestitutum a Deo et a natura et rem artificia-
210   lem transcendere suum valorem sibi prestitutum ab arte. Sed contractus
usurarius facit hoc totum, ergo ex natura rei est viciosus et malicia convolutus.

Potest insuper ex isto processu patere illud quod fuit superius decla-
randum promissum, scilicet quare usura committitur solum in istis rebus
215   circa quas mutuum consistit; nam, sicud potest patere ex dictis, sole ille
res circa quas consistit mutuum habent sibi a natura et ab arte prestitutum
determinatum valorem quem non possunt transcendere |^{L69r} nisi viciose
agatur contra naturam vel contra artem. Et quia contractus usurarius agit
contra naturam et contra artem cum faciat rem mutuatam transcendere
220   ultra suum valorem, relinquitur quod in eis solum sit possibilis fieri. In
aliis autem rebus non sic possibilis est fieri quia cum non habeant sibi de-

---

3/197 et : vel *RC*   3/198 vel : iuxta *add. RC*   3/199 denariis : denarium *R*   3/199 adinventis : inventis *C*   3/199 valorem *RC* : *om. L*   3/200 sicut *RC* : *om. L*   3/201 ex *RC* :
om. L   3/202 prestitutum *RC* : prestitum *L*   3/203 eciam : et *add. RC*   3/204 eas *C* : eos
RL   3/205 prestitutum *RC* : prestitum *L*   3/205 dicebatur : superius *add. RC*   3/207 ex
toto : exponi *R*   3/207 formari : una *add. RC*   3/209 prestitutum *RC* : prestitum *L* : a
natura *add. et del. L*   3/209 a Deo et : *om. RC*   3/210 suum : *om. RC*   3/210 prestitutum *RC* : prestitum *L*   3/213 illud : id *C*   3/214 usura *RC* : *om. L*   3/214 istis : illis
RC   3/215 nam : natura *C*   3/216 et ab : vel *RC*   3/216 prestitutum *RC* : prestitum
L   3/218 vel contra artem *RC* : *om. L*   3/218 contractus usurarius *RC* : contractata usura
L   3/221 sic : *om. RC*

3/205–6 Vid. sup. 3/129–31.   3/213–14 Vid. sup. 2/139–41, 150–1.

conceived with respect to number. And just as nature assigns weighable and measurable natural things a value in accordance with their weight and measure, so also in the same way skill assigns a value to artificially created coins in accordance with their number. Therefore, if a usurious contract is wicked and unnatural because it causes natural things to transcend the value which nature assigns them according to a fixed measure and weight, it will also be wicked with regard to artificial things, such as coins, because it causes them to transcend the value that has been assigned to them by skill. And therefore it is well said that a usurious contract causes a natural thing to transcend its nature and an artificial thing the skill that made it.

From the foregoing we may construct the following argument: a contract which causes a natural thing to transcend the value assigned to it by God and nature and an artificial thing to transcend the value assigned to it by skill is by nature wicked and bound up with vice. Now a usurious contract does all of this and therefore by its very nature it is wicked and bound up with vice.

That, moreover, which I promised to explain at the outset is clear from the foregoing, namely, why usury is committed only in those things that are the subject of a loan. For, as is clear from what has been said, only those things that are the subject of a loan have a fixed value assigned to them by nature or skill which they cannot transcend, unless this is done wickedly against nature or skill. And since a usurious contract acts contrary to nature and skill when it causes a lent thing to transcend its value, it follows that it can be committed only in such things. It cannot be committed in other things because they do not have a determinate value as-

terminatum valorem prestitutum a natura vel ab arte, non transcenderent
suum valorem vel suam naturam si in eis vel per eos exigatur aliquid ultra
sortem et per consequens nulla erit viciositas vel malicia convoluta in tali
225   exaccione.

Vlterius dicebatur secundo quod contractus usurarius faciebat quod
mutuata res que non generat fructum generat lucrum, quod est contra naturam; nam videmus universaliter quod in quacumque re que non generat
fructum quod non generat lucrum, ymmo lucrum non videtur esse aliud
230   quam fructus rei sive acquisitum per fructum. Quod autem contractus
usurarius faciat rem non generantem fructum generare lucrum apparet
quia presupponitur in precedenti processu quod res mutuabiles, in quibus
usura committitur, habeant a natura vel ab arte sibi prestitutum determinatum valorem et per consequens non possunt in eo crescere et ex hoc
235   ipso non possunt fructum generare, quia res que generat fructum semper excrescit in valore cum fructu, nam maioris valoris est quando est sub
fructu quam quando est sine fructu. Quia igitur contractus usurarius res
habentes determinatum valorem et per consequens non fructificantes facit
excrescere in valore et per consequens lucrificantes, relinquitur quod facit
240   rem non generantem fructum generare lucrum, quod omnino est contra
naturam et viciosum.

Posset igitur ita formari racio: ille contractus est ex natura rei viciosus
et malicia convolutus qui facit rem non generantem fructum generare lucrum. Contractus usurarius est talis, ergo et cetera. Vbi ulterius intelligen-
245   dum est quod ex ista racione potest corrigi prima racio superius posita pro

---

3/222 prestitutum *RC* : prestitum *L*   3/222 transcenderent : transcendet *R* : transcendent
C   3/223 per eos : pro eis *RC*   3/225 exaccione : exaccione *add. per ditt. L*   3/227 mutuata *RC* : mutua *L*   3/227 generat[2] : generaret *RC*   3/227 quod : etiam *add. RC*
3/228 nam : natura *C*   3/228 quod : *om. C*   3/228 que : quod *RC*   3/229 fructum :
lucrum *RC*   3/229 quod non : nisi quia *RC*   3/229 lucrum[1] : fructum *RC*   3/229 aliud
C : aliquid *LR*   3/230 sive : aliquid *add. RC*   3/231 non : nam *R*   3/232 presupponitur : supponitur *RC*   3/232 in[1] : ex *RC*   3/233 habeant : habent *RC*   3/233 ab :
ab *add. per ditt. L*   3/233 prestitutum *RC* : prestitum *L*   3/234 crescere : excrescere
RC   3/235 quia : res generat quia *add. R*   3/236 excrescit : crescit *C*   3/236 quando :
cum *RC*   3/237 igitur : ergo *RC*   3/239 valore *RC* : valorem *L*   3/239 facit : faciat
RC   3/240 rem : ratio *C*   3/242 igitur : ergo *RC*   3/244 talis : huiusmodi *C*   3/245 est :
om. RC

3/226 Vid. sup. 3/131–2.   3/245 Vid. sup. 3/33–41.

signed to them by nature or skill, and therefore they do not transcend their own value or their nature if something is extracted from them beyond the principal, and as a result there will be no wickedness or vice in such an exaction.

Second, it was asserted that a usurious contract causes a lent thing that does not bear fruit to do so, which is contrary to nature. We know that in general a thing that does not bear fruit does not generate a profit; indeed, profit does not appear to be anything other than the fruit of a thing or something acquired by means of the fruit. That a usurious contract causes a thing that does not bear fruit to generate a profit is clear, because it has been established in the foregoing argument that lendable things, in which usury is committed, have a determinate value assigned to them by nature or skill, and as a result cannot increase in this respect. By the same token, they cannot bear fruit, because a thing that bears fruit always increases in value along with the fruit, for it is of greater value when it is with fruit than when it is without. Therefore, inasmuch as a usurious contract causes things that have a determinate value – and as a result do not bear fruit – to increase in value and thus generate a profit, it follows that it causes a thing that does not bear fruit to generate a profit, which is completely unnatural and wicked.

The following argument may therefore be constructed: a contract that causes a thing that does not bear fruit to generate a profit is by nature wicked and bound up with vice. A usurious contract is of such a kind, therefore et cetera. Furthermore, it should be understood that the first

alia opinione si debet aliquid valere; non enim debet dici quod contractus usurarius ideo sit viciosus quia fenerator in eo acquirit lucrum de eo
quod non est suum, sicud dicebat predicta racio, sed debet dici quod ideo
est viciosus quia fenerator in eo acquirit lucrum de eo quod non est ap-
250 tum generare lucrum, eo quod non generet fructum, sicud nunc dixit ista
racio.

Vlterius dicebatur tercio quod contractus usurarius faciebat quod ista
que habent omnino eundem valorem, unum eorum excresceret in valore per alterum, quod est contra naturam; nam videmus ad sensum quod
255 cum aliqua duo ita se habent quod unum excrescit in valore per alterum,
necessario quodlibet eorum habet suum distinctum valorem. Quod autem contractus usurarius faciat hoc quod dictum est apparet; nam videmus
quod res mutuata, circa quam committitur usura, et usus talis rei habent
omnino eundem valorem, quod patet ex duobus. Primo quia unum eo-
260 rum non potest concedi vel alienari sine altero. Secundo quia unum eorum
non potest consumi sine altero; ymmo eadem alienacione alienantur et eadem consumpcione consummuntur, sicud potest discuti per singulas res
mutuabiles et earum usus, quod non potest dici in aliis rebus locabilibus,
in quibus usus rei et res habent distinctum valorem propter quod potest
265 alienari unum eorum non alienato altero, sicud patet in domo vel in equo.
Quia ergo contractus usurarius facit quod res mutuata excrescat in valore
per usum suum, cum tamen habeat omnino eundem valorem cum suo usu,
relinquitur quod faciat habencia eundem valorem, unum eorum excrescere
in valore per alterum, quod est viciosum et contra naturam.

270   Posset ergo ita formari racio: ille contractus ex natura rei est viciosus et
malicia convolutus qui facit quod duo habencia eundem valorem, unum

---

3/246 debet[1] : debeat *RC*   3/247 ideo : non *R* : *om. C*   3/247 de eo : *om. RC*   3/249–
50 aptum : natum *RC*   3/252 ista : illa *RC*   3/253 valorem : suum *add. et exp. R*
3/253–4 valore *C* : valorem *LR*   3/254 quod[1] : etiam *add. RC*   3/255 cum : quando
RC   3/255 unum : eorum *add. RC*   3/255 valore *RC* : valorem *L*   3/257 hoc : *om.*
RC   3/261 alienantur : alienatur *RC*   3/262 consummuntur : comsumitur *C*   3/262 po-
test discuti : patet discurrendo *RC*   3/263 quod : quia *R*   3/266 excrescat *RC* : excrescit
L   3/266 valore *RC* : valorem *L*   3/267 suum : unum *R*   3/267 habeat *RC* : habeant
L   3/267–8 cum suo ... valorem *RC* : *om. per hom. L*   3/268–9 excrescere *RC* : excrescit
L   3/269 valore *RC* : valorem *L*   3/269 viciosum : intensum *R*   3/271 quod : ex *R* : ut
C   3/271 duo : *om. RC*

argument cited above may be corrected by this one if it is to hold good. For it should not be said that a usurious contract is wicked because by this means a usurer obtains a profit from something that does not belong to him, as the aforesaid argument maintains, but rather that it is wicked because by this means a usurer acquires profit from a thing that is unable to generate a profit, since it does not bear fruit, as the present argument states.

Moreover, it was stated third that a usurious contract causes one of two things which share an identical value to increase in value by means of the other, which is unnatural. Now we understand by the very meaning of the words that when any two things stand in such a relationship that one increases in value by means of the other, each necessarily has its own independent value. That a usurious contract does this is clear, for we know that the thing lent – with respect to which the usury is committed – and the use of such a thing share an identical value, which is clear for two reasons. First, because one of them cannot be granted or alienated without the other. Second, because one of them cannot be consumed without the other. Indeed, they are alienated in one and the same act of alienation and consumed in one and the same act of consumption, as can be shown in relation to individual lendable things and their use. This cannot be said of rentable things, in which the use of the thing and the thing itself have separate values such that one can be alienated without the other, as is clear in the case of a house or a horse. Therefore, because a usurious contract causes a lent thing to increase in value by its use, although in fact its value is identical to its use, it follows that it causes one of two things sharing an identical value to increase in value by means of the other, which is wicked and unnatural.

The following argument may therefore be constructed: a contract that causes one of two things sharing an identical value to increase in value by

illorum excrescat in valore per alterum. Contractus usurarius est huiusmodi, ergo et cetera. Vbi ulterius sciendum est quod per istam racionem potest corrigi alia racio posita superius ab aliis; dicebatur enim in illa racione
275   quod in contractu usurario vendebatur usus rei mutuate separatim ab ipsa
re, cum sit ab ea inseparabilis, et propter hoc agebatur viciose. Hoc autem
dictum quantum ad aliquid verum et quantum ad aliquid falsum est: verum
est namque quod usus rei mutuate inseparabilis est ab ipsa re quia habet
eundem valorem cum ea, nec potest concedi nec consumi sive alienari sine
280   ea, ut patuit in precedenti racione; sed falsum est quantum ad aliud dictum,
scilicet quod in contractu usurario |L69v vendatur usus rei separatim ab
ipsa re, nam eo ipso quod habent eundem valorem et inseparabilem, non
potest unum eorum alienari sive concedi sine altero. Quapropter non est
dicendum quod in contractu usurario usus alienetur sine re, sicut dicebat
285   illa racio; ymmo dicendum est quod contractus usurarius facit quod usus
aliquid addat ad valorem rei mutuate, cum tamen non habeat ab ea distinctum valorem, sicud probavit precedens racio.

Vlterius dicebatur quarto quod contractus usurarius faciebat quod res
mutuata traheretur per abusum ad aliquid ad quod non est ordinata nec
290   principaliter nec consequenter, quod est maxime viciosum et contra naturam. Ad cuius evidenciam est intelligendum quod res possessa ab aliquo potest sine omni vicio ordinari in duplicem usum, scilicet ad unum
proprium et principalem, qui competit ei secundum suam formam, et ad
alium secundarium, qui competit ei propter necessitatem et honestatem
295   possidentis, sicut posset poni exemplum de calciamento, quod quidem
secundum suam formam ordinatur, tamquam in proprium finem, in ipsam calciacionem; ordinatur insuper, tanquam in finem secundarium, in

---

3/272 illorum : eorum *RC*   3/272 valore *RC* : valorem *L*   3/272–3 huiusmodi : talis *RC*   3/273 est : *om. RC*   3/276 cum : tamen *add. RC*   3/277 aliquid[1] : est *add.*
RC   3/278 quia : quod *RC*   3/279 nec[2] : vel *RC*   3/279 sive : vel *RC*   3/279 sine :
enim *add. R*   3/280 est : videtur *RC*   3/280 aliud : illud *C*   3/282 eo : ex *R*   3/282 habent : habet *RC*   3/282 valorem : eundem *add. L*   3/283 sive : vel *RC*   3/283 altero
RC : altera *L*   3/286 aliquid : *om. RC*   3/287 probavit : probat *RC*   3/289 ad[2] : *om.*
R   3/289 nec : *om. RC*   3/290 consequenter *RC* : communiter *L*   3/291–2 aliquo *RC* :
alio *L*   3/293 qui : et *R*   3/294 qui : et *RC*   3/294 et : vel *RC*

3/274 Vid. sup. 3/81–100.   3/280 Vid. sup. 3/253–69.

means of the other is by its very nature wicked and unnatural. A usurious contract is a contract of this kind, therefore et cetera. Furthermore, it should be understood that by means of this argument the second argument made by many and noted earlier may be corrected. For they maintain that in a usurious contract the use of the thing lent is sold separately from the thing itself, although they are inseparable, and for this reason it is contracted wickedly. This formulation is correct in one respect and wrong in another. It is true that the use of a lent thing is inseparable from the thing itself, because it shares with the thing an identical value, nor can it be granted, consumed, or alienated without the thing, as is clear in the foregoing discussion. But it is wrong when it says that in a usurious contract the use of a thing is sold separately from the thing itself, for precisely insofar as they share an identical and inseparable value, one of them cannot be alienated or granted without the other. Therefore, we ought not to say that in a usurious contract use is alienated without the thing itself, as that formulation would have it, but rather that a usurious contract causes use to add something to the value of the thing lent, although it cannot have a value independent of it, as the foregoing discussion shows.

Moreover, it was asserted fourth that usury causes a lent thing to be employed abusively for a purpose for which it was neither primarily nor secondarily intended, which is completely wicked and unnatural. By way of demonstration it must understood that a thing in someone's possession can be put licitly to a double use, namely to its own, primary, use, which belongs to it by its form, and also to another, secondary, use according to the needs and circumstances of the possessor. Take, for example, a shoe, which is intended, according to its form – that is, according to its specific purpose – to cover the foot; but it may also be employed for, as it were, a secondary purpose, say, in exchange for something of which the possessor

commutacionem alicuius rei que magis congruit ipsi possidenti quam faciat
ipsum calciamentum vel propter sublevandam eius necessitatem vel con-
300   servandam eius honestatem. Ad quemcumque ergo dictorum usuum vel
finium ordinatur ipsum calciamentum, hoc agitur sine vicio et sine abusu.
Sed si quis sive propter cupiditatem vel propter maliciam ordinaret ipsum
ad aliquem alium usum, utpote quia vellet cum eo capere alienum ut ipsum
mactaret, ipse utique eo abuteretur et eciam ageret viciose. Sic ergo debe-
305   mus ymaginari in proposito, nam in contractu usurario res in quibus committitur usura non ordinantur in suum principalem usum qui eis debetur
secundum suam formam, nec eciam in aliquem usum secundarium qui eis
debeatur propter sublevandam necessitatem ipsius possidentis vel propter conservandam eius honestatem; ymmo distrahuntur in quendam alium
310   usum qui pocius est abusus, quia venit ex cupiditate et malicia possidentis.
Et quod ita sit apparet si discurrimus per singula genera rerum in quibus
committitur usura.

Videmus enim primo in rebus que consueverant mensurari, sicut granum, vinum, et oleum, quod quodlibet istorum potest ordinari in dupli-
315   cem usum sine omni vicio, scilicet in unum, qui ei competit secundum
suam naturam vel formam, et alium, qui ei competit propter sublevandam
necessitatem vel conservandam honestatem ipsius possidentis, ut, verbi
gratia, vinum ordinatur tanquam in proprium et principalem usum in ipsum potum, quia talis usus debetur ei secundum suam naturam. Potest
320   insuper ordinari in commutacionem alterius rei que est magis necessaria
ei cuius est ipsum vinum quam sit ipsum vinum vel propter sublevandam
eius necessitatem, vel propter conservandam eius honestatem. Si quis ergo
ordinat vinum in aliquem alium usum propter suam cupiditatem vel maliciam, ipse quidem vinum distrahit et eo abutitur, et per consequens agit
325   viciose. Hoc autem facit usurarius, qui scilicet ordinat vinum ad mutuum

---

3/298 quam *RC* : quod *L*   3/299 necessitatem : vel propter sublevandum eius *add. per
ditt. R*   3/299–300 vel² ... honestatem *RC* : subsalvandam *R* : *om. L*   3/300 usuum
RC : usum *L*   3/301 finium *RC* : finem *L*   3/302 sive : *om. RC*   3/303 alienum *RC* :
vac. R*   3/303 ut : vel *RC* : ne *add. R*   3/304 mactaret : mactare *C*   3/304 et eciam
ageret : *om. RC*   3/305 res : reo *R*   3/306 non : nec *RC*   3/308 debeatur : debeat *R* :
secundum *add. et del. L*   3/309 distrahuntur *RC* : distrahentur *L*   3/310 quia *RC* : qui
L   3/310 venit : provenit *RC*   3/310 et : vel *RC*   3/311 discurrimus : discurramus
RC   3/311 rerum : eorum *C*   3/314–15 duplicem : duplicitatem enim *R*   3/318 principalem : finem vel *add. C*   3/320 insuper *RC* : enim *L*   3/321 ipsum¹ : illud *RC*
3/321 sit : *om. C*   3/325 facit : agit *C*   3/325 qui : quia *RC*

has greater need than a foot covering, or to relieve his need and preserve his circumstances. Both uses of a shoe are licit and non-abusive. But if from motives of avarice or malice someone were to employ it in another way, say, to seize or assault someone else, he would be using it abusively and wickedly. And so we ought to conceive of the present problem, for in a usurious contract, things in which usury is committed are not used according to their primary purpose, which is given them by their form, nor even according to a secondary purpose dedicated to relieving the needs of the possessor or preserving his circumstances, but rather misdirected to a use which is abusive because it arises from the avarice and malice of the possessor. And that this is so is clear if we consider in turn the various classes of things in which usury is committed.

We know, for example, that each of the things that are customarily measured, such as grain, wine, and oil, has a licit, twofold use, one of which belongs to it by nature and form, and another that serves to relieve the needs or preserve the circumstances of the possessor. So, for example, the proper and primary use of wine is drinking, which belongs to it by nature. But it may also be exchanged for something more necessary to the possessor of the wine than the wine itself, either to relieve his needs or to preserve his circumstances. Therefore if anyone uses wine for some other purpose because of avarice or malice, he misdirects and abuses it and consequently acts wickedly. But this is what a usurer does when he employs wine in a loan in order to receive something beyond the principal, for this use of wine arises from the avarice or malice of the usurer and is therefore abusive. And likewise, what has been said about things that are customarily

ut de eo recipiat ultra sortem, qui quidem usus accidit vino propter cupiditatem usurarii sive propter suam maliciam, et ideo hic est abusus. Et
sicud dictum est de rebus que consueverunt mensurari, ita potest dici de
rebus que consueverunt ponderari, ut aurum et argentum. Potest enim uti
330   quis auro et argento ad constituendum vasa decorancia ipsam ecclesiam
sive domum, et videtur eorum proprius usus. Potest eciam quolibet eorum
uti ad commutandum in alias res necessarias ad vitam, et iste videtur usus
secundarius et est licitus et honestus. Sed si quis utatur dictis metallis ad
mutuum ut de eis recipiat ultra sortem, sicut facit usurarius, ipse quidem
335   eis abutitur et agit viciose. Et eodem modo debemus ymaginari de rebus
que consueverunt numerari, sicud denarii; potest enim quis uti denariis
ad faciendum commutaciones in alias res que sunt ad vitam necessarie,
et iste videtur eorum proprius usus, quia propter tales commutaciones
sunt inventi. Potest eciam eis uti ad faciendum commutaciones in alios
340   denarios qui magis congruunt regioni in qua est vel ad quam vadit, et iste
videtur eorum usus secundarius, qui eciam convenienter eis est permissus
quia potest in eo servari equalitas iusticie. Sed si quis utatur denariis ista
intencione ad mutuum, scilicet ut de eis vel pro eis recipiat ultra sortem,
sicut facit usurarius, ipse quidem |^L70r eis abutitur, quia facit quod denarii
345   pariant denarios, quod eis non competit nec in hoc consistit eorum usus, et
ideo agit viciose. Et ista videtur fuisse intencio Aristotelis in primo *Polliticorum*, ubi vocat usuram *tokos*, quasi denariorum partum, propter quod
dicit eam maxime esse contra naturam. Quod ideo est quia certe nec a
natura nec ab arte competit denariis talis usus et talis partus sed ex propria
350   hominis malicia et cupiditate.

3/326 ut : ded *add. et del. L*   3/326 eo : ipso *RC*   3/326 quidem : quidam
R   3/327 sive : etiam *add. RC*   3/327 hic : *om. RC*   3/328 de² : in *R*   3/329 ut : sicut *RC*   2/329 et : vel *RC*   3/330 et : vel *RC*   3/331 sive : vel *C*   3/331 et : hic *add.*
RC   3/331 quolibet *RC* : quilibet *L*   3/332 videtur : eorum *add. RC*   3/333 secundarius : qui *add. RC*   3/333 et : etiam *RC*   3/334 mutuum : vel de *add. et del. L*   3/334 de :
pro *RC*   3/336 numerari : usurari *R*   3/337 necessarie *RC* : necessaria *L*   3/338 iste :
ille *RC*   3/338 commutaciones : se *add. et del. L*   3/339 eis *RC* : *om. L*   3/339 faciendum : faciendas *RC*   3/340 congruunt : congruuntur *R* : congruant *C*   3/340 qua :
quae *C*   3/340 vel : regioni *add. RC*   3/341 eis : *om. RC*   3/342 equalitas : qualitas
R   3/343 mutuum : mutua *RC*   3/344 quidem : qui de *R* : qui *C*   3/345 pariant : eorum usus *add. et del. L*   2/346 videtur *RC* : debetur *L*   3/347 tokos *Aristotle, Politica*
1.10.1258b5–8 : *vac. L* : clerios *R* : faenus *C*   3/347 quasi *RC* : quod *L*   3/347 quod :
etiam *add. RC*   3/348 contra : praeter *RC*   3/348 certe *RC* : de se *L*

3/346–8 Aristotle, *Politica* 1.10.1258b5–8 (ed. cit. p. 18).

measured may be said of things that are by custom weighed, such as gold and silver. For gold and silver can be used to make the vessels that adorn a church or a house, and this seems to be their proper use. They may also be used in exchange for other things necessary to life, and this, secondary, use also appears to be licit and honourable. But if someone employs these metals in a loan in order to receive an increment on the principal, as a usurer does, he abuses them and behaves wickedly. And we ought to think similarly of the things in which usury is usually committed, namely coins. For one can use coins as a medium of exchange for other things that are needed for life, and this appears to be their proper use, because they were devised for such exchanges. One can also exchange them for other coins that are used in the region in which one finds oneself or to which one travels, and this seems to be their secondary use, which is rightly attributed to them because in this way a certain equality is preserved between currencies. But if anyone employs coins in a loan with the intention of receiving something more than the principal in return for them or on account of them, as a usurer does, he abuses them because he causes coins to give birth to coins, which is not one of their properties and does not represent their proper use, and therefore he behaves wickedly. This appears to have been the intention of Aristotle in book 1 of the *Politics*, where he calls usury 'offspring' – as it were, 'the offspring of coins' – and therefore especially unnatural. And this is so because such use and parturition does not belong to coins either by nature or skill, but arises from human malice and avarice.

Posset ergo ex toto isto processu formari una talis racio: ille contractus ex natura est viciosus et malicia convolutus qui facit quod res aliqua distrahatur per abusum ad aliquid ad quod non est ordinata nec principaliter nec consequenter. Contractus usurarius est talis, ut patet ex dictis; ergo et cetera. Patet ergo quid dicendum quantum ad istum articulum. Tollitur similiter prima via que ingerebat dubium in ista questione, quia non potest dici quod contractus usurarius sit permissibilis ab aliquo iure quia est viciosus ex natura rei.

355

<4> <Articulus tertius>

Tercio restat videre utrum iura debeant concedere contractum usurarium propter aliquod bonum quod inde oriatur vel propter aliquod malum quod inde vitetur, ut per hoc tollatur illa via secunda que ingerebat dubitacionem in ista questione secundo loco.

5

Ad istius igitur articuli evidenciam est intelligendum quod concessio potest accipi tribus modis. Vno modo prout est idem quod simplex permissio dimittens vel indulgens penam, secundum quem modum beatus Gregorius scribens Augustino Anglorum episcopo de observancia ieiunii permisit inordinatum esum carnium diebus dominicis, ut habitum fuit supra et ponitur in decretis d. 4. c. *Denique*. Talis autem permissio fuit permissio simplex quia per solam indulgenciam pene, sicud notat glosator exponens prefata verba Gregorii ubi supra. Dixerat enim Gregorius quod

10

3/352 natura : rei *add. RC*   3/353 aliquid : aliud *add. RC*   3/355 Patet ergo : Et ita patet *RC*   3/355 quid : sit *add. RC*   3/355 articulum : quia dicendum est quod contractus usurarius est ex natura rei viciosus et malicia convolutus ac per consequens *add. RC*   3/355 Tollitur : illa *add. RC*   3/356 similiter : illa *RC*   3/356 ista : illa prima *C*   3/357 contractus usurarius : *om. RC*   3/357 quia : per *add. et del. R* : vero *add. R* : cum *C*   3/357 est : sit *C*   3/358 rei : Restat ergo videre tertio *add. RC*   4/2 Tercio restat videre *om. RC*   4/2 concedere : permictere *RC*   4/4–5 dubitacionem : dubium *RC*   4/6 igitur : ergo *RC*   4/6 intelligendum : *om. R* : sciendum *C*   4/6 concessio : permissio *RC*   4/7 idem quod : *om. RC*   4/8 beatus : Aug. *add. et exp. R* : Augustinus *add. et del. L*   4/11 ponitur : refertur *C*   4/11 in decretis : *om. C*   4/12 permissio : *om. RC*   4/13 Gregorii : in loco *add. RC*   4/13 enim *RC* : *om. L*

4/10–11 Vid. sup. 1/77–90.   4/11 Decretum Grat. D.4 c.6.   4/12–13 Gl. ord. ad Decretum Grat. D.4 c.6, v. *Venia* (ed. cit. col. 13); vid. sup. 1/80–8.

The following argument may be proposed on the basis of the foregoing reasoning: a contract that causes a thing to be employed abusively for a purpose for which it was neither primarily nor secondarily intended is by its nature wicked and unnatural. As is clear from the things that have been said, a usurious contract is such a contract, therefore et cetera. What ought to be said with respect to this article is therefore also clear, and likewise with regard to the first way in which doubt arises in this matter: because usury is wicked by nature, it cannot be asserted that it is permitted under any law.

4. Article 3

Third, it remains to be seen whether the laws should permit a usurious contract on account of some good that might follow or to avoid an evil that might thereby be avoided, so that we may dispose of the second source of doubt in this matter.

For the solution of this article, you must know that 'permission' can be understood in three ways. In one sense, that of 'simple permission,' a penalty is dispensed with or relaxed, and in this way the blessed Gregory, writing to Augustine, bishop of the English, on the observance of fasts tolerated the excessive consumption of meat on Sundays, as was noted earlier and included in the decrees at D.4 c.6. Such a permission is 'simple' because it involves only the relaxation of a penalty, as the glossator notes when expounding the words of the blessed Gregory quoted above. Greg-

illi qui sic se ingurgitabant erant relinquendi 'suo ingenio cum venia.' Dicit
15   ergo ibi glosator quod hoc intelligendum est 'de venia pene, non de venia
culpe,' quapropter relinquitur quod permissio beati Gregorii fuit simplex
per solam indulgenciam pene.

Secundo modo potest accipi concessio prout est idem quod permissio
tollens impedimentum, secundum quem modum tollerantur Iudei inter
20   nos habitantes et permittuntur inter nos ab ecclesia in observancia sui ritus, ut habitum fuit supra et ponitur in decretis d. 45. *Qui sincera.* Hec autem permissio, quamvis dicat glosator quod sit similis prime, michi tamen
non videtur, salva reverencia glosatoris, quod sit ei similis, quia ista non est
simplex sicut illa, ymmo se habet per addicionem ad eam, nam illa permis-
25   sio permittebat malum per solam indulgenciam pene, quia non fuit facta
prohibicio dicti mali per comminacionem alicuius pene, sed ista secunda
permissio plus facit, quia non solum permittit dictum malum, scilicet observanciam ritus Iudeorum subtrahendo comminacionem vel infliccionem
pene sicud prima sed eciam removendo impedimenta Christianorum, qui
30   vellent impedire observanciam dicti ritus et quantum ad hoc habet se per
addicionem ad illam.

Tercio modo potest accipi concessio prout est idem quod concessio
prestans iuvamentum, secundum quem modum ecclesia permittit quandocumque clericum occidi a potestate seculari et hec permissio se habet
35   per addicionem ad secundam quemadmodum secunda se habebat per addicionem ad primam, nam in ista permissione non solum subtrahitur com-

---

4/14 ingurgitabant : inguagitant *R* : ingurgitant *C*   4/15 hoc *RC* : *om. L*   4/16 fuit :
fuerit *RC* : permissio *add. RC*   4/18 concessio : permissio *RC*   4/18 permissio :
concessio *RC*   4/19 tollerantur : *om. RC*   4/20 et : *om. RC*   4/20 inter nos : *om.*
RC   4/20 sui : *om. C*   4/21 ponitur : habetur *C*   4/21 45. : c. *add. C*   4/23 non[1] :
om. RC   4/23 quod : non *add. C* : *om. R*   4/23 est : ita *add. RC*   4/26 mali : q *add.*
et del. L   4/26 secunda : *om. RC*   4/30 vellent : *om. R* : attentassent *C*   4/32 concessio[1] : permissio *RC*   4/32 quod concessio *RC* : *om. L*   4/33–4 quandocumque : *om.*
RC   4/35 habebat : habet *C*   4/36 primam : primum *C*

4/21 Decretum Grat. D. 45 c.3; vid. sup. 1/44–76.   4/22 Gl. ord. ad Decretum Grat. D.45
c.3, v. *Licentiam* (ed. cit. col. 210).

ory had said that those who thus gorged themselves 'are to be mercifully left to their own devices,' and therefore the glossator says of this passage that we should understand '"mercifully" with regard to the penalty, not with regard to the fault.' Therefore it follows that the permission of the blessed Gregory was 'simple' because it referred only to the relaxation of a penalty.

Permission may be granted in a second way, namely by removing an impediment, and in this way the Jews dwelling among us are tolerated and permitted by the Church to observe their rites, as was noted above and included in the decrees at D.45 c.3. Although the glossator says that this mode of permission is similar to the first, it does not – with all due respect to the glossator – appear similar to me because it is not 'simple' in the same sense, but rather involves something additional. For simple permission tolerates an evil simply by relaxing a penalty – that is, because the prohibition of the evil in question is not enforced by threatening a penalty – but the second mode of permission does more, since it not only permits the said evil, namely the observance of Jewish rites, by withholding the threat of, or refraining from imposing, a penalty, as in the first mode, but also by setting aside the objections of Christians who would hinder the observance of these rites; and to this extent it involves the addition of something beyond the first mode.

Permission may be granted in a third way and that is by active assistance, and in this way the Church sometimes permits a cleric to be executed by the secular authorities. This mode of permission involves something additional to the second mode, just as the second involved an addition to the first, for in this mode of permission not only is the threat of the

minacio pene que posset pro occisione clerici infligi, sicud fiebat in prima permissione, sed eciam ultra hoc tollitur illud impedimentum per quod posset occisio clerici impediri, quemadmodum fiebat in secunda permis-
40 sione. Et ulterius ultra hec prestatur iuvamentum in ista permissione quod non fiebat in aliqua illarum, prestat namque ecclesia iuvamentum in occisione clerici qui dignus est morte, quia ipsum degradat et postea ipsum in potestatem secularis manus dat ut crucietur et occidatur, secundum illud quod habetur Chorinthiorum prima, 'tradere huiusmodi Sathane in inte-
45 ritum carnis ut spiritus salvus sit in die domini nostri Iesu Christi.' Patet ergo quod tribus modis potest accipi concessio vel permissio.

Vlterius ad maiorem evidenciam istius articuli est sciendum quod, sicud tactum fuit superius circa principium questionis, malum potest permitti duabus de causis, scilicet vel propter bonum quod inde oritur vel propter
50 maius malum quod inde vitatur. Maius autem malum vitatur per minus malum tribus modis. Vno modo quando vitatur malum spirituale in anima quod est maius per malum corporale in corpore quod est minus. Alio modo quando vitatur unum malum spirituale quod est maius per aliud malum |L70v spirituale quod est minus, sicud sepe permittitur minus pecca-
55 tum ut vitetur maius. Tercio quando vitatur unum malum corporale maius per aliud malum quod est minus.

Ad propositum ergo applicando, cum queritur utrum iura debeant concedere contractum usurarium propter aliquod bonum quod inde oriatur vel propter maius malum quod inde vitetur, dicendum est statim quod si
60 ista questio fiat propter ius naturale, non debet esse dubium, quia dictum ius nullo modo potest vel debet concedere contractum usurarium. Racio

---

4/40 ultra : praeter *C*   4/40 hec : duo *add. RC*   4/40 ista : tercia *add. RC*   4/41–2 occisione : clericus qui *add. et del. L*   4/42 qui : quia *R*   4/42–3 postea ... dat : ponit ipsum in manibus potestatis secularis *RC*   4/43 occidatur : et *add. R*   4/44 Chorinthiorum prima : prima ad Corinthios V *R* : 1. Cor. 5 *C*   4/44 huiusmodi *C* : huius *RL*   4/48 potest : *om. RC*   4/51 malum[1] : *om. RC*   4/52 per malum corporale *RC* : pro malo corporali *L*   4/52 in corpore : *om. RC*   4/52 quod : in comparacione *add. RC* : ad illud *add. C*   4/52 Alio : Secundo *C*   4/53 malum : malum *add. per ditt. L*   4/54 minus : vero *add. et exp. R*   4/55 Tercio : modo *add. RC*   4/57 ergo : *om. RC*   4/57 applicando : descendendo *RC*   4/59 propter : aliquod *add. RC*   4/60 propter : per *R*   4/60 quia : quod *RC*   4/61 modo : et *add. et del. R*   4/61–2 Racio huius est : *om. RC*

4/44–5 1 *Cor* 5.5.   4/47–8 Vid. sup. 1/44–7.

penalty which could be imposed for the execution of a cleric withheld, as was the case in the first mode, but the impediment by which the execution of a cleric could be hindered is also removed, as in the second mode. But beyond these two concessions, this mode of permission offers assistance, which was not the case in the first two, for the Church aids in the execution of a cleric who is worthy of death by first degrading him and then by handing him over to the secular authorities for torture and execution, in accordance with the passage of 1 Corinthians: 'deliver this man to Satan for the destruction of the flesh, that his spirit may be saved in the day of the Lord Jesus.'

Moreover, for the satisfactory resolution of this article you must know – as was mentioned earlier around the beginning of the question – that an evil may be permitted for two reasons, namely, because of a good that might ensue or to avoid a greater evil. A greater evil is avoided by a lesser in three ways. First, when a spiritual evil in the soul is avoided by means of a corporeal evil, which, by comparison, is lesser. Second, when a spiritual evil is avoided by means of another, lesser spiritual evil, as a lesser sin is often tolerated in order to avoid a greater one. Third, when a corporeal evil is avoided by means of another, lesser corporeal evil.

To apply these observations to our question: when it is asked whether the laws may permit a usurious contract because of a good that may follow or to avoid an even greater evil, it must be said to begin with that if the question is asked with regard to natural law, there can be no doubt, because in no way can or should natural law permit a usurious contract.

huius est quia illud quod simpliciter est contra aliquod ius nullo modo
potest concedi ab eodem iure, alias simul esset contra ipsum et non contra
ipsum in quantum ab eo concessum. Contractus autem usurarius simplici-
65   ter est contra ius naturale, cum sit viciosus ex natura rei, ut prius patuit in
precedenti articulo, ergo et cetera. Si autem simpliciter est contra ius naturale, relinquitur quod simpliciter contra ius divinum sit, quia ius naturale
est a iure divino derivatum, propterea quidquid est contra ius naturale est
contra ius divinum.

70   Si autem fiat dicta questio propter ius civile, dicendum est quod dictum
ius potest concedere et concedit prefatum contractum concessione accepta primo modo, prout est simplex permissio per indulgenciam pene. Et
quod ita sit probo tali racione: illud ius quod non comminatur nec infligit
aliquam penam propter contractum usurarium videtur ipsum concedere
75   et permittere concessione accepta primo modo, que est simplex permissio per indulgenciam pene; sed ius civile nullam penam comminatur nec
ullam penam infligit propter dictum contractum, ergo ipsum concedit et
permittit tali concessione, scilicet primi modi. Et hec est intencio Augustini primo *de libero arbitrio*, ubi ait: 'videtur tamen mihi et legem istam
80   que populo regendo scribitur recte ista permittere et divinam providenciam vindicare.' Non tamen concedit ipsum concessione accepta secundo
modo, quia tunc tolleret eciam impedimenta a volentibus facere usuram,
quod patet esse falsum; ymmo sicud permittit fieri prefatum contractum,
ita eciam permittit prestare illa impedimenta que facit ius canonicum con-
85   tra dictum contractum.

Vlterius non concedit ipsum concessione tercia, scilicet prout est idem
quod permissio prestans iuvamentum, quia certe nullum iuvamentum,

---

4/63 ab : illo *add. RC*   4/63 alias : alioquin *RC*   4/64 eo : ipso *RC*   4/65 prius :
om. RC   4/67 relinquitur : ulterius *add. RC*   4/67 sit : est *R*   4/68 propterea : quapropter *RC*   4/68 ius : *ex* rius *corr. R*   4/68 naturale : nature *RC* : necessario *add.*
RC   4/72 modo : scilicet *add. RC*   4/72 est : idem quod *add. RC*   4/75 modo : *om.*
R   4/76–7 comminatur ... penam : *om. RC*   4/79 tamen : ergo *C* : *om. R*   4/79 mihi
RC : *om. L*   4/79 et *C* : *om. RL*   4/80 et : *om. R*   4/80–1 divinam providenciam *RC* :
divina providencia *L* : non *add. L*   4/81 tamen : autem *RC*   4/81 concedit *RC* : exce-
dit *L* : i *add. et del. R*   4/82 eciam : *om. RC*   4/82 usuram : usuras *C*   4/84 prestare :
praestari *C*   4/86 concessione : concessionem *R*   4/86 tercia : tertio modo accepta
RC   4/87 iuvamentum : et *add. C*

4/65–6 Vid. sup. 3/128–358.   4/78–81 Augustine, *De libero arbitrio libri tres* 1.40, in
CSEL 74, ed. W.M. Green (Vienna, 1956), p. 13.

The reason for this is that whatever is directly contrary to any given law cannot be permitted by the same law, otherwise the law would both forbid it and not forbid it, insofar as it permitted it. Now a usurious contract is directly contrary to natural law, since it is wicked by its very nature, as is clear from the preceding article, therefore et cetera. But if usury is directly contrary to natural law, it follows that it is also directly contrary to divine law, because natural law is derived from divine law, so that whatever is contrary to natural law is also contrary to divine law.

But if the question is asked with respect to civil law, it must be said that civil law can and does tolerate a usurious contract by means of the first mode of permission, that is, by relaxing a penalty. And that this is the case, I prove by means of the reasoning that follows: a law that does not threaten or inflict any penalty for a usurious contract appears to tolerate or permit it by the first mode of permission, that is, by simple permission that relaxes a penalty. Now the civil law neither threatens nor imposes any penalty for the said contract, therefore it tolerates and permits it by this first mode of permission. And this is the meaning of Augustine in book 1 of *On Free Will*, where he says: 'it seems to me that the law that is enacted to govern the people rightly tolerates things that divine providence redresses.' Civil law does not, however, permit usury by the second mode of permission, because it would then remove barriers to those who wish to practise usury, which is clearly false; indeed, just as it tolerates the said contract, it also permits the barriers that canon law erects against the said contract.

Furthermore, it does not allow usury by the third mode of permission, that is, by active assistance, because it offers no aid or favour to the mak-

nullum favorem prestat in contractu usurario. Si enim ius civile concederet vel permitteret contractum usurarium secundo modo, scilicet sub-
90   trahendo impedimenta per que posset dictus contractus impediri vel eciam
tercio modo, scilicet prestando iuvamenta vel auxilia per que posset prefatus contractus foveri, sequeretur necessario quod ius civile contrariaretur
iuri naturali et eciam iuri canonico, quod est omnino inconveniens quia
ius civile et ius canonicum sunt fundata in iure naturali, quapropter non
95   possunt dicto iuri naturali contrariari, nec eciam sibi invicem. Sed si ponatur quod ius civile concedat vel permittat contractum usurarium solum
primo modo, quemadmodum dictum fuit, scilicet non comminando nec
infligendo penam pro dicto contractu, non propter hoc sequitur quod
contrariaretur iuri naturali nec eciam iuri canonico, ut melius patebit in
100   quinto articulo. Hoc est ergo quod mihi videtur tenendum de isto articulo
quantum ad ius civile.

Sed si fiat questio ulterius de iure canonico, utrum scilicet dictum ius
debeat concedere vel permittere contractum usurarium propter aliquod
bonum quod inde videatur oriri vel propter maius malum quod inde vide-
105   atur vitari, sic dicendum est simpliciter quod non, quia videmus de facto
quod nullo modo ipsum concedit vel permittit. Non enim permittit ipsum
primo modo, scilicet non comminando vel infligendo penam pro dicto
contractu, quin ymmo pocius contrarium facit, quia penam comminatur
et infligit usurariis facientibus dictum contractum, sicud patet *extra, de*
110   *usuris* c. *Quia in omnibus*. Vlterius non permittit ipsum secundo modo,
scilicet subtrahendo impedimenta volentibus facere usuras, nec eciam ter-

4/88–9 concederet : et *add. et del. L* : vel *marg. L*   4/89–90 contractum … impedimenta : *om. R* : tolli impedimenta *C*   4/90 que : non *add. C*   4/90 impediri : sed hoc non
facit *add. C*   4/91 prestando : prestans *RC*   4/92 foveri : favorari *RC*   4/94 ius[2] :
om. RC   4/94 non : nec *RC*   4/95 nec … invicem *RC* : *om. L*   4/97 scilicet : supra
C   4/98 infligendo : *ex* confligendo *corr. R*   4/98 quod : in aliquo *add. RC*   4/99 contrariaretur : contrairetur *RC*   4/99 ut : sicut *RC*   4/100 mihi *RC* : *om. L*   4/102 Sed :
om. C   4/102 si : *om. R* : vero *add. RC*   4/106 ipsum[1] *RC* : *om. L*   4/106 ipsum[2] : illum
C   4/108 pocius : pocicius *R*   4/108 quia : et *add. RC*   4/108 penam : comminab *add.*
et del. L   4/109 et : penam *add. RC*   4/109 usurariis *RC* : usurario *L*   4/110 Quia *RC* :
om. L : de *add. et exp. R*   4/111 usuras : usus *R*   4/111 nec : sive *RC*

4/97 Vid. sup. 4/6–17.   4/99–100 Vid. inf. 6/1–150.   4/109–10 X 5.19.3.

ing of a usurious contract. For if civil law allowed or tolerated a usurious contract in the second mode, that is, by removing barriers by which usury could be impeded, or even in the third mode, namely, by offering active assistance or aid by which the contract might be fostered, it would necessarily follow that civil law contradicted natural law and canon law, which is completely inappropriate, because both civil and canon law are based on natural law and therefore cannot contradict it. But if it is argued that civil law allows or tolerates a usurious contract only in the first mode, as was said earlier, by not threatening or imposing a penalty for the said contract, it does not follow that for this reason it contradicts natural or even canon law, as will be shown more clearly in the fifth article. It seems to me, then, that this is what ought to be maintained so far as civil law is concerned.

Now if the question is asked with respect to canon law, that is, whether canon law should allow or tolerate a usurious contract because of some good that seems to result or to avoid some apparent evil, the answer is simply 'no,' because we know that in fact it neither allows nor tolerates usury in any way. It does not tolerate it in the first mode, that is, by not threatening or imposing a penalty, but rather the opposite, because it both threatens and imposes penalties on usurers who offer such contracts, as is clear in X 5.19.3. Moreover, it does not permit usury in the second mode, that is, by removing impediments from those who wish to commit usury, nor in the third mode, by offering aid or assistance to them; rather the

cio modo prestando auxilia vel iuvamenta eisdem, quinimmo oppositum facit, nam eo ipso quod comminatur et infligit penam, subtrahit eis auxilia, et prestat impedimenta.

115   Vlterius non solum est dicendum quod non permittit ipsum, quia videmus de facto sic esse, sed eciam quia non apparet quod posset ipsum permittere secundum aliquam racionem, teste domino papa Alexandro, ut fuit dictum supra in precedenti articulo, et habetur *extra, de usuris* c. *Super eo*, ubi dominus papa asserit se non videre quod super eo posset fieri
120   dispensacio. Nec valet si dicatur quod posset fieri dispensacio super eo propter aliquod bonum quod inde oriatur, quia ibidem idem dicit dominus papa quod 'sacra scriptura prohibuit pro alterius vita mentiri,' ut habetur in decretis 22 q. 2 *Ne quis*, ergo multo magis, sicut concludit ibidem, prohibendus est quilibet 'ne pro redimenda vita captivi involvatur crimine
125   usurarum,' cum tamen illud videatur |^{L71r} potissimum bonum quod posset ex usuris pervenire.

Vlterius non potest dici quod in dicto contractu cadat dispensacio per ius canonicum propter maius malum vitandum, quia non apparet quod per ipsum vitetur malum spirituale vel saltem non vitatur per ipsum maius
130   malum spirituale quam sit illud malum quod incurrit in dicto contractu. Videtur enim illud malum quod incurrit usurarius per dictum contractum quantum ad aliquid maximum peccatum propter quatuor: primo quia contempnit Deum audacius; secundo quia contempnit naturam expressius; tercio quia contempnit scripturam deterius; quarto quia contempnit iura
135   diucius.

Contempnit itaque ipse usurarius Deum audacius quia cum in omnibus peccatis que sunt expresse contra divina mandata homo verecundetur et

---

4/113 infligit : eis *add. RC*   4/116 posset : possit *RC*   4/118 in precedenti *RC* : preceti *L*   4/118 extra, de usuris : eodem titulo *RC*   4/119 posset : possit *RC*   4/120 posset : potest *RC* : fiel *add. et del. L*   4/121 oriatur : oritur *RC*   4/121–2 idem dicit dominus papa : idem *om. R* : per eundem dicitur *C*   4/121 idem : ibidem *add. per ditt. L*   4/123 22 *R* : 21 *L* : 12 *C*   4/123 2 : c. *add. C*   4/123 concludit : concluditur *RC*   4/125 posset : possit *RC*   4/126 ex : pro *C*   4/126 pervenire : provenire *RC*   4/128 quia : vel *add. RC*   4/129 vitetur : intelligitur *R*   4/129–30 vel saltem ... spirituale *RC* : *om. per hom. L*   4/130 incurrit : incurritur *C*   4/130–1 in dicto ... incurrit *RC* : *om. per hom. L*   4/132 quatuor : quartum *R*   4/136 itaque : namque *RC*   4/136 audacius : *om. RC*   4/137 divina *RC* : deminicum *L*   4/137 verecundetur : verecundatur *R*

4/117–18 Vid. sup. 3/22–5.   4/117–26 X 5.19.4.   4/123 Decretum Grat. C.22 q.2 c.14.

opposite, for to the extent that it threatens and imposes penalties, it also withholds aid from usurers and erects barriers against usury.

Furthermore, it must be said that not only does canon law not permit usury – because we see that this is in fact the case – but also that it cannot permit it on any grounds, for which we have the evidence of the lord pope Alexander, as was said above in the preceding article and as is noted at X 5.19.4, where the lord pope says that he does not see how any relaxation can be granted in this matter. Nor can it be said that a relaxation could be conceded with respect to usury because of some good that might follow, for, as the pope goes on to say in the same passage, 'holy scripture forbids us to lie to save the life of another,' as is maintained in the decrees at C.22 q.2 c.14; therefore, he concludes, we are much more forbidden 'to engage in the crime of usury even to save the life of a captive,' although this appears to be a particularly great good that might follow from usury.

Moreover, it cannot be said that canon law should permit a usurious contract in order to avoid an evil because it is unclear that any spiritual evil would be thereby avoided, or at least no greater spiritual evil than that which a usurer incurs by means of the said contract. For it appears that the evil the usurer incurs by means of a usurious contract is the greatest possible sin and this for four reasons: first, because he rashly treats God with contempt; second, because he openly treats nature with contempt; third, because he wickedly holds scripture in contempt; and fourth, because he habitually treats the laws with contempt.

The usurer rashly despises God because, although we should be ashamed of or embarrassed by any sin that is explicitly contrary to the Lord's com-

erubescat. In isto tamen peccato quantumcumque sit expresse contra dominicum mandatum, non videtur verecundari sed pocius gloriari.

140   Vlterius contempnit naturam expressius quia non solum contempnit
eam in uno genere rerum sed eciam in pluribus, scilicet in tribus; vult enim
contra naturam quod numerabilia, scilicet ipsi denarii, supervaleant suo
numero; vult eciam ulterius contra naturam quod ponderabilia, sicut aurum vel argentum, supervaleant suo ponderi; vult insuper contra naturam
145   quod mensurabilia, sicut granum, vinum, et oleum, supervaleant sue mensure. Quapropter bene dictum est quod contempnit naturam expressius.

Vlterius, ut dicebatur, contempnit scripturam deterius, quia videtur eam
contempnere per infidelitatem, que est opposita fidei quam in baptismo
professus est; nam si perfecte crederet, impossibile esset contra Deum et
150   contra eius scripturam sic aperte et inverecunde procedere.

Vlterius dicebatur quod contempnit iura diucius quia, non obstante
prohibicione cuiuscumque iuris adhuc, tamen in dicto peccato continue
perseverat in tantum quod ad ipsum relinquendum usque ad mortem sepius se retardat. Propter quod sibi convenienter accidit sepius quod dicit
155   Augustinus in sermone de innocentibus: 'percutitur,' inquid, 'hac animad-
versione peccator ut moriens obliviscatur sui, qui dum viveret oblitus est
Dei.' Nam sepius videmus quod usurarii decedunt sine restitucione, sine
sacramentis, sine aliqua bona spe future vite.

Propter que omnia concludo quod ius canonicum nullo modo debet
160   concedere vel permittere contractum usurarium propter maius malum
vitandum, quia regulariter loquendo non apparet quod aliquod malum
maius quam ipsum sit quod per ipsum valeat evitari. Patet ergo quid dicendum sit quantum ad istum articulum, quia dicendum est quod contractus
usurarius nullo modo potest permitti secundum ius divinum nec secun-
165   dum ius naturale et canonicum; potest tamen permicti secundum ius civile
eo modo quo dictum fuit superius.

4/138 expresse *RC* : expressum *L*   4/138–9 dominicum : divinum *RC*   4/143–4 vult
etiam ... ponderi *R* : *om. per hom. L* : eciam ulterius *om. C*   4/144 insuper : secundo *L* :
ulterius *add. R*   4/144 contra naturam : *om. C*   4/145 et *RC* : *om. L*   4/146 quod *RC* :
om. L   4/149 esset : quod *add. RC*   4/150 procedere : procederet *RC*   4/151 Vlterius :
postremo *add. C*   4/159 debet : potest *RC*   4/161 quod *RC* : *om. L*   4/162 sit *RC* : *om.*
L   4/164–5 divinum ... secundum ius *RC* : *om. per hom. L*

4/155–7 Pseudo-Augustine, *Sermo 221*, in PL 29 (Paris, 1865), col. 2153.   4/166 Vid. sup.
4/6–17.

mands, the usurer not only does not appear to be ashamed of his sin, which is utterly contrary to the Lord's command, but even to glory in it.

The usurer openly treats nature with contempt because he abuses not one but several – specifically three – classes of things. For he would cause countable things, that is, coins, to transcend their number unnaturally; weighable things, such as gold and silver, to transcend their weight unnaturally; and measurable things, such as grain, wine, and oil, to transcend their measure. Therefore it is rightly said that the usurer openly treats nature with contempt.

Moreover, as I have said, the usurer wickedly holds scripture in contempt because he violates it through infidelity, which is contrary to the faith he professed in baptism. For if his faith were genuine, it would be impossible for him to act openly and shamelessly against God and his scriptures.

I said furthermore that the usurer habitually treats the laws with contempt because, despite the prohibition of both laws, he perseveres in his sin to such a degree that he often delays repentance up to the moment of death. What Augustine says in his sermon on the Innocents is particularly applicable to the usurer: 'the sinner is subject to the punishment that he dies forgetful of himself as he lived forgetful of God.' For we often see usurers die without making restitution, without the sacraments, and with no hope of eternal life.

In the light of all these considerations, I conclude that canon law may not in any way allow or tolerate a usurious contract in order to avoid a greater evil because, properly speaking, there does not seem to be any greater evil that might be avoided by means of usury. Therefore, what ought to be said with respect to this article is clear, namely that usury may in no way whatsoever be permitted by divine, natural, or canon law, although it may be permitted by civil law in the restricted sense I noted earlier.

Vna tamen dubitacio hic occurrit, que tangetur et solvetur in quinto articulo. Per ea eciam que dicta sunt sublata est illa via que ingerebat du-bitacionem secundo loco, quia non est simile quod ibi inducebatur per si-
170   mile, nam etsi ibi permittitur observancia ritus Iudeorum, hoc est propter magnum bonum spirituale quod inde noscitur provenire, scilicet testifica-cio veritatis nostre fidei. Vlterius eciam si permisit Gregorius inordinatum esum carnium, hoc fecit propter vitandum maius malum et ideo relinque-bat eos suo ingenio ne deteriores fierent. Nichil autem talium apparet in
175   contractu usurario quo videatur debere permitti.

<5>   <Articulus quartus>

Quarto videndum est utrum in aliquo casu de facto usurarius contractus sit concessus vel permissus a iure, ut per hoc tollatur illa tercia via que ingerebat dubitacionem in tercio loco. Ad hoc autem dicendum est simpli-
5   citer quod non, nisi forte loquamur de permissione primo modo dicta, que est secundum ius civile, secundum quem modum in omni casu permittitur usura a iure civili; nullus enim casus est in quo ius civile se intromittat comminando vel infligendo penam pro usura. Et sicud ius civile se habet uniformiter affirmative ad omnes casus quia in omni casu usuram permit-
10   tit isto modo permissionis, ita suo modo ius divinum, naturale, et canoni-cum uniformiter se habent negative ad omnes casus, quia in nullo casu eam permittunt aliquo modo permissionis. Nam pari racione qua prohibent eam in uno casu debent eam prohibere in quolibet, quia in omni casu habet convolutam maliciam et per consequens pari racione qua eam concedunt

---

4/168 eciam : tamen *RC*   4/169 non : nec *RC*   4/169 inducebatur : adducebatur
C   4/169–70 per simile : pro simili *RC*   4/170 ibi : *om. RC*   4/171 provenire : pervenire
C   4/172 eciam : *om. C*   4/172 permisit : ulterius *add. et exp. R*   4/173 propter : ob
C   4/173 ideo : dicebat quod *add. RC*   4/175 quo : propter quod *RC*   4/175 videatur
RC : debeatur *L*   4/175 permitti : Restat ergo nunc quarto videre : *add. RC*   5/2 Quarto
videndum est : *om. RC*   5/4 est : *om. RC*   5/7 nullus enim : nam nullus *RC*   5/8 vel :
seu *C*   5/8 Et sicud … habet : Sicut enim iura civilia se habent *C*   5/9–11 quia in … omnes casus : *om. per hom. RC*   5/12 permissionis : ita uniformiter se habent negative *add.*
C   5/13 quolibet : quocumque *RC*   5/14 qua : quae *C*   5/14 concedunt : excederent *R* :
concederent *C*

4/167–8 Vid. inf. 6/1–151.   5/4 Vid. sup. 1/101–13.

Nevertheless, one doubt remains, which will be touched upon and re-solved in the fifth article. But from the arguments that have been advanced in this article we may lay to rest the second way in which doubt arises, because the comparison is not appropriate. For if the rites of the Jews are tolerated, this is because of a great spiritual good that is acknowledged to come from this, namely, testimony to the truth of our faith. Furthermore, even if Gregory permitted the inordinate consumption of meat, he did so to avoid a greater evil and so 'left them to their own devices lest they be-come worse.' But neither justification is applicable to a usurious contract such that it would appear permissible.

5. Article 4

Fourth, it is necessary to know whether a usurious contract is allowed or tolerated by the law in any case, so that we may dispose of the third way in which doubt arises in this matter. Now the simple answer to this ques-tion is 'no,' unless perhaps we mean the first mode of permission discussed earlier, which occurs in civil law and by which usury is permitted in all cases, for there is no situation in which civil law intervenes to threaten or impose a penalty for usury. And just as civil law takes a uniformly affirma-tive stance on all cases of usury because it tolerates usury in every case by this mode of permission, so in their own way do divine, natural, and canon law take a uniformly negative stance on all cases because there is no case in which they tolerate it by any mode of permission. For by the very logic by which they prohibit it in one case, they must prohibit it in every case, because in every case it is bound up with vice. Conversely, if they permit

15 in uno casu possunt eam concedere in quolibet, quod patet esse falsum ex
hiis que dicta sunt supra.

Sciendum tamen quod id quod facit dubium in isto articulo est ille specialis casus qui fuit tactus circa principium questionis, scilicet cum socer
assignat genero pro numerata dote aliquam possessionem in pignore, de

20 qua ipse gener postea recipit fructus, qui tamen ei non computantur in
sortem. |^{L71v}Propter istum ergo casum est intelligendum quod in eo nul-
la est usura et nullus usurarius contractus, quod apparet, nam si ibi esset
contractus usurarius, hoc ideo esset quod fructus illius possessionis perci-
perentur a genero intuitu pecunie detente a socero. Hoc autem falsum est

25 quia non intuitu pecunie dotalis quam socer detinet sed intuitu honerum
matrimonii que gener sustinet; et hoc satis innitur *extra, de usuris* c. *Salu-*
briter; vel potest dici quod dicti fructus recipiuntur a genero in recompensacionem dampni quod inde sequitur propter pecuniam dotalem que sibi
solvenda differtur. Ex quibus vobis statim apparet quod valde improprie

30 est dictum quod quandoque usura permittitur in isto casu vel in illo, quia
in nullo casu breviter est permissa; et ideo quando aliqui casus a iuristis excipiuntur, non est intelligendum quod in dictis casibus usura permittatur
sed quia in eis prima facie aliquid simile usure videtur. Sic ergo patet quod
sublata est illa via que ingerebat dubitacionem in ista questione tercio loco.

35 Patet eciam quid sit dicendum ad istum articulum.

5/15 possunt : possent *RC*   5/15 eam : agnoscere *add. et exp. R*   5/15 concedere : vel
permittere *add. RC*   5/17 id : illud *R* : *om. C*   5/17 quod^2 : *om. C*   5/17 est : *om.*
C   5/18 tactus : tractatus *C*   5/18 scilicet : 5 *C*   5/19 pignore : pignus *C*   5/20 recipit :
percipit *RC*   5/22 quod : patet *add. et del. L*   5/23 quod : quia *RC*   5/24 intuitu : intu-
ito *R*   5/24 a^2 : *marg. L*   5/24 autem : nec *R*   5/26 innitur : sumitur *RC*   5/26 c. : tunc
R   5/27 vel : ut *R* : ac *C*   5/27 fructus : percipiuntur *add. et del. L*   5/27 recipiuntur :
percipiuntur *RC*   5/27–8 recompensacionem *RC* : repensacionem *L*   5/29 vobis : nobis
RC   5/30 dictum : quando dicitur *add. RC*   5/30 quandoque : *om. RC*   5/30 isto : illo
RC   5/30 vel in illo : *om. C*   5/31 breviter : penitus *C*   5/32 permittatur : commictatur
RC   5/33 usure : fatetur *add. et del. L*   5/33 quod : quomodo *RC*   5/35 dicendum :
quantum *add. RC*   5/35 articulum : Restat ergo nunc quinto videre : *add. RC*

5/16 Vid. sup. 4/57–69, 102–65.   5/18 Vid. sup. 1/101–13.   5/26–7 X 5.19.16.

it in one case, they can, by the same logic, permit it in every case, which is clearly false in the light of what has been said earlier.

It should be understood that what inspired doubt in the first place is a special case that was touched on at the beginning of the question, namely that when a father-in-law grants his son-in-law a pledge in place of an agreed dowry, the fruits derived from the pledge are not counted against the principal. With respect to this case, it must be understood that here there is clearly neither usury nor a usurious contract; and if there were a usurious contract, this would be because the fruits of the possession are retained by the son-in-law in consideration of the money detained by the father-in-law. But this is false because the son-in-law retains the fruits not for the sake of dowry money the father-in-law detains, but rather because of the burdens of matrimony he himself sustains; and this is adequately explained in X 5.19.16. Alternatively, it can be argued that the fruits are awarded to the son-in-law by way of compensation for the damages he sustains by a delay in the payment of the dowry money owed him. From these observations it is clearly quite incorrect to say that usury is sometimes tolerated in this or that case because, to put it succinctly, it is not tolerated in any case. And therefore when the jurists make certain exceptions, it must not be thought that usury is tolerated in such cases, but rather that, on the face of it, they bear a certain resemblance to usury. And so it is clear that we have disposed of the third way in which doubt might arise in this matter; and the solution of this article is also clear.

<6> \<Articulus quintus>

Quinto videndum est utrum ius civile possit iuri canonico obviare vel
utrum dicta iura habeant ad se invicem tantam concordiam quod quidquid
est contra unum necessario sit contra alterum ac per consequens utrum
5   contractus usurarius eo ipso quod prohibitus est in iure canonico sit prohibitus eciam in iure civili, ut per hoc eciam tollatur illa via que ingerebat
dubitacionem in ista questione quarto loco.

Tria autem sunt que faciunt dubitacionem in isto articulo. Primum est
quod ius civile et ius canonicum presuppponunt ius naturale tamquam
10   fundamentum a quo sumunt originem; quapropter quidquid est contra
ius naturale necessario est contra ius civile et canonicum. Sed contractus
usurarius est contra ius naturale nec in aliquo modo est permissibilis in
prefato iure, ut patuit supra, ergo nec est permissibilis in iure civili aliquo
modo, cuius contrarium sepius est dictum.

15   Secundum quod hic facit dubium est quod ius civile et ius canonicum
subalternantur iuri divino et per consequens non possunt ei in aliquo
obviare. Si autem contractus usurarius esset permissibilis aliquo modo in
iure civili cum nullo modo sit permissibilis in iure canonico et divino, sequeretur quod ius civile se opponeret iuri divino, quod videtur absurdum,
20   quia imperator non potest tollere legem Dei; argumentum ad hoc: ff. *de*
arbi. l. *Nam et magistratus.*

Tercium quod hic facit dubium est quod imperator mandavit servari ea
que instituta sunt in Niceno concilio; sed Nicenum concilium prohibet
usuras, ut 47. di. *Quoniam,* ergo et ius civile debet eas prohibere ac per

---

6/2 Quinto videndum est : *om. RC*   6/3 se : *om. RC*   6/5 canonico : sicut nunc est,
necessario *add. RC*   6/5–6 canonico … iure : *marg. L*   6/5 sit : *om. R*   6/6 eciam[1] :
om. RC   6/7 dubitacionem : dubium *RC*   6/7 quarto : quinto *R*   6/8 dubitacionem :
dubium *C*   6/8 est *RC* : *om. L*   6/9 quod : quia *RC*   6/9 presupponunt : supponunt
RC   6/9 naturale : videtur *add. RC*   6/11 est : esse *RC*   6/12 in[1] : *om. RC*   6/13 est :
om. RC   6/14 sepius : superius *RC*   6/15 quod[2] : quia *RC*   6/16 iuri divino *RC* : iure
civili *L*   6/18 canonico et : *om. RC*   6/19 iuri : canonico *add. et del. L*   6/22 imperator :
servi *add. et del. L*   6/23 instituta : statuta *RC*   6/24 usuras : c. 17 *add. C*   6/24 ut :
patet *add. RC*   6/24 di. : c. *add. C* : di. *add. R* : Quoniam : Suam *R*   6/24 Quoniam :
multi *add. C*

6/6–7 Vid. sup. 1/114–17.   6/13 Vid. sup. 3/128–358.   6/14 Vid. sup. 4/70–100.   6/20–1
Dig. 4.8.4.   6/22–3 Cf. Nov. 131 (Auth. 119, Coll. 9.6).   6/24 Decretum Grat. D.47
c.2.   6/24–6 Cf. gl. ord. ad Decretum Grat. C.14 q.4 c.11, v. *Reddi* (ed. cit. col. 1036).

6. Article 5

Fifth, we must consider whether civil law can oppose canon law or whether the two laws are in such mutual accord that whatever is contrary to one is necessarily contrary to the other and consequently whether, by the very fact that canon law prohibits a usurious contract, civil law prohibits it as well. And thus we may dispose of the fourth way in which doubt might arise in this matter.

Three reasons give rise to uncertainty here. The first is that civil and canon law both presuppose natural law as the foundation on which they are built and from which they trace their descent. As a result, whatever is contrary to natural law is necessarily also contrary to civil and canon law. Now as we saw earlier, a usurious contract is contrary to natural law and is in no way permissible under it, therefore it is not permissible in civil law, though we have seen that the opposite is true.

The second is that civil and canon law are both subordinate to divine law and as a result cannot oppose it in any respect. But if a usurious contract were permitted in any way in civil law, though completely forbidden in canon and divine law, it would follow that civil law is opposed to divine law, which seems absurd, since the emperor cannot overturn God's law; and this may be deduced from the argument of Dig. 4.8.4.

The third reason that gives rise to uncertainty is that the emperor has ordered that the decisions of the council of Nicea be respected. Now the council of Nicea prohibits usury, as is noted at D.47 c.2, therefore civil law

25   consequens contractus usurarius non erit permissibilis aliquo modo in iure
civili, cuius contrarium superius est ostensum.

Propter ista ergo et illa que dicta fuerunt in quarto articulo consurgit
dubitacio nunc in isto articulo utrum ius civile posset obviare iuri canonico in aliquo vel utrum habeant tantam concordiam in invicem quod qui-
30   dquid est contra unum necessario est contra alterum.

Ad evidenciam ergo istius quesiti est intelligendum quod licet ius positivum sit fundatum super ius naturale, alia tamen est prohibicio iuris naturalis et alia est prohibicio iuris positivi. Nam prohibicio iuris naturalis fit
per solam vicii cognicionem et eiusdem detestacionem, quia docet ubi sit
35   vicium cognoscendum et inclinat ad ipsum detestandum; prohibicio vero
iuris positivi fit per pene comminacionem, nam sicut prefatum ius positivum se habet per addicionem ad ius naturale, ita oportet quod prohibicio
dicti iuris se habeat per addicionem ad prohibicionem illius.

Vlterius est sciendum quod duo sunt iura positiva, scilicet civile et cano-
40   nicum. Quamvis conveniant quia fundantur super ius naturale et ab ipso
eciam sumunt originem; quamvis eciam conveniant quia intendunt homines inducere in bonum commune, differant tamen quia alio modo intendit
dirigere in bonum ius civile et alio modo ius canonicum. Nam ius civile
intendit dirigere in bonum commune secundum quod congruit humane
45   societati viventi civiliter, secundum quem modum bonum commune habet mutuo conservari et promoveri per legalem iusticiam et per civilem
amiciciam. Ius vero canonicum |^L72r intendit dirigere in bonum commune
secundum quod congruit humane societati, que non solum vivit civiliter

---

6/27 consurgit : *vac. R* : movetur *C*   6/28 in : *om. RC*   6/28 isto : primo *R* : presenti *C*   6/28 posset : possit *RC*   6/29 in : ad *RC*   6/34 vicii : iuris *RC*   6/39 est :
om. RC   6/39 sunt : *om. RC*   6/40 Quamvis : eciam *add. R*   6/41 eciam¹ : *om.*
RC   6/41 eciam² : conveniant *add. et del. L*   6/41 conveniant *RC* : conveneant *L*   6/42–
3 differant ... canonicum : ius civile cum alio modo ius canonicum <ci *post* modo *add. et*
exp.> R : ius civile tamen alio modo intendit hoc quam ius canonicum *C*   6/42 intendit :
diffinere *add. et del. L*   6/44 commune *RC* : *om. L*   6/45 societati : que non solum vivit
add. per hom. et del. L   6/46 mutuo : nutriri *RC*

6/26 Vid. sup. 4/70–101.

should also prohibit usury, and consequently a usurious contract will not be permitted in any way under civil law, though we have shown earlier that the opposite is true.

For these reasons and the matters discussed in article 4, there arises the uncertainty which is the subject of this article, namely, whether civil law can oppose canon law in any respect or whether the two are in such mutual accord that whatever is contrary to one is necessarily contrary to the other.

For the resolution of this problem, it must be understood that although positive law is founded upon natural law, there is a difference between a natural law prohibition and a prohibition in positive law. For a natural law prohibition arises solely from the recognition and execration of a vice, because it indicates where a vice must be recognized and proceeds to execrate it. But a prohibition in positive law consists in threatening punishment, for just as positive law builds upon natural law by elaborating it, it is fitting that a positive law prohibition elaborates upon the natural law prohibition.

Furthermore, it must be understood that positive law is twofold, namely civil and canon. Although they are in accord inasmuch as they are both founded upon natural law, from which they trace their descent, and although they agree to the extent that their objective is to guide humans to the common good, they differ insofar as civil law guides humans to the common good in one way, canon law in another. For the objective of civil law is to guide humans to the common good in a way that is adapted to human society living in accordance with civic norms, and therefore it must nourish, preserve, and advance the common good through legal justice and civic friendship. The objective of canon law is to guide humans to the com-

sed eciam regulariter secundum fidem in Deum tendendo et vitam aliam
50   expectando. Nam cum ius canonicum sit quedam explicacio iuris divini,
oportet quod idem finis intendatur ab utroque; bonum autem commune
isto modo acceptum, scilicet secundum quod congruit humane societati
non solum viventi civiliter sed eciam regulariter secundum fidem in Deum
tendendo, non potest mutuo conservari nec promoveri per solam legalem
55   iusticiam vel per solam civilem amiciciam, sed ultra hoc requiritur quedam celestis amicicia, quam caritatem vocamus, sine qua est impossibile
aliquem hominem in Deum tendere. Quapropter sicud potissima virtus ad
quam conatur inducere ius civile est ipsa legalis iusticia sive civilis amicicia,
ita potissima virtus ad quam conatur inducere ius canonicum est illa celes-
60   tis amicicia, quam caritatem vocamus.

Ad propositum ergo applicando primum dictum, scilicet de prohibicione iuris naturalis et positivi, dico quod non est inconveniens quod aliquid
sit prohibitum in iure naturali quod tamen non est prohibitum in iure civili, quia prohibicio iuris civilis se habet per addicionem ad prohibicionem
65   iuris naturalis; nec tamen per hoc debet deputari inter predicta iura contrarietas sed solum alterius modi prohibendi diversitas.

Vlterius possumus colligere ex secundo dicto quod non est inconveniens
aliquod peccatum esse prohibitum in iure canonico quod tamen non est
prohibitum in iure civili prohibicione que fit per comminacionem pene,
70   cum nullum sit peccatum prohibitum in iure civili quod non sit eciam prohibitum in iure canonico. Racio autem huius diversitatis potest accipi ex
dictis, nam quia ius civile intendit conservare bonum commune multitudinis per iusticiam legalem, quod tamen est impossibile attingi a tota multi-
tudine, ymmo eciam a maiori parte multitudinis, idcirco sufficit dicto iuri

6/52 isto : ipso *R* : secundo *C*   6/54 tendendo : *ex* tempdendo *corr. R*   6/54 mutuo :
nutriri *RC*   6/54 nec : vel *RC*   6/58 inducere *RC* : *om. L*   6/59 inducere *C* : *om.*
RL   6/63 tamen : *om. C*   6/63 non : si *R*   6/65 per : propter *RC*   6/65 deputari : putari *RC*   6/65 predicta : dicta *RC*   6/69 comminicionem : consummacionem
R   6/70 cum : quamvis *RC*   6/70 sit² : quod non sit *add. per ditt. R*   6/71 huius : dictae
C   6/71 accipi : sumi *C*   6/72 nam *RC* : *om. L*   6/73 quod : quam *RC*   6/74 idcirco :
ideo *C*

6/61 Vid. sup. 6/31–8.   6/67 Vid. sup. 6/39–60.

mon good in a way that is adapted to human society living not only in accordance with civic norms, but also according to rules that lead via faith to God and in expectation of eternal life. Since canon law is an elaboration of divine law, it is fitting that both canon and civil law share the same objective; but since it understands the common good in this way, namely, as adapted to human society living not only in accordance with civic norms, but also according rules that lead via faith to God and in expectation of eternal life, canon law cannot nourish, preserve, and advance the common good solely by legal justice, but requires something additional, that is, heavenly friendship, which we call charity, without which it is impossible for anyone to turn to God. And so, just as the highest virtue civil law strives to inculcate is legal justice or civic friendship, likewise, the highest virtue canon law strives to induce is the heavenly friendship we call charity.

In response to the question, then, I maintain in accordance with the first observation, that is, with regard to natural and civil law prohibitions, that there is no inconsistency in the fact that something prohibited in natural law is not prohibited in civil law, because the civil law prohibition proceeds by elaborating upon the natural law prohibition. Nor for this reason should one posit a contradiction between the two laws but only the diversity that arises from the different modes of prohibition.

We can, moreover, deduce from the second observation that there is no inconsistency in the fact that something that is prohibited as a sin in canon law is nevertheless not prohibited in civil law by threat of punishment, since there is no sin prohibited in civil law that is not also forbidden by canon law. The reason for the difference may be deduced from what has been said: the objective of civil law is to preserve the common good of the many by means of legal justice; but legal justice cannot be obtained by everyone, or even by a majority, therefore it suffices that civil law preserves

75   quod posset pro maiori parte conservare bonum commune per viam civilis
      amicicie, nam secundum Aristotelem octavo *Ethicorum*, 'amicicia videtur
      civitates continere,' ymmo secundum quod ipse dicit ibidem 'legisposito-
      res magis circa ipsam student quam circa iusticiam,' quod potest contingere
      propter duplicem causam. Vna est quod facilius est homines inducere ad
80   amiciciam quam ad legalem iusticiam; alia est quia habentes legalem iusti-
      ciam indigent amicicia eo quod in vita civili et domestica maxime sit neces-
      saria, quapropter videtur quod a iure civili maxime sit intenta et ideo ius
      civile videtur quod debeat prohibere primo et per se per comminacionem
      pene illa vicia que possunt dictam amiciciam impedire. Secundo tamen et ex
85   consequenti potest prohibere quecumque alia vicia altero duorum modo-
      rum, utpote vel quia prohibicio illorum iuri divino et canonico obsequitur
      vel quia illorum prohibicione amicicia non leditur et bono iusticie et virtu-
      tis favoratur. Vbi autem prohibicione aliquorum viciorum civilis societas et
      amicicia lederentur, a tali prohibicione ius civile se preservat et ea relinquid
90   divino iudicio punienda, teste beato Augustino I *de libero arbitrio*, ubi ait
      'lex inquam ista que regendis civitatibus fertur multa concedit ac impunita
      relinquid, que per divinam providenciam vindicantur.'
         Applicando ergo hec ad propositum, apparet statim quod contractus
      usurarius non est necessario prohibitus in iure civili quia non habet civi-
95   lem societatem et amiciciam impedire. Est tamen necessario prohibitus in
      iure canonico quia ius canonicum ex fine quem intendit habet necessario
      vicia omnia prohibere; intendit namque ius canonicum dirigere multitu-
      dinem fidelium in Deum, quod non potest fieri nisi per caritatem, et quia

---

6/75 posset : possit *RC*   6/75 pro maiori parte : provere et *add. RC*   6/75 commune
RC : *om. L*   6/76 Aristotelem : in *add. RC*   6/76 videtur : etiam *add. C*   6/77–8 legis-
positores *R* : legisperitores (!) *L* : legislatores *C*   6/78 circa ipsam : ipsi *C*   6/78 circa
iusticiam : iustitiae *C*   6/78 quod : quia *RC*   6/80 alia : Secunda *RC*   6/83 prohibere :
providere *R*   6/83 se : et *add. R*   6/84 Secundo : Secundario *RC*   6/85 prohibere :
probare *R*   6/86 prohibicio : per prohibicionem *RC*   6/87 prohibicione : per prohibicionem *RC*   6/87 amicicia : et *add. R*   6/88 prohibicione : per prohibicionem *RC*
6/90 teste : testante *RC*   6/91 lex inquam *RC* : lex in agnicionem *L*   6/94 est : statim
add. L

6/76–8 Aristotle, *Ethica Nichomachea* 8.1.1155a (*Ethica Nichomachea: translatio Roberti
Grosseteste Lincolniensis sive Liber ethicorum recensio pura*, ed. R.A. Gauthier, Aristoteles
Latinus 26.1–3, fasc. 4, Leiden, 1973, p. 520).   6/90–2 Augustine, *De libero arbitrio* 1.40
(ed. cit. p. 13).

the common good for the majority by means of civic friendship, for, according to Aristotle in book 8 of the *Ethics*, 'friendship appears to be the bond of the state.' Indeed, he adds immediately that 'lawgivers seem to set more store by friendship than they do by justice,' and this is so for two reasons. First because it is easier to foster friendship among people than legal justice. Second because those who seek only legal justice lack the friendship so necessary for civic and domestic life, which appears to be the principal objective of civil law. Therefore it seems that civil law should first and foremost prohibit by threat of punishment vices that impede civic friendship. Secondarily, and as a consequence, it may prohibit all other vices in one of two ways: either because their prohibition defers to divine and canon law or because their prohibition does not harm friendship and fosters the good of justice and virtue. But when civil society and civic friendship are harmed by their prohibition, civil law abstains from such prohibition and leaves such vices to divine punishment, as the blessed Augustine observes in book 1 of *On Free Will*, where he says that 'it seems to me that the law that is enacted to govern the people rightly tolerates things that divine providence redresses.'

With respect to the point at issue, it is immediately clear that a usurious contract will not necessarily be prohibited by civil law, because it does not impede civil society and civic friendship. But it is necessarily prohibited in canon law because the objective of canon law necessarily demands that it prohibit all vices; for the objective of canon law is to direct the mass of believers to God, and this cannot be accomplished except by means of

omnia peccata mortalia sunt opposita caritati et habent eam tollere, idcirco
100   ius canonicum debet omnia talia merito prohibere. Quapropter si contingeret quod ius civile in aliquo casu vel pro aliquo tempore de futuro
contractum usurarium prohiberet per comminacionem pene, hoc faceret
in obsequium iuris canonici, utpote vel quia pena comminata per ius canonicum non sufficeret vel quia non posset per iudicem ecclesiasticum suffi-
105   cienter execucioni mandari.

Ex quibus omnibus apparet quod controversia que est inter iuristas de
permissione contractus usurarii non videtur esse racionabilis, quia utraque
pars potest dicere verum. Nam illi qui dicunt |^{L72v} quod talis contractus est
permissus et debet permitti in iure civili, si intelligant quod sit permissus
110   simplici permissione non comminante vel infligente penam, verum dicunt;
si autem intelligant quod sit permissus permissione tollente impedimentum facientibus usuras vel permissione prestante eis iuvamentum, falsum
dicunt. Et eodem modo dicendum est de aliis ex alia parte; nam si dicat
glossa, et illi qui eam sequuntur, quod contractus usurarius non est per-
115   missus in iure civili et intelligunt quod non ibi sit permissus secundo modo
vel tercio modo, verum dicunt; si vero intelligant quod non sit permissus
primo modo, falsum dicunt.

Vlterius eciam per hoc apparet quid sit dicendum ad illa dubia superius
introducta. Ad primum namque dicendum est quod non obstante quod
120   ius civile sit fundatum super ius naturale, potest tamen aliquid esse prohibitum in iure nature quod non est prohibitum in iure civili, quia prohibicio iuris civilis addit super prohibicionem iuris nature, ut superius
patuit.

Ad secundum dicendum quod non sequitur propter hoc quod ius civi-
125   le se opponat iuri divino, quia talis permissio non est per opposicionem,

---

6/101 futuro : facto *RC*   6/103 comminata : concusata (!) *R*   6/105 mandari : mandati
R   6/106 inter : ius *R*   6/108 talis : ille *C*   6/110 comminante vel infligente : commi-
nande vel infligere *R* : pro indulgentia comminandae vel infligendae *C*   6/111–12 impedimentum : aliquod *add. RC*   6/114 illi : *om. C*   6/115 intelligunt *RC* : intelligant
L   6/115 modo : *om. RC*   6/118 eciam : *om. C*   6/118 hoc : haec *C*   6/119 introducta :
inducta *C*   6/119 est : *om. RC*   6/120 naturale : nature *RC*   6/120–1 prohibitum :
prohibitus *R*   6/121 in iure^2 *RC* : *om. L*   6/122 super : supra *C*   6/124 quod^1 *RC* : *om.*
L   6/125 opponat : opponit *R*

6/118–19 Vid. sup. 6/8–26.   6/122–3 Vid. sup. 6/31–8.

charity. Because all mortal sins are opposed to charity and seek to destroy it, canon law rightly prohibits them. Therefore if it should happen that civil law in some case or at some future time prohibits a usurious contract by threatening a penalty, it would do so out of deference to canon law, either, let us say, because the penalty threatened by canon law is insufficient or because it could not be imposed effectively by an ecclesiastical judge.

In summary, then, it is clear that the disputes among the jurists about the permissibility of a usurious contract are unjustified, since each side can claim to be right. For those who maintain that the contract is and should be permitted in civil law, provided they mean that it is permitted by the mode of 'simple permission' by which no penalty is threatened or imposed, are correct. If, on the other hand, they mean that it is permitted in such a way that all obstacles to the exercise of usury are removed or that aid is given to usurers, they are wrong. And similarly those who take the opposite side; for if the gloss and those who adhere to it say that a usurious contract is not permitted in civil law and they mean that it is not permitted by the second or third mode of permission, they are correct; but if they mean that it is not permitted in the first mode, they are wrong.

Moreover, it is now clear what should be said in response to the questions raised earlier. The response to the first is that even if civil law is founded on natural law, something that is prohibited in the law of nature need not be prohibited by civil law, since a civil law prohibition builds upon a natural law prohibition by way of addition, as was demonstrated earlier.

The response to the second is that it does not follow from this that civil law is in opposition to divine law, for civil law permits usury not in oppo-

quia per obmissionem, quasi negative, non comminando penam, eo quod obmisit et reliquit talem contractum prohibendum vel puniendum iuri canonico et divino, quibus magis congruit.

Ad tercium dicendum, si imperator mandat servari ea que statuta fuerunt in Nyceno concilio, quod non vult quod ea que fuerunt in dicto concilio prohibita sint a iure civili permissa per amocionem alicuius impedimenti vel per concessionem alicuius auxilii, non tamen propter hoc intendit quod quecumque ibi prohibita sunt, prohibita sint a iure civili per pene comminicionem. Vel potest dici quod imperator mandavit illa servari per approbacionem, quia approbavit illa tanquam rite facta; non autem mandavit servari quecumque ibi statuta sunt per pene comminacionem.

Apparet insuper ex omnibus dictis quid dicendum sit quantum ad istum articulum; nam cum queritur utrum ius civile valeat iuri canonico obviare vel utrum habeant in invicem tantam concordiam quod quidquid est contra unum necessario sit contra alterum, dicendum est statim quod duobus modis potest intelligi ista obviacio. Vno modo propter contradiccionem, et isto modo dicendum quod non, quia ubi lex civilis contradicit canonice, nullius est momenti, sicud habetur in decretis d. 10 *Constituciones*. Alio modo ut capiatur ista obviacio per obmissionem sive dereliccionem, ut ita dicam, quia certe obmittit prohibere aliquid cuius prohibicionem sive punicionem relinquid iuri canonico et divino, quibus magis hic congruit; et isto modo videtur quod sit dicendum. Et ita patet quid sit dicendum quantum ad totam questionem, quia ostensum est quomodo contractus usurarius sit aliquo modo permissibilis in iure civili, scilicet permissio-

_____

6/126 quia : sed *RC*   6/126 negative : negati *R* : ut *add. R*   6/127 obmisit : obmittit *RC*   6/127 reliquit : relinquit *RC*   6/127 vel : et *RC*   6/127 puniendum *RC* : permittendum *L*   6/128 congruit : videtur congruere *RC*   6/129 si : quod *RC*   6/129 mandat : mandavit *RC*   6/129 ea : eam *C*   6/129–30 fuerunt : fuerant *RC*   6/130 quod[1] : quia *RC*   6/130 ea : illa *RC*   6/130 fuerunt : sunt *RC*   6/131–3 prohibita sint ... prohibita sunt *RC* : *om. per hom. L*   6/135 autem : tamen *C*   6/136 statuta : *om. RC*   6/137 dictis : istis *RC*   6/139 in : ad *RC*   6/141 propter : per *RC*   6/142 dicendum : dico *RC*   6/142 contradicit : legi *add. RC*   6/143 sicud : ut *C*   6/143 in decretis : *om. RC*   6/143 d. : pisti. *R*   6/143 10 : V *R* : c. *add. C*   6/144 sive : per *add. RC*   6/144 dereliccionem : predilectionem *R*   6/145 sive : et *RC*   6/146 hic : *om. C*   6/147 quod sit dicendum : dicendum quod sic *RC*   6/149 modo *RC* : *om. L*

_____

6/143 Decretum Grat. D.10 dictum Grat. ante c.1.

sition to divine law but, as it were, negatively, by omission, by not threatening a penalty, leaving the question of whether to prohibit or punish this contract to canon and divine law as the more appropriate norms.

The response to the third is that the emperor orders that the decrees of the council of Nicea be respected because he does not want the things that have been prohibited at the council to be allowed by civil law through the removal of some impediment or the extension of aid, not because he intended that everything prohibited by the council should be prohibited by civil law by threat of penalty. Or it may be said that the emperor ordered that the decrees be respected as a sign of approval, because he approved of them as things rightly ordained; but he did not thereby order that the decrees be approved by threatening penalties for their violation.

Moreover, from all that has been said, the resolution of this article is clear. For when it is asked whether civil law can oppose canon law or whether the two laws are in such mutual accord that whatever is contrary to one is necessarily contrary to the other, it must be said that 'opposition' may be understood in two ways. In one sense it can mean 'contradiction,' but that is not the meaning here, because where civil law contradicts canon law it is void, as is noted in the decrees at D.10 dictum Gratiani ante c.1. In another sense, 'opposition' may be understood as, so to speak, 'omission' or 'dereliction,' because civil law certainly omits to prohibit something whose prohibition and punishment it leaves to canon and divine law as the more appropriate norms; and it seems that this is the sense in which we should say that civil law 'opposes' canon law. And so it is clear what ought to be said with regard to this question as a whole, for we have shown how

150   ne indulgente penam, non autem permissione tollente impedimentum vel
prestante iuvamentum.

<7> <Solutio rationum ad oppositum>

Sexto et ultimo dicendum est de solucione racionum ad oppositum.

Ad primum principale dicendum quod ubi aliquid donatur non pro pacto vicioso et malicia convoluto, illud utique potest licite recipi; et sic maior
5 est vera sub isto intellectu. Sed tunc minor est falsa, quia in contractu usurario lucrum usurarium donatur pro pacto explicito vel implicito, ut potest
patere ex hiis que dicta sunt in primo articulo, quando inquisitum fuit quid
est usura et in quibus rebus commitatur.

Ad secundum cum dicitur quod contractus usurarius non est contra ca-
10 ritatem quia vergit in utilitatem utriusque partis, dicendum quod quamvis
quandoque non sit contra caritatem tamquam aliquid inutile, est tamen
contra eam tamquam aliquod inhonestum et viciosum. Nam ostensum fuit
supra in secundo articulo quod contractus usurarius ex natura rei sit viciosus et malicia convolutus et ex hoc ipso necessario contra caritatem.

15 Ad tercium cum dicitur quod liceat accipere lucrum de re sua; res autem
mutuata est ipsius mutuantis, nam quamvis transferat eam quantum ad
substanciam, retinet tamen sibi potestatem quantum ad valorem. Dicendum est ad istud quod unusquisque potest licite accipere lucrum de re sua
dummodo sit apta nata lucrifacere. Res autem mutuata non est apta nata

---

6/151 iuvamentum : vel tollente culpam *add. C*   7/1 Solutio ... oppositum : *ed.*   7/2–
201 Sexto ... palmarum : *om. RC*   7/2 Sexto ... oppositum : Restat ergo nunc ultimo
solvere rationes que in actu disputationis allegate videntur esse in oppositum *V*   7/2 racionum *scripsi* : racione *L*   7/3 dicendum : dico *V*   7/3 pro : pretio *V*   7/4 convoluto
V : convoluta *L*   7/5 est[1] : sit *V*   7/5 isto : ill *V* : intellecto *add. et del. L*   7/5 tunc :
om. V   7/5 est[2] : erat *V*   7/6 usurarium : *om. V*   7/6 pro : pretio *V*   7/6 vel : saltem
add. V   7/7 sunt : fuerunt *V*   7/7 inquisitum : quesitum *V*   7/8 est : esset *V*   7/9 dicitur : dicebatur *V*   7/9 quod *V* : *om. L*   7/9 est : erat *V*   7/10 vergit : vergebat
V   7/10 quamvis : licet *V*   7/12 eam *V* : eum *L*   7/13 sit : est *V*   7/14 malicia : malo
V   7/14 ex : *om. V*   7/15 tercium : vero *add. V*   7/15 dicitur : dicebatur *V*   7/15 liceat :
licebat *V*   7/18 istud : illud *V*   7/18 accipere : recipere *V*   7/19 dummodo : res illa *add.*
V   7/19 Res autem : Sed res *V*   7/19–20 apta nata lucrifacere : talis *V*

7/3 Vid. sup. 1/4–9.   7/7 Vid. sup. 2/2–29, 62–8.

a usurious contract is in a certain sense permissible in civil law, namely by remitting any penalty, but not by removing impediments to usury or abetting it.

7. Solution of arguments to the contrary

Sixth and lastly, something must be said regarding the solution of the arguments to the contrary.

To the first principal argument, it should be said that when something is given, but not by means of a wicked agreement or in a way that is bound up with vice, it may be accepted licitly; and so the major premiss is true in this sense. But the minor premiss is false because in a usurious contract usurious profit is given by means of an explicit or implicit agreement, as is clear from what was said in the first article, when it was asked what usury is and in what things it is committed.

To the second argument, which asserts that a usurious contract is not contrary to charity because it serves the utility of both parties, it should be said that although it is sometimes not contrary to charity in the sense that it is useless, it is nevertheless contrary to charity because it is dishonest and wicked. For it was demonstrated above in the second article that a usurious contract is by its very nature wicked and bound up with vice and for this reason is necessarily contrary to charity.

The third argument asserts that one may derive profit from private property. A lent thing belongs to the lender, for although he transfers the substance of the thing to the borrower, he nevertheless retains ownership so far as the value is concerned. The response to this argument is that anyone may licitly derive profit from private property so long as it is adapted

20   lucrifacere, ymmo quod lucrifacet est omnino contra naturam, ut patuit
supra in secundo articulo.

Ad quartum cum dicitur quod domus est quoddam artificiale nec est
apta nata parere domum, et tamen videmus quod per licitum contractum
una domus posset parere plures domus, nam posset aliquis per pensio-
25   nem domus usque ad certum |^{L73r} tempus recipere unam aliam domum, et
iterum usque ad aliud tempus unam aliam, et sic de multis; et per consequens una domus isto modo pareret multas. Ergo eodem modo de pecunia quantumcumque sit quoddam artificiale poterit parere pecuniam per
licitum contractum, et per consequens contractus usurarius non videbitur
30   illicitus isto modo. Ad quod dicendum quod causa quare pecunia non parit pecuniam non est quia quoddam artificiale sed quia habet prestitutum
determinatum valorem ab ipsa arte, ut patuit supra in secundo articulo,
et ideo non potest excrescere in suo valore ita ut recipiatur per eam ultra,
nisi per cupiditatem et maliciam ipsius mutuantis. Non potest autem sic
35   dici de domo, quia quamvis sit quoddam artificiale, non tamen habet sibi
prestitutum determinatum valorem ab arte et ideo potest excrescere in suo
valore ita ut recipiatur pro ea aliquid lucrum sine omni vicio.

Ad quintum cum dicitur quod contractus usurarius debet permitti quia
per ipsum vitantur multa mala, ut dampna in rebus, periculum in personis;

7/21 articulo : *om.* V   7/22 quartum : vero *add.* V   7/22 dicitur : dicebatur
V   7/22 quoddam : quid V   7/24 domus² : alias V   7/25 unam : *om.* V   7/26 aliud :
quoddam V   7/26 unam : *om.* V   7/26 de multis : deinceps V   7/26–7 consequens : unam domum *add. et del.* L   7/27 pareret : parere V   7/27 multas. Ergo : *om.*
V   7/27 modo² : dicebatur *add.* V   7/27 de : *om.* V   7/28 quoddam : quid V   7/28 poterit : potest V   7/28 parere : petere V   7/29 per consequens : sic V   7/29 videbitur :
videbatur V   7/30 isto modo : *om.* V   7/30 Ad quod : *om.* V   7/30 dicendum : ad istam
rationem *add.* V   7/30–1 parit V : pareat L   7/31 quia : sit *add.* V   7/31 quoddam :
om. V   7/31 habet : sibi *add.* V   7/31 prestitutum V : prestitum L   7/33 non V : *om*
L   7/33 excrescere : exercere V   7/33 ut : quod V   7/33 per eam : pro eo V   7/33 ultra :
sortem *add.* V   7/34 sic : hoc V   7/35 quamvis : habet *add. et del.* L   7/35 quoddam :
quid V   7/36 prestitutum *scripsi* : prestitum L : pristinum V   7/36 excrescere : exercere
V   7/37 ea : eo V   7/38 quintum : vero *add.* V   7/38 dicitur : dicebatur V   7/38 debet :
deberet V   7/39 ut : utpote V   7/39 dampna : damnum V

7/20–1 Vid. sup. 3/226–51.   7/32 Vid. sup. 3/137–212.

by nature to bearing a profit. But a thing lent by means of a strict loan contract is not by nature profit-bearing, indeed it is utterly contrary to nature that it should bear a profit, as is clear above in the second article.

The fourth argument observes that a house is an artificial thing that is not adapted by nature to producing another house, but nevertheless it is clear that a house may produce several houses by means of a legitimate contract. For, by renting out a house for a period of time, one might obtain another house by means of the profits, and by re-renting it, yet another, and so on. In this way, therefore, a house appears to produce several houses. In the same way, then, money, which is also an artificial thing, could also produce money by means of a legitimate contract, and consequently a usurious contract will not appear to be illicit in this respect. The response to this argument is that the reason money cannot produce money is not because it is something artificial but because it has a determinate value assigned to it by skill, as is clear in the second article, and therefore cannot increase in value in such a way that something additional accrues to it, except through the avarice and malice of the lender. The same cannot be said of a house because, although it is an artificial thing, it does not have a determinate value assigned to it by skill, and therefore it can grow in value in such a way that something additional accrues to it without vice.

The fifth argument maintains that a usurious contract should be permitted because by means of it many evils may be avoided, such as material

40   item quia per ipsum sequuntur multa bona, utpote pauperum sustentacio
et mercacionum salvacio. Dicendum ad istam racionem quod ista mala que
possunt vitari per contractum usurarium, ut plerumque sunt mala corporalia, illa autem que possunt sequi, ut plerumque sunt bona corporalia.
Malum autem spirituale numquam debet permitti propter quodcumque
45   malum corporale vitandum et propter quodcumque bonum corporale
consequendum, ut patuit supra in tercio articulo. Vlterius eciam dato quod
per contractum usurarium vitaretur aliquod malum spirituale aliquo casu,
illud tamen malum regulariter loquendo non videretur esse posse maius
quam sit illud peccatum quod committitur in dicto contracto usurario, ut
50   patuit supra in tercio articulo. Maius autem malum numquam debet permitti propter vitandum minus malum.

Ad sextum, cum dicitur quod iuriste excipiunt aliquos casus in quibus
usura permittitur, dicendum quod cum iuriste dicunt usuram in quibusdam casibus permitti, talis, inquam, modus dicendi aut nullo modo est
55   verus vel est omnino improprius, nam dicti casus non excipiuntur quasi in
eis sit usura sed quia videtur in eis aliquod simile usure, ut patuit supra in
quarto articulo.

Ad septimum cum dicitur quod si usura esset permissibilis saltem in
iure civili, non videretur ius civile iuri canonico obviare, cuius contrarium
60   videtur haberi in decretis d. 10. *Lege imperatorum.* Ad istam rationem patet solucio per id quod dictum est inmediate in isto articulo, quia verum
est quod ius civile non obviat iuri canonico vel divino per contradiccio-

---

7/40 sequuntur : sequebantur *V*   7/40 multa : *om. V*   7/40 utpote : scilicet *V*   7/41 mercacionum : mercantiarum *V*   7/41 Dicendum : utique *add. V*   7/42 plerumque : pluri-
mum *V*   7/42 mala : *om. V*   7/43 illa autem … corporalia : *om. V*   7/44 Malum autem :
Sed malum *V*   7/44 quodcumque : aliquod *V*   7/45 et : nec etiam *V*   7/46 tercio *V* :
secundo *L*   7/46 Vlterius eciam : et *V*   7/48 malum : *om. V*   7/48 videretur : videtur
V   7/49 usurario : *om. V*   7/50 tercio : eodem *V*   7/50 malum : *om. V*   7/52 sex-
tum : vero *add. V*   7/52 cum dicitur : quod dicebatur *V*   7/53 permittitur : ergo vide-
tur permissibilis *add. V*   7/53 iuriste : hoc *add. V*   7/53–4 usuram … permitti : *om.*
V   7/54 inquam : *om. V*   7/54 aut : *om. V*   7/55 est : *om. V*   7/56 aliquod : aliquid
V   7/58 septimum : et octavum *add. V*   7/58 dicitur : dicebatur *V*   7/58 si : *om.*
V   7/58 usura : non *add. L* : *om. V*   7/59 civile : in aliquo *add. V*   7/60 haberi : habere
V   7/62 quod : per *add. V*   7/62 obviat : obviatur *V*   7/62 iuri : *om. V*

7/46 Vid. sup. 4/102–65.   7/56–7 Vid. sup. 5/2–35.   7/60 Decretum Grat. D.10
c.1.   7/61 Vid. sup. 4/70–101.

damage and personal risk; and likewise many good things follow from it, such as aid for the poor and the promotion of trade. In response to this argument, it must be noted that most of the evils that can be avoided by means of a usurious contract are corporeal evils and that most of the goods that can follow from it are also corporeal. But a spiritual evil can never be permitted in order to avoid a corporeal evil or to obtain a corporeal good, as is clear above in the third article. But moreover, granted that in some case a spiritual evil might be avoided by means of a usurious contract, properly speaking such an evil would not seem to be greater than the sin which is committed in the usurious contract, as is clear above in the third article, and a greater evil can never be permitted in order to avoid a lesser.

The sixth argument observes that the jurists make an exception of certain cases in which usury is permitted. In response to this argument, I say that when the jurists say that usury is permitted in certain cases, and so forth, this manner of speaking is entirely untrue and completely incorrect, for these cases are not exceptions in the sense that they really involve usury, but rather they contain an element that appears similar to usury, as is clear above in the fourth article.

The seventh argument maintains that if usury were permissible at least in civil law, it would not seem that civil law is opposed to canon law, although the contrary opinion is maintained in the decrees at D.10 c.1. The solution to this argument is clear from what was said just above in the third article, namely, that civil law does not oppose canon or divine law

nem, quia sic nullius esset momenti, ut superius dicebatur. Potest tamen ei obviare per simplicem permissionem indulgentem penam, ut superius est
65   ostensum. Nam talis obviacio non est contrarietas vel contradiccio sed solum quedam obmissio. Si autem obviaret ei per contradiccionem, sequeretur quod ius civile esset contra deum et contra racionem et per consequens non esset ius.

Ad octavum quando arguitur per id quod habetur in auttentica *In ec-*
70   *clesiasticis titulis* c. 1 collatione 9, ubi imperator mandat servari quatuor concilia, et tamen constat quod in Niceno concilio usure prohibite fuerunt et ita videtur presumi quod in iure civili debeant esse prohibite; ad hoc dicendum, sicud dicebatur superius, quod imperator mandat servari ea que statuta sunt in dictis conciliis per approbacionem non contradicendo et
75   non per prohibicionem quorumcumque malorum penam comminando.

Ad novum cum arguitur quod duobus malis concurrentibus semper minus malum est eligendum, quod probatur per ius divinum et ius civile. Per ius divinum primo quia invenimus in lege moysaica, scilicet *Gene-si* 19, quod Loth voluit tradere filias suas fornicacioni ut vitaretur maius
80   malum, scilicet sodomiticum. Idem videmus de iure civili quia minor restituitur regulariter ex contractu quem ipse facit et tamen ius civile vult quod non ex omni contractu, quia tunc nullus secum contraheret, et sic minus malum eligitur, ff. *de mino. Etsi sine* § I. Ergo eodem modo usuram fieri: cum sit minus malum quam ipsam non fieri, videtur quod de iure
85   sit eligendum et permittendum ipsam fieri. Quod autem ipsam sive ipsum fieri sit minus malum quam ipsam non fieri probatur per hoc, scilicet quod si nullus prestaret ad usuram sepe pauperes morirentur fame. Ad

---

7/63 sic : tunc *V*   7/63–71 ei ... constat : *om. V*   7/66 ei : quod *add. et del. L*
7/67 deum *scripsi* : dampnum *L*   7/72 ad hoc : *om. V*   7/73 superius : supra *V*
7/74 contradicendo : scilicet *add. V*   7/75 per *C* : *om. L*   7/76 cum : quando *V*
7/76 arguitur : arguebatur *V*   7/77 malum : *om. V*   7/77 ius² : *om. V*   7/79 19
scripsi : 23 *L* : xviii *V*   7/79 voluit : *om. V*   7/79 tradere : tradidit *V*   7/80 Idem :
Item *V*   7/80 quia : quod *V*   7/80 minor *V* : *vac. L*   7/81 quem : fuit *add. et del.*
L   7/83 mino. *V* : immo *L* : l. *add. V*   7/83 Etsi *V* : Et *L*   7/83 § I *V* : c. *L*   7/85–6 sive
ipsum : *om. V*   7/86 per hoc, scilicet : *om. V*   7/87 quod : quia *V*   7/87 usuram : usuras
V   7/87 morirentur : morerentur *V*

7/69–71 Nov. 131 (Auth. 119, Coll. 9.6).   7/73 Vid. sup. 129–30.   7/78–80 *Gen* 19.1–11.   7/83 Dig. 4.4.7.8.

by contradicting them, for then it would be void, as was said above; but it can, nevertheless, oppose them by way of 'simple permission' that waives a penalty, as was shown above. Opposition of this sort is not contradiction or negation, but only a certain type of omission; if it were to oppose divine law by flat contradiction, it would follow that civil law is contrary to divine law and reason, and consequently is not law.

The eighth argument refers to the content of the authentic 'On ecclesiastical titles,' in chapter 1 of collation 9, where the emperor orders that the four ecumenical councils are to be respected; since the council of Nicea prohibited usury, it is apparently presumed that it is also prohibited in civil law. The response to this argument, as was said earlier, is that the emperor orders that the things decreed by the said councils are to be respected in order to demonstrate his approval by not contradicting them, rather than to prohibit any particular wickedness by threatening penalties.

The ninth argument maintains that it may be proven by both divine and civil law that when confronted by two simultaneous evils, the lesser must always be chosen. It can be proven by divine law, because we know from the law of Moses, namely at Genesis 19, that Lot preferred to give his daughters over to fornication in order to avoid the great evil of sodomy. Similarly, we see in civil law that a minor is routinely freed of contracts he has made, but the law does not wish this to be so of every contract, for then no one would enter into agreements, and thus the lesser evil is chosen; see Dig. 4.4.7.8. And likewise with a usurious agreement: since it is a lesser evil that it be made than not made, it seems that it ought to be approved and permitted by the law. And that it is a lesser evil that it be made than not made is proven by the fact that if nobody would lend at interest,

hoc dicendum quod ubi concurrunt duo mala, semper minus malum est eligendum ab illo qui necesse habet incidere in alterum illorum duorum, unde pauper pocius debet eligere recipere |^{L73v} mutuum ad usuram quam eligere mori fame. Ipse autem usurarius non necessario incidit in alterum illorum duorum malorum quia potest mutuare sine usura et isto modo vitabit famem et mortem pauperis, et per consequens non incidit in alterum illorum duorum malorum. Et ex hoc apparet inmediate quod unus et idem actus potest esse viciosus respectu unius qui tamen non est viciosus respectu alterius. Contractus ergo usurarius, quamvis sit viciosus respectu eius qui mutuum prestat, non est tamen viciosus respectu eius qui mutuum recipit, sicud eciam possemus ponere exemplum. Nam passio Christi fuit viciosa respectu Iudeorum, qui eam intulerunt; non autem ex parte Christi, qui eam recepit, ymmo summe virtuosa. Vel possumus nos ex isto argumento breviter expedire dicendo quod e duobus malis semper est minus malum eligendum illi qui esset causa illius mali, quod non potest dici in proposito. Nam dato quod pauper moriatur ex eo quod non invenit pecuniam ad usuram, ille tamen qui potuit eam prestare non proprie sit causa sue mortis; fuisset tamen causa illius peccati quod committitur in usura si suam pecuniam ad usuram prestasset, et ideo pocius debuit velle vitare hoc peccatum cuius causa ipse fuisset quam illud aliud in quo nullam culpam habuisset.

Ad decimum cum dicitur quod ea que parificantur in effectu debent parificari in iuris disposicione ff. *de verborum obligationibus*, l. *A Titio* et l. *Illud, ad legem Aquiliam.* Sed pecunia et opera parificantur, ut l. *Societates*

7/88 dicendum : ergo *add.* V   7/88 concurrunt : concurrerunt V   7/88 malum : *om.* V   7/89 illorum duorum : de duobus V   7/90 unde : et ideo V   7/90 pocius : i *add. et del.* L   7/90 eligere : *om.* V   7/93–4 alterum : aliquod V   7/94 duorum : *om.* V   7/94 ex : *om.* V   7/97 est : *om.* V   7/97 viciosus : *om.* V   7/97 qui² V : *om.* L   7/97–8 mutuum : *om.* V   7/98 eciam : et V   7/98 possemus ponere : potest poni V   7/98 Nam passio : In passione V   7/98 Christi : quia *add.* V   7/100 recepit : recipit V   7/100 summe : valde V   7/100 ex : de V   7/101 e : de V   7/102 illius : utriusque V   7/103 moriatur : fame *add.* V   7/103 invenit : inveniat V   7/104 proprie : *om.* V   7/104 sit : fuit V   7/106 prestasset : prestaret V   7/106 debuit : velle *add. et eras.* L   7/107 vitare : *marg.* L   7/107 hoc : illud V   7/107 illud : *om.* V   7/108 habuisset : et de hoc XIII di. in summa et IX di. c. I *add.* V   7/109 dicitur : dicebatur V   7/110 ff. de verborum obligationibus V : *vac.* L   7/110 Titio V : Titia L   7/110 et l. V : *om.* L   7/111 parificantur : in effectu *add.* V   7/111 ut : *om.* V

7/110–11 Dig. 45.1.116; Dig. 9.2.32.

paupers would often die of hunger. In response to this argument, it should be said that when confronted by two simultaneous evils, the lesser must always be chosen by the one who must necessarily succumb to one or the other, and so a pauper should rather elect to take a loan at usury than to die of hunger. But the usurer will not necessarily succumb to one or the other of those evils, because he can lend without usury and thus avoid both the hunger and the death of the pauper, and consequently he is not subject to a choice between evils. And from this example, it is evident that one and the same act can be wicked with respect to one person but not with respect to another. Therefore, although a usurious contract is wicked with respect to one who lends at interest, it is not wicked for the recipient; and this can be illustrated by an example. The passion of Christ was wicked as far as the Jews who inflicted it upon him were concerned, but not with respect to Christ, who endured it, but rather it was supremely virtuous. We can dispense with this argument more efficiently by saying that of two evils, the lesser must always be chosen by the author of the evil, and this cannot be said in the case under discussion. For granted that the pauper should die if he did not find money at usury, he who could lend it is not, properly speaking, the author of his death; but if he had lent his money at usury, he was the author of the sin that is committed in usury, and so he should rather wish to avoid this sin, of which he was the author, than the other, for which he bears no responsibility.

The tenth argument states that things that are equivalent in effect should also be equivalent in the disposition of the law; see Dig. 45.15.116 and 9.2.32. But money and work are equivalent, as in Dig. 17.2.5.1, therefore

§ I, ff. *Pro socio*, ergo idem ius statuerunt in utroque, quia de similibus ad similia procedunt. Sicud ergo in casu ubi cum opera mea percipis tantum de lucro quantum tu de pecunia ponis, sic et ubi ego meam pecuniam dabo
115 etiam sine opera tua potero de ea licite lucrum recipere. Ad hoc dicendum quod non est simile quia opera sine pecunia potest fructificare nec habet determinatum valorem a natura vel ab arte et ideo de ea sola possumus licite lucrum recipere. Pecunia autem sine opera non est apta nata ad fructificandum et habet determinatum valorem ab arte; quapropter nullus potest
120 de ea sola licite exigere lucrum.

Ad undecimum cum dicitur quod illud quod est licitum in uno casu presumitur semper licitum. Vsura autem videtur esse licita in quodam casu ut, verbi gratia, ego qui habeo molendinum do pecuniam Tytio ut magis veniat ad molendinum meum quam ad vicinorum. Et tamen si alibi ivis-
125 set, tantum de labore habuisset et tantum de pensione solvisset, nec hoc obstante tenetur quod recepcio talis sit licita, cum videatur usura quia recipit ultra sortem et laborem. Ad hoc dicendum quod, sicut patuit supra in quarto articulo, usura nullo casu est permissibilis, nec ex matrimonio, quod declaratum fuit in articulo secundo. In casu ergo nunc habito, si esset
130 usura nullo modo esset licita, quapropter dicendum quod nulla est ibi usura, quia cum usura generetur naturaliter de ipso mutuo, ut patuit supra in primo articulo, et in dicto casu nullum sit mutuum, relinquitur simpliciter quod in eo nulla sit usura.

7/112 § V : *om.* L   7/112 statuerunt : statuendum V   7/113 cum : ex V   7/113 percipis : participo V   7/114 de² : *om.* V   7/114 pecunia : pecuniam V   7/114 ego : *om.* V   7/115 etiam V : et L   7/116 nec V : ut L : fieri *add.* V   7/116 habet V : habeat L   7/117 ea : ipsa V   7/117 sola : *om.* V   7/119 determinatum : terminatum V   7/121 cum V : *om.* L   7/121 dicitur : dicebatur V   7/122 esse : *om.* V   7/122 casu V : *om.* L   7/123 gratia : ut *add.* L   7/124 ad² : *om.* V   7/125 tantum¹ ... et : *om.* V   7/126 obstante V : *vac.* L : communiter *add.* V   7/126 talis : pecuniae *add.* V   7/126 cum : tamen ea V   7/128 quarto : III V 7/128 usura : in *add.* V   7/128–9 nec ... secundo : nisi eo modo quo allegatum fuit supra in III articulo V   7/129 nunc : hic V   7/130 modo V : *om.* L   7/130 licita : receptio dictae pecuniae *add.* V   7/131 quia : nam V   7/131 naturaliter : maxime V

7/111–12 Dig. 17.2.5.1.   7/128 Vid. sup. 5/1–35.   7/129 Vid. sup. 3/355–8.   7/131–2 Vid. sup. 2/32–46.

they demand equivalent legal treatment in each case, because we reason from like to like. Therefore, just as in the case where I receive with my labour as much profit as you from the money you contribute, likewise can I licitly take a profit in the case where I grant my money even without your labour. The response to this argument is that there is no similarity here, because work can generate a profit without money and does not have a value determined by nature or skill, and therefore we can licitly take a profit from it. But money is not adapted to bear fruit and has a value determined by skill. As a result, no one may licitly may extract a profit from money alone.

The eleventh argument maintained that what is licit in one case may be presumed to be licit in every case. Now usury appears to be licit in one case, as, for example, when I, as the owner of a mill, give money to Titius so that he might use my mill rather than that of my neighbours. Nevertheless, notwithstanding the fact that if Titius had gone elsewhere it would have involved the same effort and payment of a similar fee, it is considered licit for me to accept such a benefit, although it appears to be usury, because I receive something in excess of the principal and the labour. The response to this argument is that, as is clear above in the fourth article, usury is never permissible, not even on account of marriage, as was stated in the second article. In this case, then, if it were usury, it would not be permissible in any way. Therefore, the response is that this case does not involve usury: since by its nature usury arises in a loan, as is clear from the first article, and since there is no loan in this case, it clearly follows that there is no usury here.

135 Ad duodecimum cum dicitur quod si homo non pecuniam mutuaret, esset deperdita et non multiplicaretur, nec ex ea communis utilitas resultaret et per consequens videtur quod usura sit licita et permissibilis quia illud ex quo aliquod bonum utile multiplicatur videtur licitum et permissibile. Ad hoc dicendum quod illud ex quo bonum utile multiplicatur, salvato bono honesto, est licitum et permissibile. Hoc autem in proposito non est ita;

140 nam quamvis per contractum usurarium multiplicetur sepius utile bonum, non tamen salvatur ibi bonum honestum et virtuosum, cum habeat convolutam maliciam, ut patuit supra in secundo articulo.

Ad tertiumdecimum cum dicitur quod usure sint permissibiles omni iure quia sancte, et probatur per hoc, quia illius condicionis sive nature est

145 causatum, cuius est causans. Sed usure sunt permisse ex legibus civilibus, que sunt sancte, ergo et cetera. Ad hoc dicendum quod si leges civiles ita permitterent usuras, quod essent causa earum, tunc argumentum concluderet. Nunc autem ita eas permittunt quod non sunt cause earum, quia non permittunt eas tamquam eas fieri precipientes vel eis auxilium prestantes,

150 sed solum tamquam penam non infligentes, ut superius fuit dictum.

Ad quartumdecimum cum dicitur quod usura est causa mutui, quod est bonum, ergo ipsa est bona et licita. Dicendum ad istam racionem quod ubi usura est finis mutui, ibi tale mutuum non est bonum et ideo melius est a tali mutuo cessare.

155 Ad quintumdecimum |^L74r cum dicitur quod si usura non est licita, tunc alienatio rei acquisite per usuram non est licita, quod videtur esse falsum. Dicendum ad hoc quod alienatio talis rei ideo est licita quia si aliquod

---

7/134 duodecimum : vero *add.* V   7/134 dicitur : dicebatur V   7/134 mutuaret :
corr. ex imutuaret L   7/135 ea : eo V   7/136 videtur : videbatur V   7/136 sit : esset
V   7/138 hoc : ergo *add.* V   7/139 Hoc autem : Sed V   7/140 multiplicetur : multiplicaretur V   7/143 tertiumdecimum : vero *add.* V   7/143 dicitur : dicebatur V   7/143 sint :
essent V   7/144 iure V : *om.* L   7/144 condicionis sive : *om.* V   7/145 cuius : omni
add. L   7/145 ex : a V   7/146 ergo V : *om.* L   7/146 Ad hoc : *om.* V   7/147 tunc
V : *om.* L   7/148 eas : *om.* V   7/148 permittunt : permittitur V   7/148 cause : causa
V   7/148 earum V : eorum L   7/150 superius : sepius V   7/151 dicitur : dicebatur
V   7/152 ergo : et *add.* V   7/152 est : *om.* V   7/154 cessare : se praeservare V   7/155 dicitur : dicebatur V   7/155 est : esset V   7/156 est : esset V   7/157 ad hoc : *om.* V

7/142 Vid. sup. 3/137–358.   7/150 Vid. sup. 4/70–101.

The twelfth argument stated that if a person did not lend out his money, it would be wasted and would not multiply, nor would any common good arise from it; therefore it seems that usury is licit and permissible because anything that augments the common good seems to be licit and permissible. To this argument the response is that anything that augments the common good, provided it is an honest good, is licit and permissible. But this is not so in the case proposed, for although the common good is often augmented by a usurious contract, an honest and virtuous good is not thereby preserved since it is bound up with vice, as is clear from the second article.

The thirteenth argument maintained that usury is permissible by law because it is sacred. The proof is as follows: a caused thing shares the condition and nature of its cause; usury is permitted by civil law, which is sacred, therefore et cetera. The response to this is that if civil law permitted usury as cause, then the argument would hold. But it does not permit usury as cause, because it does not permit it by urging its commission or by offering assistance, but only by waiving the penalty, as was said earlier.

The fourteenth argument asserted that usury is the cause of a loan, which is a good, therefore usury itself must be good and licit. The response to this argument is that when usury is the objective of a loan, the loan is not a good and it is better to abstain from such loans.

The fifteenth argument maintained that if usury is illicit, the alienation of a thing acquired by means of usurious profit is also illicit, which appears to be false. The response to this argument is that the alienation of such a

lucrum ex ea oritur, id non pervenit ex sola pecunia usuraria sed ex opera illius alienantis cum pecunia.

160   Ad sextumdecimum cum dicitur de eo qui habet molendinum, quod potest prestare pecuniam Tycio ut magis vadat ad molendinum suum quam ad molendinum vicinorum, et tamen dicitur quod in dicto casu non sit usura quantumcumque propter dictum mutuum recipiat lucrum quod antea non recipisset si mutuum non prestasset, et ita videtur secundum istam
165   viam quod iste casus omnino non sit alius ab illo qui fuit positus in undecimo argumento. Ad hoc dicendum quod habens molendinum, si prestat Tÿcio cum ista intencione quod Ticius magis vadat ad suum molendinum quam vicinorum, ex hoc ipso debet iudicari usurarius in mente quia ubicumque aliquis intuitu mutui intendit recipere aliquod commodum ultra
170   sortem, quod quidem commodum per pecuniam potest emi, tantum valet acsi reciperet pecuniam ultra sortem et per consequens eodem modo est censendus usurarius. Si tamen queratur ulterius utrum teneatur ad restitucionem, dico quod si sua intencio sit nota Tycio eunti ad molendinum, tenetur ad restitucionem propter causam superius assignatam in primo
175   articulo, quando agebatur de usura mentali. Si autem queratur ulterius utrum teneatur restituere totum quod a Ticio recepit pro pensione sui molendini, dico quod non, sed tenetur restituere tantum quantum reputat sibi valuisse illud commodum quod recepit propter hoc, quod Ticius ivit ad molendinum suum, ad quod non ivisset si pecuniam non prestasset. In-
180   telligo autem per id commodum concursum gencium usurancium quem consequitur suum molendinum ex hoc quod Ticius ivit ad ipsum et ideo debet tantum restituere Ticio quantum reputat sibi valere illud tale com-

---

7/158 id : illud *V*   7/159 alienantis : simul *add. V*   7/160 dicitur : dicebaur *V*   7/160 eo : illo *V*   7/160-2 potest ... quod : *om. V*   7/163 quantumcumque : licet *V*   7/163 mutuum recipiat lucrum : lucrum mutuum <*del.*> recipiat mutuum *inv. L*   7/163-4 antea : *om. V*   7/164 et : ut *V*   7/165 non *V* : *om. L*   7/166 hoc : ergo *add. V*   7/166 prestat : pecuniam *V*   7/167 Tÿcio *V* : Tycioni *L*   7/168 iudicari : videri *V*   7/171 acsi : reciperet *add. et del. L*   7/178 valuisse : voluisse *V*   7/178 illud : inde *V*   7/179 prestasset : prestitisset *V*   7/180 id : illud *V*   7/180 usurancium : vel notitiam *V*   7/180 quem : quam *V*   7/182 Ticio : *om. V*

7/165-6 Vid. sup. 7/121-33.   7/174-5 Vid. sup. 2/85-112.

thing is licit because if any profit arises from usurious profit it does not derive from the usurious profit alone but from a combination of the money and the labour of the usurer.

The sixteenth argument concerns a miller who lends money to Titius so that he might frequent his mill rather than that of his neighbours. It is said that there is no usury in this case despite the fact that because of the loan the miller receives a profit that he would not have received if he had not made it; and thus it is clear, from this perspective, that the case is completely different from the case proposed in the eleventh argument. The response to this argument is that if the miller lends to Titius with the intention that Titius should frequent his mill rather than that of his neighbours, he ought to be judged a mental usurer because whenever somebody intends to receive a benefit in excess of the principal for the sake of a loan – if the benefit is something that can be bought by means of money – this is tantamount to receiving money in excess of the principal, and consequently he should be censured as a usurer. But if you ask further whether he is bound to make restitution, I say that if his intention was known to Titius who frequented his mill, he is obliged to make restitution for the reasons given above in the first article, where I dealt with mental usury. But if you ask yet further whether he is obliged to restore everything that he received from Titius as a milling fee, I say that he is not, but only as much as much as he reckons the benefit of Titius using his mill – which he might not have done if the miller had not offered him a loan – profited him. By 'benefit' I mean the volume of customers that frequent his mill for the same reason that Titius frequented it, namely to mill corn, and therefore he should restore to Titius only as much as he reckons the benefit he sought thereby –

modum quod consecutus est per eum, dato quod deberet ipsum emere. Si
tamen queratur ulterius cui debeat fieri ista restitucio, dico quod ista re-
185   stitucio non debet fieri Tycio, quia ad illud lucrum quod contulit illi cuius
est molendinum obligabatur ex solo servicio quod habuit ex molendino,
circumscripto omni servicio mutui. Et ista duo stant valde bene simul, scilicet quod iste cuius est molendinum teneatur restituere et tamen ille qui
ivit ad molendinum non debeat recipere, quia ille cuius est molendinum
190   recipit aliquod benefactum vel aliquod lucrum intuitu mutui quod antea
non recepisset si mutuum non fuisset; ille vero qui ivit ad molendinum
non contulit aliquod lucrum intuitu mutui quod antea non contulisset,
sed solum cui non contulisset, et ideo in nullo potest se probare gravatum,
quapropter nulla debet sibi fieri restitucio. Ex quibus omnibus racionabi-
195   liter potest concludi quod restitucio prefata debet eodem modo fieri quo
fit restitucio de usura incerta. Intelligendum tamen quod si ille qui ivit ad
molendinum fuisset ex hoc consecutus aliquod dampnum quod non fuisset consecutus eundo ad molendinum alterius, debet ei dicta restitucio fieri
usque ad quantitatem illius dampni.
200   Finit anno domini millesimo 338, 4 nonas aprilis in Bodonis insula, tunc
feria 5 ante festum palmarum.

7/183 eum : Titium V   7/183 Si : tamen *add. et del. L*   7/186 ex² : de V   7/187 mutui
V : mut- L   7/187 valde : *om.* V   7/190 aliquod² : *om.* V   7/191 si mutuum non fuisset :
om. V   7/192 non¹ : *om.* V   7/193 sed ... contulisset : *om.* V   7/193 probare : putare
V   7/194 quapropter : ergo V   7/194 omnibus : potest *add. et del. L*   7/195 fieri : *om.*
V   7/196 restitucio : que est *add.* V   7/196 Intelligendum : Sciendum V   7/196 tamen :
om. V   7/199 usque : *om.* V   7/199 dampni : Io. And. *add.* V   7/200–1 Finit ... palmarum : *om.* V   7/201 festum *scripsi* : *om.* L

given that Titius was obliged to pay for the benefit anyway – profited him. But if you ask yet further to whom restitution should be made, I say that it should not be made to Titius, because he was obliged to pay the miller anyway simply for the service he derived from using the mill, setting aside any service he had from the loan. And these two are not at odds, namely, that the miller is obliged to make restitution but the user of the mill should not receive it, because the miller enjoys a certain benefit or profit he would not otherwise have enjoyed on account of the loan, but the customer did not confer a benefit for the sake of the loan he would not otherwise have conferred, but simply made a choice of the miller he would confer it upon, and therefore he cannot show that he was somehow inconvenienced, and so, he should not receive restitution. From these considerations it may be concluded reasonably that restitution should be made in the way that the restitution of 'uncertain usury' is made. You should understand nevertheless that if the customer incurred some damage by using the mill that he would not have incurred had he frequented the mill of another, he ought to be compensated to the extent of the damage.

Completed in the year of our Lord 1338 on the second of April in Bodenwerder, which was the Thursday before Palm Sunday.

Tractatus de restitutione

A Treatise on Restitution

<8> <Tractatus de restitutione>

R214r Hic incipit tractatus de restitucione usurarum et quorumcumque male ablatorum editus a fratre Gerardo de Senis in sacra scriptura magistro ordinis fratrum heremitarum sancti Augustini.

5   Intelligendum tamen quod quia hic se intulit materia de usuris et multi sunt qui dubitant de modo faciendi restitucionem usurarum et quorumcumque male ablatorum, idcirco istam materiam decrevi hoc modo disponere. Quia primo inquiram utrum usurarius acquirat aliquod dominium in usura per quod vero videatur non teneri ad restitucionem. Secundo, dato

10 quod teneatur ad restitucionem, utrum dicta restitucio requirat aliquam formam cum debitis circumstanciis servatam. Tertio utrum non reddendo usuras possit liberari ab earum obligacione per remissionem vel aliquam aliam viam. Quarto utrum teneatur restituere non solum usuram extortam sed eciam id quod per usuram extortam lucratus est. Quinto utrum

15 in restituendo debeat servare aliquem ordinem ita quod prius restituat uni quam alteri. Est ergo primo videndum.

<9> <Articulus primus>

Primus articulus, in quo ostenditur quod usurarius non potest acquirere aliquod dominium in usura.

    Vtrum usurarius acquirat aliquod dominium in usura per quod videa-
5 tur non teneri ad restitucionem. Sciendum ergo quod quidam dicunt quod

---

8/2–4 Hic ... Augustini : *om. C*   8/5 hic ... et : *om. W*   8/6 faciendi *C* : *om. RW*   8/7–8 istam ... inquiram : volui sub brevibus verbis de dicto tractatu aliqua recolligere hoc modo, quia primo in brevibus recolligam aliqua de primo articulo in quo dicitur queritur *W*   8/7–8 disponere *C* : *om. R*   8/8–9 in usura : *om. W*   8/9 vero : *om. CW*   8/9 dato : de secundo qui est supposito *W*   8/10 utrum : da *add. et exp. R*   8/10 dicta : *om. W* 8/10 requirat *CW* : requiratur *R*   8/11 servatam : mensuratam *C*   8/11 Tertio : de tertio, qui est *add. W*   8/12 vel : per *add. W*   8/13 Quarto : de quarto, qui est *add.* *W*   8/13 usuram : usuras *W*   8/14 Quinto : de quinto qui est *add. W*   8/16 Est ... videndum : *om. W*   9/2 Primus articulus : in primo articulo *W*   9/2–3 Primus ... usura : *om. C*   9/4–136 Vtrum ... propositum est : est ergo istud specialiter retinendum *W*   9/4 non *C* : *om. R*

9/5 Cf. gl. ord. ad Decretum Grat. C.14 q.4 c.10, v. *Si quis* (ed. cit. col. 1036).

A Treatise on Restitution

8. *Here begins the treatise on the restitution of usury and other things wickedly appropriated composed by Brother Gerard of Siena, master of sacred scripture, of the order of the hermit brothers of Saint Augustine.*

It should be understood that because it is related to the question of usury and because there are many who ask how to make restitution of usury and other things appropriated wickedly, I have decided to organize my discussion as follows. First, I shall consider whether the usurer acquires ownership by means of usury such that he might appear free of the obligation to make restitution. Second, assuming that he is bound to make restitution, whether restitution must take a particular form in view of the circumstances. Third, whether he may be freed from the obligation to make restitution by remission or some other means. Fourth, whether he is obliged to restore not only the usury he extorted but any profits he derived from it. Fifth, whether some order of priority is to be observed in making restitution such that one creditor receives restitution before another.

9. Article 1

Article 1, in which it is shown that a usurer cannot acquire ownership by means of usury.

First, then, we must see whether a usurer acquires ownership by means of usury such that he might appear free of the obligation to make restitu-

hec est differencia inter usuram et rapinam, quia in rapina non transfertur dominium in ipsum raptorem; in usura vero transfertur dominium in ipsum usurarium. Cuius racio est, secundum eos, quia res quam capit raptor per rapinam acquiritur ei invito domino suo, et idcirco non transfertur in
10 eum dominium sed remanet apud illum cui est facta oblacio, propter quod videmus quod semper ei competit repeticio; in usura vero ideo transfertur dominium, quia res quam capit usurarius per usuram acquiritur ei de voluntate domini sui, qui sufficiens est ad transferendum dominium, quamvis et voluntas domini sic transferentis rem suam in usurarium sit
15 coacta in tali casu, quia non libere consentit sed cogitur consentire propter indigenciam mutui, quo metuit carere. Hoc tamen non impedit propositum, secundum eos, quia voluntas propter coactionem non desinit esse voluntas, nam coacta voluntas vere est voluntas, ut dicunt, et potest haberi XV q. I *Merito* et XXII q. IIII *Inter cetera*, et XXIII q. IIII
20 *Displicet.*

Hec autem opinio non videtur mihi vera propter quatuor. Primo ex eo quod distinccio dominiorum est de iure gencium, ut patet ff. *de iusticia et iure* l. *Ex hoc iure*, ideo oportet quod omnis acquisicio dominii innitatur iuri gencium sive iuri naturali directe vel indirecte, ut eciam fuit dictum
25 in questione de prescripcione in articulo quarto. Si ergo in usura esset acquisicio dominii, sequeretur quod contractus usurarius concordaret iuri naturali directe vel indirecte, quod patet esse falsum ex hiis que dixi in illa questione quam de usuris determinavi. Posset ergo ex isto fundamento formari una talis racio ad propositum: ille contractus qui ex toto discordat
30 a iure naturali ita quod nec concordat ei directe vel indirecte non potest esse causa ex qua acquiratur aliquod dominium alicui. Contractus usurarius est huiusmodi, ut suppono ex questione prehabita, ergo et cetera.

Secundo patet hec racio ex eo quod per usuram fit usurpacio rei aliene, ut patuit supra in primo articulo. Hoc ergo supposito, posset ita forma-

---

9/14 et : *om.* C   9/14 domini C : dominii R   9/19 XXII C : XXXII R   9/28 quam : modo *add.* C   9/30 ei : illi C   9/30 vel : nec C   9/32 huiusmodi C : huius R   9/33 ex : *om.* C   9/34 articulo : superioris questionis *add.* C

9/19–20 Decretum Grat. C.15 q.1 c.1; C.22 q.4 c.22; C.23 q.4 c.38. Cf. Guido de Baisio, *Rosarium*, ad Decretum Grat. C.14 q.4 c.10, n.3 (Lyons, 1549, repr. Frankfurt am Main, 2008, fol. 240vb).   9/22–3 Dig. 1.1.5.   9/24–5 Vid. inf. 18/117–235.   9/28–9 Vid. sup. 3/128–358.   9/32 Vid. sup. 3/128–358; 6/1–151.   9/34 Vid. sup. 2/1–112.

tion. You should know that some maintain that the difference between usury and robbery is that a thief does not acquire ownership by his theft, but in usury ownership is transferred to the usurer. The reason for this, they maintain, is that what a thief takes by robbery is acquired without the consent of the owner, and therefore ownership does not transfer but remains with him from whom the thing was taken; for this reason, it is always subject to an action for recovery. But in usury ownership does transfer, because whatever the usurer obtains by means of usury is acquired with the consent of the owner, who is capable of transferring ownership even though his consent is coerced, for he does not consent freely to the transfer of his property but is compelled to consent because of his need of a loan and his fear of not obtaining it. But this consideration, they say, does not weaken their case, because coerced consent does not cease to be consent; or, as they say, coerced consent is a real form of consent, as is held in C.15 q.1 c.1, C.22 q.4 c.22, and C.23 q.4 c.38.

This opinion seems to me false for four reasons. First, because individual ownership derives from the law of nations, as is clear at Dig. 1.1.5, and therefore it is fitting that any acquisition of ownership is based directly or indirectly upon the law of nations or natural law, as is also noted in the fourth article of the question on prescription. Therefore, if ownership were acquired in usury, it would follow that a usurious contract accords directly or indirectly with natural law, which is clearly false for the reasons I gave in the question I determined on usury. On these grounds, we may formulate an argument against the proposition: no contract that completely departs from natural law such that it accords with it neither directly nor indirectly can effect a transfer of ownership. Now a usurious contract is such a contract, as I have shown in the said question, therefore et cetera.

Second, the argument is clear because usury involves the usurpation of another's property, as is clear above in the first article of the question on

35 ri secunda racio: ille contractus qui est causa usurpacionis rei aliene ipsi
usurario non potest esse sibi causa acquisicionis dominii in eadem re, quia
tunc eadem res simul et semel per eundem contractum fieret sua et remaneret aliena, quod est impossibile, ut de se patet. Contractus autem usurarius est causa usurpacionis rei aliene ipsi usurario, ut dictum est, ergo non
40 potest sibi esse causa acquisicionis dominii in eadem re.

Tercio patet hoc idem ex eo quod lucrum usurarium aquiritur usurario
ex causa non lucrativa, scilicet ex ipso mutuo, quod quidem mutuum, cum
habeat sibi taxatum valorem a natura vel ab arte, non potest lucrificare, ut
declaravi in illa questione quam de usuris determinavi. Hoc ergo supposi-
45 to, potest ita formari tercia racio: illud lucrum quod acquiritur usurario ex
causa non lucrativa non transfertur in suum dominium; lucrum usurarium
acquiritur usurario ex causa non lucrativa, ut dictum fuit, ergo non transfertur in suum dominium. Minor iam patet. Maiorem probo quia illud
lucrum quod acquritur ex causa non lucrativa non est dicendum lucrum;
50 et si non est lucrum, non est super ipsum de novo dominium acquisitum.

Quarto apparet hoc idem ex eo quod translacio rei acquisite per usuram
fit de voluntate domini sui coacta, que magis debet dici non voluntas quam
voluntas, ut statim patebit. Hoc ergo supposito, potest ita formari quarta
racio: ille qui transfert rem suam in alium magis nolens quam volens non
55 transfert nec intendit transferre rei sue dominium; sed ille qui dat usurario
lucrum propter mutuum transfert rem suam in usurarium magis nolens
quam volens, ergo et cetera. Maior patet quia eciam contraria opinio concederet eam; accipit enim contraria opinio pro fundamento quod coacta
voluntas sit sufficiens ad transferendum dominium, quia magis voluntas
60 quam non voluntas ac per consequens magis volens quam nolens. Vbi
ergo voluntas transferentis est magis non voluntas quam voluntas et magis

---

9/36 eadem : rei *add. R*   9/38 se *C* : *om. R*   9/39 causa *C* : *om. R*   9/40 acquisicionis :
om. C   9/44 quam … determinavi : paulo superioris de usuris *C*   9/46 suum dominium : usurarium *C*   9/47 dictum *C* : *om. R*   9/48 suum dominium : ipsum usurarium
C   9/52 domini *C* : dominii *R*   9/57–8 concederet *C* : concedet *R*   9/58 enim *C* : eam
R   9/58 quod : contracta *add. R*

9/44 Vid. sup. 3/128–358.   9/53 Vid. inf. 9/67–151.

usury. On these grounds, we may formulate a second argument: no contract that effects the usurpation of another's property by a usurper can effect the transfer of the ownership of a thing, for then a thing would at one and the same time become the property of the usurper and remain the property of the usurped, which is clearly impossible. Now as I have said, a usurious contract effects the usurpation of another's property by the usurer, therefore it cannot be a means by which ownership of a thing is acquired.

Third, the argument is likewise clear because a usurer acquires usurious profit from something which cannot produce a profit, namely, a loan, which, because it has a value assigned to it by nature or skill, cannot produce a profit, as I explained in the question on usury that I determined. On these grounds, we may formulate a third argument: the profit a usurer acquires from a thing that does not produce a profit cannot become his property; but usurious profit derives from something that cannot produce a profit, as has been said, therefore the usurer cannot acquire ownership. The minor premiss is clear. I prove the major premiss thus: a profit that derives from something that cannot produce a profit cannot be called a profit; and if it is not a profit, it is impossible to obtain ownership of it.

Fourth, the argument is likewise clear because the transfer of a thing acquired by means of usury is effected by the coerced consent of the owner, which is better described as non-consent than consent, as will immediately be made clear. On these grounds, we may formulate a fourth argument: he who transfers his property to another more unwillingly than willingly does not intend to transfer ownership. But he who gives a usurer profit because of a loan transfers ownership of his property more unwillingly than willingly, therefore et cetera. The major premiss is clear, because even those maintaining the opposite opinion would concede it, for they maintain as fundamental the fact that coerced consent is sufficient to transfer ownership, since it is more consent than non-consent, and as a result more

nolens quam volens, ibi non est efficax ad transferendum dominium. Ita autem est in proposito, ut dicebat minor proposicio, quia voluntas illius qui transfert rem suam in usurarium propter mutuum quod ab eo habu-
65 it magis est nolens quam volens, ac per consequens magis non voluntas quam voluntas.

Ad cuius evidenciam est intelligendum quod voluntas coacta quando-que est magis voluntas quam non voluntas, quandoque vero magis non vo-luntas quam voluntas. Contingit enim quandoque quod voluntas cogitur
70 volens et tunc est magis voluntas quam non voluntas; quandoque vero co-gitur nolens et tunc est magis non voluntas quam voluntas. Et quod ita sit apparet, potest enim contingere quod voluntati proponuntur duo mala, ad que ita se habet quod necessario cogitur alterum illorum eligere. Si ergo in-ter illa duo preeligat maius malum, tunc cogitur volens, quia ex natura rei
75 non habet quod debeat magis acceptare malum maius quam minus; ÿmo ex natura rei deberet contrarium. Si ergo preacceptat maius malum minori malo, hoc procedit ex sua malicia et ex sua libertate, quia sic vult, quamvis non sic debeat, et ideo in tali casu voluntas coacta magis dicitur voluntas quam non voluntas, et magis voluntas volens quam voluntas nolens. Et de
80 hoc habemus exemplum a beato Augustino XV q. I *Merito*. Queritur enim ibi a beato Augustino utrum sint aliqua peccata que debeant dici peccata nolencium et hoc propter quosdam qui videntur quandoque peccare inviti, ut ponitur ibi exemplum de illo qui nollet peccare peccato periurii; si tamen in casu mortis imminentis possit mortem evadere propter periurium, quasi
85 coactus videtur periurare ut possit mortem vitare. In tali ergo casu volun-tas coacta est magis voluntas quam non voluntas, nam debemus ÿmaginari quod ei qui est in tali casu proponuntur duo mala, scilicet periurium et mors corporalis, ad que duo |^R214v ita se habet quod necessario cogitur alterum illorum eligere. Si ergo preeligat periurium, eligit illud quod ex
90 natura rei est minus eligendum, quia periurium, per quod moritur anima, est maius malum quam mors corporalis, per quam moritur corpus; et ideo

---

9/67 cuius : in te *add. et exp. R*   9/73 cogitur : cogatur *C*   9/76 deberet : debet *C*
9/80 Augustino : Quaest. lib. 4 q. 24 et refertur *add. C*

9/80 Decretum Grat. C.15 q.1 c.1.

willing than unwilling. But where the consent of one who transfers ownership is more non-consent than consent and more unwilling than willing, then it is insufficient to transfer ownership. But this is the situation in the proposed case, as the minor premiss indicates, because the consent of one who transfers his property to a usurer because of a loan he obtained from him is more unwilling than willing, and as a result he exhibits more non-consent than consent.

For the clarification of this point you must understand that coerced consent sometimes contains a greater element of willing than unwilling, at other times a greater element of unwilling than willing. For sometimes consent is willingly coerced and in such cases the element of willing predominates; but sometimes consent is unwillingly coerced and so the element of unwilling is dominant. And that this is true is evident because it is possible for the will to be confronted by a choice of two evils such that it is compelled to choose one. If it selects the greater evil of the two, then it may be said to choose willingly, for it does not belong to the nature of the thing itself that it is necessary to choose the greater evil in preference to the lesser; indeed the opposite. If, then, the will chooses a greater over a lesser evil, the choice proceeds from its own malice and freedom, because it so chooses without needing to do so; and so in such a case, coerced consent is said to be more consent than non-consent, and more willing than unwilling. We have an example of this from the blessed Augustine at C.15 q.1 c.1. There the blessed Augustine asks whether there are sins that may be called unwilling sins, because people sometimes seem to sin unwillingly, and he gives the example of someone who does not wish to commit the sin of perjury. If, however, he is threatened with death and can evade it by perjury, he is, as it were, coerced into perjury in order to escape death. In such a case, coerced consent is more consent than non-consent, for we must imagine that he who confronts the two evils of perjury and execution is so placed that he must choose one or the other. If he chooses perjury, he chooses that which by its nature is the greater evil, for perjury, which kills the soul, is a greater evil than physical death, by which only the body dies.

quantumvis voluntas in volendo alterum illorum malorum cogatur nolens
in preacceptando, tamen periurium, quod est maius malum, non cogitur
nolens sed volens, quia non ideo sic preeligit vel preacceptat quia ex natura
95 rei sic cogatur et sic debeat ita quod non possit aliud preeligere, sed quia
sic est male disposita, quia sic vult et magis ei placet per periurium animam
ledere, quod est maius malum quam mortem corporalem suscipere, quod
est malum minus. Ex quo apparet immediate quod talis voluntas coacta
magis dicitur voluntas quam non voluntas et magis voluntas volens quam
100 voluntas nolens. Et ad istam intencionem videtur tendere beatus Augustinus in loco supra assignato, nam videtur ibi dicere quod si ille qui peccat
isto modo invitus diceretur peccare nolens, tunc quilibet peccans peccaret
nolens, quia omnis qui peccat ita peccat quod tamen non vult ipsum peccatum sed vult aliquid quod est adnexum peccato, propter quod adnexum
105 magis eligit peccare ut illud adnexum habeat quam velit illud adnexum
perdere ut peccatum dimictat. Et ita apparet ex omnibus istis quomodo
voluntas coacta quandoque cogitur volens et tunc est magis voluntas quam
non voluntas et magis voluntas volens quam voluntas nolens.

Vlterius dicebatur quod voluntas coacta quandoque cogitur nolens et
110 tunc est magis non voluntas quam voluntas et magis voluntas nolens quam
voluntas volens. Hoc autem possumus videre in quodam alio exemplo
quod eciam habemus ab Augustino et ponitur in decretis XXII q. IIII *Inter cetera*. Ibi enim respondet Augustinus Severo episcopo super uno casu
cuiusdam sui parrochiani nomine Ubaldi, qui compulsus iuraverat quan-
115 dam suam concubinam uxorem accipere et matrem et fratres de domo ex-
pellere, propter quod perplexus quasi videbatur inter duo mala, scilicet vel
ut iuramentum non servaret vel quod matrem et fratres relinqueret. Quia
tamen in isto casu non servare iuramentum est minus malum, cum dictum iuramentum fuerit coactum et omnino temerarium, idcirco consulit
120 Augustinus quod ille debeat matrem et fratres fovere et iuramentum non
servare. Ex quo apparet immediate quod in isto casu voluntas istius coacta
erat inservare iuramentum et cogebatur magis nolens quam volens, quia ita
cogebatur quod non poterat hoc non velle nisi vellet in maius malum incidere, utpote ut matrem et fratres relinqueret. Propter quod eciam in isto

9/94 ideo : *om.* C   9/94 preacceptat : acceptat C   9/97 suscipere : sustinere C
9/100 beatus : dominus C   9/101 peccat : primo *add. et exp.* R   9/102 nolens C : volens R   9/112 ponitur : refertur C   9/117 quod : ut C   9/122 inservare C : non servare
R   9/124 ut : quod C

9/112–13 Pseudo-Augustine at Decretum Grat. C.22 q.4 c.22.

Therefore, however much consent is unwillingly coerced in choosing between the two, nevertheless it is not unwillingly, but rather willingly, coerced to accept the greater evil of perjury, for it does not choose or accept it because it is compelled to by the nature of the thing such that it could not choose otherwise, but because it is wickedly disposed, preferring to injure the soul by the greater evil of perjury than to endure the lesser evil of physical death. From this it is clear that such coerced consent contains a greater element of consent than non-consent and that it is more willing than unwilling. And it appears that the blessed Augustine inclines to this interpretation in the passage cited above, for he seems to say that if he who sins in this way can be said to sin unwillingly, then every sinner sins unwillingly, because every sinner desires not the sin itself but something that comes with it, and it is to obtain this thing that he prefers to sin than to lose it by resisting the sin. From this, then, it is clear how coerced consent is sometimes coerced willingly and so contains a greater degree of consent than non-consent, and more willing than unwilling.

I also said that coerced consent is sometimes coerced unwillingly, and in this case there is a greater degree of non-consent than consent, and more unwilling than willing. We can see this in another example we have from the blessed Augustine included in the decrees at C.22 q.4 c.22, where he advises the bishop Severus on the case of a certain Ubaldus, one of Severus' parishioners. Ubaldus had sworn under compulsion to marry his concubine and expel his mother and brothers from his house. As a result, he was confronted by a choice of two evils, namely to violate his oath or to abandon his mother and brothers. Because in this case to violate the oath – since it was coerced and altogether improper – is the lesser evil, Augustine advises that he should prefer his mother and brothers and renounce the oath. It is obvious that in this case Ubaldus' consent to keep the oath had been coerced and this more unwillingly than willingly, because he was placed in a position where he could not choose to observe it without falling into the greater evil of abandoning his mother and brothers. For this reason he appears to be excused from perjury in whole or in part, and this

125 casu videbatur a periurio excusari vel a toto vel a tanto, et hoc videtur intendere Augustinus ibidem ubi sic ait 'nec enim ullo modo ad obprobrium
coacte voluntatis trahitur quod illicita condicio necessitatis extorsit.'
      Ex quibus omnibus possumus colligere tria notabilia ad propositum.
Primum est quod voluntas coacta non semper est dicenda voluntas, ÿmo
130 quandoque voluntas, quandoque non voluntas, ut superius est expressum.
Secundum est quod non bene dicunt illi qui volunt ex duobus locis preal-
legatis accipere quod voluntas coacta sit voluntas, nam quamvis ex primo
loco, qui est XV q. I, hoc habeant, ex secundo tamen loco, qui est XXII
q. IIII, magis habeant contrarium, scilicet quod voluntas coacta sit non
135 voluntas, quia magis est coacta nolens quam volens. Tertium notabile quod
ex dictis possumus colligere et quod eciam erit magis ad propositum est
quod voluntas transferentis rem suam in usurarium propter mutuum magis est dicenda non voluntas quam voluntas et magis nolens quam volens.
Et quod ita sit apparet, ille enim qui indiget ab usurario mutuum accipere
140 ponitur quasi perplexus inter duo mala, scilicet ut vel mutuo careat vel
quod pro mutuo non lucrificante aliquod lucrum in usurarium transferat,
ad que duo mala ita se habet quod cogitur alterum illorum eligere. Si ergo
indigencia mutui sit tanta quod nullo modo possit eo carere pocius eliget
aliquod lucrum pro illo mutuo in usurarium transferre quam mutuo care-
145 re, in quo casu sua voluntas est voluntas coacta et magis est dicenda non
voluntas quam voluntas, quia magis cogitur nolens quam volens. Nam ita
cogitur ad volendum tale lucrum transferre quod non potest non velle ipsum transferre nisi velit in maius malum incidere, utpote nisi velit mutuo
carere, et quia talis voluntas est magis nolens quam volens et magis non
150 voluntas quam voluntas, idcirco non est sufficiens ad transferendum dominium, ut superius dicebatur.
      Apparet ergo ex omnibus quod usurarius non acquirit aliquod domi-
nium in usura per quod non videatur teneri ad restitucionem, nisi forte
volumus loqui de dominio secundum simulacionem iuris. Et ideo si velle-

---

9/129 dicenda *C* : danda *R*   9/132 accipere : colligere *C*   9/133 est[2] : habetur *C*
9/134 habeant : habebunt *C*   9/136 eciam : *om. C*   9/139 mutuum : apparet *add. R*
9/139 accipere : recipere *W*   9/141 lucrificante *C* : lucificante *R*   9/148 malum *CW* :
maius *R*   9/148 incidere : cadere *W*   9/150 quam *C* : quod *R*   9/151–72 ut superius …
actionem : *om. W*   9/153 nisi *C* : ubi *R*

9/131–2 Vid. sup. 9/79–127.   9/133 Decretum Grat. C.15 q.1 c.1.   9/133–4 Decretum
Grat. C.22 q.4 c.22.   9/151 Vid. sup. 9/51–66.

seems to be what Augustine means when he says that 'what the unlawful condition of necessity has extorted is not in any way to be handed over to the great shame of a constrained will.'

Three points relevant to the question may be deduced from the foregoing. The first is that coerced consent should not always be described as consent, but sometimes consent, sometimes non-consent, as was explained above. The second is that those who wish to conclude from the two passages cited earlier that a coerced consent is consent are mistaken, for although they can come to this conclusion on the basis of the first passage, namely, C.15 q.1 c.1, on the basis of the second, that is, C.22 q.4 c.22, they should conclude the opposite, namely, that coerced consent is not consent because it is more unwilling than willing. The third point – and one even more pertinent to the proposition – that we may take from the foregoing is that the consent of one who transfers his property to a usurer because of a loan is better described as non-consent than consent, and more unwilling than willing. And that this is so is clear, for he who needs to accept a loan from a usurer is confronted by two evils, namely, that he either go without the loan or transfer to the usurer profit on account of a non-profit-bearing loan; and he is thus confronted by two evils of which he must choose one. If, then, his need of the loan is so great that he can in no way do without it, he does better to transfer some profit for the loan to the usurer than to do without it, and in this case his consent is coerced and more non-consent than consent, more unwilling than willing. For he is compelled to consent to the transfer of a profit which he cannot not wish to transfer unless he wants to incur the greater evil of doing without the loan. Since such consent is more unwilling than willing, and more non-consent than consent, it is insufficient to effect a transfer of ownership, as was said earlier.

In the light of these arguments, it is clear that the usurer does not acquire any ownership by means of usury such that he might appear free of the obligation to make restitution, unless perhaps we wish to speak of

155 mus, possemus distinguere de acquisicione dominii dicendo quod duobus
modis potest alicui dominium acquiri: uno modo per omnis iuris approbacionem, alio modo per alicuius iuris simulacionem. Primus modus habet locum quando acquisicio dominii concordat iuri naturali directe vel
indirecte, nam illud quod concordat iuri naturali videtur esse secundum
160 approbacionem omnis iuris. Secundus modus maxime habet locum in proposito, nam quamvis usurarius non acquirit dominium in usura secundum
alicuius iuris approbacionem, videtur tamen in ea acquirere dominium secundum iuris civilis simulacionem, quia, ut patuit supra in questione quam
de usuris determinavi, ius civile permictit contractum usurarium permis-
165 sione non infligente penam et ideo nec infligit penam pro usure exactione nec eciam pro usure non restitucione, quia nec usurarium per aliquam
penam impedit ut non possit usuras exigere nec ipsum per aliquam penam
compellit usuras restituere, ÿmo videtur ipsum simulare ita ut per dicti iuris simulacionem videatur usurario dominium acquisitum, et ista est causa
170 quare ei a quo usura est extorta non competit repeticio, quia scilicet propter civilis iuris simulacionem non habet in curia civili contra usurarium
aliquam actionem.

Patet ergo quantum ad istum articulum quod usurarius non acquirit aliquod dominium in usura per quod non videatur teneri ad restitucionem.
175 Et ideo restat videre secundo.

<10> <Articulus secundus>

Secundus articulus, in quo ostenditur quibus circumstanciis restitucio
usurarum debeat mensurari.

9/157 simulacionem : seu dissimulationem *add. C* 9/157 Primus modus : Primo modo
C 9/158 concordat *C* : concordare *R* 9/161 acquirit : acquirat *C* 9/162 acquirere :
dicioni *add. et del. R* 9/163 simulacionem : dissimulationem *C* 9/163–4 quam ... determinavi : de usura *C* 9/165 infligente : *corr. al. man. ex* intelligente *R* 9/167 ut non :
quominus *C* 9/167 nec : in *add. R* 9/168 ipsum : idipsum *C* 9/168 simulare : dissimu-
lare *C* 9/169 simulacionem : dissimulacionem *C* 9/169 et *C* : ut *R* 9/170 repeticio :
seu actio ad repetendum *add. C* 9/171 simulacionem : dissimulacionem *C* 9/175 Et
ideo ... secundo : *om. W* 10/2–3 Secundus ... mensurari : *om. C* : In secundo articulo in
quo queritur *W*

9/163–4 Vid. sup. 6/61–92, 106–28.

legally fictive ownership. We could, if we wished, make a distinction by saying that there are two ways in which someone can acquire ownership: one is with the approval of the law, the other by feigning the appearance of law. The first way is applicable when the acquisition of ownership accords directly or indirectly with natural law, for that which agrees with natural law appears to be legally approved. The second is particularly applicable to question at issue, for although the usurer does not acquire ownership by means of usury in a legally approved manner, he nevertheless appears to acquire legally fictive ownership by means of civil law because, as was explained above in the question I determined on usury, civil law tolerates a usurious contract by not imposing a penalty. It imposes a penalty neither for demanding usury nor even for not restoring it, because it neither inhibits the usurer by a penalty such that he could not exact usury nor compels him by means of any penalty to restore it, to the extent, indeed, that by means of a civil law fiction the usurer appears to acquire ownership. For this reason, namely, the civil law fiction, he from whom usury has been extorted has no action for recovery, because he has no action against the usurer that would stand in a civil court.

With respect to this article, it is clear that the usurer does not acquire any ownership by means of usury such that he might appear free of the obligation to make restitution; let us, therefore, now consider the second article.

10. Article 2

Article 2, in which it is shown by what circumstances the restitution of usury is measured.

Vtrum restitucio usurarum requirat aliquam formam cum aliquibus cir-
5   cumstanciis servatam. Vbi sciendum quod restitucio videtur esse quidam
actus oppositus illi actui quem vocamus usurpacionem rei aliene. Constat
autem quod usurpacio rei aliene est actus iniusticie, quapropter relinquitur
necessario quod restitucio sit actus iusticie, et quia actus iusticie et cuiuscumque virtutis debet esse formatus et secundum debitas circumstancias
10   mensuratus, cogimur ulterius dicere quod restitucio usurarum requirat aliquam formam debitis circumstanciis mensuratam. Si ergo volumus videre
que sit ista forma et que ille cicumstancie ex quibus |R215r constituitur et
mensuratur, debemus inspicere que sit forma usurpacionis rei aliene per
contractum usurarium et que circumstancie eam constituentes et mensu-
15   rantes, quia 'opposita iuxta se posita melius elucescunt.'

Sciendum ergo quod usurpacio rei aliene facta per usuram sic est cir-
cumstancionata quod singulariter est odiosa Deo, singulariter est odiosa
ecclesie, singulariter est odiosa nature, singulariter est odiosa fortune, singulariter odiosa speciei humane. Est, inquam, singulariter odiosa omnibus
20   istis quia in tali actu magis quam in furto et rapina Deus contempnitur;
secundo quia magis in eo quam in furto et rapina ecclesia decipitur; tercio
quia magis in eo natura pervertitur; quarto quia magis in eo fortuna extinguitur; ultimo quia magis in eo species humana offenditur.

Quod autem in tali actu Deus magis contempnatur quam in furto et
25   rapina apparet ex eo quod usurarius nullum tempus, nullum locum in tali
actu exspectat sed omne tempus et omnem locum ad usurpandum rem
alienam per usuram coaptat. Fur vero vel raptor certum locum et certum

---

10/5 servatam *W* : servatis *R* : mensuratam *C*   10/5 Vbi : *om. W*   10/11 mensuratam
CW : mensurato *R*   10/12 ille : iste *W*   10/15 quia … elucescunt : *om. W*   10/15 posita :
secundum Philosophum *add. C*   10/15 elucescunt *C* : eluscescunt *R*   10/16–17 circum-
stancionata : circumstantiata *C*   10/19 singulariter : est *add. W*   10/20 tali : casu *add.*
et exp. R   10/22 eo[1] : quam in furto et rapina *add. C*   10/22 pervertitur *CW* : pervertit
R   10/23 ultimo : quinto *W*   10/25 usurarius : vult *add. et exp. R*   10/26 exspectat :
spectat *W*   10/27 coaptat : coadaptat *W*   10/27–8 certum … tempus : certum tempus
certumque locum *C*

10/15 Cf. Walther, ed., *Proverbia sententiaeque Latinitatis Medii Aevi*: 3:650, no. 20276.

Is it necessary to observe some form in the restitution of usury that takes into account the relevant circumstances? It must be understood in this regard that, as an act, restitution appears to be the opposite of the act we call usurpation of another's property. Now it is the case that the usurpation of another's property is an act of injustice, so it follows necessarily that restitution is an act of justice. And because an act of justice – and of any other virtue – should be framed with respect to the relevant circumstances, we are further compelled to say that restitution of usury demands a certain form measured with respect to the relevant circumstances. If, then, we want to know what that form is, and what the circumstances are by which it is established and measured, we must first consider the form assumed by the usurpation of another's property in a usurious contract and the circumstances that establish and measure it, the better by comparison to illuminate its opposite.

It must be understood, therefore, that the usurpation of another's property by means of usury is conditioned by the fact that it is uniquely hateful to God, to the Church, to nature, to fortune, and to the human race. It is uniquely hateful to all these, I maintain, because usury displays greater contempt of God than theft or robbery. Second, because usury deceives the Church more than theft or robbery. Third, because usury perverts nature more than they. Fourth, because usury extinguishes fortune more than they. And finally, because usury is more offensive to the human race than they.

That usury exhibits greater contempt of God than theft or robbery is clear because the usurer awaits no time or place to usurp the property of another, but exploits every opportunity to this end, whereas a thief or robber must await his opportunity. For example, a thief searches out a time

tempus exspectant, utpote fur exspectat locum et tempus in quo dominus
rem suam non videat ut per hoc possit eam latenter subripere; raptor vero
30 exspectat locum et tempus in quo dominus rei potenciam resistendi non
habeat ut per hoc possit rem suam violenter accipere. Et ideo ex hoc ipso
videtur quod usurarius magis contempnat Deum super eum superbiendo
quam faciat fur vel raptor, nam quamvis quilibet eorum sit transgressor divini mandati in usurpando rem alienam, ipse tamen usurarius cum maiori
35 superbia et audacia divinum mandatum transgreditur, quia maiori posse
in tali transgressione utitur, nam utitur tali posse vel tali potencia que se
extendit ad omnem locum et ad omne tempus. Ipse vero fur vel raptor
in transgressione divini mandati per usurpacionem rei aliene non habet
posse vel potenciam que se extendat ad omnem locum et ad omne tempus
40 sed que se tantum extendit ad certum locum et ad certum tempus ac per
consequens utitur minori posse sive minori potencia. Et quia ille qui in
transgressione mandati sui superioris utitur maiori potencia videtur contra
ipsum incedere cum maiori audacia et superbia, idcirco relinquitur quod
usurarius contra Deum magis superbiat ac per consequens magis ipsum
45 contempnat quam faciat fur vel raptor. Et ita patet quomodo in usura magis quam in furto et rapina Deus contempnitur.
　　Secundo dicebatur quod in usura magis quam in furto et rapina ecclesia
decipitur; et quod ita sit apparet, nam propter simulacionem iuris civilis
possidet usurarius rem alienam pacifice sine reclamacione et secure sine
50 temporalis pene timore acsi esset sua, quod non potest dici de fure vel
raptore, ut de se patet, et ideo non potest ecclesia certificari de consciencia
usurarii sicut de consciencia furis vel raptoris, quia si velit usurarius ecclesiam decipere dicendo quod non possideat rem alienam sed suam, non
habet ecclesia contra eum aliquam viam per quam possit suum mendacium
55 deprehendere, quia nec potest ipsum deprehendere per alicuius pene temporalis vel corporalis inflictionem, nec eciam per iuris civilis persecucio-
nem. Peccatum autem furis vel raptoris utroque modo potest deprehendi,
ut de se patet. Ex quo apparet immediate quod in usura magis quam in
furto et rapina ecclesia decipitur.

10/31 ideo : et *add. R*　10/32 super : contra *W*　10/34 tamen : *om. W*　10/36 nam utitur : utitur enim *C*　10/36 tali³ : *om. C*　10/39 vel : sive *C*　10/39 extendat *CW* :
extendit *R*　10/39 extendat : nisi *add. W*　10/39–40 ad omnem ... extendit *C* : *om. per
hom. RW*　10/43 incedere : procedere *C*　10/46–7 Deus ... rapina : *om. per hom. W*
10/49 reclamacione *CW* : reclamacionem *R*　10/50 acsi *CW* : si *R*　10/51 de se patet :
usurario *W*　10/53 suam *CW* : sua *R*　10/54 ecclesia : *om. W*　10/54 mendacium : mandatum *W*

and place when the owner of a thing cannot see it so that he might carry it off secretly; and the robber waits for a time and place when the owner lacks the power to resist so that he might take his property from him by force. And so the usurer seems to mock God, vaunting himself more arrogantly than the thief or robber, for although all three transgress a divine command by usurping the property of another, the usurer transgresses the divine command with greater insolence and temerity, for in his transgression he employs greater capacity, namely, one which extends to every time and place. In their transgressions of the divine command, the thief and robber lack this capacity which extends to every time and place, employing one that is confined to specific times and places, and consequently they employ a lesser capacity. And because he who deploys a greater capacity to transgress the command of a superior appears to act with greater temerity and insolence, it follows that the usurer vaunts himself against God and mocks him more arrogantly than the thief or the robber. And so it is clear how usury exhibits more contempt for God than theft or robbery.

It was said second that usury deceives the Church more than theft or robbery, and it is clear that this is so, for, by a fiction of the civil law, the usurer possesses the property of another peacefully and securely as if it were his own, with no fear of an action for recovery or of temporal punishment, which obviously cannot be said of the thief or robber, and therefore the Church cannot be certain about the usurer's conscience in the way it can be of that of the thief or the robber. For if the usurer wants to deceive the Church by asserting that he does not possess the property of another but rather his own, the Church has no means to unmask his lie, since it cannot threaten any temporal penalty or corporeal punishment, nor can it prosecute him under civil law. But the sin of the thief or robber can obviously be unmasked by both means. It is clear, then, that usury deceives the Church more than theft or robbery.

60　　Tercio dicebatur quod in usura magis quam in furto et rapina natura pervertitur et quod ita sit apparet, quia quamvis usurpacio rei aliene
sit contra naturalem equitatem, illa tamen que fit per furtum et rapinam
non pervertit rerum naturas. Illa autem que fit per usuram rerum naturas
pervertit quia, sicut patuit in questione quam de usuris determinavi, fa-
65　cit transcendere res mutuatas suum valorem, quem habent sibi taxatum et
prestitutum a natura vel ab arte, quapropter convenienter est dictum quod
in ea magis quam in furto et rapina natura pervertitur.

　　Quarto dicebatur quod in usura magis quam in furto et rapina fortuna
extinguitur, nam secundum Aristotelem in libello de bona fortuna bono-
70　rum exteriorum fortuna est domina. Quicumque ergo vult lucrari et ditari non inherendo fortune vult ipsam fortunam extinguere; ita autem facit
usurarius, vult enim lucrari et ditari non inherendo fortune, quia fortuna
excludit securitatem et certitudinem. Ipse autem vult esse securus et certus
de lucro, ergo vult fortunam extinguere. Qui autem vult extinguere fortu-
75　nam vult eciam extinguere divinam influenciam, quia fortunati inpelluntur
et diriguntur a superiori principio, ut patet in libello supra assignato, scilicet de bona fortuna. Hoc autem non potest dici de fure et raptore, quia
neuter eorum habet securitatem vel certitudinem de lucro, ÿmo quilibet
eorum dubitat utrum debeat ditari vel non ditari per aliquem duorum mo-
80　dorum, scilicet furando vel rapiendo, eo quod in quolibet eorum immineat
periculum non solum de rebus sed eciam de persona. Quapropter bene est
dictum quod in usura magis quam in furto et rapina fortuna extinguitur,
quamvis in quolibet eorum extinguatur, quia nec fur nec raptor potest dici
fortunatus, eciam si per furtum vel rapinam locupletentur; sufficit tamen
85　quantum ad propositum quod magis in usura quam in furto et rapina.

　　Quinto dicebatur quod in usura, quamvis non simpliciter, quantum
tamen ad aliquid magis quam in furto et rapina, species humana offenditur, quod patet ex duobus. Primo quia usurarius facit iniusticiam prox-

---

10/61–85 et quod … et rapina : sed quomodo hoc declaratur ad presens non dico, quamvis
sit pulcherrima declaracio. Dimitto eciam declaracionem quarti membri propter brevi-
tatem *W*.　10/66 prestitutum : praescriptum *C*　10/67–8 natura … rapina *C* : *om. per
hom. R*　10/69 extinguitur : quod patet *add. C*　10/70 Quicumque : autem *add. et exp.
R*　10/71 extinguere *C* : extingere *R*　10/75 inpelluntur : impellantur *C*　10/76 assignato : signato *C*　10/83 fur *C* : fuit *R*　10/84 vel : per *add. C*　10/86 Quinto : Vltimo *C*

10/64 Vid. sup. 3/128–358.　10/69 Cf. Hamesse, *Les Auctoritates Aristotelis*, p. 249, lin.
32–3.

Third, it was said that usury, more than theft or robbery, perverts nature, and it is clear that this is so, because although the usurpation of another's property is contrary to natural justice, the usurpation of theft or robbery does not pervert the nature of the stolen things themselves. But usurious usurpation perverts the nature of things because, as is clear in the question on usury that I determined, it causes lent things to exceed the value that is assigned to them by nature or skill. Thus it is well said that usury, more than theft or robbery, perverts nature.

It was said fourth that, more than theft or robbery, usury thwarts fortune, for, according to Aristotle in his book *On Good Fortune*, 'fortune is the mistress of external goods.' Anyone, therefore, who would profit and enrich himself without regard to fortune chooses to thwart her. But this is what the usurer does, for he wishes to profit and enrich himself with no regard to fortune, because fortune precludes security and certainty. But the usurer wants to be secure and certain about his profit, and so he wishes to thwart fortune. Now he who wishes to thwart fortune also wishes to thwart divine influence, because the fortunate are guided and directed by a higher principle, as is clear in the book cited above, namely, *On Good Fortune*. But this cannot be said of the thief or the robber, because neither can be secure in, or certain of, his profit; indeed, each is in doubt whether or not he will be enriched by his theft or robbery, because each crime involves material and personal risk. Thus it is well said that usury, more than theft or robbery, thwarts fortune – although all three in some sense thwart it – since neither the thief nor the robber can be called fortunate, even if he is enriched by his theft or robbery. And this suffices with regard to the proposition that usury thwarts fortune more than theft or robbery.

It was said fifth that usury is largely, if not completely, more offensive to the human race than theft or robbery, and this is clear for two reasons. First, because the usurer commits an injustice against his neighbour with

imo cum maiori malicia; secundo quia communem iusticiam ledit cum
90 maiori securitate et superbia. Primum patet quia quamvis fur et raptor et
eciam usurarius faciunt iniuriam proximo in eo quod usurpant rem suam,
malicia tamen usurarii in tali usurpacione in tantum superhabundat quod
compellit voluntatem istius cui usurpat rem suam ad volendum et consenciendum in talem usurpacionem, in quo apparet maxima malicia, quia
95 per hoc simulat usurarius se non facere aliquam iniuriam vel iniusticiam
proximo suo. Nam quia nullus potest pati iniusticiam volens, ut probatur in quinto Ethicorum, idcirco eo ipso quod ille cui usurarius usurpat
rem suam vult et consentit in talem usurpacionem, non videtur ei facere
aliquam iniusticiam. Secundum eciam patet, scilicet quod usurarius ledat
100 communem iusticiam cum maiori securitate et superbia, tum quia usurpat
rem alienam sine timore persecucionis, tum eciam quia eam detinet sine
timore repeticionis.

Apparet ergo ex omnibus istis quod usurpacio rei aliene facta per usuram
quantum ad circumstancias superius memoratas redditur magis viciosa et
105 odiosa quam usurpacio rei aliene facta per furtum et rapinam. Intelligendum tamen quod quamvis sit magis viciosa quantum ad circumstancias
prefatas, non tamen propter hoc simpliciter inferri potest quod sit magis
viciosa universaliter, quia possunt esse quedam alie circumstancie speciales
que magis viciant usurpacionem rei aliene factam per furtum vel rapinam,
110 utpote quia usurpacio rei aliene facta per furtum vel rapinam magis quam
per usuram ledit rem publicam; ulterius quia proximo infert maiorem iniuriam. Et ideo quantum ad presens sufficit scire quomodo usurpacio rei
aliene per usuram ex suis specialibus circumstanciis redditur singulariter
viciosa et odiosa. Vtrum autem per hoc sit magis viciosa simpliciter vel
115 universaliter de hoc nihil ad presens.

10/90 et superbia : *om.* W   10/90 quia CW : quod R   10/91 faciunt : faciant C
10/93 istius : illius CW   10/95 per : in C   10/96 iniusticiam : iniustum CW   10/97 in :
om. W   10/98 non W : *om.* RC   10/105 quam : sit *add.* C   10/105–16 Intelligendum …
visis : *om.* W   10/107 quod C : *om.* R   10/107 sit C : sicut R   10/109 viciant : vitient
C   10/110 facta C : *om.* R   10/112 sufficit C : sufficitur R   10/114 sit C : *om.* R

10/97 Aristotle, *Ethica Nichomachea* 5.11.1136a (ed. cit. p. 470).

greater malice than the thief or robber; and second, because he harms collective justice with greater complacency and arrogance than they. The first point is clear, because even though the thief, the robber, and the usurer each commits an injustice against his neighbour by usurping his property, the malice displayed by the usurer in his usurpation is excessive, because he coerces the consent of the one whose property he is usurping such that the debtor wills and agrees to the usurpation. In this respect, the usurer exhibits excessive malice, because he pretends he is not inflicting an injury on, or committing an injustice against, his neighbour. After all, nobody willingly endures an injustice, as is shown in book 5 of the *Ethics*, but because he whose property the usurer is usurping wills and consents to the usurpation, it appears that the usurer does him no injury. The second point is also clear, namely, that the usurer harms collective justice with greater complacency and arrogance, because he both usurps the property of another without fear of punishment and detains it with no fear of an action against him for recovery.

It is obvious on the basis of all the foregoing that the usurpation of another's property by means of usury, by virtue of the circumstances outlined above, is rendered more vicious than usurpation by means of theft or robbery. Nevertheless, it should be understood that even though usury is more vicious than theft or robbery with respect to these circumstances, we should not conclude that it is always and without exception more vicious, because under certain circumstances the usurpation of another's property by means of theft or robbery may be considered more vicious, for instance, because such usurpation harms the state more than usury does, or because it inflicts a greater injury on a neighbour. But so far as the present article is concerned, it is sufficient to know that usurpation of another's property by means of usury is rendered particularly vicious and hateful because of its peculiar circumstances; whether it is always and without exception vicious is irrelevant.

Hiis ergo visis, possumus ad illud quod quesitum est in isto articulo facilius respondere. Cum ergo queritur utrum restitucio usurarum requirat
aliquam formam cum debitis circumstanciis servatam,|^R215v dicendum est
statim quod sic. Debet enim sic esse mensurata ut per eam tollatur illa obli-
120　gacio que ex illicita usurpacione et detencione rei aliene nascitur. Tollantur
insuper omnes ille circumstancie superius memorate que illam usurpacionem et detencionem singulariter viciabant, nam quia restitucio, secundum
quod de ea loquimur, directe opponitur illicite usurpacioni et detencioni
rei aliene, idcirco debet primo tollere illam obligacionem que ex ea in-
125　nascitur, consequenter vero omnes circumstancias que eam concomitan-
tantur, utpote quia debet tollere Dei contemptum et illusionem, ecclesie
decepcionem, nature perversionem, fortune extinctionem, specie humane
offensionem. Si ergo prefata obligacio cum dictis circumstanciis auferatur
habebit restitucio illam formam quam ex sui natura exigit optinere.

130　Et ita patet quid sit dicendum quantum ad illum articulum. Restat ergo
videre tercio.

<11> <Articulus tertius>

Tercius articulus, in quo ostenditir quod usurarius vel quicumque habet
male ablata non potest liberari a sua obligacione per viam remissionis nec
per aliquam aliam viam nisi reddat vel sufficientem caucionem faciat.

5　Vtrum usurarius non reddendo usuras nec aliquam caucionem pro eis
reddendis faciendo possit liberari ab earum obligacione per viam remissionis vel per aliquam aliam viam que attingit formam restitucionis in

---

10/116 possumus : ergo *add.* W　10/116 illud : istud W　10/116 isto : primo W
10/118 servatam : mensuratam C　10/119 statim : *om.* W　10/119 mensurata C : mensura RW　10/120 Tollantur CW : Tollant R　10/121 ille : iste W　10/121 illam : istam
W　10/123 directe : *om.* W　10/123 usurpacioni CW : usurpacionem R　10/123 detencioni CW : detencionem R　10/125 consequenter : ex consequenti C　10/125–6 concomi-
tantur C : concomitant R　10/126 et illusionem : *om.* C　10/128 dictis : suis C
10/129 quam : qua W　10/130–1 Et ita … tercio : et cetera W　10/130 illum : istum C
11/2 Tercius articulus : De tercio articulo W　11/2–4 Tercius … faciat : *om.* C　11/2 habet W : *om.* R　11/5–8 Vtrum … quidam : *om.* W

In the light of these observations, we are now in a position to respond clearly to the question posed in this article. When it is asked, then, whether the restitution of usury should assume a form that takes into account the relevant circumstances, the simple answer is 'yes.' The measure of this is that it removes the obligation that arises from the illicit usurpation and retention of another's property. Moreover, it should remove all the circumstances noted above that render this usurpation and retention particularly vicious. Now as we have said, since restitution is the complete opposite of the illicit usurpation and retention of another's property, it should first of all remove the obligation that arises from the usurpation, and then all the circumstances that accompany it, specifically, contempt and mockery of God, deception of the Church, the perversion of nature, the thwarting of fortune, and offence against the human race. If, therefore, the said obligation and circumstances are to be removed, restitution must by its very nature take such a form as to accomplish these ends.

And so it is clear what should be said with respect to the second article. Let us, therefore, now consider the third article.

11. Article 3

The third article, in which it is demonstrated that a usurer or anyone else who has appropriated something illicitly cannot be freed of his obligation by remission or in any other way unless he makes restitution or posts an adequate pledge to make restitution.

Can a usurer, without making restitution or posting a pledge to make restitution, be freed of this obligation either by remission or in some other way, which touches on the very form of restitution treated in the preced-

precedenti articulo traditam. Vbi sciendum quod quidam tenent partem affirmativam, dicentes quod usurarius potest liberari ab obligacione usu-
10   rarum per solam viam remissionis, dato quod eas non reddat nec aliquam caucionem pro eis reddendis faciat, nam si ille cui debet fieri restitucio usurarum libere eas remictat, non tenebitur usurarius amplius ad restitu-cionem et per consequens erit liberatus ab illa obligacione qua antea tene-batur, secundum quod dicunt, non obstante quod ibi non fuit usurarum
15   reddicio nec eciam pro eis reddendis aliqua caucio. Hoc autem probant una racione, que potest sic formari: illud quod in aliquo particulari casu statuitur non valere videtur extra illum casum generaliter et ubique valere; sed statutum est per ius canonicum quod remissio non valeat in eo casu in quo iudex ecclesiasticus tenetur ad restitucionem omnium eorum que pro
20   danda sentencia recepit sive per seipsum exigendo sive cum assessore et notariis lucrum participando; et de hoc habemus *extra, de rescriptis* in VI c. *Statutum* § *Si quid*. Vlterius statuit ius canonicum quod remissio non valeat in eo casu in quo visitator ecclesie tenetur ad restitucionem mune-rum que pro visitacione recepit; et de hoc habemus *extra* in eodem VI *de*
25   *censibus* c. *Exigit* in fine. Ergo videtur quod extra dictos duos casus valeat remissio generaliter et ubique, et per consequens valebit in restituendis usuris ita quod si remictatur antequam reddantur non tenebitur usurarius amplius ad restitucionem, quia erit liberatus ab illa obligacione qua antea tenebatur.
30   Posset autem hec oppinio confirmari per V rationes, quarum prima sumitur ex parte satisfaccionis, quia satisfactum accipimus eum modum quem creditor acceptavit, ut ff. *de pi. acc. Si rem* § *Satisfactum*. Ex primo

---

11/9 dicentes *C W* : dicentis *R*   11/10 nec aliquam : vel sufficientem *W*   11/11 pro eis reddendis : *om. W*   11/11 nam : motivum eorum est istud quod *W*   11/12 tenebitur *C* : tenditur *R* : tenetur *W*   11/13 antea : amplius *W*   11/14 non[2] : *om. W*   11/14 fuit : fuerit *W*   11/15 eciam : *om. W*   11/15–29 Hoc autem ... tenebatur : *om. W*   11/20 per *C* : *om. R*   11/25 dictos : hos *C*   11/27 remictatur *C* : remictantur *R*   11/28 qua *C* : contra *R*   11/30 Posset ... rationes : Hanc autem opinionem confirmant quinque racionibus *W*   11/32–9 de pi. acc. ... obligacione : et cetera *W*

11/8–25 Cf. Hostiensis, *Summa aurea*, ad X 5.19 *de usuris*, n.12 (ed. cit. fol. 251vb); gl. ord. ad VI *de reg. iur.* 4, *Peccatum*, v. *Restituatur* (Lyons, 1559, col. 719); Dino of Mugel-lo, *Commentaria in regulas iuris*, in 4 *Peccatum*, nn.5–6 (Venice, 1570, p. 60); Giovanni d'Andrea, *In titulum de regulis iuris novella commentaria* ad VI *de reg. iur.* 4, *Peccatum*, n.3 (Venice, 1581, repr. Turin, 1963, fol. 62rb).   11/21–2 VI 1.3.11.7.   11/24–5 VI 3.20.2.   11/32 Dig. 13.7.9.3.

ing article? It must be understood in this connection that some respond affirmatively, maintaining that a usurer may be freed of the obligation if he has been forgiven, even if he has not made restitution or posted a pledge, for if the one who is owed restitution of usury freely forgives it, the usurer will no longer be bound to make restitution and will consequently be freed of his earlier obligation, notwithstanding (they maintain) the fact that no restitution was offered or pledge posted. They demonstrate this by means of an argument that goes like this: something that has been declared invalid in a particular case appears otherwise to be generally and universally valid. Now canon law declares that remission is invalid in the case of an ecclesiastical judge, who is obliged to restore anything he received for pronouncing sentence, whether he alone demanded the bribe or did so with the complicity of his assessor and notaries, as in VI 1.3.11.7. Moreover, canon law declares that remission is invalid in the case of an ecclesiastical visitor, who is obliged to restore gifts he received for the visitation, as in VI 3.20.2, towards the end. It appears, therefore, that beyond the these two cases, remission is generally and universally valid, and consequently that remission is valid with regard to the restitution of usury such that if it is forgiven before it is offered the usurer will no longer be bound to make restitution, because he will be free of his earlier obligation.

This opinion could be strengthened by five arguments, of which the first is based on the meaning of 'satisfaction,' for we understand by satisfaction whatever is acceptable to the creditor, as at Dig. 13.7.9.3. On this basis, the

ergo fundamento potest formari una talis racio pro dicta opinione. Ille
debitor qui facit quod suus creditor acceptet eum absolvi a sua obligacione
35   videtur per talem absolucionem veraciter liberatus ab illa obligacione. Sed
usurarius eciam non reddendo usuras potest quandoque facere ex amicicia
vel ex aliqua alia causa quod ille cui debet restituere acceptet eum tanquam
absolutum a sua obligacione, ergo sine aliqua reddicione vel restitucione
poterit liberari ab usurarum obligacione.
40   Secunda vero racio sumitur ex parte solucionis, quia potest solvi obligacio in qua aliquis tenetur obligatus absque eo quod solvatur res illa in qua
est obligatus, sicut patet ff. *de solucionibus et liberacionibus* l. *Solucionis*
verbum. Dicitur enim in dicta lege quod 'verbum solucionis pertinet ad
omnem liberacionem quocumque modo factam magisque ad substanciam
45   obligacionis refertur quam ad nummorum solucionem.' Quapropter videtur quod secundum intencionem dicte legis aliquis possit solvere substanciam obligacionis absque eo quod solvat vel tradat rem illam in qua erat
obligatus; poterit ergo usurarius solvere obligacionem usurarum in quibus
tenetur non solvendo vel non tradendo usuras. Ex istis autem verbis pos-
50   set formari una talis racio ad propositum: quicumque solvit substanciam
alicuius obligacionis liberatur ab illa obligacione eo modo quo solvit illius
obligacionis substanciam; sed usurarius potest solvere substanciam obligacionis usurarum non solvendo usuras, ergo potest liberare seipsum ab
obligacione usurarum sine earum reddicione. Maior est nota. Minor eciam
55   apparet per illam legem superius allegatam que vult quod possit solvi substancia obligacionis sine solucione rei obligante.
          Tercia racio ad idem potest sumi ex parte translacionis dominii, quia
potest contingere quod ille cui debet fieri restitucio usurarum transferat
earum dominium in ipsum usurarium, qui est earum possessor, nam quili-
60   bet homo potest transferre dominium sue rei in illum qui eam possidet, ut
patet ff. *de acquirendo rerum dominio* l. *Si servus.* Dicitur enim in prefata
lege quod si aliquis habet rem suam apud alium et velit eam fieri ipsius

---

11/34 quod *C* : qui *R*   11/35 per *C* : quod *R*   11/37 acceptet *C* : acceptat *R*   11/40 racio : *om. W*   11/40 solucionis *C* : satisfaccionis *R*   11/41 solvatur *CW* : solvantur *R*
11/41 in[2] : pro *C*   11/42 sicut : ut *W*   11/42–56 patet ... obligante : et cetera *W*
11/55 possit : loqui *add. et exp. R*   11/57 racio ad idem : *om. W*   11/58 ille *CW* : illo
R   11/61–9 ff. de acquirendo ... reddicione : et cetera *W*

11/42–3 Dig. 46.3.54.   11/61 Dig. 41.1.21.

following argument in support of this position can be constructed: a debtor who causes his creditor to consider him absolved of his obligation appears in truth to be freed of the obligation. But even without restoring usury, a usurer can sometimes arrange – for reasons of friendship or for some other reason – that one to whom he ought to make restitution will declare him absolved of the obligation, and therefore he could be freed of the obligation to restore usury without any actual restitution or restoration.

The second argument is based on the meaning of 'payment,' for someone under an obligation need not pay by means of the things in which the obligation consists, as is clear at Dig. 46.3.54, where it is said that 'the term "payment" pertains to any release, however effected, and relates to the substance of the obligation rather than to the payment of coins.' The sense of this law suggests that one can satisfy an obligation without paying or handing over the thing in which the obligation consists. Therefore a usurer can satisfy the obligation to restore usury without actually paying or handing back the usury. On this basis, the following argument in support of this opinion could be constructed: whoever satisfies the substance of an obligation is freed from it because he has repaid its substance. Now a usurer can satisfy the substance of his obligation to restore usury without repaying the usury itself, therefore he can free himself of the obligation to restore usury without any actual repayment. The major premiss is clear. The minor premiss is likewise clear on the authority of the law just cited, which holds that the substance of an obligation can be satisfied without the repayment of the thing that forms the basis of the obligation.

The third argument is based on the meaning of 'transfer of ownership,' because it sometimes happens that one to whom usury should be restored transfers ownership of it to the usurer, who is in possession, for anybody can transfer ownership of his property to the possessor, as clear at Dig. 41.1.21, where it says that if someone has lodged his thing with someone else and wishes it to become the possessor's, it will immediately become

possessoris apud quem est, statim efficitur ipsius. Ex isto ergo fundamento potest formari una talis racio ad propositum: ille qui potest acquirere
65   dominium in re aliena quam possidet antequam eam reddat, potest liberari
ab obligacione illius rei sine reddicione; sed usurarius potest acquirere dominium in usura quam possidet antequam eam reddat, ut patet ex preha-
bito fundamento, ergo potest liberari ab eiusdem usure obligacione sine
reddicione.

70   Quarta racio ad idem potest sumi ex parte donacionis, nam illud proprie donari videtur quod nulla necessitate cogente sed ex mera voluntate
conceditur, sicut patet ff. *de donacionibus* l. *Donari.* Hoc ergo supposito, potest ita formari racio ad propositum: ille cui potest fieri donacio rei
alienae quam habet antequam eam reddat potest liberari ab obligacione
75   dicte rei sine reddicione, quia postquam est sibi facta donacio talis rei, non
obligatur amplius ad eam reddendam; usurario autem potest fieri donacio
usurarum, non ex necessitate sed ex mera voluntate antequam eas reddat,
ergo poterit liberari ab earum obligacione sine reddicione.

Quinto ad idem potest sumi racio ex parte renunciacionis, quia illud
80   quod semel quis renunciavit non potest ipsum repetere, ut patet VII q. I
Quam periculosum. Hoc ergo supposito, fiat talis racio ad propositum: ille
qui habens rem alienam et eam non reddens desinit esse obligatus alteri
in dicta re videtur posse liberari a rei aliene obligacione sine reddicione;
usurarius autem est huiusmodi, nam si contingat quod ille cui debet fieri
85   restitucio usurarum renunciet iuri suo quod in usuris habet antequam ei
reddantur, desinet usurarius esse obligatus eidem sine reddicione, quia ipse
cui debebat fieri dicta restitucio non poterit amplius usuras repetere.

Iste ergo videntur mihi raciones precipue propter quas forte videretur
alicui quod usurarius posset liberari ab usurarum obligacione sine reddi-

---

11/70 ad idem : *om. W*   11/70 sumi *CW* : sum *R*   11/70 illud : istud *W*   11/72–8 de donacionibus ... reddicione : et cetera *W*   11/72 donacionibus *scripsi* : donacionis *R* : donat.
C   11/79 ad idem : *om. W*   11/79 racio *C* : *om. R*   11/80–91 VII q. I ... dico et : et
cetera *W*   11/79 sumi *C* : sum *R*   11/84 huiusmodi *C* : huius *R*   11/85 renunciet *C* : rei
modo et (!) *R*   11/88 precipue *C* : precipuo *R*

11/67–8 Vid. sup. 11/60–1.   11/72 Dig. 39.5.29.   11/80–1 Decretum Grat. C.7 q.1 c.8.

his. On this basis, therefore, the following argument can be constructed in support of the proposition: he who can acquire ownership of the property of another which he possesses before returning it can also be freed of the obligation arising from it without restoring it. Now a usurer can acquire ownership of usury that he possesses before returning it, as is clear from the law I cited, therefore he can be freed of the obligation to restore usury without making restitution.

The fourth argument is based on the meaning of 'gift,' for a gift, properly speaking, is something that is given freely and without constraint, as is clear at Dig. 39.5.29. On this basis, the following argument can be constructed in support of the proposition: he who is in possession of another's property, which he then receives as a gift before returning it, may be freed of the obligation to return the said thing without restoring it, because after the gift has been granted, he is no longer obliged to restore it. Now the usury owed by a usurer may be given to him freely and without constraint before he has restored it, therefore he can be freed of the obligation to restore or return it.

The fifth argument is based on the meaning of 'renunciation,' because one cannot at once renounce and reclaim the same thing, as is clear at C.7 q.1 c.8. On this basis, the following argument may be advanced in support of the proposition: if someone is in possession of the property of another and fails to return it to him because the owner has renounced it, thus ceasing to be obliged to the owner for the thing, he appears to be free of the obligation to restore the thing without first returning it. Now the usurer is in precisely this situation, for if it happens that he to whom restitution of usury is owed renounces any right to it before repayment, the usurer ceases to be obligated without restoration, since he to whom restitution should be made can no longer launch an action for recovery.

These, then, seem to me the arguments by which it might appear that a usurer could be freed of the obligation to restore usury without actu-

90 cione, que quidem raciones concludunt non solum de usuris sed eciam
de |R216r quacumque re male ablata. Hiis tamen non obstantibus, dico et
teneo quod usurarius qui est potens restituere non possit liberari ab usurarum obligacione nisi prius eas reddat vel aliquid equipollens faciat, utpote
quia si eas non reddat debet facere sufficientem caucionem que equippol-
95 let restitucioni. Ad hoc autem probandum tenebo istum ordinem: quia
primo probabo quod non potest tolli vel dissolvi illa obligacio generaliter qua obligatur habens rem male ablatam ad eam reddendum nisi prius
eam reddat, et per consequens non poterit dissolvi obligacio qua usurarius
est obligatus in reddendis usuris nisi prius eas reddat; secundo probabo
100 specialiter quia nisi prius usure reddantur, non possunt tolli ille circumstancie superius memorate, que in usura singulariter sunt reperte. Primum
probo VII racionibus, quarum VI procedent opposito modo ad illas que
sunt inducte superius pro contraria opinione; ostendam namque quod illa
obligacio qua usurarius est obligatus ad reddendum usuras non potest tol-
105 li sine tradicione vel reddicione per aliquam de viis superius memoratis,
scilicet nec per viam remissionis nec per viam satisfaccionis nec per viam
solucionis nec per viam translacionis dominii nec per viam donacionis nec
per viam renunciacionis.

Probo ergo primo quod non possit tolli dicta obligacio sine reddicio-
110 ne per viam remissionis quia illud quod necessario tollitur antequam fiat
remissio non potest tolli per viam remissionis, tolleret enim aliquid antequam esset, quod est impossibile. Nunc autem illa obligacio qua usurarius est obligatus ad reddendas usuras necessario tollitur antequam fiat
ei remissio, quia stante tali obligacione non potest usurarius recipere re-
115 missionem, ergo non potest tolli per viam remissionis. Confirmo autem
racionem quia nullus est capax remissionis nisi prius a peccato desistat;
usurarius autem et quilibet habens rem alienam male ablatam, quamdiu

---

11/92 teneo : tenendum est *W*   11/92–3 usurarum : *om. W*   11/94–5 equipollet : equi-
polleat *W*   11/95–6 Ad hoc … probabo : Ostendo ergo primo *W*   11/96 illa : *om. W*
11/98 dissolvi : solvi *W*   11/99–101 secundo … reperte : *om. W*   11/101–8 Primum …
renunciacionis : et hoc per septem raciones *W*   11/103 ostendam *C* : ostendendam *R*
11/105 tradicione vel : *om. C*   11/106 nec per viam satisfaccionis *C* : *om. R*   11/109 Probo ergo primo : Prima est *W*   11/110 illud : istud *W*   11/111 enim *C* : *om. R* : quia tunc
W   11/111–12 antequam : quod non *W*   11/113 obligatus *C* : obligacione *R*   11/114 tali
CW : tamen *R*   11/115–31 Confirmo … remissionis : *om. W*

11/101 Vid. sup. 10/1–130.   11/105 Vid. sup. 11/30–87.

ally repaying anything; and these arguments apply not only to usury but to anything else that has been appropriated illicitly. Nevertheless, I assert and maintain that a usurer who is capable of making restitution may not be freed of this obligation unless he has actually made restitution or the equivalent, for example, by posting an adequate pledge to this effect. By way of demonstration, I shall observe the following plan: first, I shall prove in general that the obligation to return something that has been illicitly appropriated cannot be set aside or dissolved unless the thing appropriated has first been restored, and that, as a result, a usurer cannot be absolved of his obligation to restore usury before he has actually done so; second, I shall prove in particular that unless usury has first been restored, the circumstances peculiar to usury mentioned earlier cannot be set aside. I prove the former by means of seven arguments, six of which respond to the arguments just outlined in support of the opposite conclusion; for it must be shown that the obligation of a usurer to make restitution cannot be set aside without actual repayment or restoration in any of the ways mentioned above, that is, by way of remission, satisfaction, payment, transfer of ownership, gift, or renunciation.

Therefore, I prove first that this obligation cannot be set aside by way of remission without prior restoration because that which must be removed before remission is granted cannot be removed by way of remission, for then something would be removed before it was removed, which is impossible. Now a usurer's obligation to restore usury must be removed before he is granted remission of the obligation because, so long as the obligation persists, he cannot be granted remission, and therefore the obligation cannot be removed by way of remission. I confirm this argument thus: no one has a right to remission unless he has first desisted from sin. But the usurer

manet obligatus ad eam reddendam, tamdiu a peccato non desistit, ergo
non est capax remissionis, stante tali obligacione, ac per consequens sua
120 obligacio non poterit tolli per viam remissionis sed tolletur necessario per
aliquam aliam viam priorem remissioni. Et hoc videtur intendere illa regula que habetur *extra, de re. iuris* in VI, ubi dicitur quod 'non remictitur
peccatum nisi restituatur ablatum.' Nam sicut patet ex verbis istius regule,
restitucio est per quam tollitur obligacio et ideo notanter dicit regula quod
125 non dimicititur peccatum nisi restituatur ablatum. Si enim remissio in usuris et in quacumque re male ablata posset precedere remocionem obligacionis, quemadmodum fit econtrario; tunc utique sicut dicimus quod non
remictitur peccatum nisi restituatur ablatum, ita eciam possemus dicere
econtrario quod non restituatur ablatum nisi remictatur peccatum, quod
130 patet esse falsum et ideo concludo quod dicta obligacio non potest tolli per
viam remissionis.

Secundo probo quod non possit tolli sine reddicione per viam satisfaccionis, sicut ponebat contraria opinio, quia satisfaccio non fit nisi causa
peccati decidatur, ita enim dicitur *de penitencia* distinctione III, quod sa-
135 tisfaccio est dum peccati causa exciditur et eius subgescioni additus non
apperitur. Constat autem quod usurpacio et detencio rei aliene est causa
peccati et ideo nisi ista causa peccati, scilicet detencio rei aliene, excidatur
per suum oppositum, scilicet per reddicionem vel restitucionem, non videtur posse satisfaccio fieri quantumcumque creditor acceptet. Et confirmo
140 racionem quia cum satisfaccio sit quedam emenda, oportet quod per eam
reparetur non solum amicicia sed eciam equalitas et iusticia; equalitas autem et iusticia reparari non potest nisi primum illud quod fuit inequalitatis
et iniusticie causa auferatur. Et quia detencio rei aliene est causa inequa-

---

11/121 priorem *C* : primam *R*   11/121 remissioni : remissione *C*   11/122 VI *scripsi* : V
R : IV in VI *C*   11/122 VI : et est Augustini ad Maced. Epistula 54 *add. C*   11/123 nisi
C : nec *R*   11/123 istius : illius *C*   11/124 est *C* : *om. R*   11/124 dicit : dicitur in ista
C   11/125 dimicititur : remittitur *C*   11/132 probo : probatur *W*   11/132 reddicione :
reddi *W*   11/134 III : c. Satisfactionis *add. C*   11/135 eius subgescioni *C* : eis subgestionis
R : ei subgestionis *W*   11/137 excidatur *C* : decipiatur *R* : decidatur *W*   11/138 scili-
cet *C* : *om. R* : ut *W*   11/139–51 Et confirmo ... violavit : *om. W*   11/141 eciam : *om.*
C   11/143 auferatur *C* : afferatur *R*

11/122 VI *de reg. iur.* 4, *Peccatum.*   11/133 Vid. sup. 11/30–9.   11/134 Decretum Grat.
D.3 *de poen.* c.3.

– and anyone else who has illicitly appropriated the property of another – does not desist from sin so long as he remains obliged to make restitution, therefore he has no right to remission so long as the obligation stands, and consequently his obligation cannot be set aside by means of remission, but must be removed in some way prior to remission. And this appears to be the intention of the rule cited at VI *de reg. iur.* 4, where it says that 'sin is not remitted, unless the stolen good is returned.' For as the very words of the rule make clear, restitution is the way in which the obligation is removed, and therefore the rule states clearly that sin is not forgiven unless the stolen thing is returned. Now if remission preceded the removal of the obligation in the case of usury or anything illicitly appropriated, the opposite would be true. In that case we could equally assert that the sin is not forgiven unless the stolen thing is returned or the opposite, namely, that the stolen thing is not restored unless the sin is forgiven, which is clearly false. I conclude therefore that the obligation cannot be removed by way of remission.

Second, I prove that it cannot be removed without restitution by way of satisfaction, as is maintained above, because satisfaction is not made unless the cause of the sin has been excised, and so it is said in D.3 *de poen.* c.3 that 'the satisfaction of penance is to excise the causes of sins and not to allow entry to their suggestion.' Now it is the case that the usurpation and detention of the property of another is a cause of sin, and that unless it is excised by its opposite, namely, by restoration or restitution, it does not appear that satisfaction can be made, whatever the creditor agrees to. I confirm this argument by the observation that since satisfaction is a type of correction, it is fitting that it restores not only friendship, but also equality and justice. But equality and justice cannot be restored unless the cause of the inequality and injustice is first removed. Now because the detention of

litatis et iniusticie in usurario et fure et raptore, idcirco necessarium est
145   istam causam per suum oppositum tolli, scilicet per reddicionem et restitucionem, si debeat per satisfaccionem iusticia et equalitas reparari. Ex
quo apparet immediate quod ad satisfaccionem pro re aliena male ablata
non sufficit accepcio creditoris sine reddicione et restitucione debitoris,
quia reparacio equalitatis et iusticie que fit in tali satisfaccione debet fieri
150   non per ipsum creditorem sed per debitorem, qui equalitatem et iusticiam
violavit.

Vlterius probo tercio quod prefata obligacio non possit tolli sine reddicione per viam solucionis, sicut probatur superius pro contraria opinione,
nam sicut habetur *extra, de re. iur.*: 'omnis res' et omnis obligacio 'per
155   quascumque causas nascitur et per easdem dissolvitur.' Nunc autem obligacio usurarii sive eciam furis et raptoris nascitur per solam voluntatem
ipsius sive ipsorum depravatam in usurpando et detinendo, ergo non poterit dissolvi nisi per eorumdem voluntatem rectificatam in reddendo et
restituendo. Et ex hoc apparet immediate quod voluntas illius cui debet
160   fieri restitucio non videtur sufficiens ad solvendum talem obligacionem,
quia nullo modo fuit causa ipsius.
Vlterius probo quarto quod dicta obligacio non possit solvi sine reddicione per viam translacionis et acquisicionis dominii, sicut fuit superius probatum pro contraria opinione. Hoc autem potest probari ex parte
165   usurarii, qui ante reddicionem non potest in usura dominium acquirere ac
eciam per consequens nec ille cui debet restitucio fieri potest in usurarium
tale dominium transferre. Quod autem usurarius non possit acquirere
dominium in usuris antequam eas reddat et restituat leviter apparet, nam
antequam usuras reddat possidet eas iniusto titulo et ideo non potest sibi
170   advenire iustus titulus per dominii acquisicionem nisi prius auferatur titu-

---

11/148 accepcio : acceptatio *C*   11/148 creditoris : *corr. ex* conditoris *R*   11/150 creditorem : *corr. ex* conditorem *R*   11/150 sed per debitorem *C* : *om. R*   11/152–3 Vlterius
... reddicione : Tercio quod non *W*   11/153–4 sicut ... nam : quia *W*   11/154 et omnis
obligacio : *om. C*   11/157 depravatam : deputatam *W*   11/159 restituendo : et *add. et
exp. R*   11/159 ex : *om. W*   11/159 quod : quia *W*   11/162–313 Vlterius ... faciat : Alias
autem raciones causa brevitatis ad presens dimitto *W*   11/166 ille *C* : illi *R*   11/167 tale
C : talem *R*

11/153 Vid. sup. 11/40–56.   11/154–5 X 5.41.1.   11/163–4 Vid. sup. 11/57–69.

another's property is the cause of inequality and injustice in usury, theft, and robbery, it is necessary that it be removed by its opposite, namely, restoration and restitution, if justice and equality are to be restored by means of satisfaction. From this it is quite clear that the creditor's assent in the absence of restoration and restitution by the debtor is insufficient satisfaction for the illicit appropriation of another's property, because the restoration of equality and justice required by satisfaction cannot be accomplished by the creditor, but only by the debtor, who violated equality and justice in the first place.

Furthermore, I prove third that the obligation cannot be removed without restitution by way of payment, as was argued above in support of this proposition, for, as is noted in X 5.41.1, 'every thing and every obligation is dissolved by the very causes that gave rise to it.' Now the usurer, the thief, or the robber incurs an obligation solely on account of his perverse decision to usurp and detain the property of another, and therefore it cannot be dissolved unless this decision is corrected by restoration and restitution. From this it is quite clear that the assent of him to whom restitution is owed is insufficient to remove this obligation by way of repayment because he was not the source of the obligation in the first place.

Furthermore, I prove fourth that the obligation cannot be dissolved without restitution by means of transfer and acquisition of ownership, as was argued above in support of this proposition. This can be demonstrated in the case of the usurer who, prior to restitution, cannot acquire ownership of his usury; nor can he to whom restitution is owed transfer ownership to the usurer. That the usurer cannot obtain ownership of his usury before restoring it is perfectly clear because before he restores the usury he possesses it by means of an unjust title; he cannot obtain just title by transfer of ownership unless the unjust title is removed by restitu-

lus iniustus per usurarum reddicionem, quapropter relinquitur quod dicta
obligacio tolli non possit nisi per usurarum reddicionem. Posset ergo ita
formari racio: nulli potest advenire titulus iustus in re detinenda nisi prius auferatur titulus iniustus, nam quia iniustus titulus potest tolli absque
175 eo quod iustus titulus acquiratur et econtrario, idcirco erit alia actio per
quam iniustus titulus tollitur et per quam iustus titulus acquiritur; nulli
ergo poterit advenire titulus iustus per aliquam actionem nisi prius tollatur
titulus iniustus per primam actionem. Sed illi qui acquirit dominium in re
detinenda advenit titulus iustus per dominii acquisicionem, ergo si prius
180 habuit titulum iniustum per rei aliene illicitam usurpacionem et detencionem, oportet quod dictus titulus auferatur per eiusdem rei restitucionem
ante dominii acquisicionem. Et ex hoc apparet immediate quod quantumcumque ille cui debet restitucio fieri velit transferre dominium usurarum
in usurarium, quia tamen ipse non est capax talis dominii antequam eas
185 reddat, idcirco non potest per hoc dissolvi sua obligacio.

Vlterius probo quinto quod non potest tolli prefata obligacio sine reddicione per viam donacionis, sicut inducebatur superius pro contraria opinione, quia nec ille cui debet restitucio fieri potest donare antequam sit
restitutus nec ipse usurarius antequam restituat potest certificari de tali
190 donacione utrum sit vera donacio. Ad cuius probacionem suppono quod
nisi donacio sit libera non est donacio, ut patet ff. *de adimendis legatis*
l. *Rem legatum*. Ille autem qui donat antequam sit restitutus non libere
donat, quia illud solum quod quis libere habet potest libere donare; ille
autem qui nondum est restitutus non habet libere illud quod sibi debet
195 restitui, ergo non potest ipsum libere donare. Nec valet si dicatur quod re-
stituendus potest |[R216v] libere habere ac per consequens libere donare quia
usurarius paratus est reddere. Ista siquidem instancia non valet quia resti-
tuendus non potest certificari quod usurarius vel quicumque alius habens
male ablata sit paratus ad ea reddendum nisi ea statim, dum potest, reddat
200 vel pro eis reddendis sufficientem caucionem faciat, nam etsi appareant
aliqua signa per que videatur paratus ad restituendum, illa quidem non

---

11/171 reddicionem : restitutionem *C*   11/172 non possit : nequeat *C*   11/175 econtrario : e converso *C*   11/176 acquiritur : in hoc ergo *add. et exp. R*   11/178 primam *C* :
secundam *R*   11/182 quod *C* : *om. R*   11/183 velit : vellet *C*   11/186 potest : possit
C   11/191 donacio[1] : Ad *add. et exp. R*

11/187 Vid. sup. 11/70–8.   11/191–2 Dig. 34.4.18.

tion of the usury, and so it follows that the obligation cannot be dissolved except by restitution. The following argument can therefore be proposed: nobody can acquire just title to a thing he has appropriated unless the unjust title is first dissolved; but because unjust title can be removed without acquiring just title, and vice versa, unjust title must be removed by some other action by which, in turn, just title is obtained. No one can obtain just title by any action unless unjust title is first removed; but he who secures ownership of a thing he has appropriated obtains just title by acquisition of ownership. Therefore, if he first held unjust title by the illicit usurpation and detention of another's property, it is necessary that it be dissolved by restitution of the property before acquisition of ownership. From this it is quite clear that even if he to whom restitution is due wants to transfer ownership to the usurer, he cannot, because the latter lacks the capacity to own before he has made restitution; consequently, the obligation cannot be dissolved in this way.

Furthermore, I prove fifth that the obligation cannot be dissolved without restitution by means of gift, as was argued above in support of this proposition, for neither he to whom restitution is due nor the usurer can be certain before restitution whether the gift is real. By way of demonstration, I assume that unless a gift is freely given, it is not really a gift, as is clear at Dig. 34.4.18. Now he who offers a gift before restitution has been made does not do so freely because no one can freely give something he does not actually possess; but he who has not yet received restitution does not possess freely that which ought to be restored, therefore, he cannot freely offer it as a gift. Nor can it be argued that if the usurer is prepared to make restitution, the recipient possesses and consequently gives freely. This example does not hold because the recipient cannot be certain that the usurer – or anyone else in possession of a thing illicitly appropriated – is prepared to restore the usury unless he actually does so at that moment, or posts an adequate pledge to repay. For even if there are certain indications that suggest he is prepared to make restitution, they are insufficient to

sufficiunt ad propositum, quia quibuscumque talibus signis ita potest uti
ille qui non habet intencionem reddendi sicut ille qui habet intencionem
reddendi. Et per eamdem viam apparet quod usurarius cui fit talis donacio
205 ante restitucionem non potest eam acceptare ut veram donacionem, quia
non potest certificari utrum fiat ei libere vel non libere, quia eisdem signis
et eisdem verbis utitur ille qui non donat libere, et per consequens non donat, et ille qui libere donat. Posset ergo ex toto isto processu formari una
talis racio ad propositum: ubi non potest esse libera donacio, ibi non po-
210 test tolli obligacio per viam donacionis. Sed antequam fiat restitucio non
potest fieri usurario libera donacio usurarum, ut ex dictis patet, ergo sua
obligacio non potest tolli ante restitucionem per viam donacionis.

Vlterius probo sexto quod dicta obligacio non potest tolli sine reddicione per viam renunciacionis, sicut assumebatur superius pro alia opi-
215 nione, quia ubi non potest esse renunciacio, ibi non potest tolli obligacio
per viam renunciacionis, sed antequam fiat restitucio usurarum non potest
ille cui debet fieri restitucio renunciare, ergo obligacio usurarii antequam
reddat non poterit tolli per viam renunciacionis. Maior est nota. Minorem
probo quia illa renunciacio que fit a spoliato ante restitucionem ab ipso
220 iure decernitur esse nulla, sicut patet III q. I *Episcopis* et *extra, de re. spo.* c.
Sollicite, et hoc racionabiliter, quia renunciacio debet esse libera. Illa autem
que fit ante restitucionem presummitur non fore libera et ideo dominus
papa Alexander dicit in prefato capitulo quod 'non est verisimile quod
iuri suo sponte renunciaverit qui renunciat spoliatus.' Ita ergo videtur di-
225 cendum in proposito quia si quis renunciet usuris que ei deberent restitui,
non videtur renunciare spontanee, ÿmo pocius videtur renunciare coactus,
nam eo ipso quod talis renunciacio fit ante restitucionem potest provenire
ex timore sive eciam ex verecundia vel desperacione non recipiendi, propter que omnia merito presumitur non fore libera.

11/208 et : atque C   11/214 assumebatur : asserebatur C   11/215 potest[2] : esse *add. et*
exp. R   11/223 Alexander : *om.* C   11/225 deberent : debent C

11/214 Vid. sup. 11/79–87.   11/220–1 Decretum Grat. C.3 q.1 c.1; X 2.13.2.

sustain the proposition, since one who is prepared to make restitution and one who is not would make the very same gestures. By the same token, it is clear that a usurer who is offered such a gift before making restitution cannot accept it as a genuine gift, because he cannot be certain whether it is offered freely or not, for one who does not freely offer – and therefore does not really offer – a gift and one who does would make the very same gestures. In the light of this reasoning, the following argument can be made with respect to the proposition: if a gift is not free, it cannot remove the obligation. Now a free gift of usury cannot be made to the usurer prior to restitution, as is clear from what has been said, therefore his obligation cannot be removed by way of a gift prior to restitution.

Furthermore, I prove sixth that the obligation cannot be dissolved by way of renunciation without restitution, as is maintained above in support of the opposite position, because where the conditions for renunciation do not exist, an obligation cannot be dissolved by way of renunciation; but prior to the restitution of usury, he to whom it is owed cannot renounce it, and therefore the usurer's obligation cannot be removed prior to restitution by way of renunciation. The major premiss is clear. I prove the minor premiss thus: the law decrees that the renunciation of one who has been despoiled of his property is null unless the spoils have been previously restored to him, as is clear at C.3 q.1 c.1 and X 2.13.2, and for good reason, because a renunciation must be free. Anything done before restitution is presumed to be coerced, and therefore the lord pope Alexander says at X 2.13.2 that 'it is improbable that one who has been despoiled would freely renounce his right.' Therefore, it seems that what should be said in response to the proposition is that if someone renounces usury that should be restored to him, he does not appear to renounce it freely but rather does so under duress, since any such renunciation made before restitution can be presumed to proceed from fear, or even from the shame and anxiety of not receiving [further credit], and for this reason is rightly considered to be coerced.

230   Apparet ergo ex omnibus istis VI racionibus quod obligacio qua usura-
       rius est obligatus ad reddendas usuras non potest tolli sine reddicione per
       aliquam illarum viarum que videbantur posse prestare favorem contrarie
       opinioni.

       Vlterius probo septimo eamdem conclusionem specialiter ex parte resti-
235   tucionis, suppono namque per illam regulam que habetur *extra, de re. iu.*
       IIII quod 'non remictitur peccatum nisi restituatur ablatam,' et ideo illa
       obligacio qua usurarius est obligatus ad reddendas usuras oportet necessa-
       rio quod tollatur vel per viam restitucionis vel per aliquam aliam viam que
       restitucioni equippolleat. Queratur ergo que sit illa via que restitucioni
240   equippollet et que potest talem obligacionem tollere. Si ergo dicatur quod
       ista via sit remissio vel donacio, de quibus videtur maxime, cadimus in
       quatuor inconvenientia magna.

       Primum est inconveniens quia sequeretur quod non solum habens unde
       restituat sed eciam non habens posset restituere, quod patet esse falsum
245   per illud quod habetur XIIII q. VI *Si res.* Nam sicut ibidem per Augu-
       stinum restitucio est necessaria ad remissionem peccati ubi est possibile
       reddere, sed ei cui non est possibile reddere non possumus dicere ut resti-
       tuat, secundum Augustinum, quapropter relinquitur quod solum habens
       unde reddat restituere valeat. Et tamen constat quod ita potest consequi
250   remissionem ille qui non habet unde sicut ille qui habet unde reddat; si
       ergo remissio que fit ante restitucionem equippollet resticutioni, videtur
       necessario sequi quod eciam non habens unde reddat restitutere valeat,
       quod est omnino absurdum.

       Secundum inconveniens quod ad hoc sequitur est quia posset aliquis
255   dici restitutus et tamen non esset positus in possessione, quod patet esse
       falsum per illud quod habetur ff. *de ver. et rerum significacione* l. *Plus est
       in restitucione.* Dicitur enim in prefata lege quod restituere est non solum

---

11/236 IIII *scripsi* : III *R* : *om. C*   11/239 restitucioni[1] *C* : restitucionem *R*   11/239 restitucioni[2] *C* : restitucionem *R*   11/240 tollere *C* : tolle *R*   11/242 magna : *om.*
C   11/244 patet *C* : posset *R*   11/245 Si res *C* : Vires *R*   11/245–6 per Augustinum :
dicit Augustinus *C*   11/248 Augustinum : propter *add. et exp. R*   11/249 unde *C* : non
R   11/251 restitucioni *C* : restitucionem *R*   11/256 l. *C* : infra *R*   11/257 in restitutione : *om. C*

11/235–6 VI *de reg. iur.* 4, *Peccatum.*   11/245 Decretum Grat. C.14 q.6 c.1.   11/256–
7 Dig. 50.16.22.

It is clear from these six arguments, then, that the obligation by which a usurer is obliged to make restitution of usury cannot be dissolved by any of the means that seemed to offer support to the contrary view.

Finally and seventh, I prove the same conclusion with respect to restitution in particular, for I presume on the basis of the rule at VI *de reg. iur.* 4, namely, that 'sin is not remitted, unless the stolen good is returned,' that the usurer's obligation to restore usury is necessarily removed either by way of restitution or something equivalent to restitution. The question, therefore, is what is equivalent to restitution such that it can dissolve the obligation? If the response is that it is remission or gift, which seem the most likely, we encounter four serious inconsistencies.

The first is that it would follow that not only one with the wherewithal to make restitution but even one without it could make restitution, which is clearly false in the light of what is said at C.14 q.6 c.1. For, as Augustine states in this passage, restitution, if possible, must be made before the sin can be forgiven; by the same token, one who lacks the wherewithal cannot be said to make restitution. Therefore it follows, in Augustine's view, that only one who has the wherewithal to make restitution can do so. But if remission prior to restitution were equivalent to restitution, it would be the case that both one who has no wherewithal to make restitution and one who has can seek remission. Therefore, if remission made before restitution is equivalent to restitution, it seems to follow necessarily that even one who has no wherewithal to make restitution has made restitution, which is utterly absurd.

The second inconsistency that follows is that it could be said that someone has received restitution without being put in possession, which is clearly false in the light of what is said at Dig. 50.16.22, where it says that 'to restore' something is not only 'to provide the presence of a thing,' but

'presenciam rei prebere' sed 'eciam possessorem facere fructusque reddere.' Quapropter nullus videtur posse dici restitutus nisi in possessione
260 sit positus, et tamen constat quod si remissio que fit ante restitucionem
equippolleat restitucioni quod eciam non positus in possessione dicetur
restitutus, quia talis remissio non ponit creditorem in possessione.

Tercium inconveniens quod ad hoc sequitur est quia exhibicio haberet
maiorem efficaciam quam restitucio, quod patet esse falsum per illam le-
265 gem superius allegatam ff. *de ver. et rerum significacione*, ubi dicitur quod
'plus est in restitucione quam in exhibicione.' Si tamen ponatur quod remissio que fit ante restitucionem equippolleat restitucioni, sequitur quod
plus sit in exhibicione quam in restitucione, quia maiorem efficaciam habet
exhibicio quam illa remissio que restitucioni ponitur equippollere. Et quod
270 ita sit apparet, constat namque remissio vel donacio que fit ante restitucionem non est actus illius qui debet restituere, ÿmo est actus illius cui debet
fieri restitucio; exhibicio autem potest esse actus illius qui debet restituere
ac per consequens potest esse magis satisfactoria exhibicio quam remissio, quia satisfaccio debet esse actus illius qui tenetur restituere. Si autem
275 exhibicio est magis satisfactoria quam remissio, relinquitur ulterius quod
sit eciam magis satisfactoria quam restitucio, quia secundum illam viam
remissio et restitucio equippollent. Si autem est magis satisfactoria quam
restitucio sequitur necessario quod habeat maiorem efficaciam, quod est
absurdum. Est ad eamdem racionem quod habeatur ad intencionem le-
280 gis nunc allegate: videtur enim quod restitucio se habeat per addicionem
ad exhibicionem et ideo debet fieri per restitucionem totum quod fit per
exhibicionem et adhuc aliquid plus; per exhibicionem autem prebetur rei
presencia ei cui fit exhibicio, sicut patet ex prehabita lege, ergo per restitucionem et per consequens per remissionem, que ei equippollet, debet
285 preberi rei restituende presencia ei cui fienda est restitucio. Debet insuper
fieri aliquid plus et tamen constat quod illa remissio que fit sine reddicione
non prebet rei restituende presenciam, quia non est actus illius qui illam

---

11/258 fructusque *Dig. 50.16.22* : fructus quia *R* : fructus et cetera *C*   11/261 re-
stitucioni *C* : *om. R*   11/261 possessione : possessionem *C*   11/264 quam *C* : quod
R   11/267 restitucioni *C* : restitucionem *R*   11/269 restitucioni *C* : restitucionem
R   11/278 efficaciam : quam restitutio *add. C*   11/279 Est : Et *C*   11/279 quod *C* : quia
R   11/279 habeatur : magis fit *C*   11/280 enim *C* : *om. R*   11/281 totum *C* : totam *R*

11/265 Dig. 50.16.22.

'also to make someone the owner and hand over the produce.' Therefore nobody can be said to have received restitution unless he has been put in possession. But if remission prior to restitution were equivalent to restitution, even someone who has not been put in possession could be said to have received restitution, but such remission does not put the creditor in possession.

The third inconsistency that follows is that 'presentation' would have a greater effect than restitution, which is clearly false in view of Dig. 50.16.22, where it is said that 'more is conveyed by restitution than by presentation.' But if it is argued that remission made prior to restitution is equivalent to restitution, it follows that more would be conveyed by presentation than by restitution, because presentation would have a greater effect than the remission that is said to be equivalent to restitution. And that this is so is clear, for it is a fact that a remission or gift offered prior to restitution is not an act of the one who should make restitution, but rather the act of the one to whom restitution should be made. Now presentation is the act of the one who is obliged to make restitution and consequently can be more atoning than remission, because satisfaction should be the act of the one obliged to make restitution. But if presentation is more atoning than remission, it follows as well that it is more atoning than restitution because, by this reasoning, remission is equivalent to restitution. But if it is more atoning than restitution, it necessarily follows that it has a greater effect, which is absurd. This is confirmed by the intention of the law just cited: restitution represents something more than presentation and therefore restitution accomplishes everything accomplished by presentation plus something more. Presentation provides the presence of the thing exhibited, as is clear from the citation, therefore restitution and, by extension, remission, to which it is supposedly equivalent, should provide the presence of the thing plus something more. But it is a fact that remission offered without restitution does not provide the presence of the thing that should be restored, because it is not the act of him who possesses the thing

rem habet et tenetur eam restituere, immo est actus illius qui eam non habet et debet eam recipere. Si autem remissio non prebet rei restituende
290 presenciam, multo minus facit illud plus quod addit restitucio super exhibicionem.

Quartum inconveniens quod ad hoc sequitur est quia talis remissio que fit sine tradicione rei restituende erit magis satisfactoria quam sit solucio, quod patet esse falsum, quia remissio non est actus debitoris ad quem per-
295 tinet satisfacere, ÿmo est actus creditoris cui debet satisfieri. Solutio autem est actus debitoris ad quem pertinet satisfacere et ideo |^{R217r} talis remissio vel nullo modo est satisfactoria vel saltem est minus satisfactoria quam solucio. Si tamen ponitur quod talis remissio possit liberare usurarium ab illa obligacione usurarum, sequitur quod ipsa sit magis satisfactoria quam
300 solucio. Et quod ita sit apparet, videmus namque quod illa solucio per quam non ponitur creditor in plena possessione non liberat, sicut patet ff. *de solucionibus et liberacionibus*, id est, 'qui sic solvit ut reciperet non liberatur'; quod non videtur esse propter aliud nisi quia per talem solucionem creditor in plena possessione non ponitur. Cum ergo remissio que fit sine
305 tradicione rei restituende nullo modo ponat creditorem in sua possessione, si ponatur quod talis remissio possit usurarium liberare, necessario sequitur quod ipsa sit magis satisfactoria quam solucio, quod tamen evidenter est falsum.

Apparet ergo ex omnibus istis racionibus illud primum quod superius
310 promittebatur probandum, scilicet quod usurarius sive quicumque alius habens rem male ablatam non potest liberari ab illa obligacione qua est obligatus ad eam restituendam nisi prius eam reddat, si potens sit ad reddendum, vel bonam caucionem pro ea reddenda faciat.

Et ideo restat probare secundum quod specialiter pertinet ad usuras,
315 scilicet quod nisi usure reddantur non possunt tolli ille circumstancie superius memorate que in usura simpliciter sunt reperte. Probo ergo primo quod usurarius qui usuras non reddit dum potest et tamen credit se esse

---

11/289 eam : restituere *add. et exp. R*   11/298 liberare *C* : liberari *R*   11/300 ita : *corr. ex* ipsa *R* : ita *C*   11/302–3 ut … liberatur : *om. C*   11/309 racionibus : racionibus *add. per ditt. R*   11/314 Et ideo … secundum : Sed in hoc eodem articulo est unum *W*   11/316 simpliciter : singulariter *C*   11/316 Probo ergo primo : Et probatur hoc valde bene; primo ergo probatur *W*   11/317 reddit *CW* : reddat *R*

11/301–3 Dig. 46.3.55.   11/309–10 Vid. sup. 11/5–8.   11/315–16 Vid. sup. 10/1–129.

and is obliged to restore it, but rather of him who does not possess it and ought to receive it. But if remission does not provide the presence of the thing that should be restored, it accomplishes much less than what restitution adds to presentation.

The fourth inconsistency that follows is that remission made without delivery of the thing that ought to be restored would be more atoning than payment, which is clearly false, because remission is not an act of the debtor, who should make satisfaction, but rather of the creditor, who merits satisfaction. Now payment is an act of a debtor, who should make satisfaction, and therefore remission either has no atoning value or is at least less atoning than payment. But if it is argued that remission could free the usurer from the obligation to restore usury, it follows that it is more atoning than payment. That this is so is clear, because we know that payment that does not put the creditor in full possession does not extinguish the debt, as is clear at Dig. 46.3.55, where it says that 'he who pays on such terms that he may recover is not released,' that is, a payment by which the creditor is not put in full possession. Since remission without delivery of the thing that should be restored does not put the creditor in possession, if it is argued that remission of this kind can liberate the usurer, it necessarily follows that it is more atoning than payment, which is clearly false.

These arguments suffice to demonstrate what I promised above to prove, namely, that neither a usurer nor anyone else in possession of illicitly appropriated property can be freed of the obligation to make restitution unless he first returns it, if he can do so, or posts an adequate pledge to restore it.

It remains, then, to prove the second proposition, which pertains particularly to usury, namely that, unless usury is restored, the circumstances noted above that pertain peculiarly to usury cannot be removed. First, I prove that a usurer who does not restore usury when he can, but neverthe-

liberatum a peccato per solam remissionem creditoris non cessat Deum
contempnere et offendere, quia ille qui non decidat illud quod fuit cau-
320 sa maioris contemptus divini in usura quam in furto et rapina non cessat
Deum contempnere. Talis autem est usurarius, qui usuras non reddit dum
potest et tamen per solam remissionem liberatum se credit; ergo qui sic facit non cessat Deum contempnere. Maior videtur esse nota, quia ubi causa
ad peccandum assumpta non deciditur, ibi a peccato non cessatur; unde ei
325 qui talis est recte convenit illud verbum quod ponitur in decretis distinctione III et est verbum Ÿsodori: 'irrisor,' inquid Ÿsodorus, 'est et non
penitens qui adhuc agit quod penitet, nec videtur Deum poscere subditus
sed subsanare superbus.' Probo ergo minorem, constat namque per ea que
dicta fuerunt in precedenti articulo quod causa maioris contemptus in usu-
330 ra quam in furto et rapina est maius posse quo usuarius utitur in detinendo rem alienam quam faciat fur vel raptor, et ideo peccatum usurarii non
poterit extirpari nisi illud posse totaliter deciditur ita ut quemadmodum
primum potuit detinere rem alienam pro quolibet tempore et pro quolibet loco, ita postea per oppositum pro nullo tempore et nullo loco habeat
335 tale posse. Ille autem qui usuras non reddit eciam in ipso actu remissionis
utitur eo posse quo prius, nam dato quod creditor eas remictere vellet,
adhuc ipse eas detinere posset sicut prius et ideo quamdiu utitur tali posse,
causam divini contemptus non decidit. Si ergo utendo eodem posse quo
prius remissionem petat et remissio ei fiat, videtur quasi Deum subsanare
340 superbus; et ita patet quomodo si fiat remissio usurarum sine earum reddicione non tollitur illa prima circumstancia que singulariter reperiebatur
in usura, scilicet Dei contemptus.

Vlterius probo secundo quod per viam remissionis facte sine reddicione non tollatur secunda circumstancia, scilicet ecclesie decepcio, quia illa

---

11/319 offendere : irridere W   11/319–42 quia ille … contemptus : *om.* W   11/319 decidat : reddit C   11/324 deciditur : reciditur C   11/325 decretis : de poen. *add.*
C   11/326 III C : IIII R   11/326 III : cap. *add.* C   11/326 et … Ÿsodori : *om.*
C   11/329 dicta : sunt *add. et exp.* R   11/329 precedenti : praesenti C   11/332 deciditur : reciditur C   11/333 detinere : retinere C   11/338 decidit : recidit C   11/343 Vlterius probo : *om.* W   11/344–62 quia illa … reddicione : *om.* W

11/325–8 Decretum Grat. D.3 *de poen.* c.11.   11/328–9 Vid. sup. 10/1–129.

less thinks himself free of sin solely on account of the creditor's remission, does not cease to mock and offend God, because he who does not excise what makes usury a greater offence to God than theft or robbery does not cease to mock God. Such is the case of the usurer who does not restore usury when he can, but nevertheless thinks himself free of sin solely on account of the creditor's remission; therefore he does not cease to mock God. The major premiss seems to be clear because when the presumed cause of a sin is not excised, there is no abstention from the sin. Hence, the saying of Isidore included in the decrees at D.3 *de poen.* c.11 is rightly applied to the usurer: 'he is a derider, and not a penitent, who still does now what he has repented. Nor does he appear to be a subject who pleads with God, but a proud mocker.' I prove the minor premiss thus: it is clear from what was said in the preceding article that what makes usury a greater offence than theft or robbery is the greater capacity of the usurer, compared to the thief or robber, to appropriate the property of another. Consequently, the sin of usury cannot be extirpated unless it is completely excised, so that just as the usurer was first able to detain another's property at any time and at any place, now, by contrast, he should not be permitted to possess it for any period of time or at any place. But the usurer who does not restore usury, even if he is forgiven, enjoys the same capacity he enjoyed earlier, for granted that the creditor wants to forgive the usury, the fact that the usurer still retains the usury as he did earlier, and so enjoys the same capacity, shows that he has not excised the source of his contempt for God. If he seeks and obtains remission by employing the capacity he enjoyed earlier, then it appears that he arrogantly mocks God. And so it is clear how remission of usury without restitution does not remove the first circumstance that uniquely attends usury, namely contempt of God.

Furthermore, I prove second that remission without restitution does not remove the second circumstance, that is, deception of the Church, for

345   via per quam ecclesia non potest certificari utrum remissio sit libera vel
non libera relinquit ecclesiam in decepcione. Sed ubi fit remissio vel donacio usurarum sine reddicione non potest certificari ecclesia utrum talis
remissio vel donacio sit libera vel non libera, quia usurarius non minus
habet pacificam possessionem post talem remissionem quam haberet ante
350   remissionem, saltem quantum ad curiam civilem. Ex quo apparet immediate quod ista racio idem non potest applicari ad furtum et rapinam quemadmodum nec precedens, nam ubi ille cui sublata est res per furtum et
rapinam nolit remictere, non potest fur vel raptor rem illam ulterius detinere pacifice propter timorem pene temporalis, et ideo non optenta tali
355   remissione non habet idem posse in detinendo quod prius habuit in usurpando, cuius contrarium ponebatur superius de usurario. Propter quam
causam poterit ulterius ecclesia melius certificari de remissione facta furi
vel raptori utrum sit libera vel non libera quam de remissione facta usurario, quamvis proprie loquendo numquam remissio vel collacio sit vere
360   libera in quacumque re male ablata nisi prius res illa reddatur. Et ita patet
quomodo non tollitur secunda circumstancia, facta remissione usurarum
sine reddicione.

Vlterius probo tertio quod per viam remissionis factae sine reddicione non tollitur tercia circumstancia, scilicet nature perversio, quia illa via
365   per quam usurarius non cessat lucrificare cum mutuo non tollit nature
perversionem, sed ubi fiat remissio usurarum sine earum reddicione non
cessat usurarius lucrificare cum mutuo, ergo talis via non tollit nature perversionem. Maior est nota, quia sicut patuit supra in questione de usuris
ideo usura pervertit naturam, quia facit lucrificare mutuum, contra cuius
370   naturam est lucrificare; quamdiu ergo usurarius non cessat lucrificare cum
mutuo non tollitur nature perversio. Minor eciam apparet quia quamdiu
usurarius usuras non reddit si potest reddere, videtur velle habere lucrum
de suo mutuo. Et ita patet quomodo per istam viam non tollitur tercia

---

11/346 Sed *C* : sicut *R*   11/349 haberet : habuerit *C*   11/351 idem : *om. C*   11/353 nolit : noluerit *C*   11/355 quod : quam *C*   11/355–6 usurpando : *ex* usurpacione *corr.*
R   11/359 collacio : donatio *C*   11/359 sit *C* : in *R*   11/361 non : sequitur secunda *add.*
et del. R   11/363–4 Vlterius … reddicione *C* : *om. per hom. R*   11/363–4 Vlterius …
non : Tercio quod nec *W*   11/364 tollitur : tollatur *C*   11/364–75 quia illa … in usura :
om. W   11/365 lucrificare : lucrifacere *C*   11/367 lucrificare : lucrifacere *C*   11/369 lucrificare : lucrifacere *C*   11/370 lucrificare[1,2] : lucrifacere *C*

11/356 Vid. sup. 10/86–102.   11/368 Vid. sup. 3/226–51.

if the Church cannot be certain whether remission is free or not, it remains deceived. Now when usury is forgiven or granted as a gift without restitution, the Church cannot be certain whether the remission or gift is really free because the usurer enjoys precisely the same peaceful possession with remission that he enjoyed without it, at least in the eyes of a secular court. It is quite clear that the same argument does not apply to theft and robbery, because when someone whose property has been taken by theft or robbery does not choose to forgive the theft, the thief or robber may not peacefully detain the thing any longer for fear of temporal punishment, and so without remission, the thief or robber does not enjoy the same capacity to detain a thing that he enjoyed in usurping it; but the opposite is true of the usurer. For this reason, the Church can be more certain that remission granted to a thief or robber is free than it can be of remission granted a usurer, though properly speaking remission or concession of a thing illicitly appropriated is never truly free unless the thing has first been returned. And so it is clear that remission of usury without restitution does not remove the second circumstance.

Furthermore, I prove that the third circumstance, namely perversion of nature, is not removed by way of remission without restitution, because so long as the usurer does not cease to profit from his loan, perversion of nature is not removed. But when usury is forgiven without prior restitution, the usurer does not cease to profit from his loan, therefore perversion of nature cannot be removed in this way. The major premiss is clear because, as was made clear in the question on usury, usury perverts nature by causing a loan to bear fruit contrary to its nature. Therefore, so long as the usurer does not cease to profit from his loan, perversion of nature is not removed. The minor premiss is also clear because so long as the usurer does not restore usury if he can, he appears to want to retain the profit

circumstancia. Hec autem racio non potest applicari ad furtum et rapinam,
375   quia in eis non pervertuntur nature rerum sicut in usura.

Vlterius probo quarto quod si quis petat remissionem usurarum sine
reddicione non tollit fortune extinctionem, quia ille qui est securus de
lucro sicut prius, si prius extinguebat fortunam eciam postea non cessat
fortunam extinguere. Sed usurarius, qui petit remissionem usurarum sine
380   earum reddicione, videtur velle esse securus de lucro usurario sicut prius,
ergo non cesssat fortunam extinguere. Maior est nota. Minor eciam apparet quia tota causa quare usurarius petit remissionem usurarum eas non
reddendo est quia vult esse securus. Et ex hoc apparet quod ista via non
sufficiat ad tollendam quartam circumstanciam. Haec autem racio non po-
385   test applicari ad furtum et rapinam, quia in eis non habet locum fortunae
extinctio.
Vlterius probo quinto quod ille qui petit remissionem usurarum sine
earum reddicione non cessat proximo iniuriam per maliciam facere. Et
quod ita sit apparet, nam sicut prius, ut fingeret se non facere iniuriam in
390   usurpacione rei aliene, compulit voluntatem proximi ad consenciendum
in talem usurpacionem, ita eciam postea, ut fingat se non obligari ad restitucionem, compellit voluntatem proximi ad consenciendum in sue rei detencionem. Est enim quedam coactio in secundo consensu sicut in primo,
nam sicut prius ille a quo facta est extorsio usurarum consensit in talem
395   extorsionem non libere sed quia voluit magis talem extorsionem a se fieri
quam voluerit mutuo carere, ita eciam postea ipse idem consentit in sue
rei detencione non libere sed quia magis vult rem suam perdere lucrando
amiciciam per remissionem quam simul perdere rem et |^R217v amiciciam
propter non remictere, et ideo sic remictentibus videtur convenire illud
400   commune proverbium, scilicet quod 'quis non potest vendere debet se fin-
gere donare.' Ex hoc apparet quod ista racio est specialis in usura, quia furi

---

11/374 racio : racio *add. per ditt. R*   11/375 pervertuntur *C* : pervertitur *R*   11/376 Vlterius probo : *om. W*   11/377 tollit : tollet *W*   11/377–86 quia ille … extinctio : *om.*
W   11/378 eciam : et *C*   11/387–8 Vlterius … reddicione : Quinto quod *W*   11/388–
405 nam sicut … ex mutuo : et cetera *W*   11/394 consensit : consentit *C*   11/395 magis : et alicui *add. et exp. R*   11/397 detencione : detentionem *C*   11/399–400 illud
commune proverbium : illud quod communi proverbio fertur *C*   11/401 Ex *C* : Eciam
R   11/401 furi *C* : fur *R*

11/400–1 *Non inveni.*

from his loan. And so it is clear how the third circumstance is not removed in this way. This argument cannot be applied to theft and robbery because neither perverts nature in the way that usury does.

Furthermore, I prove fourth that if a usurer seeks remission of usury without restitution, he does not cease to thwart fortune, because one who remains secure in his profit with remission continues to thwart fortune just as he did earlier without it. Now the usurer who seeks remission of usury without restitution appears to wish to remain as secure in his profit as he was before remission, therefore he continues to thwart fortune. The major premiss is clear. The minor premiss is also clear because the very reason why a usurer seeks remission of usury without restoring it is because he wishes to remain secure. And thus it is clear that the fourth circumstance cannot be removed in this way. This argument does not apply to theft and robbery because neither involves the extinction of fortune.

Furthermore, I prove fifth that a usurer who seeks remission of usury without restitution does not desist from maliciously injuring his neighbour. That this is true is clear, because just as he previously coerced the will of his neighbour to consent to the usurpation of his property so that he could pretend that he was not injuring him, so now he coerces his neighbour's will to consent to the detention of his property so that he might pretend that he is not obliged to make restitution. For in both cases, consent is coerced, and just as he from whom usury was extorted in the first place did not freely consent to the extortion because he preferred extortion to the refusal of the loan, so now he consents to the retention of his property, not freely, but because he prefers to lose his property by cultivating the goodwill of the usurer through remission than to lose both his property and the goodwill of the usurer by refusing it; and so those who forgive usury seem to conform to the common saying: 'he who cannot sell should pretend to give.' From this it is clear that this argument is unique

vel raptori non convenit usurpare vel detinere rem alienam cum consensu illius cuius est res illa, quia nec apparet aliqua causa racione cuius possit querere vel extorquere talem consensum sicut in usura, in qua potest ex-
405 torqueri dictus consensus ratione servicii impensi ex mutuo.

Vlterius probo sexto quod ille qui petit remissionem usurarum sine ea-rum reddicione non cessat ledere communem iusticiam cum securitate et superbia. Et quod ita sit apparet, nam si contingat quod ille cui queritur remissio nolit remictere adhuc ipse usurarius vult posse usuras retinere
410 sine timore pene temporalis sicut prius, et ideo videtur uti eadem securi-tate nunc in remissione qua prius utebatur in usurpacione. Ex istis autem duabus racionibus ultimo apparet quod ubi sit remissio usurarum sine reddicione non tollitur sexta circumstancia superius memorata in prece-denti articulo. Apparet insuper quod ista sexta racio est specialis in usura
415 quia fur et raptor semper timent ne per penam temporalem restituere com-pellantur.

Concludo ergo ex omnibus istis quod usurarius potens restituere usuras non potest liberari ab illa obligatione per viam remissionis nec per aliquam aliam viam nisi prius usuras reddat vel pro eis reddendis sufficientem cau-
420 cionem faciat.

Hic respondetur ad rationes domini Iohannis Andree, qui tenet con-trariam conclusionem et ad alias raciones que fuerunt inducte pro eadem conclusione.

Hiis autem visis, possumus respondere ad raciones que fuerunt superius
425 facte pro contraria opinione.

Ad primam ergo racionem, que sumitur ex parte remissionis, dicendum quod ideo forte ius canonicum declaravit remissionem in illis duobus casi-bus non valere quia in eis nullo modo potest prestare favorem, nam extra

---

11/402 raptori *C* : raptor *R*   11/405 servicii *C* : servi cum *R*   11/406–7 Vlterius … red-dicione : Sexto quod *W*   11/406 qui *C* : *om. R*   11/407 cum : maiore *add. C*   11/408–16 Et quod … compellantur : *om. W*   11/411 utebatur *C* : utebat *R*   11/417 Concludo : Concluditur *W*   11/418 illa : ista *W*   11/421–3 Hic … conclusione : *om. CW*   11/424–525 Hiis autem … videre quarto : *om. W*

11/413–14 Vid. sup. 10/1–129.   11/421–3 Cf. Giovanni d'Andrea, *In titulum de regulis iuris novella commentaria*, ad VI *de reg. iur.* 4, *Peccatum*, n.3 (ed. cit. fol. 62rb). Cf. Hos-tiensis, *Summa aurea*, ad X 5.19 *de usuris*, n.12 (ed. cit. fol. 251vb); gl. ord. ad VI *de reg. iur.* 4, *Peccatum*, v. *Restituatur* (ed. cit. col. 719); Dino of Mugello, *Commentaria in regulas iuris*, in 4 *Peccatum*, nn. 5–6 (ed. cit. p. 60).   11/424–5 Vid. sup. 11/30–87.   11/427–8 Vid. sup. 11/9–29.

to usury because neither the thief nor the robber can usurp or retain the property of another with the owner's consent, nor are there any grounds on which he can seek or extort such consent as can the usurer in view of the benefit the borrower derives from the loan.

Furthermore, I prove sixth that he who seeks remission of usury without restitution does not cease to harm collective justice with complacency and arrogance. And that this is so is clear, for if it should happen that he whose remission is sought refuses, it is clear that the usurer seeks to retain his usury without fear of temporal punishment as he did earlier; and so it appears that he is invoking the same complacency in remission that he enjoyed earlier in usurpation. Finally, for these two reasons, it is clear that the sixth circumstance noted earlier is not removed by remission of usury without restitution. Moreover, it is also clear how this circumstance is peculiar to usury, because the thief or robber always fears that he will be compelled to make restitution by means of temporal punishment.

On the basis of all these arguments, I conclude that a usurer who is able to make restitution cannot be freed of the obligation by way of remission or by any other means unless he first restores the usury or posts adequate guarantees of repayment.

Here he responds to the arguments of messer Giovanni d'Andrea, who holds the opposite position, and to other arguments in support of the same opinion.

In the light of the foregoing, we are now in a position to respond to the arguments advanced earlier in support of the opposed position.

In response to the first argument, which is based on the meaning of 're-mission,' it must be said that canon law declares remission in these two cases invalid because it cannot be beneficial in any way. But beyond these two

duos prefatos casus potest remissio quandoque prestare favorem duo-
430 bus modis, ut, verbi gratia, si usurarius nolit recipere usuras quas potest
exigere sive per actum sive per iusticiam vel per pignora, et debitor velit
omnino eas tradere liberaliter remictendo, tunc remissio in tali casu pre-
stabit favorem ipsi usurario quia non tenebitur ad restitucionem. Vlterius
secundo si contingat quod usurarius restituat usuras et ille cui facta est
435 restitucio velit eas iterato reddere usurario liberaliter remictendo, tunc in
tali casu remissio erit favorabilis ipsi usurario, quia non amplius tenebitur
ad restitucionem. Intencio ergo iuris canonici fuit quod quia in duobus
casibus superius memoratis numquam remissio est favorabilis, idcirco debet exceptuari omnino ad differenciam aliorum casuum in quibus potest
440 esse quandoque favorabilis, sicut nunc est ostensum. Intelligendum tamen
quod numquam remissio sic est favorabilis quod obligacionem debitoris
solvat sicut facit restitucio, quia tunc equippolleret restitucioni, cuius contrarium superius est ostensum. Erit ergo favorabilis quia quamvis obligacionem non solvat, ab ipsa tamen obligatione preservat; preservat enim
445 illum cui fit remissio ne obligacionem incurrat, sicut potest patere per ea
que nunc fuerunt inducta, et ideo habet se remissio non ad modum medicine expellentis morbum sed ad modum medicine preservantis a morbo.
Possumus insuper respondere secundo: quamvis remissio in nullo casu sit
efficax ad liberandum, in illis tamen duobus casibus a iure exceptuatis est
450 magis inefficax, nam quamvis in aliis casibus sit inefficax ex parte recipien-
tis, quia non est habilis ad recipiendum talem remissionem, non est tamen
inefficax ex parte remictentis quasi sit impotens ad dictam remissionem
faciendam. In illis vero duobus prefatis casibus a iure exceptuatis est inefficax utroque modo. Racio autem huius differencie sumitur ex eo quod ex
455 dictis duobus casibus non posset fieri remissio sine alienacione bonorum
ecclesiasticorum ex parte remictentis, quorum alienacionem vult dominus
papa penitus prohibere, propter quam causam voluit ulterius declarare
quod remissio nullam haberet efficaciam nec ex parte remictentis nec ex

---

11/430 ut : *om. C*   11/430 si : enim *add. R*   11/434 si *C* : non *R*   11/436 amplius : *om.*
C   11/438 memoratis *C* : inebriatis (!) *R*   11/438–9 debet : debeat *C*   11/442 equipolle-
ret *C* : equipollet *R*   11/444 tamen *C* : cum *R*   11/445 ne *C* : ut *R*   11/450 inefficax *C* :
ibi efficax *R*   11/453 prefatis : *om. C*   11/453 exceptuatis : *corr. al. man. ex* acceptuatis *R* :
exceptuatis *C*

11/443 Vid. sup. 11/109–31.   11/453 Cf. VI 1.3.11; 3.20.2; vid. sup. 11/9–29.

cases, remission can sometimes be beneficial in two ways. For example, if a usurer does not wish to accept the usury he is entitled to demand by means of an action, a lawsuit, or a pledge, and the debtor genuinely wishes to pay it, freely forgiving him any further obligation, then remission is beneficial to the usurer because he is no longer bound to make restitution. Or second, if it happens that a usurer restores usury and he to whom restitution is made wishes in turn to repay it to the usurer, freely forgiving him any further obligation, in this case, too, remission is beneficial to the usurer because he is no longer bound to make restitution. But the intention of the canon law is that remission can never be beneficial in the two cases cited above, and therefore must be completely distinguished from other cases in which it can sometimes be so, as I have just indicated. But it must be understood that remission that dissolves the obligation of a debtor as if he had made restitution (without actually doing so) is never beneficial, because then it would be equivalent to restitution, and we showed above that the opposite is true. Remission is beneficial not because it dissolves an obligation but because it preserves the debtor from it, for it preserves the one forgiven from incurring an obligation, as is clear in the examples I just provided, so that the remission is analogous not so much to a medicine that cures an illness as to one that prevents it. Moreover, we can also respond that, although remission is never capable of freeing the recipient of an obligation, this is particularly true in the two cases singled out by the law. For in other cases, the incapacity refers to the one forgiven because he is incapable of accepting remission, but not to the one forgiving, as if he were incapable of offering remission. But in the two cases singled out by the law, remission is invalid on both sides. The reason for the difference is that in both cases remission would involve the alienation of ecclesiastical property by the forgiver, something the pope intends to prohibit entirely. For this reason, he wished to declare that remission had no effect either on the side of the forgiver or on that of the forgiven in these cases, and so,

parte illius cui fit remissio in prefatis duobus casibus, et ideo in eis singula-
460   riter talem remissionem penitus anullavit. Vlterius possumus dare terciam
solucionem dicendo utique quod prefati duo casus sunt quasi similes aliis
casibus in quibus aliquis tenetur ad restitucionem. Vbi autem sunt similes
casus magis debet sumi argumentum a sensu simili quam a sensu contrario,
quia 'de similibus idem iudicium est habendum,' ut patet *extra, de transla-*
465   *cione episcopi* c. *Inter corporalia* § *Sicut ergo.*

Ad secundam vero racionem, que sumitur ex parte satisfaccionis, dicendum quod satisfaccio potest accipi duobus modis. Vno modo prout
est equalitatis reparativa; alio modo ut est aequalitatis conservativa. Alia
namque satisfaccio est illa qua quis satisfacit reddendo depositum; alia
470   vero qua quis satisfacit reddendo male ablatum. Nam prima satisfaccio
habet equalitatem et iusticiam conservare, quia ille qui depositum non redderet inequalitatem et iniusticiam commicteret; secunda vero satisfaccio
habet equalitatem et iusticiam reparare, quia ille qui habet male ablatum,
quamdiu ipsum non reddidit, inequalitatem et iniusticiam commisit, et
475   ideo isto casu inventa est satisfaccio ad reparandam inequalitatem et iniusticiam iam commissam. Prima ergo satisfaccio potest recipere mensuram
iuxta voluntatem et acceptacionem ipsius creditoris, nam quia creditor in
tali casu separavit rem suam a se ipso per suam voluntatem, idcirco debitor sufficienter ei satisfaciet si de re illa agat iuxta eiusdem creditoris vo-
480   luntatem. Secunda vero satisfaccio non potest mensurari iuxta voluntatem
ipsius creditoris, quia in tali casu fuit separata res sua ab eo contra suam
voluntatem et per maliciam ipsius usurpantis fuit ipsi usurpanti vel alicui
alteri iniuste unita, et ideo si debeat equalitas et iusticia reparari non satisfacit recurrere ad ipsam voluntatem creditoris, ẙmo debemus recurrere ad
485   ipsam naturam rei secundum quam inequalitas et iniusticia est commissa
ex eo quod res aliqua separata est ab eo cui debet esse unita et est unita ei
a quo debet esse separata. Idcirco non reparabitur iusticia et equalitas nisi
res illa vel ei equippollens separaretur ab eo cui fuit unita et reuniatur ei a
quo fuit separata. Et ita patet quid sit dicendum ad secundam racionem.

11/459 illius : eius *C*   11/461 solucionem *C* : remissionem *R*   11/465 episcopi : episcoporum *C*   11/466–7 dicendum ... saitsfaccio *C* : *om. per hom. R*   11/468 alio ... conservativa *C* : *om. per hom. R*   11/474 commisit : committit *C*   11/475 inventa : adinventa
C   11/475 reparandam : reparandum *C*   11/483–4 satisfacit : satis est *C*   11/484 ipsam :
om. C   11/488 separaretur : separetur *C*   11/488 fuit *C* : finis *R*

11/464–5 X 1.7.2.pr.   11/466 Vid. sup. 11/3–9.

in these unique cases, he nullified remission. Furthermore, we can suggest a third solution by arguing that the said two cases are only superficially similar to other cases in which someone is bound to make restitution. But when cases are similar, the argument should rather proceed on the basis of similarity than difference, because 'judgment should be passed on the basis of similarities,' as is clear at X 1.7.2.pr.

In response to the second argument, which is based on the meaning of 'satisfaction,' it must be said that satisfaction can be understood in two ways: in one way it repairs equality, in the other it preserves it. There is a difference between the satisfaction involved in restoring a deposit and the satisfaction involved in restoring something which has been illicitly appropriated. In the first, satisfaction preserves justice and equality, for one who failed to restore a deposit would be guilty of an injustice. In the second, satisfaction repairs equality and justice, for the possessor of a thing illicitly appropriated has committed an act of inequality and injustice so long as he has not returned it, and so in this case satisfaction serves to repair an earlier act of inequality and injustice. The first kind of satisfaction takes its measure from the will and agreement of the creditor, for inasmuch as the creditor in this case parted with his property willingly, the debtor adequately satisfies the creditor if the creditor approves his handling of the property. The second kind of satisfaction cannot be measured by the will of the creditor because he was parted from his property unwillingly, and it acceded unjustly to the usurper or someone else by the usurper's malice. If, therefore, equality and justice are to be repaired, it is inadequate to appeal to the will of the creditor; rather we must appeal to the nature of the thing with respect to which inequality and injustice were committed, because the thing has been separated from one who should have it and possessed by one from whom it should be separated. Justice and equality cannot be repaired unless the thing or something equivalent is removed from the one who possesses it and handed over to the one from whom

490   Ad terciam vero racionem, que sumebatur ex parte solucionis, dicendum quod duplex est obligacio: una que per mutuum et liberum consensum duorum constituitur, sicut patet in deposito et gratuito mutuo; alia vero que per solam pravam voluntatem obligati exoritur, sicut patet in fure et raptore ac eciam usurario, namque quilibet istorum facit aliquid unde
495 postea relinquitur obligatus. Prima ergo obligacio potest tolli sine reddicione per solum consensum illorum inter quos est, quia per easdem causas dissolvitur per quas innascitur, ut supra dicebatur, et in tali casu verum est directe quod solucio magis refertur ad substanciam obligacionis quam ad nummorum solucionem. Secunda autem obligacio non potest tolli nisi
500 previa reddicione, quia talis obligacio generata est per solam voluntatem illius obligati depravatam in usurpando et detinendo ac per consequens non poterit dissolvi nisi per eamdem voluntatem ipsius rectificatam in reddendo et restituendo, et ideo in tali casu solucio non |^{R218r} solum refertur ad substanciam obligacionis sed eciam ad ipsam rem obligatam.

505   Ad quartam vero racionem, que sumebatur ex parte translacionis dominii, per ea que dicta sunt supra patet quid sit dicendum: quia usurarius vel quicumque alius habens rem male ablatam non est habilis ad capiendum dominium in ea nisi prius eam reddat, nam quia possidet eam iniusto titulo non potest ei advenire titulus iustus per dominii acquisicionem nisi prius
510 tollatur titulus iniustus per restitucionem.

    Ad quintam vero racionem, que sumebatur ex parte donacionis, dicendum quod usurario non potest fieri donacio usurarum antequam eas restituat, tum quia non potest acquirere titulum iustum per donacionem nisi prius deponat titulum iniustum per restitucionem, tum eciam quia non
515 potest certificari de tali donacione utrum sit libera vel non libera, cum eadem signa appareant in eo qui non libere donat et in eo qui libere donat.
    Ad sextam et ultimam racionem iam apparet quid sit dicendum ex hiis

---

11/491 et liberum : liberumque *C*   11/493 obligati *C* : obligari *R*   11/494 namque : nam *C*   11/499 nummorum : numorum *RC*

11/490 Vid. sup. 11/40–56.   11/496–7 X 5.41.1.; vid. sup. 11/154–5.   11/505 Vid. sup. 11/57–69.   11/511 Vid. sup. 11/70–8.   11/517 Vid. sup. 11/79–87.

it was separated. And so it is clear what should be said in response to the second argument.

In response to the third argument, which is based on the meaning of 'payment,' it must be said that there are two kinds of obligation: the first is created by the mutual and free consent of two parties, as in a deposit or interest-free loan; the second arises from the wicked choice of someone who is thereby placed under an obligation, as is the case of the thief, robber, or usurer, for each of these does something that leaves him under an obligation. The first kind of obligation can be dissolved simply by the consent of the parties without restoration of the thing involved, for it 'is dissolved by the very causes that gave rise to it,' as was said earlier, and in this case, it is true that 'payment relates to the substance of the obligation rather than to the payment of coins.' But the second kind of obligation cannot be dissolved without restitution because it arose solely from the wicked choice of the obligor to usurp and detain another's property; consequently it can only be dissolved by the choice of the obligor to make restitution. In this case, payment does not relate only to the substance of the obligation, but to thing itself.

In response to the fourth argument, which is based on the meaning of 'transfer of ownership,' what ought to be said is clear from what was said earlier, namely, that a usurer or anyone else in possession of an illicitly appropriated thing has no capacity to acquire ownership in it unless he has first restored it. Because he possesses it by means of an unjust title, he cannot obtain just title by transfer of ownership unless the unjust title is first removed by restitution.

In response to the fifth argument, which is based on the meaning of 'gift,' it should be said that a usurer cannot accept a gift of usury before he has restored it, for he can neither obtain just title through a gift before he has set aside the unjust title by restitution, nor can he be certain that the gift is truly free, since the same gestures would be employed by one who made a free gift and one who did not.

What ought to be said in response to the sixth and final argument is

que dicta sunt supra, quia illa renunciacio que fit a spoliato ante restitucionem penitus determinatur nulla, ut superius est ostensum.

520   Et ideo concludo quantum ad totum istum articulum quod nec usurarius nec aliquis alius habens rem male ablatam potest liberari ab obligacione illius per viam remissionis nec per aliquam aliam viam nisi prius dictam rem reddat et restituat, dummodo habeat unde restituere valeat vel bonam caucionem pro ea restituenda faciat.

525   Restat ergo videre quarto.

<12> <Articulus quartus>

Quartus articulus, in quo ostenditur quod usurarius tenetur restituere quandoque non solum usuram extortam sed eciam id quod per eam lucratus est, quandoque vero non tenetur.

5   Vtrum usurarius teneatur restituere non solum usuram extortam sed etiam totum illud quod per eam lucratus est. Ad istum ergo articulum quidam respondent dicentes quod usurarius tenetur restituere non solum usuram sed eciam totum id quod per eam lucratus est; nam quia 'difficile est ut bono peragantur exitu ea que malo sunt inchoata principio,' ut pa-

10 tet I q. 1 *Principatus*, idcirco, ut dicunt, lucrum id quod per usuram est habitum, quia est a mala radice et a malo principio derivatum, difficile est ut sit bonum, ÿmo videtur penitus malum, quia radice existente corrupta quidquid de ea procedit corruptum est. Similiter enim de radice sancta non potest procedere aliquid nisi sanctum, quia 'si radix sancta et rami,' ut dicit

15 Apostolus ad Romanos XI, ita eciam de radice corrupta non videtur posse procedere aliquid nisi corrupcio. Quapropter videtur quod lucrum quod de usura est habitum penitus sit corruptum ac per consequens omnino restituendum pariter cum usura.

11/522 nec *C* : *om. R*   11/523 dummodo : modo *C*   12/2 Quartus articulus : Ad quartum articulum *W*   12/2–4 Quartus … tenetur : *om. C*   12/5–6 Vtrum … articulum : *om. W*   12/5–6 sed … eam *C* : *om. R*   12/8 id : illud *CW*   12/8–18 nam quia … cum usura : *om. W*   12/10 q. 1 Principatus *C* : q. 2 Primatus *R*   12/10 id : illud *C*   12/11 a² : enim *add. et exp. R*   12/12 existente : extante *C*   12/13 Similiter : Sicut *C*   12/15 XI : 6 *C*   12/16 corrupcio : corruptum *C*

11/519 Vid. sup. 11/213–29.   12/7 Cf. Guido de Baisio, *Rosarium*, ad Decretum Grat. C.14 q.4 c.10, n.2 (ed. cit., fol. 240vb).   12/8–10 Decretum Grat. C.1 q.1 c.25.   12/14–15 *Rom* 11.16.

already clear from what has been said above, for renunciation by one who has been despoiled of his property before restitution must be considered completely null, as was shown earlier.

Therefore, with respect to the question posed in this article, I conclude that neither a usurer nor anyone else in possession of an illicitly appropriated thing can be freed of the obligation to make restitution by way of remission or in any other way, unless he has first restored the thing, provided he has the wherewithal, or posted an adequate pledge to do so.

Let us now, therefore, consider the fourth article.

12. Article 4

The fourth article, in which it is demonstrated that a usurer is sometimes obliged to restore not only the usury he extorted but also the profit he gained from it, sometimes not.

Is a usurer obliged to restore not only the usury he extorted but also all the profits he gained by means of it? To this question some respond that a usurer is indeed obliged to restore not only the usury he extorted but all the profits he gained by means of it. They argue that because 'it is difficult that something that has had a bad beginning should achieve a good end,' as it says at C.1 q.1 c.25, it is impossible that profit gained from usury, which is rooted in evil and derived from a wicked principle, should be good; indeed, it seems particularly wicked, because whatever springs from a corrupt root is itself corrupt. For just as nothing can spring from a holy root but what is holy, because 'if the root is holy, so too are the branches,' as the Apostle says in Romans 11, so likewise it seems that nothing but corruption can spring from a corrupt root. Therefore, it seems that profit gained from usury is completely corrupt and consequently must be restored along with the usury.

Hec autem opinio mihi non placet nec videtur racionabilis propter tria.
20   Primo quia supponit quod principalis radix lucri quod usurarius lucratur
per usuram sit ipsa usura, quod tamen non est universaliter verum, nam
potest contingere quod industria et sollicitudo usurarii est principalis causa talis lucri et ideo in tali casu debet iudicari dictum lucrum bonum vel
malum non penes usuram, que fuit eius causa instrumentalis, sed penes
25   industriam usurarii, que fuit ipsius causa principalis. Vlterius secundo non
videtur vera dicta opinio quia sicut de bona materia, si sit male tractata,
potest provenire malus effectus, ita e contra et de mala materia, si sit bene
tractata et deducta, poterit provenire bonus effectus. Patet exemplo de vi-
pera, ex qua fit mitridatum, atque de saccaro, ex quo fit potio laetalis; nunc
30   autem versamus in artefactis. Vlterius si prefata sit opinio vera, sequitur
quod sicut usurarius ponitur teneri ad restitucionem eius quod lucratus
est per usuram, ita pari racione et ille qui accepit ab usurario mutuum
tenebitur ad restitucionem eius quod lucratus est per illud mutuum, quod
patet esse falsum. Quod autem istud sequitur apparet, quia potest contin-
35   gere quod usura extorta per mutuum sit eiusdem racionis cum mutuo, ut
cum quis usurariam pecuniam alteri mutuat, et ideo in tali casu si usurarius
non potuit tenere illud lucrum quod lucratus est cum usura, pari racione
nec ille qui recepit ab usurario mutuum poterit tenere illud quod lucratus
est cum dicto mutuo. Et ideo propter ista et plura alia que possunt induci
40   videtur quod in isto articulo sit aliter procedendum, nam quia videmus
quandoque quod usurarius tenetur ad restituendum non solum usuram
sed eciam illud quod per usuram lucratus est, quandoque vero videmus
contrarium, idcirco videtur necessario distinguendum de usura.
Dico ergo quod usura extorta per mutuum potest accipi duobus modis.
45   Vno modo prout est de genere illarum rerum que possunt lucrificare quia
non habent determinatum valorem a natura vel ab arte, quemadmodum est

---

12/19 mihi non placet : non est bona *W*   12/20–39 Primo ... mutuo : que causa brevitatis dimitto *W*   12/22 industria *C* : industris *R*   12/22 sollicitudo *C* : ellicitudo (!)
R   12/27 materia : potest *add. et exp. R*   12/28 poterit : potest *C*   12/28–30 Patet ...
artefactis *C* : *om. R*   12/30 Vlterius : est *add. R*   12/34 quia *C* : quod *R*   12/35 sit
C : *om. R*   12/35–6 ut ... mutuat *C* : *om. R*   12/39 que : que *add. R*   12/39 ista : tria
add. W   12/41 usurarius : quandoque *add. W*   12/42–3 quandoque ... usura : *om.*
W   12/43 necessario *C* : necessarium *R*   12/45 lucrificare : lucrifacere *C*   12/45 quia :
que *W*   12/46 habent *C* : habet *R*

12/19–92 Cf. Thomas Aquinas, *Summa theologiae*, 2ª 2ᵃᵉ, q.78 art.3, in *Opera omnia*, vol. 9
(ed. cit.), p. 165b.

But I am unhappy with this opinion, and it seems unreasonable on three grounds. First, because it supposes that the principal root from which the usurer profits is the usury itself; but this is not always so, for it can be that the industry and care of the usurer himself is the principal cause of such profit, and so, in this case, profit should be judged good or bad not with respect to the usury, which was its instrumental cause, but with respect to the usurer's industry, which was the principal cause. Second, this opinion does not appear to be true because just as a bad effect can proceed from good matter badly treated, by contrast, a good effect can proceed from bad matter treated well and wisely. This is clear from the example of the adder, from which is made an antidote to its own poison, or sugar, from which a lethal poison can be made, to speak only of artifacts. Finally, if this opinion were true, it follows that just as the usurer is obliged to the restitution of profit he gained by means of the usury, so also will his debtor be obliged to restore any profit he gained by means of the loan, which is clearly false. That this follows is clear, because usury extorted by means of a loan is of the same character as the loan itself, as it is when someone lends money to another at usury; in this case, if the usurer cannot keep the profit he earned by means of the usury, by the same token, neither can his debtor keep the profit he earned by means of the loan. And so, for these reasons and several other that can be adduced, it seems that we must proceed otherwise in this article; for inasmuch as we see that sometimes a usurer is bound to restore not only usury but what he gained by means of it and sometimes the opposite, it seems necessary to makes some distinctions about usury.

I maintain, therefore, that usury extorted by means of a loan can be obtained in two ways. One is from the class of things that can bear fruit because they do not have a value assigned by nature or skill, such as a

vinea vel ager; alio modo prout est de genere illarum rerum que non possunt lucrificare vel quia habent determinatum valorem a natura, ut ponderabilia et mensurabilia, vel quia habent determinatum valorem ab arte, ut
50 numerabilia, sicut denarii. Si ergo accipiatur usura primo modo, sic dicendum est simpliciter quod usurarius tenetur restituere non solum usuram
sed eciam id quod per talem usuram lucratus est, nam res que de sui natura
habet lucrum et fructum est restituenda cum suo lucro et fructu, et ideo
si usurarius per suum mutuum extorsisset agrum vel vineam, deberet re-
55 stituere non solum illum agrum vel illam vineam sed eciam omnes fructus
quos inde percepisset, deductis tamen expensis, et hoc propter duo. Primo
quia nullus debet recipere fructum de re non sua; vinea autem vel ager qui
per usuram extorquentur non sunt ipsius usurarii extorquentis, quapropter tenetur non solum ad restitucionem talis vinee vel talis agri sed eciam
60 omnium fructuum quos de eis percepit. Secundo apparet racio hec: quia
si usurarius posset recipere fructum de illa re quam per usuram extorsit,
sequeretur quod usura fieret ei favorabilis, quod patet esse falsum, quia
nullum peccatum potest esse favorabile ipsi peccanti. Vsura autem peccatum est, ut patet ex hiis que dicta fuerunt in precedenti questione, ergo
65 non potest esse favorabilis ipsi usurario. Apparet ergo quid sit dicendum
si accipiatur usura primo modo.

    Si vero accipiatur usura secundo modo, scilicet prout est de genere il-
larum rerum que non possunt lucrificare vel quia habent determinatum
valorem a natura, ut ponderabilia et mensurabilia, vel quia habent deter-
70 minatum valorem ab arte, ut numerabilia, sicut denarii, sic dicendum est
quod usurarius tenetur restituere solam usuram quam extorsit et non id
quod per eam lucratus est, quod patet ex duobus. Primo ex eo quod usura accepta in isto secundo modo non habet de sui natura quod lucrificet,

---

12/47 prout : ut *C*   12/48 lucrificare : lucrifacere *C*   12/48 quia : que *W*   12/48–9 a
natura ... valorem *C* : *om. per hom. RW*   12/50 sicut denarii : *om. C*   12/55 illum
... vineam : haec *C* : illum *om. W*   12/57–66 quia nullus ... primo modo : et cetera *W*   12/57 qui : quae *C*   12/58 extorquentur : extorquerentur *C*   12/59 agri *C* :
om. R   12/60 de : ex *C*   12/60 racio hec : hoc ratione *C*   12/61 recipere : percipe-
re *C*   12/61 fructum : fructus *C*   12/68 lucrificare : lucrifacere *C*   12/69 ut *C* : vel
R   12/70 sicut *supplevi* : *om. RC* : denarii *om. C*   12/72–108 ex eo ... sollicitudine : et
cetera *W*   12/73 de : ex *C*

12/64 Vid. sup. 3/128–357.

vineyard or a field. The other is from the class of things that cannot bear fruit either because they have a value assigned by nature, such as weighable or measurable things, or because they have a value assigned by skill, such as countable things, for example, coins. If usury is obtained in the first way, it must be said that the usurer is obliged to restore not only the usury but also whatever he gained by means of it, for a thing that by nature generates a profit and fruits must be restored along with the profit and fruits. Therefore, if a usurer has extorted a field or vineyard by means of a loan, he should restore not only the field or vineyard but also any fruits he derived from it, minus expenses, and this for two reasons. First, because nobody may receive fruit from something which is not his own. Now a vineyard or field extorted by means of usury does not belong to the usurer who has extorted it, therefore he is obliged to restore not only the vineyard or field but also any fruits he derived from it. The second reason is this: if a usurer could derive fruits from something he extorted by usury, it would follow that usury was advantageous to him, which is clearly false, because no sin is advantageous to the sinner. Now usury is a sin, as is clear from what was said in the preceding question, therefore it cannot be advantageous to a usurer. And so it is clear what should be said if usury is obtained in the first way.

But if usury is obtained in the second way, namely, from the class of things that cannot bear fruit either because they have a value assigned by nature, such as weighable or measurable things, or because they have a value assigned by skill, such as countable things, for example, coins, it must be said that the usurer is obliged to restore only the usury that he extorted and not any profit he gained by it, which is clear for two reasons. First, because usury obtained in the second way does not by nature bear

quia habet determinatum valorem a natura vel ab arte, et ideo si usurarius
75   aliquid lucratur per eam legitimo modo, illud lucrum non est ascribendum
usure sed sue proprie industrie et sollicitudini per quam causam poterit
usurarius convenienter tale lucrum tenere. Vlterius secundo apparet hoc
idem ex eo quod usura isto secundo modo accepta est eiusdem racionis
cum ipso mutuo de quo est genita vel per quod est extorta, nam sicut mu-
80   tuum habet determinatum valorem a natura vel ab arte propter quod non
potest lucrificare, ut patuit supra in questione de contractu usurario, ita
eciam talis usura que extorta est per dictum mutuum. Quia eciam ipsa,
cum talis est, ponitur de genere numerabilium vel ponderabilium vel mensurabilium, et ideo hoc supposito poterimus sic arguere, sicut se habet ille
85   qui accipit mutuum ab usurario ad ipsum mutuum, ita usurarius ad usuram quam extorsit per dictum mutuum. Sed ille qui accipit mutuum tenetur reddere usurario solum mutuum et non id quod lucratus est per tale
mutuum, ergo eodem modo usurarius tenebitur restitutere |[R218v] solum
talem usuram quam extorsit per mutuum et non id quod lucratus est per
90   talem usuram. Minor est nota; maior eciam quia supponebatur quod talis
usura esset eiusdem racionis cum mutuo ita quod neutrum eorum posset
de sui natura lucrificare.

Nec valet si dicatur quod per istam viam videbitur quod usura sit favorabilis ipsi usurario, cuius contrarium superius ponebatur. Ista siquidem
95   instancia non valet quia in tali lucro usura non prestat favorem ipsi usurario tanquam causa illius lucri, quia causa a qua derivatur dictum lucrum
non est ipsa usura sed industria et sollicitudo usurarii, concurrit tamen
ibi usura tanquam causa sine qua non. Nec hoc debet reputari inconveniens vel mirabile, quia sepe videmus quod illud quod est malum potest
100   concurrere ad aliquod bonum, non quidem tamquam causa propter quam
sic, sed tamquam causa sine qua non. Constat namque quod causa a qua
est bonum iusticie vindicative est ipse iustus iudex, qui penam condignam
infligit, concurrit tamen ibi necessario malum culpe tanquam causa sine

---

12/77 hoc *C* : sed *R*   12/81 lucrificare : lucrifacere *C*   12/83–4 vel[1] ... mensurabilium *C* :
om. R   12/84 poterimus *C* : positus *R*   12/92 lucrificare : lucrifacere *C*   12/93 per *C* :
om. R   12/94 ponebatur : fuit positum *C*   12/96 illius : ipsius *C*   12/101 sed *C* : quia
R   12/101 non *C* : si *R*   12/101 Constat : *ex* Consistat *corr. R*   12/102 condignam *C* : et
dignum *R*

12/81 Vid. sup. 3/226–51.   12/94 Vid. sup. 12/5–18.

fruit, since it has a value assigned by nature or skill, and so if the usurer legitimately gained some profit from it, the profit cannot be ascribed to the usury but to his industry and care, and for this reason the usurer can appropriately retain such profit. Second, it is clear because usury obtained in the second way is of the same character as the loan itself from which it arises or through which it is extorted, for just as a loan has a value assigned to it by nature or skill such that it cannot bear fruit, as is clear above in the question on the usurious contract, so also does the usury extorted by means of the loan. For the usury itself is such that it belongs to the class of countable, weighable, or measurable things, and therefore we could argue that the debtor who borrows from the usurer stands in the same relation to his loan as does the usurer to the usury he extorts by means of it. Now the borrower is obliged to return to the usurer only the amount borrowed and not any profit he made by means of it, therefore, by the same token, the usurer will be obliged to restore only the usury he extorted through the loan and not any profit he gained by means of the usury. The minor premiss is clear. The major premiss is clear as well, because it was supposed that the usury is of the same character as the loan, such that neither can by nature produce a profit.

Nor is it true to say that usury obtained in the second way is somehow advantageous to the usurer, although the opposite was maintained earlier. But the example is irrelevant because in this case usury does not confer an advantage on the usurer, as if it were somehow the cause of the profit, for here the cause of the profit is not the usury itself but the industry and care of the usurer; by contrast, in the first case, the usury represents an indispensable condition of the profit. Nor should this be considered inappropriate or remarkable, because we often see that an evil stands in relation to a good not as a final cause, but as an indispensable condition. For example, although the efficient cause of the good of penal justice is a just judge who imposes a fitting penalty, nevertheless the evil of sin represents

qua non, quia si nulla esset culpa, nulla foret iusticia vindicativa. Et per
105 hoc apparet ulterius quod fundamentum contrarie opinionis non procedit,
quia quando usurarius lucratur per usuram secundo modo acceptam, tale
lucrum tanquam de radice procedit non de ipsa usura sed de sua propria
industria vel sollicitudine.

Et ita patet ex omnibus hiis quid sit dicendum quantum ad istum articu-
110 lum. Restat ergo quinto et ultimo videre.

<13> <Articulus quintus>

Quintus articulus, in quo ostenditur quem ordinem debet servare usurarius in restituendo et quomodo prius uni quam alteri.

Vtrum usurarius in restituendo debeat servare aliquem ordinem, ita
5 quod prius restituat uni quam alteri. Vbi sciendum quod circa istum articulum occurrunt plura dubia. Primum est utrum usurarius prius debeat
restituere ei cui tenetur ex aliquo contractu quam illi cui tenetur ex simplici extorsione usurarum. Ad hoc ergo dico statim quod sic, nam quia
restitucio est quedam obligacionis solucio, idcirco ibi debet precedere re-
10 stitucio ubi est maior obligacio. Maior autem est obligacio qua usurarius
est obligatus alicui ex contractu mutui vel empcionis quam illa qua est
obligatus alicui alteri ex simplici extorsione usurarum, quod patet ex tribus: primo quia per ipsum creditorem est volita et expressa; secundo quia
per ipsum usurarium est promissione firmata; tercio quia per ipsius iuris
15 civilis favorem approbata. Primum patet, constat namque quod ille qui
mutuat vel vendit aliquid ipsi usurario vult expresse ipsum usurarium sibi
esse obligatum in tantum quod, si expediat, vult dictam obligacionem fir-
mari et declarari per testes sive eciam per publicum instrumentum, quod
non est propter aliud nisi quia talis obligacio est per ipsum volita et ex-
20 pressa. Secundum eciam patet, constat namque quod usurarius cum accipit ab aliquo mutuum vel aliquam aliam rem nomine empcionis promittit
se illud mutuum reddere vel pro illa re solvere, sive eciam in eo tempore
quod per utriusque consensum fuerit ordinatum. Talis autem promissio
habet dictam obligacionem firmare, propter quod bene dicebatur quod

---

12/109 ex omnibus hiis : *om.* W   12/110 Restat ... videre : *om.* W   12/110 quinto et : *om.*
C   13/2–3 Quintus ... alteri : *om.* C   13/4–6 Vtrum ... est : Queritur primo W   13/6 debeat : debet W   13/8 Ad hoc ... sic : Dico quod sic W   13/8 ergo : ego C   13/10 obli-
gacio² : illa *add.* W   13/13–36 primo ... secundo modo : et cetera W   13/21 nomine : et
titulo *add.* C   13/24 dictam : talem C

the indispensable condition; for if there were no sin, there would be no penal justice. And so it is clear that the foundation of the opposed opinion does not hold, because when a usurer profits by means of usury received in the second way, his profit derives fundamentally not from the usury itself but from his own industry and care.

From the foregoing, it is clear what should be said with respect to the fourth article. Let us now, therefore, consider the fifth and final article.

13. Article 5

The fifth article, in which it is shown what order the usurer should observe in making restitution and how one is given preference over another.

Should a usurer observe some order in making restitution such that he makes restitution to one in preference to another? It must be understood that several questions arise in connection with this issue. The first is whether the usurer should make restitution to him to whom he is obliged by contract before him to whom he is obliged by the simple extortion of usury. To this I respond directly that the answer is 'yes'; for inasmuch as restitution is the discharge of an obligation, where there is a greater obligation, there should also be priority of restitution. Now the obligation that binds a usurer to someone by a contract of loan or sale is greater than the obligation that binds him to someone by the simple extortion of usury; and this is clear for three reasons. First, because it was willed and expressed by the creditor; second, because it was confirmed by the usurer by means of a promise; and third, because it was approved with the blessing of the civil law. The first is clear because it is a fact that one who lends or sells something to a usurer clearly wishes the usurer to be obliged to him to the degree that, if it is convenient, he wishes the obligation to be confirmed and witnessed by witnesses, or even by means of a public instrument, which would not be the case unless the obligation was willed and expressed by the creditor. The second is also clear because it is a fact that when a usurer accepts a loan or something by way of purchase from someone, he promises that he will repay the loan or render payment for the thing bought at

25 dicta obligacio erat per ipsum usurarium promissione firmata. Tercium
patet eciam, constat namque quod si usurarius mutuum non reddat vel
pro re empta non solvat eo tempore quo promisit, compellitur per penam
a iure civili mutuum reddere et pro re empta solvere, quod non esset nisi
dicta obligacio foret per iuris civilis favorem approbata. Hec autem tria
30 non possunt dici de illa obligacione que innascitur ex simplici extorsione usurarum, ut de se patet, propter que tria convenienter est dicendum
quod illa que innascitur ex contractu mutui vel empcionis est maior quam
illa que innascitur ex simplici extorsione usurarum, et ideo prius solvenda
illa, cum sit maior quam alia, que est minor, ac per consequens prius debet
35 usurarius restituere ei cui est obligatus primo modo quam ei cui est obligatus secundo modo.

Secundum dubium circa istum articulum est quod supposito quod usurarius non possit solvere in solidum ei cui est obligatus ex contractu mutui vel empcionis et ei cui est obligatus ex simplici extorsione usurarum,
40 utrum debeat cuilibet eorum solvere pro rata vel utrum soli alteri cui tenetur ex contractu mutui vel emptionis. Ad quod dicendum est quod prius
solvere in solidum ei cui tenetur ex contractu mutui vel empcionis propter
duo. Primo quia obligacio que innascitur ex contractu mutui vel empcionis
est legitima et favorabilis ex utraque parte et ideo solucio ipsius non debet
45 impediri per solucionem alterius que ex non legitima causa nascitur nec ex
utraque parte favorabilis redditur. Secundo quia dicta obligacio est firmata
promissione integre solucionis et ideo non debet impediri per solucionem
illius obligacionis que nullius solucionis promissione firmatur.

Tercium dubium quod occurrit circa istum articulum est utrum usura-
50 rius prius debeat restituere ei cui aliquid extorsit per usuram quam ei cui
aliquid extorsit per furtum vel rapinam. Ad hoc ergo dico quod prius ei
cui aliquid extorsit per furtum vel rapinam propter duo. Primo quia, cum

---

13/28 et : vel *C*   13/28 esset : fieret *C*   13/29 dicta : ipsa *C*   13/30 ex *C* : quod *R*
13/32 quod *C* : pro *R*   13/35 modo : secundo modo *add. R* : *om. C*   13/37 quod[1] *C* :
circa *R* : *om. W*   13/40 vel utrum : an *C*   13/40–1 vel utrum … empcionis : *om. W*
13/40–1 cui … prius *C* : *om. R*   13/41 Ad quod … prius : Dico quod debet soli alteri *W*
13/42 solidum : scilicet *add. W*   13/42 tenetur *C* : *om. R*   13/43–8 quia … firmatur :
om. W   13/49 quod … articulum : *om. W*   13/50–1 quam … furtum *W* : an prius ei
cui abstulit per furtum *C* : *om. R*   13/51 Ad hoc ergo : *om. W*   13/51 ergo : ego *C*
13/52 cui aliquid extorsit : a quo abstulit aliquid *C*   13/52–67 Primo … usuram : *om. W*

a time mutually agreed by the parties. This promise has the function of confirming the obligation, so it is well said that the obligation was confirmed by the usurer by means of a promise. The third is likewise clear because it is a fact that if the usurer does not repay the loan or pay for the thing bought at the agreed time, he is compelled by a civil law penalty to do so, which would not be the case if the obligation were not approved by civil law. These three characteristics cannot be ascribed to the obligation that arises from the simple extortion of usury, as is self-evident, and for these three reasons it can be maintained appropriately that the obligation that arises from a contract of loan or purchase is greater than that which arises from the simple extortion of usury and therefore ought to be paid first, since it is greater than the other, which is less. Consequently, a usurer should first make restitution to him to whom he is obliged in the first way and only then to him to whom he is obliged by the second.

A second question that arises in connection with this issue is whether, assuming the usurer cannot completely repay both the one to whom he is obliged by a contract of loan or purchase and the one to whom he is obliged by simple extortion of usury, he should pay each proportionately or one or other of the two. The response is that he is bound to repay completely the one to whom he is bound by a contract of loan or purchase for two reasons. First, because an obligation that arises from a contract of loan or purchase is lawful and advantageous to both parties, and so its payment should not be impeded by the payment of another obligation that arises from a non-lawful source and is disadvantageous to both parties. Second, because the obligation was confirmed by a promise of complete payment and therefore should not be impeded by payment of an obligation that was not confirmed by any promise of payment.

A third question that arises in connection with this issue is whether a usurer should make restitution to him from whom he has extorted usury before him from whom he has extorted something by theft or robbery. I respond that he from whom he extorted something by theft or robbery

restitucio sit ordinata ad satisfaccionem, ibi debet prius restitucio fieri ubi
est opus maiori satisfaccione. Nunc autem maiori satisfaccione opus est
55 in furto et rapina quam in usura quia in eis infertur maior iniuria, nam
usurpacio rei aliene facta per furtum vel rapinam est penitus involuntaria; illa autem que fit per usuram est aliquo modo voluntaria; quapropter
relinquitur quod prius sit fienda restitucio ei cui facta est usurpacio per
furtum vel rapinam quam ei cui facta est per usuram. Secundo patet hoc
60 idem quia ubi usurarius magis de iure compellitur, ibi prius tenetur. Nunc
autem magis de iure compellitur ad restituendum illud quod extorsit per
furtum vel rapinam quam illud quod extorsit per usuram; nam videmus
quod ad restituendum furtum et rapinam compellitur non solum a iure
divino et canonico sed eciam a iure civili; ad restituendam vero usuram
65 compellitur solum a iure canonico et divino. Ergo relinquitur quod prius debeat restituere illud quod extorsit per furtum et rapinam quam illud
quod extorsit per usuram.

Quartum dubium quod hic occurrit est, dato quod usurarius non possit
restituere in solidum ei cui extorsit aliquid per furtum et rapinam et ei cui
70 extorsit per usuram, utrum debeat restituere cuilibet pro rata vel solum
alteri eorum in solidum. Ad hoc autem dico quod debet restituere in solidum ei cui aliquid extorsit per furtum et rapinam, quod patet ex duobus.
Primo quia videmus quod compellitur a iure civili ad restituendum in solidum furtum et rapinam, non obstante quod per hoc reddatur impotens ad
75 restituendum usuras in solidum. Secundo apparet hoc idem quia restitucio
illius qui spoliatus est omnino contra suam voluntatem non debet impediri
per restitucionem illius qui spoliatus est consenciente sua voluntate. Ita
autem est in proposito, nam ille qui spoliatus est omnino contra suam voluntatem est ille cui facta est usurpacio rei sue per furtum et rapinam. Ille
80 autem qui spoli-|^{R219r}-atus est consenciente aliquo modo illa voluntate est
is cui facta est usurpacio rei sue per usuram et ideo nullo modo restitucio
primi debet impediri per restitucionem secundi.

Quintum dubium est utrum usurarius prius teneatur restituere usuram

---

13/53 prius *C* : peius *R*   13/61 restituendum *C* : restitucionem *R*   13/63 et : vel *C*
13/64 restituendam *C* : restituendum *R*   13/68 quod hic occurrit : *om. W*   13/69 et rapinam : *om. C*   13/71 Ad hoc autem : *om. W* : autem : *om. C*   13/75–82 quia ... secundi : et
cetera *W*   13/80 illa : illius *C*   13/81 cui *C* : cuius *R*   13/81 rei sue : *om. C*   13/83 teneatur *CW* : tenetur *R*

should come first for two reasons. First, because although restitution is directed to satisfaction, restitution should be directed where there is greater need of satisfaction. Now there is greater need of satisfaction in the cases of theft and robbery than in usury, because greater injury is inflicted in these two, for the usurpation of another's property by theft or robbery is utterly involuntary, while the usurpation of usury is, in a sense, voluntary. And so it follows that restitution should be made to the victim of usurpation by theft or robbery before the victim of usury. Second, this is clear because the greater the legal compulsion, the more urgent the obligation to make satisfaction. Now there is greater legal compulsion to restore something extorted by theft or robbery than something extorted by usury. For we see that one is compelled to restore something stolen or robbed not only by divine and canon law but also by civil law; but usury only by canon and divine law. And so it follows that the usurer should restore something extorted by theft or robbery before something extorted by usury.

A fourth question that arises in connection with this issue is whether, assuming a usurer cannot completely repay the one from whom he has extorted something by theft or robbery and one from whom he has extorted something by usury, he should pay each proportionately or one or other of the two. I respond that he should make complete restitution to the one from whom he extorted something by theft or robbery, and this is clear for two reasons. First, because we see that he is compelled by civil law to make complete restitution of theft or robbery, notwithstanding this should render him incapable of restoring usury in full. Second, this is clear because restitution to one who has been despoiled completely against his will should not be inhibited by restitution to one who was willingly despoiled. But such is the situation in the proposed case, for he who has been despoiled completely against his will is the victim of usurpation by theft or robbery, and he who has been despoiled, in a sense, of his own free will is the victim of usurpation by usury, therefore the restitution of the first should under no circumstances be impeded by restitution of the second.

A fifth question is whether a usurer is obliged to restore usury extorted

quam extorsit pauperibus quam illam quam extorsit divitibus. Ad hoc au-
85 tem dicendum quod ex caritate prius debet restituere pauperibus quam
divitibus, et quod ita sit apparet, nam illa restitucio prius videtur fienda
ex caritate per quam magis vitatur dampnum proximi. Nunc autem magis
vitatur dampnum proximi per restitucionem que fit pauperibus quam per
illam que fit divitibus, quia pauperes magis leduntur per dilacionem resti-
90 tucionis quam divites; ergo prius est fienda restitucio usurarum ex caritate
pauperibus quam divitibus. Si tamen queratur ulterius, dato quod usurarius non possit satisfacere in solidum pauperibus et divitibus, utrum debeat
satisfacere in solidum solis pauperibus aut utrisque pro rata, dico quod
debet satisfacere utrisque pro rata, nam quia illa obligacio qua per usura-
95 rum extorsionem est obligatus pauperibus et divitibus est eiusdem racionis, idcirco solucio illius obligacionis eodem modo se extendit ad omnes.

Sextum et ultimum dubium circa istum articulum est utrum usurarius
debeat prius restituere illis a quibus prius usuras extorsit. Ad hoc ergo
dicendum quod ubi dilacio restitucionis non inferat maius dampnum pos-
100 terioribus quam prioribus sed equaliter se habent condiciones ex parte
utrorumque, ibi racionabiliter videtur quod debeat restitucio fieri secundum illum ordinem secundum quem facta est usurarum extorsio, dummodo possit hoc congrue fieri, nam ubi ex parte restituendorum ponuntur
condiciones equales, qui prius fuit spoliatus est magis gravatus propter di-
105 lacionem restitucionis et ideo prius debet restitui, quia qui magis gravatus
est prius allevari debet. Intelligendum tamen quod si usurarius non posset
omnibus in solidum restituere, deberet pro rata omnibus solvere, quia cum
obligacio sit eiusdem racionis respectu omnium, non debent posteriores
pati detrimentum in restitucione propter priores.
110 Ista ergo sunt dubia que circa istum articulum mihi sunt visa posse mo-
veri. Apparet ergo ex hiis omnibus quem ordinem debeat servare usurarius
in restituendo.

Apparent insuper omnia illa que superius promisi declarare circa restitucionem usurarum.

13/84–5 Ad hoc autem dicendum : Dico *W*   13/87 vitatur *CW* : videatur *R*   13/87 autem *CW* : nec *R*   13/90–1 prius … divitibus : et cetera *W*   13/92 satisfacere : satisfaccio
W   13/93 solis : *om. W*   13/93–4 dico … rata *W* : Ad quod dicendum quod pro rata
utrisque *C* : *om. per hom. R*   13/94–6 nam quia … ad omnes : *om. W*   13/97 circa
istum articulum : *om. W*   13/98–9 Ad hoc ergo dicendum : Dico *W*   13/98 ergo : *om.*
C   13/101 debeat : debet *W*   13/101 fieri *CW* : *om. R*   13/103 hoc : id *C*   13/106 allevari : alleviari *C* : levari *W*   13/109 pati *CW* : patet *R*   13/110 mihi : *om. W*   13/111 debeat : debet *W*   13/113–14 Apparent … usurarum : et cetera. Gerardus de Senis. *W*

from the poor before that which he extorted from the rich. The response is that charity demands he make restitution first to the poor and only then to the rich, and that this is so is clear, for charity demands that the restitution that rectifies a greater injury to your neighbour should take priority. Now a greater injury to your neighbour is rectified by restitution to the poor than to the rich because the poor suffer greater injury by the postponement of restitution than do the rich, and so charity demands that restitution be made to the poor before the rich. But if it is asked further whether, assuming the usurer cannot completely satisfy both poor and rich, he should make complete satisfaction to the poor alone or to both proportionately, I say that he should satisfy each proportionately, for inasmuch as the grounds of his obligation to restore extorted usury is the same for both poor and rich, so should the payment of the obligation be the same for each.

The sixth and last question of this article is whether a usurer should restore usury first to those from he extorted it first. The response is that when the deferral of restitution would not impose a greater injury on more recent than on earlier creditors, but rather all things are equal, it seems reasonable that restitution follow the order of extortion, provided this can be done appropriately. For, all things being equal, from the perspective of those who should receive restitution, he who was despoiled first is more burdened by delay of restitution and so should be compensated first, for he who is more burdened should be relieved first. But it should be understood that if a usurer cannot make complete restitution to all, he ought to pay them proportionately, because although the grounds for his obligation is the same with respect to all, later creditors should not suffer some injury in restitution on account of earlier ones.

Such therefore are the questions that it seems to me ought to be raised with regard to this article. It is clear from what has been said what order a usurer should observe in making restitution.

Moreover, all the things I promised earlier to clarify regarding the restitution of usury are now clear.

Questio de prescriptione

A Question on Prescription

\<14\> \<Questio de prescriptione\>

^{R219r} Incipit questio de prescripcione cum VI articulis infrascriptis deter-
minata a fratre Gerardo de Senis in sacra scriptura magistro fratrum heremitarum ordinis sancti Augustini.

5   Vtrum prescripcio sit contra ius nature. Et videtur quod non, quia nullum ius positivum prestat favorem ei quod est contra ius nature; sed ius canonicum et civile prestant favorem ipsi prescripcioni, ergo prescripcio non
est contra ius nature. Maior videtur nota, quia quodlibet ius positivum
supponit ius nature sicut suum fundamentum et per consequens nullum
10   tale ius potest prestare favorem ei quod est contra ius nature; minor autem
apparet de facto, quia prescripcio est introducta a iure canonico et civili et
per consequens utrumque ius prestat ei favorem.

Ad oppositum arguitur: quia contra ius nature est quod aliquis ditetur
cum detrimento alterius iuxta illud quod habetur ff. *de regulis iuris*: 'iure,'
15   inquit, 'nature equum est neminem cum alterius detrimento et iniuria fieri
locupletiorem.' In prescripcione autem fit prescribens dicior cum detrimento alterius, ut de se apparet, ergo et cetera.

Respondeo: in ista questione VI sunt videnda. Primo quid est prescripcio? Secundo utrum prescripcio sit contra ius nature. Tertio utrum pre-
20   scripcio iuris canonici debuerit esse alia et distincta a prescripcione
iuris civilis. Quarto utrum in prescripcione acquiratur dominium. Quinto
utrum prescribens mala fide sit censendus cum raptore vel in aliqua alia
specie peccati locandus et utrum teneatur ad restitucionem sicut raptor;
et per hoc patebit quid sit dicendum ad illud quod in ista questione prin-
25   cipaliter est quesitum. Sexto erit videndum utrum mala fides adveniens
prescripcione completa obliget ad restitucionem.

\<15\> \<Articulus primus\>

Primus articulus, in quo ostenditur quid sit prescripcio et datur quedam
nova descripcio.

14/2–4 Incipit ... Augustini *om. C*   14/13 ditetur *C* : dicitur *R*   14/16 locupletiorem
corr. al. man. ex locupletionem *R*   15/2 Primus articulus ... nova descriptio : *om. C*

14/14–16 Dig. 50.17.206(207).

A Question on Prescription

14. *Here begins the question on prescription in six articles determined by Brother Gerard of Siena, master of sacred scripture of the hermit brothers of the order of Saint Augustine.*

The question is whether prescription is contrary to the law of nature. And it appears that it is not, because no positive law approves anything contrary to the law of nature; but canon and civil law approve prescription, therefore it is not contrary to the law of nature. The major premiss seems clear because all positive law presupposes the law of nature as its foundation and consequently no such law can approve anything contrary to the law of nature. The minor premiss is evident inasmuch as prescription has been introduced by canon and civil law, and consequently both laws approve it.

On the contrary it may be argued that something that enriches someone to the detriment of another is contrary to the law of nature, in accordance with the rule of law in the Digest that says, 'by the law of nature it is fair that no one become richer by the loss and injury of another.' But it is evident that in prescription the prescriber is enriched to the detriment of another, therefore et cetera.

I respond that there are six points to be considered in this question. First, what prescription is. Second, whether prescription is contrary to the law of nature. Third, whether prescription in canon law is different from prescription in civil law. Fourth, whether ownership is acquired by means of prescription. Fifth, whether one who prescribes in bad faith is to be condemned as a robber. In this way it will be clear what the principal response to the question will be. But sixth, we must see whether bad faith emerging after prescription is complete imposes an obligation to make restitution.

15. Article 1

The first article, in which it is shown what prescription is and it is given a new definition.

Est ergo primo videndum quid sit prescripcio, quia nisi hoc sciatur non
5 poterunt bene sciri ea que in sequentibus sunt tractanda. Intelligendum
autem quod prescripcio sic uno modo consuevit describi: 'est exceptio ex
tempore substantiam capiens.' Hec descripcio ponitur a glossatore XVI q.
III *Quod autem*; in qua descripcione duo ponuntur, ex quibus prescripcio
notificari videtur. Primum est effectus quem prescripcio efficit; secundum
10 est causa que prescripcionem inducit. Effectus quem prescripcio efficit
tangitur cum premictitur 'prescripcio est excepcio,' ut intelligatur ista pre-
dicacio esse causalis et non essencialis. Et secundum hoc erit talis sensus:
'prescripcio est excepcio,' id est, est causa excepcionis, quemadmodum si
diceremus fumalis evaporacio pomi est odor, non quod sit essentialiter
15 odor sed quia est causa odoris. Intelligendum tamen quod quamvis prescripcio possit habere aliquem alium effectum, utpote acquisicionem dominii, secundum quosdam, quia tamen dictus effectus non est ei necessario
adnexus, cum possit esse aliqua prescripcio sine acquisicione dominii, scilicet prescripcio male fidei, in qua acquiritur sola excepcio, cuius signum
20 quia si prescribens mala fide a possessione cadat, non habet actionem ulterius respondendi, ut patet XVI q. III *Placuit*. Idcirco talis effectus non
debuit poni in sua descripcione, nam ubi causa describitur per effectum
oportet quod effectus qui ponitur in eius descripcione sit ei semper et necessario adnexus. Exceptio autem est talis effectus qui semper et necessario
25 adnectatur ipsi prescripcioni.

Quod patet per racionem et induccionem. Per racionem quidem quia
nisi prescripcio haberet semper et necessario adnexum istum effectum,
sequeretur quod erit sine omni effectu, nam ubi tollatur ab ea excepcio,
oportet dicere quod tollatur ab ea acquisicio dominii et quicumque alius
30 effectus, et per consequens frustra fuisset inducta, quia ibi nullam haberet
efficaciam, quod nullus diceret. Secundo patet hoc idem per induccionem,

---

15/6 sic *C* : sit *R*   15/6–7 est exceptio … capiens *C* : *om. R.*   15/8 III : c. *add.*
C   15/9 notificari : verificari *C*   15/21 III : c. *add. C*   15/22 sua : eius *C*   15/22 per :
suum *add. C*   15/23 semper *C* : senis (!) *R*   15/25 adnectatur : adnectitur *C*   15/26 et
induccionem. Per racionem *C* : *om. per hom. R*   15/28 erit : esset *C*

15/6–8 Gl. ord. ad dictum Grat. ante Decretum Grat. C.16 q.3 c.1, v. *Quod autem praescriptione* (ed. cit. col. 1114).   15/21 Decretum Grat. C.16 q.3 c.15.

We must first understand what prescription is because, unless we grasp this, it is impossible to understand the things that will be treated in the following articles. It should be understood, then, that one way in which prescription is customarily described is as follows: 'prescription is a defence that takes its substance from time.' This definition is noted by the glossator at C.16 q.3 c.1 and contains two features by which it seems that prescription is recognized: the first is the effect of prescription, the second its cause. The effect of prescription is touched on in the phrase 'prescription is a defence,' by which we must understand that the predication is causal not essential. Accordingly, the sense of 'prescription is a defence' is that prescription is the cause of a defence, just as we might say that the gassy exhalation of an apple is an odour, not in the sense that it is an odour in essence but that it is the cause of an odour. It must be understood, therefore, that although prescription could have some other effect, such as (according to some) the acquisition of ownership, nevertheless such an effect is not necessarily inherent in it, because prescription can exist without acquisition of ownership – for example, prescription in bad faith, by which only a defence is obtained – and the evidence of this is that if the prescriber loses possession, he has no further grounds for legal action, as is clear at C.16 q.3 c.15. Therefore, such an effect cannot be included in the definition, for when a cause is described by its effect it is necessary that the effect included in the definition be one that always and necessarily inheres in it. Now defence is an effect that always and necessarily attaches to prescription.

This is clear by reason and induction because unless an effect always and necessarily adhered to prescription, it would follow that it had no effect, for if the defence were removed, then one could also say that acquisition of ownership and every other effect is removed, and consequently the reasoning would be meaningless, because it would be completely without effect, which no one would argue. Second, the same is clear by induction,

nam si inducamus in singulis speciebus prescripcionis semper inveniemus quod ipse prescribens habet exceptionem excludentem actionem que contra se fieret in re prescripta; quia cum longum esset per omnes species
35   prescripcionis transcurrere, sufficit si in duabus vel in tribus inducamus.

Sciendum ergo quod una species prescripcionis est que currit spacio duorum vel trium dierum contra non appellantem, ut patet 2 q. VI *Biduum*. In hac ergo prescripcione acquiritur excepcio excludens accionem, quia non appellans, transcurso dicto spacio dierum, non habet ulterius accionem
40   ad sententiam contra se latam. Est alia prescripcio que currit spacio trium mensium, que currit capitulo non eligente, ut patet L dist. *Postquam*. In qua eciam prescripcione acquiritur excepcio excludens accionem, quia capitulum non eligens transcurso spacio trium mensium non habet ulterius actionem per quam possit resumere vel recuperare ius eligendi. Vlterius est
45   alia prescripcio que currit spacio trium annorum cum dimidio contra episcopum qui aliquem locum ad suam cathedram pertinentem negligit convertere ad catholicam unitatem, ut patet *extra de prescrip*-|^{R219v}-*cionibus* c. I *Placuit*. Nam sicut notat ibi glosa que concordat illud capitulum cum illo alio capitulo quod habetur XVI q. III et incipit eodem modo, si aliquis
50   episcoporum vicinorum moneat talem episcopum negligentem et ipse non obstante tali monicione negligens fuerit per VI menses, poterit episcopus monens dictum locum seu dictam plebem convertere quod, si post illos VI menses possederit eam postea per tres annos, excepcione tutus erit. Ex quo apparet immediate quod in hac eciam prescripcione acquiritur excepcio
55   excludens accionem quia transcurso spacio trium annorum et VI mensium quibus precessit amonicio non habet episcopus negligens ulterius accio-

---

15/34 quia : quare *C*   15/35 tribus : si *add. R*   15/36 est *C* : *om. R*   15/36–7 duorum vel trium *C* : *om. R*   15/37 Biduum *C* : Bunum *R* : c. *add. C*   15/39 transcurso : transacto *C*   15/39 habet : habetur *C*   15/41 dist. : capitulo *add. C*   15/42-3 capitulum *C* : capituli *R*   15/43 transcurso : transacto *C*   15/48 I : *om. C*   15/48 Placuit : ut si quisquam et 16 q. 3 c. Placuit ut quicunque *add. C*   15/48-9 illud capitulum … eodem modo : ibi utrumque capitulum *C*   15/50 ipse *C* : ipso *R*   15/51 poterit : dictus *add. C*   15/52 seu *C* : ut *R*   15/52 dictam : *om. C*   15/53 postea : *om. C*   15/55 transcurso : transacto *C*   15/55 et : insuper *add. C*   15/56 amonicio : monitio *C*   15/56 negligens : negligligens *per ditt. R*

15/37 Decretum Grat. C.2 q.6 c.29.   15/41 Decretum Grat. D.50 c.11.   15/47–8 X 2.26.1.   15/48 Gl. ord. ad X 2.26.1, v. *Per ipsum triennium* (ed. Lyons, 1559, col. 782).   15/49 Decretum Grat. C.16 q.3 c.15.

for if we consider specific examples of prescription, we shall always find that the prescriber has a defence that excludes an action against him for the thing prescribed. Since it would take too long to review all the forms of prescription, it will suffice if we consider one or two examples.

One form of prescription lasts for a period of two or three days if unchallenged, as is clear at C.2 q.6 c.29. This form of prescription confers a defence that excludes an action, because after the period of two or three days has elapsed, the appellant has no further action against the sentence pronounced against him. A second kind of prescription lasts for a period of three months and occurs when a chapter fails to elect, as is clear at D.50 c.11. This form of prescription confers a defence that excludes an action because after the period of three months has elapsed and the chapter has not elected, it has no further action by which it could resume or recover the right of election. A third form of prescription lasts for a period of three and a half years against a bishop who neglects to convert some place under his jurisdiction to Catholic unity, as is clear at X 2.26.1. For as the gloss – which relates this decretal to the chapter in the decrees at C.16 q.3 c.15 that begins with the same word – says, if a neighbouring bishop admonishes his colleague for negligence and he nevertheless fails to act for six months, the admonisher is free to convert the place or parish; if he remains in possession for three years, he is secure in his defence. Now it is quite clear that this form of prescription confers a defence precluding an action, because once a period of three years and six months from the admonition has elapsed, the negligent bishop has no further action for recovering the parish that belonged to his see. And so it is true to say that

nem ad recuperandum plebem que ad suam cathedram pertinebat, et ita
ut sic ad unum dicere sicut in istis tribus speciebus prescripcionis ita et in
omnibus aliis semper acquiritur ipsi prescribenti excepcio excludens ac-
60   cionem. Quapropter bene dicebatur superius quod primum quod ponitur
in descripcione prescripcionis, est effectus quem prescripcio efficit, et iste
effectus est excepcio excludens accionem, ut superius est ostensum.

Secundum quod ponitur in eius descripcione est causa que prescripcionem inducit, et ista tangitur cum in dicta descripcione additur 'ex tempore
65   substanciam capiens,' nam secundum istam clausulam videtur quod ipsum tempus sit causa inducens prescripcionem. Quod eciam videtur posse
probari racione, illud namque quod exspectat temporis determinacionem
et temporis implecionem videtur capere suam substanciam ex tempore.
Prescripcio est huiusmodi quia videmus quod prescripcio nulla est nisi
70   sit prima determinacio temporis facta per legem. Vlterius videmus quod
prescripcio non currit nec habet vim nisi impleto illo tempore quod est per
legem determinatum, quapropter bene dictum est quod exspectat temporis determinacionem et temporis implecionem ac per consequens quod ex
tempore capiat illam substanciam.

75   Ex quibus omnibus apparet quod diffinicio vel descripcio superius data
de prescripcione sit satis racionabilis, tum quia tangit effectum quem prescripcio efficit, tum eciam quia tangit causam que prescripcionem inducit.
Intelligendum tamen quod quamvis dicta descripcio possit racionabiliter
sustineri, videtur tamen diminuta et insufficiens propter tria. Primo quia
80   videtur pretendere quod tempus sit causa ex qua prescripcio suam efficaciam capit, quod patet esse falsum, nam cum tempus sit quid naturale,
sequeretur quod prescripcio haberet causam naturalem ac per consequens
ipsa et sua virtus esset quid naturale et a natura, quod nullus diceret.

Secundo defficit dicta descripcio quia pretermictit causam principalem,
85   ex qua prescripcio suam efficaciam capit, scilicet legum auctoritatem. Capit enim prescripcio suam efficaciam non ex tempore sed ex legum auctoritate.

15/58 sic ad unum : sit verum *C*   15/58 prescripcionis *C* : prescripcionibus *R*
15/59 omnibus *C* : racionibus *R*   15/60 ponitur : ponebatur *C*   15/63–4 prescripcionem
C : perscripcionem *R*   15/64 tangitur : in ista *add. et exp. R*   15/68 implecionem *C* :
impleciorem *R*   15/74 substanciam : ei *add. et exp. R*   15/86 ex^2 : *om. C*

15/62 Vid. sup. 15/10–25.   15/64–5 Vid. sup. 15/6–7.

just as these three forms of prescription confer a defence that precludes an action, likewise all the others. Therefore, the first element of the definition of prescription offered above is well formulated, namely, that the effect of prescription is a defence that precludes an action.

The second element included in the definition of prescription is its cause, which is indicated by the phrase 'takes its substance from time,' which seems to suggest that time is the cause that gives rise to prescription. This appears to be demonstrable by reason, for that which looks to time for its limit and completion appears to derive its substance from time. Now prescription seems to be such a thing, for we see that prescription is nothing other than a limit of time established by law. Furthermore, we see that prescription has no force unless the period of time set by law has expired. Thus it is well said that prescription looks to time for its limit and completion, and consequently that it derives its substance from time.

From these points it is clear that the definition of prescription offered above conforms to reason because it embraces both the effect of prescription and its cause. Nevertheless, it must be understood that although the definition can be sustained by reason, it appears inadequate and insufficient for three reasons. First, because it seems to indicate that time is the cause from which prescription draws its efficacy, which is clearly false: because time is a natural thing, it follows that prescription has a natural cause and consequently that its force is something natural derived from nature, which no one would maintain.

Second, the definition is wanting because it ignores the principal cause from which prescription draws its efficacy, namely the authority of the law. For prescription draws its efficacy not from time, but from the authority of the law.

Tercio, defficit et est diminuta eadem descripcio quia pretermictit causam finalem propter quam fuit inventa prescripcio, que tamen causa finalis
90 maxime debet accipi in diffinicione vel descripcione cuiuscumque rei eo
quod per eam maxime habet quecumque res innotescere et notificari.

Et ideo propter omnia ista videtur danda alia descripcio de prescripcione, que talis sit que tangat modum secundum quem tempus ad prescripcionem concurrit; tangat eciam causam efficientem, que prescripcioni
95 efficaciam tribuit; tangat insuper causam finalem propter quam prescripcio adinventa fuit.

Ad que tria explicanda videtur quod prescripcio sic possit diffiniri vel
describi: prescripcio est ius quoddam ex tempore congruens legum auctoritate vim capiens, penam negligentibus inferens, et finem litibus ponens.
100 In hac ergo descripcione tanguntur illa tria que superius sunt prefata. Primo namque tangitur modus secundum quem tempus ad prescripcionem
necessario concurrit, non enim concurrit ibi tamquam causa prebens ei efficaciam, sicut pretendebat prima descripcio, sed tamquam causa prebens
ei congruenciam quemadmodum pretendit descripcio nunc data. Nam nisi
105 esset determinatum tempus per quod posset deffectus negligencium deprehendi non congrue nec iuste vel racionabiliter posset contra eos ius
prescripcionis institui.

Tota ergo causa quare prescripcio temporis determinacionem et implecionem expectat est ut, scilicet per illius determinati temporis cursum,
110 defectus negligencium inexcusabilis cognoscatur. Illius autem negligencie
inexcusabilis cognicio prebet congruam et iustam materiam prescribendi, nam cognito quod negligencia illius in repeticione sue rei est omnino
inexcussabilis, congruum est et iustum ut per penam excepcionis a legibus
puniatur. Tunc autem leges per penam excepcionis puniunt negligentem
115 quando contra eum auctoritatem tribuunt prescribendi.

Ex quo apparet immediate quod sicut prescripcio trahit suam congruenciam ex temporis determinacione, ita eciam trahit suam efficaciam ex

---

15/92 videtur : dicenda *add. et exp.* R   15/94 tangat C : tangeat R   15/108 Tota : ratio et
add. C   15/109 est C : *om.* R   15/110 cognoscatur C : cognoscat R   15/114 puniunt C :
puniuntur R

Third, the definition is wanting because it ignores the final cause on account of which prescription was devised, although the final cause should certainly be included in the definition of any thing, because it is above all the final cause that allows us to recognize and understand a thing.

For these reasons, it appears necessary to provide a second definition of prescription which is such that it embraces the function of time in prescription, the efficient cause of prescription (which gives it its efficacy), and the final cause on account of which prescription was devised.

Taking all three into account, it seems that prescription could be defined or described as follows: 'prescription is a certain right that derives its fitness from time, draws its force from the authority of law, imposes a penalty on the negligent, and places a limit on lawsuits.' This definition embraces all three elements mentioned above. First of all, it touches on the way in which time is implicated in prescription, not as the cause that endows it with efficacy, as the first definition suggested, but as a cause that endows it with fitness, as the second definition suggests. For unless there is a defined period of time during which the fault of the negligent is revealed, the right of prescription could not be fitly, justly, or reasonably invoked against them.

The entire reason why prescription looks to time for its limit and fulfilment is so that, in the course of a determined period of time, it might reveal the inexcusable fault of the negligent. Now the revelation of such inexcusable negligence confers a fit and just ground for prescription, for when it has been revealed that the negligence of someone in recovering his property is inexcusable, it is fitting that he be punished by the law through the penalty of the defence granted to the prescriber; and the laws punish the negligent by the penalty of the defence when they grant the authority to prescribe against him.

From this it is quite clear that just as prescription draws its fitness from the determination of time, it also draws its efficacy from the authority of

legum auctoritate, propter quod bene dicebatur supra quod prima descripcio est diminuta et insufficiens, eo quod ponit tempus esse causa ex qua
120   prescripcio efficaciam capit ac per consequens deficiebat. Quapropter di-
camus quod in ista secunda descripcione tangitur primo modus secundum
quem tempus ad prescripcionem necessario concurrit, nam concurrit ibi
tamquam causa prebens congruenciam et non tamquam causa prebens efficaciam; propter quod bene dicitur in prima particula descripcionis quod
125   prescripcio est ius ex tempore congruens. Secundo, ut dicebatur in eadem
descripcione, tangitur causa principalis prescripcioni tribuens efficaciam,
et hec est auctoritas legum, ut superius est dictum, et ista tangitur in secunda particula prefate descripcionis, in qua dicitur quod prescripcio est ius
auctoritate legum vim capiens.

130   Tercio, in eadem descripcione tangitur causa finalis propter quam prescripcio adinventa fuit, enim inventa prescripcio propter duplicem finem,
scilicet ut penam negligentibus inferret et ut finem litibus imponeret,
quemadmodum et usucapio, ut patet ff. *de usucapionibus* l. *Bono publico*;
dicitur enim ibi quod 'usucapio est introducta ne quarumdam rerum do-
135   minium diu et fere semper incerta essent.' Ex hoc autem sequitur duplex
prefatus finis, quia tam usucapio quam eciam prescripcio dominia distin-
guendo penam negligentibus infligit et finem litibus imponit. Iste autem
duplex finis tangitur in tercia particula prefate descripcionis cum dicitur
quod prescripcio est ius penam negligentibus inferens et finem litibus im-
140   ponens.

       Intelligendum tamen omnibus ulterius quod Papias ponit tria significata
de prescripcione que videntur respondere tribus prefatis particulis posi-
tis in dicta descripcione. Dicit enim quod prescribere uno modo idem est
quod predicere, alio modo idem est quod contradicere, tercio modo idem
145   est quod diffinire. Hec autem tria significata recte concordant cum tribus

---

15/118 legum : a *add. et exp.* R   15/119–20 est diminuta … prescripcio C : *om.* R
15/123 congruentiam : congruentia C   15/126 tribuens C : tribuit R   15/131 fuit : fuit
add. C   15/131 propter C : per R   15/133 usucapio C : usupacio R   15/134–5 dominium : dominia C   15/136 quam C : quod R   15/141 tamen omnibus : *om.* C   15/142 de
prescripcione : praescriptionis C   15/144 tercio : alio C

15/118–19 Vid. sup. 15/79–83.   15/124–9 Vid. sup. 15/98–9.   15/130–2 Vid. sup.
15/99.   15/133 Dig. 41.3.1.   15/139–40 Vid. sup. 15/99.   15/141–5 Papias, *Elementarium doctrinae erudimentum*, v. *Prescribit* (ed. Venice, 1491, fol. 133vb).

the law, and for this reason it was noted earlier that the first definition is insufficient because it posits time as the cause from which prescription draws it efficacy, and is consequently defective. Thus, we should say that the second definition embraces first the way in which time is necessarily involved in prescription, namely as a cause endowing it with fitness, not as a cause endowing it with efficacy. For this reason it was well put in the first element of the definition that 'prescription is a right that derives its fitness from time.' Second, it embraces the principal cause that endows prescription with its efficacy and this, as was noted above, is the authority of the law. And this is the second element of the definition, where it is said that 'prescription is a right that draws its force from the authority of law.'

Third, the definition includes the final cause on account of which prescription was devised, because it was devised for a twofold purpose, namely, to impose a penalty on the negligent and to place a limit on lawsuits, as was usucapion, as is clear at Dig. 41.3.1, where it is said that 'usucapion was introduced so that the ownership of certain things should not be for a long period, possibly permanently, uncertain.' From this follows its twofold purpose, because, by clarifying ownership, both usucapion and prescription impose a penalty on the negligent and place a limit on lawsuits. This double purpose is included in the third element of the definition, where it is said that 'prescription is a right that imposes a penalty on the negligent, and places a limit on lawsuits.'

Moreover, it should be known that Papias assigns three meanings to 'prescription' that seem to correspond to the three elements of our definition. He says that, in one sense, 'to prescribe' is equivalent to 'to declare'; in another, 'to contradict'; and in a third, 'to define.' Now these three meanings accord with the three elements of the definition, for prescrip-

prefatis particulis, nam tunc prescripcio vere predicit quando tempus determinatum et congruum ad prescribendum instituit. Nunc vero contradicit quando contra negligentem auctoritate legum vim capit; tunc vero diffinit quando penam negligentibus infligit et finem in litibus imponit.

150   Ex quibus omnibus apparet quid sit prescripcio. Apparet et ulterius quod diffinicio vel descripcio superius data de ea sit bene assignata. Ideo est videndum secundo.

\<16\> \<Articulus secundus\>

Secundus articulus: utrum prescripcio sit contra ius nature.

Vtrum prescripcio sit contra ius nature. Vbi sciendum quod iurisperiti videntur communiter dicere quod ipsa sit contra |^{R220r} ius nature quia
5   contra naturalem equitatem, ut dicunt. Et ista oppinio manifeste habetur ff. *de usucap.* l. I, que incipit *Bono publico.* Dicit in glosa ergo ibi glossator quod usucapio introducta est 'ad utilitatem omnium communem contra naturalem equitatem' quia 'aliud est bonum, aliud est equum, ut C. *de pactis conve. supra dote* l. *Hac lege.*' Et quod dictum est de usucapione
10   potest dici de prescripcione; si ergo usucapio est introducta contra naturalem equitatem, et prescripcio. Insuper habetur eadem opinio XVI q. III *Quicumque*; in glosa dicit enim glosator quod 'de iure civili non sunt prescripciones inducte.' Fundamentum autem dicte opinionis sumitur ex una regula que habetur ff. *de regulis iuris*, que regula taliter est in scripto: 'iure,'
15   inquit, 'nature est equum neminem cum alterius detrimento fieri et iniuria

---

15/147 instituit : est *add. R*   15/147 Nunc : Tunc *C*   15/149 penam : veram *add. et exp. R*   15/149 infligit : inflligit *R*   15/149 in : *om. C*   15/151 diffinicio vel : *om. C*   16/2 Secundus ... nature : *om. C*   16/3 Vbi : *om. C*   16/4 quod *C* : *om. R*   16/6 l. I *C* : II *R*   16/6 Dicit ... glossator : ubi glossator inquit *C*   16/7 est : fuit *C*   16/8 equitatem : a *add. et exp. R*   16/9 conve. supra dote : *om. C*   16/9 l. : Ex *add. RC*   16/9 dictum est : dicendum est *C*   16/10 potest dici : dicendum est *C*   16/11 et prescripcio *C* : *vac. R*   16/11 III : q. *add. C*   16/12 in glosa ... glosator : ubi glosator inquit *C*   16/12–13 prescripciones *C* : prescripcionis *R*   16/14–16 que regula ... nature : quae inquit *C*

16/6 Dig. 41.3.1.   16/8–9 Gl. ord. ad Dig. 41.3.1, v. *Bono publico* (ed. Lyons, 1627, repr. Frankfurt am Main, 2007, col. 452); citing C. 5.14.8 (*recte* Hac lege).   16/11–13 Decretum Grat. C.16 q.3 c.4; gl. ord. ad Decretum Grat. C.16 q.3 c.4, v. *Legis* (ed. cit. col. 1116). For 'civili' the gloss reads 'naturali.'   16/13–16 Dig. 50.17.206(207).

tion 'declares' when it sets a determinate and fitting time for prescription; it 'contradicts' when it takes action against the negligent by the authority of the law; and it 'defines' when it imposes a penalty on the negligent and places a limit on lawsuits.

From the foregoing observations it is clear what prescription is. Furthermore, it is clear that the definition of it offered above is good. Let us, therefore, proceed to the second article.

16. Article 2

Article 2: whether prescription is contrary to the law of nature.

Is prescription contrary to the law of nature? It should be known that the jurists commonly say that prescription is contrary to the law of nature because it is contrary to natural equity. This opinion is clearly maintained at Dig. 41.3.1, and therefore the glossator notes there that usucapion was introduced 'for the common utility of all contrary to natural equity, because the good and the equitable are not the same thing, as at C. 5.14.8.' What is said of usucapion can also be said of prescription, so if usucapion was introduced contrary to natural equity, so was prescription. The same opinion, moreover, is maintained at C.16 q.3 c.4, for in the gloss the glossator says that 'prescriptions were not introduced by civil law.' The foundation of this opinion is taken from a rule of law at Dig. 50.17.206, which reads thus: 'by the law of nature it is fair that no one become richer by the loss and injury of another.' But it is the case that in prescription the pre-

fieri locuplectionem.' Constat autem quod in prescripcione fit prescribens locuplectionem cum alterius detrimento et iniuria ac per consequens videtur quod prescripcio sit contra ius nature.

Hiis tamen non obstantibus, videtur mihi quod nullo modo prescripcio sit contra ius nature seu contra equitatem naturalem; ymmo pocius iuri naturali et naturali equitati concordat, sicut infra probabitur. Ad maiorem tamen evidenciam omnium eorum que dicenda sunt, videndum est primo quid debeamus intelligere per ius naturale et quid per ius legale.

Sciendum ergo quod omne ius consistit in rectitudine quadam, nam ideo 'ius dictum est quia iustum est,' ut habetur in decretis di. I 'iusticia autem non est aliud quam quedam rectitudo.' Omne ergo ius, sive sit naturale sive sit legale, in rectitudine quadam consistit. Intelligendum tamen quod quamvis ius naturale et ius legale sint iura distincta, non tamen est eorum rectitudo diversa, immo est eadem rectitudo aliter et aliter sumpta; nam si bene consideramus, ius legale non addit supra ius naturale quandam aliam rectitudinem sed specificat illam eandem, ita ut verum sit dicere quod ius legale est quedam specificacio naturalis rectitudinis expressiva. Habet enim ius legale specificare et explicare naturalis iuris rectitudinem tripliciter, scilicet quandoque eam determinando per congruos modos, quandoque vero eam applicando ad varios actus, quandoque vero eam declarando per quosdam euentus; et quod ita sit apparet si discurramus per omnes istos tres modos. Videmus enim quandoque quod ius legale assumit rectitudinem iuris naturalis et eam specificat determinando per congruos modos, sicut, verbi gratia, assumit a iure naturali quod rectum est quod ille qui peccat puniatur sed non habet ab eo determinatum modum punicionis. Et ideo postea determinat istam rectitudinem per congruos modos, utpote determinat quod ille qui peccat tali peccato puniatur tali poena, ille vero qui peccat alio peccato puniatur alia pena secundum quod conditor iuris legalis viderit talem vel talem penam magis vel minus congrue tali peccato.

Vlterius videmus secundo quod ius legale quandoque assumit rectitudinem iuris naturalis et eam specificat applicando ad varios actus, sicut,

---

16/25 ut : quod *exp. R* : ut *interlin. al. man. R* : sic *C*   16/28 sint *C* : sit *R*   16/31 sed *C* : si *R*   16/32 est : sit *C*   16/33 rectitudinem : simpliciter *add. et exp. R*   16/35 vero[1] : *om. C*

16/25–6 Decretum Grat. D.1 c.2. Cf. gl. ord. ad Dig. 1.1.1, v. *Iustitia* (ed. cit. col. 14).

scriber is enriched at the expense and injury of another, and consequently it seems that prescription is contrary to the law of nature.

These observations notwithstanding, it seems to me that prescription is not at all contrary to the law of nature or to natural equity, but rather in accordance with them, as shall be demonstrated below. By way of a clearer demonstration of all that will be said, it is necessary first to consider what we understand by natural and positive law.

Now it should be understood that all law consists in a certain equity, for 'law (*ius*) is so called because it is just,' as is held in the decrees at D.1 c.2: 'justice is nothing other than a certain equity.' Therefore every law, whether natural or positive, consists in a certain equity. But it must be understood that although natural and positive law are distinct, they do not differ with respect to equity; indeed, equity is presupposed by each. For on consideration, it is clear that positive law does not add some additional equity to natural law but simply renders it more specific, so that it is true to say that positive law represents a specification of natural equity. For it is the office of positive law to specify and explicate the equity of natural law in three ways: sometimes by expressing it by appropriate means; sometimes by applying it to various actions; and sometimes by declaring it through certain results. And that this is so is clear if we review these three ways. Thus we see that positive law assumes and specifies the equity of natural law by appropriate means as, for example, when it assumes on the basis of natural law that something is right and that he who sins should be punished, but does not deduce from natural law a specific form of punishment. And so it proceeds to give equity a determinate form by appropriate means insofar as it specifies that one kind of sinner is punished in one way, another in another, as it seems good to the lawmaker that the punishment fits the sin.

Second, it must be understood that positive law sometimes assumes and specifies the equity of natural law by applying it to various acts as, for

verbi gratia, assumit a iure naturali quod rectum est nulli subtrahere quod suum est; non tamen habet ab eo qui sunt illi actus qui a dicta rectitudine deviant et qui illi actus qui dictam rectitudinem servant. Et ideo ut pos-
50   sint cognosci illi actus ad quos dicta rectitudo potest applicari distinguit ius legale omnes illos actus qui possunt a dicta rectitudine deviare, utpote distinguit inter actum furandi, rapiendi et fenerandi, quia omnes isti actus a dicta rectitudine deviare videntur. Ostendit insuper ius legale quomodo unus istorum actuum magis deviat ab illa rectitudine quam alius, et quo-
55   modo unus et idem actus aliter et aliter circumstancionatus magis et minus ab illa rectitudine deviat. Propter quod eciam ulterius prohibet omnes dictos actus comminando penam per quodlibet eorum maiorem vel minorem secundum quod a dicta rectitudine magis vel minus deviat. Prohibicio autem dictorum actuum est illius naturalis rectitudinis applicacio, quia per
60   hoc quod dictus actus cavetur, prefata rectitudo iuris naturalis in humanis actibus invenitur. In tali ergo casu apparet manifeste quod ius legale non addit supra ius naturale quandam specialem rectitudinem sed specificat illam eandem eo modo quo superius est expressum. Quemadmodum eciam videmus in scienciis speculativis quod in suis conclusionibus non addunt
65   quasdam speciales veritates distinctas a veritatibus principiorum generalium, immo specificant illas easdem applicando eas ad varias conclusiones quia illa eadem veritas que in principiis generalibus est confusa et indeterminata, applicata ad speciales conclusiones specificatur et sit distincta et determinata, ita ergo suo modo debemus ymaginari in proposito, quia
70   rectitudo iuris naturalis confusa et indeterminata existens applicatur per ius legale ad varios actus in quibus postea specificatur ac per consequens distincta et determinata efficitur.

Vlterius videmus tercio quod ius legale quandoque assumit rectitudinem iuris naturalis et eam specificat declarando per quosdam eventus,
75   sicut verbi gratia assumit a iure naturali quod rectum est neminem cum alterius detrimento et iniuria esse locuplectiorem. Non potest tamen haberi a dicto iure utrum sit possibile ad eventus vel aliquis casus in quo quis possit locuplectari cum alterius detrimento et sine eius iniuria, et ideo postea specificat et declarat intellectum dicte regule in quibusdam casibus in

---

16/47 assumit : enim *add. R* : *om. C*   16/47 iure : civili *add. et exp. R*   16/49 qui illi :
om. C   16/53 videntur *C* : *om. R*   16/56–7 dictos : istos *C*   16/61 manifeste : veritas *C*
16/65 a veritatibus *C* : et veritates *R*   16/68 applicata : *om. C*   16/69 quia : quod *C*
16/71 postea : prius ea *C*   16/77 vel aliquis : nullus *C*   16/78 sine : cum *C*

example, when it assumes on the basis of natural law that it is right not to take what belongs to another, but does not deduce from natural law which acts deviate from, and which ones preserve, equity. In order, therefore, that the acts to which equity is applicable may be recognized, positive law makes distinctions between acts that may deviate from equity when it distinguishes between acts of theft, robbery, and usury, all of which appear to deviate from equity. Moreover, positive law shows how one of these deviates from equity more than the other and how one and the same act deviates more or less from equity under different circumstances. For this reason, it prohibits all such acts by threatening a greater or lesser punishment for each according as it deviates more or less from equity. The prohibition of such acts is the application of natural equity because the equity of natural law is revealed in human deeds to the degree that we guard against such acts. In this case, it is completely clear that positive law does not add some special equity to natural law, but rather renders it more specific in the way described above. In the same way, we see that in their conclusions the speculative sciences do not add certain special truths distinct from those of general principles, but rather render them more specific by application to various conclusions. For when a truth that is indistinct and indeterminate in general principles is applied to specific conclusions, it is rendered specific, distinct, and determinate. Likewise with regard to the proposition: we should conceive of the equity of natural law as indistinct and indeterminate until it is applied by positive law to various acts, in which it is then rendered specific and consequently distinct and determinate.

Third, it must be understood that positive law sometimes assumes and specifies the equity of natural law by declaring it through certain results, as, for example, when it takes from natural law the principle that it is right that no one be enriched to the detriment and injury of another. For it cannot be deduced from the natural law as it stands whether in practice there is any case in which someone could be enriched to the detriment of another but with no injury to him, and so positive law specifies and declares

80   quibus aliquis potest locuplectari cum alterius detrimento et sine eius iniu-
     ria, sicut in prescripcionibus et usucapientibus, eo quod in eis inferuntur
     alicui dampna et tamen non inrogatur ei iniuria. Nam videmus manifeste
     quod ille contra quem currit prescripcio, quamvis patiatur dampnum, non
     patitur iniuriam, quia ipse propter suam negligenciam meretur pati dam-
85   pnum et idcirco in tali casu, quamvis videatur recedi ab intellectu quem re-
     gula pretendit secundum literam, non tamen receditur ab intellectu quem
     regula intendit secundum veram intelligenciam. Nam si dicta regula iuris
     nature in omni casu ad literam servaretur, a duabus aliis regulis iuris nature
     expresse recederet. Et quod ita sit apparet: non enim potest dicta regula
90   in omni casu ad literam servari nisi prescripcio et usucapio tollantur; si
     autem prescripcio et usucapio tolluntur, peccatum negligentie, quod est
     contra bonum publicum, non punitur et per consequens receditur ab illa
     regula iuris nature que dicit quod rectum est peccantem puniri et maxime
     peccantem contra bonum publicum. Et ita facit ille qui magno tempore
95   negligit repetere rem suam; peccat enim contra bonum publicum quia dat
     materiam licium et rixarum. Vlterius, eciam si prescripcio et usucapio tol-
     luntur, receditur ab illa regula iuris naturalis que dicit quod bonum publi-
     cum et commune est preferendum cuicumque bono speciali et proprio.
     In remocione autem prescripcionis et usucapionis fit totum contrarium,
100 quia preelegitur bonum proprium illius qui negligit repetere rem suam et
     dat materiam licium et rixarum, ac per consequens pretermictitur bonum
     commune quia consistit in pacifico communitatis convictu; nam data ma-
     teria licium et rixarum per remocionem prescripcionis vel usucapionis,
     convictus communitatis pacificus perturbatur.

105 Et ideo per omnia hoc est nobis attendendum, quod ius naturale habet
     diversas regulas, que ita sunt intelligende quod una alteri non contrarietur;
     ita eciam sunt servande |^{R220v} quod cum una servatur contra aliam non

---

16/80 sine : cum *C*   16/81 inferuntur *C* : infertur *R*   16/83 non *scripsi* : *om. R* : et *C*
16/86 pretendit *C* : precedit *R*   16/86 receditur : recedit *C*   16/88 nature : nec *C*
16/90 omni : tali *C*   16/96 eciam : *om. C*   16/98 cuicumque : cuilibet *C*   16/100 quia :
quare *C*   16/102 quia : quare *C*

its interpretation of the rule in certain cases in which someone can be enriched to the detriment of another but with no injury to him, as is in fact the case in prescription and usucapion, insofar as these both impose damages but no injury on someone. For we see clearly that although someone against whom prescription lies suffers damage, he suffers no injury, for he deserves to suffer damage on account of his negligence. Although in this case positive law seems to depart from the literal sense of the natural law rule, nevertheless it does not depart from its real sense. For if this natural law rule were observed literally in every case, it would clearly depart from two other natural law rules. And this is clear because the rule cannot be observed literally in every case unless prescription and usucapion are abolished. But if prescription and usucapion are abolished, the sin of negligence, which is contrary to the common good, will not be punished, and consequently there will be a departure from the natural law rule that says it is right to punish a sinner and, above all, the one who sins against the common good. But this is precisely what someone who neglects to claim his own for a lengthy period of time does, for he sins against the common good by giving cause for quarrels and strife. Moreover, if prescription and usucapion are abolished, there will also be a departure from the natural law rule that says the public and common good is to be preferred to any particular and subjective good. But the abolition of prescription and usucapion accomplishes just the opposite, because it gives preference to the subjective good of one who neglects to claim his own and gives cause for quarrels and strife, and consequently neglects the common good, which consists in the peaceful intercourse of the community; for, by giving cause for quarrels and strife, the abolition of prescription and usucapion would disturb the peaceful intercourse of the community.

What we must note in all of this is that natural law has various rules, but that they must not be understood as contradictory, and that their observance is such that adherence to one does not imply departure from an-

eatur. Et quamvis istud satis appareat per ea que dicta sunt, possunt tamen
ad hoc alia induci exempla. Videmus enim quod de iure nature rectum est
110   quod depositum reddatur, ut patet in decretis di. I *Ius naturale*. Hec ergo
regula sic est intelligenda atque servanda ut contra alias regulas iuris nature non eatur. Nam si quis gladium quem deposuisset furendo repeteret et
sibi redderetur atque per illum homo occideretur, contra duas regulas iuris
nature iretur, quarum una dicit quod non est occidendum ac per conse-
115   quens nec favor prestandus ipsi occidenti; ille vero qui illo modo gladium
depositum redderet, favorem occidenti prestaret. Illa vero regula iuris nature dicit quod bonum publicum est conservandum ac per consequens pax
inter homines nullatenus perturbanda; ille vero qui dicto modo gladium
depositum redderet pacem communem hominum perturbaret vel saltem
120   esset occasio perturbandi. Quapropter dicta prima regula non est servanda
secundum sensum quem pretendit sed secundum veram intelligenciam, ut
intelligatur depositum semper esse reddendum nisi in casibus in quibus
adest aliqua circumstancia maliciam involvens, racione cuius aliqua regula
iuris nature superveniens depositum reddendum prohibeat, sicut nunc est
125   in proposito; nam regula iuris nature que dicit non esse occidendum et
non prestandum favorem occidenti in prefato casu superveniens mandat
depositum gladium furenti homini non reddendum. Nec tamen propter
hoc in tali casu contra ius nature itur; immo magis contra ius nature iretur
si in dicto casu gladius redderetur. Nam quamvis non reddens gladium in
130   prefato casu videatur recedere a iure nature secundum illam regulam que
dicit depositum esse reddendum, revocatur tamen ad ius nature secundum
duas alias regulas, quarum una dicit favorem occidenti non prestandum
et alia dicit pacem inter homines esse servandam, et hinc est quod si quis
promississet se gladium reddere et in tali casu ipsum non redderet, non
135   propter hoc mendacio involvetur, ut patet XXII q. II *Ne quis*.

Ex quibus omnibus apparet quod ius legale non addit supra ius naturale
quandam specialem et novam rectitudinem sed specificat et declarat illam

---

16/109 ad hoc : *om. C*   16/112–13 et sibi : et ei si *C*   16/113 occideretur *C* : occidetur
R   16/114 iretur *C* : videtur *R*   16/116 Illa : Iam *C*   16/121 sed *C* : *om. R*   16/124 prohibeat *C* : prohibebat *R*   16/125–6 et non : nec *C*   16/126 favorem *C* : amorem *R*
16/130 prefato : tali *C*   16/133 alia : quae *add. C*   16/134 promississet : quod *add. et
exp. R*   16/134 se : *om. C*   16/137 quandam : quorundam *C*

16/109–35 Cf. *Republic* 331c–332b; Thomas Aquinas, *Sententia libri Ethicorum*, lib. 5
lectio 12, 1134b24, in *Opera omnia*, vol 47.2 (Rome, 1969), 306.   16/110 Decretum Grat.
D.1 c.7.   16/135 Decretum Grat. C.22 q.2 c.14.

other. And although this should be sufficiently clear from what has been said, nevertheless other examples may be adduced. We see, for example, that by natural law it is right to return a deposit, as is clear in the decrees at D.1 c.7. But this rule must be understood and observed in such a way that it does not contradict other rules of natural law. For example, if a madman seeks to recover a sword he has placed in deposit, and it is returned to him, and with it he kills a man, two natural law rules are violated, one of which says that we must not kill, and consequently that no assistance should be offered to a killer. But he who returns the deposited sword in this case offers assistance to a killer. There is also a natural law rule that says that the public good must be preserved, and consequently that peace among men should not be disturbed in any way. But he who returns the deposited sword in this case disturbs the common peace or at least provides an occasion for disturbance. Therefore, the first rule should not be observed in a literal sense but according to its real meaning, such that it is understood that a deposit should always be returned except in cases where the circumstances involve vice, and then a supervening rule of natural law prohibits its return, as in the case under discussion. For the supervening rule of natural law that prohibits killing and giving assistance to a killer decrees that a deposited sword should not be returned to a madman. Nor does this involve any contravention of natural law, but rather natural law is more seriously violated if the sword is returned to the madman. For although not returning the sword in this case appears to depart from natural law – specifically, the rule that says a deposit must be returned – nevertheless it adheres to it with regard to two other rules, one of which says that no assistance should be given to a killer, and the other that the peace is to be preserved among men. And thus it is that if someone has promised to return a sword but, in a case like this, does not, he is not for that reason guilty of deception, as is clear at C.22 q.2 c.14.

In the light of the foregoing, it is clear that positive law does not add some special or novel equity to natural law, but rather specifies and ex-

eandem per quosdam casus in quibus, etsi non servetur rectitudo iuris naturalis secundum unam regulam, servatur tamen secundum aliam, ut superius est ostensum; vel possumus dicere quod in talibus casibus licet non servetur sensus quem pretendit secundum literam, servatur tamen sensus quem eadem regula intendit secundum veram intelligenciam.

　　Propter que omnia videtur bene dictum illud quod superius dicebatur, scilicet quod rectitudo iuris naturalis et iuris legalis non est alia et alia sed est una et eadem aliter et aliter sumpta. Potest autem hoc totum quod dictum est confirmari per unam legem, que habetur ff. *de iusticia et iure* l. *Ius civile*. Dicit enim illa lex quod 'ius civile est quod nec in totum a naturali vel iure gencium recedit, nec per omnia conservit, itaque vel addimus vel detrahimus iuri communi ius proprium, id est, civile efficimus.' Ex verbis ergo istius legis statim apparet quod rectitudo iuris naturalis et iuris legalis non est alia et alia sed una et eadem aliter et aliter sumpta, nam si alia et alia, tunc ius legale esset rectum ex sua propria rectitudine et non ex rectitudine iuris naturalis, ac per consequens in totum recederet a iure naturali, cuius oppositum dicit lex prefata. Quapropter debemus ymaginari quod ideo ius legale dicitur non recedere in totum a iure naturali quia assumit suam rectitudinem ab illo; ideo vero dicitur non per omnia ei proportionari, quia illam rectitudinem videtur mutare quandoque per addicionem, quandoque per detractionem. Per addicionem siquidem quando addit ei varios actus ad quos habet applicari vel congruos modos per quos habet determinari; per detractionem vero quando in aliquo casu videtur ei subtrahere rectitudinem secundum unam regulam, quam tamen sibi conservat secundum aliam regulam.

　　Occurunt tamen contra istud dictum duo dubia. Primum est: quia cum

---

16/139–40 superius est ostensum : *corr. e* super est ostensum ius *R*　16/141 servetur : serveretur *C*　16/141 quem : qui *C*　16/143 Propter que omnia : Quapropter *C*　16/143–4 illud ... scilicet : *om. C*　16/146 confirmari : contrariari *C*　16/148 conservit : confirmatur *C*　16/148 itaque : ita quod *C*　16/150 istius *scripsi* : istis *R* : ex istis ergo legibus *C*　16/151 aliter[1] : tamen *add. C*　16/153 ac : et *C*　16/153 recederet *C* : redderet *R*　16/155 assumit : sumit *R*　16/156 ab illo *C* : *om. R*　16/156–7 proportionari *C* : pro iure *R*　16/157 mutare : imitari *C*　16/158 Per addicionem *C* : *om. R*　16/158 siquidem : quidem *C*　16/159 congruos : et *add. R*　16/159 congruos modos : aliquos terminos *C*

16/139–40 Vid. sup. 16/73–104.　16/143 Vid. sup. 16/24–37.　16/146–9 Dig. 1.1.6.

plicates it through individual cases in which, even if the equity of natural law embodied in one rule is not observed, it is nevertheless observed according to another rule, as we showed above. Or we can say that in such cases, even if the literal sense of a rule is not observed, its real meaning nonetheless is.

For all of these reasons, it appears that I spoke well when I said earlier that the equity of natural and positive law are not two different things, but rather one and the same thing viewed from two different perspectives. Moreover, all that I have just said may be confirmed by a single law, which is found at Dig. 1.1.6, where it says that 'the civil law is that which neither wholly diverges from natural law and the law of nations nor follows the same in every particular. And so whenever we add anything or take anything away from it we make a law special to ourselves, that is, civil law.' From the very words of this law, it is at once clear that the equity of natural and of positive law are not two different things, but rather one and the same viewed from two perspectives. For if they were two different things, positive law would be right by its own equity and not by the equity of natural law, and consequently it would depart entirely from natural law, which is the opposite of what the law just cited says. Therefore, we should rather conceive that positive law does not depart from natural law but derives its equity from it, though not in every respect proportionately, because it seems to adapt natural law equity by sometimes adding to it, sometimes subtracting from it. It does so by addition when it adds acts to which it must apply or appropriate means by which it should be explicated; by subtraction when in a specific case it seems to diminish natural law equity with regard to one rule, but preserves it with respect to another.

Two questions, however, arise that cast doubt on this conclusion. The

quodlibet ius in rectitudine consistat, ut superius dicebatur, videtur sequi
165   necessario quod non est eadem rectitudo utriusque iuris; quia tunc utrumque ius sit idem ius, quod patet esse falsum. Secundum dubium est: quia
ius naturale est mensura iuris legalis ac per consequens si est eadem rectitudo, videtur quod idem sit mensura iuris legalis sui ipsius.

Ad primum ergo dubium videtur dicendum quod quamvis sit sola una
170   rectitudo, sunt tamem diversa iura propter duas causas. Vna est quia dicta
rectitudo una existens habet duplicem vim directivam in actibus humanis;
alia est enim vis directiva istius rectitudinis secundum quod pertinet ad ius
legale et alia secundum quod pertinet ad ius naturale. Nam secundum quod
pertinet ad ius naturale dirigit in actibus humanis quantum ad id quod est
175   in eis omnibus equaliter certum; secundum vero quod pertinet ad ius legale
dirigit in eisdem quantum ad id quod in eis est dubium, sicut verbi gracia
quia iste peccavit tali peccato certum est quod debeat puniri et ideo ius
naturale dirigit nos in tali actu per suam certitudinem quantum ad id quod
in eo est certum; ius vero legale per eandem rectitudinem dirigit nos in eo
180   actu quantum ad id quod in eo est dubium. Ex quo apparet immediate quod
quamvis sit una et eadem rectitudo, in quantum tamen est aliter et aliter
sumpta habet aliam et aliam vim directivam absolute et sumptam, sed prout
habet vim directivam actuum humanorum. Alia causa distinccionis inter
ista iura est quia alia est noticia istius rectitudinis prout pertinet ad ius na-
185   turale et alia prout pertinet ad ius legale. Nam prout pertinet ad ius naturale
eius noticia omnibus est aperta, prout vero pertinet ad ius legale eius noticia non est aperta omnibus, ymmo solum quibusdam paucis et sapientibus
hominibus, et quia ius non dicit solam rectitudinem sed rectitudinem cum
noticia, idcirco non obstante quod sit una rectitudo, quia tamen est alia
190   noticia que de ea habetur secundum unum modum et alia que de ea habetur
secundum alium modum, poterit facere distincta iura.

Ad secundum vero dubium dicendum quod non est inconveniens quod
unum et idem sumptum alio et alio modo sit sui ipsius mensura, nam si aliquid sumptum uno modo habeat maiorem certitudinem quam sumptum

---

16/164 quodlibet *C* : quolibet *R*   16/165 quia tunc *C* : quod eciam *R*   16/165–6 utrumque : utrumquam *C*   16/166 sit : esset *C*   16/169 Ad : *om. C*   16/173 et alia …
naturale *C* : *om. R*   16/179 eo *scripsi* : eos *R* : ea *C*   16/182–3 absolute … directivam : *om. per hom. R* : *suppl. al. man. marg.*   16/182 sed : *om. C*   16/183 Alia : Secunda *C*   16/184 iura : *om. C*   16/186 aperta *C* : apta *R*   16/187 aperta *C* : apta
R   16/190 que de ea habetur[2] : *om. C*   16/192 vero dubium dicendum quod : dicitur
C   16/192 est : esse *C*   16/194 habeat : habet *C*

first is that although each law consists in equity, as was said above, it seems to follow necessarily that equity is not exactly the same for each, for then the two laws would be identical, which is false. The second is that natural law is the measure of positive law and consequently, if equity is the same for both, then it seems that positive law is the measure of itself.

It seems that the response to the first is that although the two share the same equity, they are nevertheless distinct laws for two reasons. One is because the same equity has a double directive force in human actions: one is its directive force as it pertains to positive law, the other as it pertains to natural law. Now as it pertains to natural law it has a directive force in human actions with respect to what is equally certain in them all; as it pertains to positive law it has a directive force with respect to what is uncertain. Thus, for example, because someone has sinned by means of a specific sin it is certain that he should be punished, and therefore natural law has a directive force in such an act by its certainty regarding what is certain in that act; but positive law has a directive force in such an act by the same equity with respect to what is uncertain. From this it is clear that although equity is the same for both laws, insofar as it is viewed from different perspectives it has a different directive force, absolute or applied, so far as human actions are concerned. The second cause of the difference between the two laws is that the knowledge of what is equitable is one thing in natural law and another in positive law. With respect to natural law, knowledge of what is equitable is evident to everyone, but with respect to positive law it is not, but rather only to a few learned men. But because law does not mean simply equity but equity combined with knowledge of what is equitable, notwithstanding the fact that equity is the same for both laws, it is possible to distinguish them because knowledge of equity is different in each.

The response to the second question is that it is not inappropriate that one and the same thing understood in two ways should be the measure of itself, for if something understood in one way possesses a greater degree

195 alio modo, erit seipso nocius et cercius et per consequens poterit esse sui
ipsius mensura. Ita autem est in proposito, nam dicta rectitudo prout pertinet ad ius naturale habet maiorem certitudinem quam prout pertinet ad
ius legale. Quia primo modo sumpta, tantam habet certitudinem quod
omnibus est aperta et nota; prout vero sumitur secundo modo, est nota

200 solum quibusdam paucis et sapientibus hominibus, ut superius dicebatur,
et ideo non est inconveniens quod accepta penes primum modum habeat
racionem regule et mensure; ipsa vero eadem accepta penes secundum modum habeat racionem regulati et mensurati.

Declaratis ergo omnibus istis, lene est descendere ad illud quod in isto
205 articulo superius promittebatur probandum, scilicet quod ius de prescripcionibus non sit contra ius nature, immo magis iuri nature concordet. Et
quod ita sit probo quattuor racionibus.

Prima talis: illa iura que habent rectitudinem eandem, unum eorum non
potest alteri contrariari; sed ius naturale et ius legale de prescripcionibus
210 habent eandem rectitudinem, ergo unum eorum, scilicet ius legale de prescripcionibus, non poterit contrariari iuri naturali. Maior apparet de se;
minor autem potest esse nota ex dictis.

Secunda|[R221r] racio ad illud potest esse talis: illud ius quod habet con-
gruam et racionabilem causam concordat iuri naturali; sed ius de prescrip-
215 cionibus habet congruam et racionabilem causam, ergo concordat iuri
naturali. Maior videtur satis nota, quia quidquid est congruum et racio-
nabile concordat naturali racioni et per consequens iuri naturali; minorem
vero probo per id quod dicebatur superius in primo articulo, ubi ostende-
batur quod longitudo determinati temporis a legibus prebet congruam et
220 racionabilem causam prescribendi. Nam sicut patet ff. *de usuc.* l. I que in-

---

16/198 sumpta : *om. C*   16/199 prout ... nota : secundo vero modo *C*   15/200 et sapientibus : *om. C*   16/201 inconveniens *C* : illi conveniens *R*   16/201 penes primum modum :
primo modo *C*   16/202-3 penes scundum modum : secundo modo *C*   16/204 illud : id
C   16/206 iuri nature : ei *C*   16/206 concordet : concordare *C*   16/208 talis : sic *C*
16/209 ius[2] : *om. C*   16/211 apparet : patet *C*   16/211 se : et *add. C*   16/212 autem : *om.*
C   16/213 Secunda racio : Secundo *C*   16/213 ad illud ... talis : *om. C*   16/216 naturali
C : *om. R*   16/216 satis : *om. C*   16/217 iuri *C* : *om. R*   16/219 temporis : tempori *C*

16/218 Vid. sup. 15/97–115.   16/220–1 Dig. 41.3.1.

of certainty than when it is understood in another way, it will then be better known and more certain to itself, and consequently it could be its own measure. But this is so in the case proposed, for what is equitable possesses a greater degree of certainty as it pertains to natural law than it does as it pertains to positive law. Understood in the first way, it possesses such a degree of certainty that it is open and clear to everyone; understood in the second way, it is known only to a few learned men, as was said earlier. Therefore, it is not inappropriate that equity understood in the first way has the character of a rule and measure; in the second way, the character of the regulated and measured.

These issues having been clarified, then, it is a simple matter to return to what I promised to prove earlier in the article, namely, that the law of prescriptions is not contrary to the law of nature, but rather completely in accordance with it. That this is so I shall prove by four arguments.

The first is as follows: of two laws that share the same equity, one cannot be contrary to the other. Now natural law and the positive law of prescriptions share the same equity, therefore one of them, namely, the positive law of prescriptions, could not be contrary to natural law. The major premiss is clear and the minor premiss may be understood from what has been said already.

The second argument is as follows: a law that has a fit and reasonable cause is in agreement with natural law. But the law of prescriptions has a fit and reasonable cause, therefore it agrees with natural law. The major premiss is sufficiently clear, because whatever is fit and reasonable agrees with natural reason and consequently with natural law. The minor premiss I prove by means of what was said above in the first article, where it was shown that the length of time determined by the laws presents an appropriate and reasonable cause for prescribing. For, as is clear at Dig. 41.3.1,

cipit *Bono publico* ideo introducta fuit usucapio, ac per consequens etiam prescripcio, ne dominia rerum diu et fere semper essent amittenda, cum sufficiat dominus ad inquirendas res suas intra statuti temporis spacium, ut dicitur ibidem. Quia ergo statutum tempus per leges sufficit unicui-
225 que ad requirendam rem suam, si eam in tam longo tempore non requirat, congrue et racionabiliter currit prescripcio contra eum; ex quo apparet immediate quod prescripcio habet congruam et racionabilem causam ac per consequens concordat racioni naturali et iuri.

Tercio ad idem est talis: illud ius legale quod punit peccatum negligen-
230 cie, quod est contra bonum publicum, concordat iuri naturali; sed ius de prescripcione est huiusmodi, ergo concordat naturali iuri. Maior videtur nota, quia regula iuris nature est quod peccans puniatur et maxime peccans contra bonum publicum; minor eciam apparet quia ille qui negligit repetere rem suam tam longo tempore maxime peccat contra bonum publicum,
235 quia prebet materiam licium et rixarum que non possunt facile terminari, et per consequens de iure nature est equum quod puniatur; ius autem prescripcionis punit sic negligentes, ut patet per descripcionem superius datam de ea.

Quarta racio ad idem est talis: illud ius legale quod imponit finem liti-
240 bus que non videntur possibiles terminari maxime concordat iuri naturali; sed ius legale de prescripcione est huiusmodi, ergo et cetera. Maior videtur nota, quia bonum publicum maxime impeditur per lites que non facile terminantur et ideo illud ius legale quod imponit finem talibus litibus maxime concordat iuri naturali; minor eciam apparet tum ex descripcione
245 superius data de prescripcione, que dicebat quod erat ius quoddam finem

---

16/222 amittenda *C* : *om. R*   16/223 intra *C* : *om. R*   16/227–8 ac per consequens : et sic *C*   16/229 Tercio ... talis : Tertio sic *C*   16/230 sed *C* : *om. R*   16/231 ergo ... iuri : ergo et cetera *C*   16/232 peccans[2] : si peccat *C*   16/233 minor *C* : maior *R*   16/234 peccat : videtur peccare *C*   16/236 per consequens : sic *C*   16/237 sic : huiusmodi *C*   16/238 ea : ergo et cetera *add. C*   16/239 Quarta ... talis : Quarto ad idem sic *C*   16/240 possibiles : facile *add. C*   16/241 sed *C* : *om. R*   16/241 legale : *om. C*   16/241 et cetera : *om. C*   16/243 legale : *om. C*   16/243 imponit *C* : imponitur *R*   16/245 data : *om. C*   16/245 dicebat *C* : tacebat *R*

16/237–8 Vid. sup. 15/130–40.   16/245 Vid. sup. 15/130–40.

usucapion was introduced – and consequently prescription as well – to prevent the ownership of things from lapsing for an extended period or even forever, since the statutory period of time should suffice an owner to look after his possessions, as is said there. Therefore, because the time laid down by the laws is sufficient for anyone to look after his own property, if he fails to do so for a considerable period, it is appropriate and reasonable that prescription run against him. From this it is evident that prescription has an appropriate and reasonable cause and consequently that it is in accordance with natural reason and law.

The third argument is as follows: a positive law that punishes the sin of neglect – which in turn is contrary to the public good – is in accordance with natural law. Now the law of prescription is of this nature, therefore it is in accordance with natural law. The major premiss seems clear, because it is a rule of natural law that a sinner should be punished, particularly one who sins against the public good. The minor premiss is also clear, because he who neglects to look after his property for a long period of time especially sins against the public good, because he gives cause for quarrels and strife, which are not easily settled, and consequently it is just, according to the law of nature, that he be punished. Now the law of prescription punishes those who are guilty of such negligence, as is clear from the definition of prescription provided earlier.

The fourth argument is as follows: a positive law that imposes a limit on quarrels that appear impossible to settle is especially in accordance with natural law. Now the positive law of prescription is of this nature, therefore et cetera. The major premiss seems clear, because the public good is especially harmed by interminable lawsuits, and therefore a positive law that limits such quarrels is especially in agreement with natural law. The minor premiss is also evident both from the definition of prescription pro-

litibus imponens, tum eciam ex illa lege superius allegata ff. *de usucap.*,
que dicit quod usucapio est introducta propter bonum publicum, et pari
racione eciam prescripcio.

Ex istis autem duabus ultimis racionibus apparet quod quamvis pre-
250   scripcio videatur deviare a iure naturali secundum illam regulam que dicit
quod nullus debet locuplectari cum alterius detrimento et iniuria, revocatur tamen ad ius nature secundum duas alias regulas, quarum una dicit
quod peccans debet puniri, alia vero dicit quod debet finis litibus imponi.
Quod eciam patet ulterius quomodo tollitur fundamentum contrarie opi-
255   nionis, quam glose tenent, nam quamvis sit equum simpliciter neminem
ditari cum detrimento alterius, in tali tamen casu in quo currit prescripcio,
non est rectum, quia iretur contra duas regulas alias iuris naturalis. Nec
valet id quod inducebatur in contrarium per aliam legem, que dicit quod
'aliud est bonum, aliud est equum,' nam quanto aliquid recedit ab equi-
260   tate tanto eciam recedit a bonitate. Quapropter est dicta lex intelligenda
hoc modo, utpote quia aliquid est quod apparet bonum secundum unam
regulam quod tamen non apparet equum secundum aliam; vel potest dici
alio modo quod aliquid est quod apparet equum secundum aliquam regulam iuxta veram intelligenciam quod tamen non apparet equum secundum
265   eandem regulam intellectam apparenter ad aliquam literam.
Intelligendum autem circa totum istum articulum quod si velimus bene
attendere ea que superius dicta sunt, possumus uti una distinccione que
sufficit ad tollendas omnes cavillaciones et iuristarum dubitaciones. Dicemus ergo quod prescripcionem esse de iure nature vel concordare iuri
270   nature potest dupliciter intelligi, uno modo quod sit directe ab eo exorta,
et iste intellectus est falsus, quia tunc nulla regula iuris nature ei obviaret
aliquo modo, cuius contrarium superius est ostensum, quia obviat ei illa
regula que habetur ff. *de re. iuris* que dicit 'iure,' inquam, 'nature equum est neminem cum alterius detrimento et iniuria fieri locuplectorem.'

16/250 iure : a iure *add. per ditt. R*   16/250 naturali *C* : *om. R*   16/254 Quod : Ex
quo *C*   16/262 non : *om. C*   16/267–8 que sufficit : sufficiente *C*   16/268–9 Dicemus : Dicimus *C*   16/269 concordare : concordari *C*   16/270 potest ... modo *C* : *om.*
R   16/272 modo : pacto *C*   16/273–4 equum : *om. C*   16/274 locuplectorem : locupletiorem *C*

16/246 Dig. 41.3.1; vid. sup. 16/5–13.   16/259 Gl. ord. ad Dig. 41.3.1, v. *Bono publico* (ed.
cit. col. 452); vid. sup. 16/8.   16/272 Vid. sup. 16/73–87.   16/273–4 Dig. 50.17.206(207);
vid. sup. 14/14–16.

vided earlier – which states that it is a law that imposes a limit on lawsuits – and from the law that we cited earlier, namely, Dig. 41.3.1, which says that usucapion was introduced to serve the common good, and, for the same reason, prescription.

From the last two arguments it is clear that although prescription appears to depart from the rule of natural law that says no one should be enriched at the expense and injury of another, it nevertheless reflects two other natural law rules, one of which says that a sinner should be punished and the other that a limit should be imposed on quarrels. Furthermore, it is also clear how the basis of the contrary opinion maintained by the glosses may be undermined, for although it is clearly just that no one be enriched at the expense of another, in a case where prescription runs, it is not, because this would contradict the two other natural law rules. Nor does the law that says that 'the good and the equitable are not the same thing' adduced in support of the contrary argument avail, for to the extent that anything departs from equity it also departs from goodness. Therefore, this law should be interpreted to mean that something might seem good by one rule but inequitable by another. Alternatively it could be said that something might seem just according to a rule understood correctly, but inequitable according to the same rule interpreted literally.

With respect to the article as a whole, it should be understood that if we are prepared to consider carefully the things which were said above, we can employ a single distinction that suffices to remove all the quibblings and doubts of the jurists. Let us say, therefore, that prescription belongs to the law of nature or is in accordance with the law of nature, and that this may be understood in two ways. In one way, it arose directly from natural law and this understanding is false, because then no rule of natural law would obstruct it in any way. But we demonstrated the opposite above, because it is obstructed by the rule of the Digest which says 'by the

275 Ista enim regula obviat prescripcioni, saltem quantum ad sensum quem
pretendit ad literam; et hoc est forte quod movet iuristas ad dicendum
quod prescripcio sit contra ius nature, quia non directe est ab eo exorta.
Potest tollerari eorum opinio, quamvis simpliciter non sit bona, quia magis est verum eam concordare iuri nature quam eam esse contra ius natu-
280 re; concordat namque iuri nature iuxta secundum intellectum, qui modo
ponetur.

Dico ergo quod secundo modo potest intelligi prescripcionem concordare iuri nature quia quamvis non sit directe ab eo exorta, est tamen ad ipsum indirecte reducta et iste intellectus est verus, quia ostensum est supra
285 quod quamvis prescripcio videatur directe deviare a iure nature secundum
unam regulam, reducitur tamen ad ipsum indirecte per duas alias regulas,
ymmo quod plus est, ista reductio potest fieri secundum unam et eamdem
regulam, ut superius est ostensum. Propter que omnia simpliciter debemus
dicere quod ipsa non sit contra ius nature, ymmo magis quod iuri nature
290 concordat, et ita patet quid sit dicendum quantum ad secundum articulum.
Restat ergo videre tercio.

<17> <Articulus tertius>

Tertius articulus, in quo probatur quod prescripcio iuris canonici debet
esse alia ad prescripcionem iuris civilis.
 Vtrum prescripcio iuris canonici debuit esse alia et distincta a prescrip-
5 cione iuris civilis. Vbi sciendum quod in isto articulo est aliquid certum
et aliquid dubium, nam certum est quod prescripcio que currit secundum

---

16/275 obviat : prestita *add. et exp. R*   16/275 prescriptioni *C* : prescripta *R*
16/277 exorta *C* : extorta *R* : et *add. C*   16/278 bona *C* : bene *R*   16/279–80 eam ...
nature : eidem contrariare *C*   16/280 secundum : veram *C*   16/283 exorta *C* : extorta
R   16/283–4 ipsum : saltem *add. C*   16/284 quia ... supra : est enim superius ostensum
C   16/288 Propter que omnia : Quapropter *C*   16/289 ipsa : *om. C*   16/289 sit : sic
C   16/289 ymmo : sed *C*   16/290 concordat : concordet *C*   17/2–3 Tertius ... civilis :
om. C   17/4 debuit : debeat *C*   17/4 et distincta : *om. C*   17/5 civilis : vel eadem *add.*
C   17/5 Vbi : *om. C*

16/288 Vid. sup. 16/87–104.

law of nature it is fair that no one become richer by the loss and injury of another.' This rule obstructs prescription, at least with regard to its literal meaning; and possibly it is this that leads the jurists to say that prescription is contrary to the law of nature, because it does not arise directly from it. Their opinion can be maintained, although plainly it is not sound, because it is more true that it is in accordance with the law of nature than that it is contrary to it, for it accords with the law of nature according to a second interpretation, which I shall now explain.

I maintain, therefore, that prescription can be understood to accord with the law of nature in the second way, because although it did not arise directly from natural law, it can nevertheless be traced back to it indirectly, and this is the correct interpretation. For it was shown above that although prescription seems to depart explicitly from the law of nature with regard to one rule, it can nevertheless be traced back to it by two others; moreover, this derivation can be established by one and the same rule, as was shown above. In the light of all these considerations, we can say plainly that prescription is not contrary to the law of nature; indeed more, that it accords with the law of nature, and so the response to the second question is clear. Let us now turn to the third article.

17. Article 3

The third article, in which it is proved that canon law prescription should be different from civil law prescription.

Should prescription in canon law be different and distinct from prescription in civil law? It must be known that there is a degree of both certainty and uncertainty in this article, for it is certain that prescription in

ius canonicum est alia et distincta a prescripcione que currit secundum ius
civile, quia prescripcio que currit secundum ius civile non requirit necessario bonam fidem in prescribente, ut patet C. *de prescripcionibus XXX*
10   *annorum* l. I, l. *Omnes*, et l. *Cum notissimi*. Prescripcio autem que currit
secundum ius canonicum necessario requirit bonam fidem in prescribente,
sicut patet *extra de prescripcionibus* c. *Vigilanti* et c. *Si diliguntur bene*, et
una regula iuris canonici dicit quod 'possessor male fidei ullo tempore non
prescribit,' ut habetur *extra de regulis iuris* in VI. Illud autem est dubium
15   in isto articulo, scilicet utrum ista diversitas prescripcionis inter dicta iura
sit racionabilis seu utrum fuerit racionabiliter posita. Illud autem quod
facit hic aliquam difficultatem est quia si prescripcio male fidei concordat
equitati iuris nature, videtur quod ambo dicta iura debuerint concordare
in eam statuendo; si vero dicta prescripcio sit iniqua et contra equitatem
20   iuris nature, videtur quod nullum ius legale debuerit eam statuere, ac per
consequens dicta prescripcio, sicut non currit secundum iura canonica, ita
eciam non curret secundum hec aliqua diversitas inter dicta iura.

Sciendum ergo quod dicta prescripcio uno modo est equa quia concordat equitati iuris nature et alio modo iniqua quia ab eius equitate recedit.
25   Nam si consideramus intencionem iuris civilis eam statuentis, sic est equa
et concordat equitati iuris nature; si vero consideramus intencionem ipsius
prescribentis sic est iniqua et discordat a iure nature. Et quod ita sit apparet: intendit enim ius civile per prescripcionem male fidei duplicem finem,
scilicet negligentes punire et finem litibus imponere, et utrumque dictorum
30   finium iuri naturali concordat, ut superius fuit visum, et ideo ex ista parte
merito est dicenda equa et iusta talis prescripcio. Ipse vero prescribens
per eamdem prescripcionem intendit rem alie-|^R221v-nam usurpare propter
quod merito ex ista parte est dicenda iniqua et iniusta, quia discordat ab
illa regula iuris nature que dicit 'quod tibi non vis fieri alteri ne feceris,'

17/8 que currit ... civile : iuris civilis *C*   17/10 l. I : 6 *C*   17/10 Omnes : Omnis *C*
17/10 notissimi : notissimum *C*   17/10 autem : vero *C*   17/10–11 que currit ...
canonicum : iuris canonici *C*   17/13 ullo : nullo *C*   17/13 non : *om. C*   17/17 hic : ibi
C   17/23 ergo : *om. C*   17/23 quia : nec *C*   17/24 modo : est *add. C*   17/24 recedit
C : recedat *R*   17/26 concordat : concordans *C*   17/26 equitati iuris nature : iuri naturae
C   17/26 consideramus : consideremus *C*   17/27 discordat *C* : discordet *R*   17/34 alteri
ne feceris : et cetera *C*

17/9–10 C. 7.39.1, 4, 7.   17/12 X 2.26.5, 17.   17/13–14 VI *de reg. iur.* 2, *Possessor.*
17/30 Vid. sup. 16/229–48.

canon law is different and distinct from prescription in civil law, because civil law prescription does not necessarily require that the prescriber act in good faith, as is clear in C. 7.39.1, 4, and 7. But canonical prescription necessarily requires that the prescriber act in good faith, as is clear in X 2.26.5 and 17, and the rule of canon law at VI *de reg. iur.* 2 that says that 'a possessor in bad faith never prescribes.' The element of doubt is whether the difference in prescription between the two laws is reasonable or reasonably asserted. What creates a difficulty here is that if prescription in bad faith accords with natural law equity, it seems that both laws should agree in sanctioning it. If, on the other hand, such prescription is unjust and contrary to natural law equity, it seems that no positive law should sanction it, and consequently prescription of this kind should not hold in civil law just as it does not hold in canon, since there should be no diversity between the two.

It must be understood that civil law prescription is in one sense just, because it accords with natural law equity, and in another sense unjust, because it departs from it. For if we consider the intention of civil law in sanctioning prescription, it is just and accords with natural law equity; if we consider the intention of the prescriber, it is unjust and contrary to natural law equity. And that this is the case is clear, for the civil law has a double objective by means of prescription in bad faith, namely, to punish the negligent and to impose a limit on quarrels, each of which accords with natural law, as we saw above, and therefore prescription of this sort is rightly called just and equitable. But the prescriber intends to usurp another's possession by means of prescription in bad faith, and for this reason it is rightly said to be inequitable and unjust because it departs

35   que regula in lege et evangelio continetur. Et hinc apparet que fuerit causa
     quod prescripcio male fidei est a iure civili inducta; remanet tamen dubium
     quare ius canonicum in dicta prescripcione a iure civili discordet.

     Sciendum ergo quod prescripcio male fidei partim est a iure civili in-
     ducta, partim est ab eodem iure permissa, nam si consideramus eam ex
40   parte duplicis finis ipsam consequentis, sic est a iure civili inducta quia,
     sicut patuit supra, ius civile eam induxit propter duplicem finem, scilicet
     ut negligentes puniret et ut lites terminaret. Si vero consideramus eam ex
     parte prescribentis, sic est solum ab eodem iure civili permissa, quia isto
     modo accepta est iniqua et iniusta, ut supra fuit ostensum. Ius autem civile
45   non potest inducere aliquid iniquum et iniustum, nam 'omne ius ideo ius
     dictum est quia iustum est,' ut patet in decretis di. I. Quapropter relinqui-
     tur quod prescripcio male fidei in quantum se tenet ex parte prescribentis
     non sit a iure civili inducta sed solum permissa, quia ius civile et quodli-
     bet aliud ius, quamvis non possit aliquid iniquum et iniustum inducere,
50   potest tamen et debet quandoque aliquid iniustum et iniquum permittere
     propter aliquod bonum et iustum quod inde potest oriri et quod ad ipsum
     tale ius magis spectat intendere, sicut utique nunc est in proposito, nam
     permittit quod prescripcio istius ex mala fide et iniquitate procedat ut per
     eam duplicem prefatum finem eliciat, scilicet ut negligentes puniat et ut
55   finem litibus imponat. Hoc autem ideo facit quia ius civile, cum intendat
     ultimo de fine conservare civilem societatem, cui fini maxime debetur ne-
     gligencium punicio et licium terminacio, idcirco magis dicitur intendere ad
     hoc ut negligentes puniat et ut finem litibus imponat quam ut iniquitatem
     prescribentis corrigat vel removeat, nam magis ad ipsum spectat illius du-
60   plicis finis equitas prosequenda quam ipsius prescribentis iniquitas corri-

---

17/36 est : sit *C*   17/37 discordet *C* : discordat *R*   17/39 consideramus *C* : conside-
ram *R*   17/42 consideramus : consideremus *C*   17/43 iure *C* : iuris *R*   17/44 supra :
superius *C*   17/47 in quantum : prout *C*   17/50 et iniquum : *om. C*   17/51 oriri *C* :
obire *R*   17/52 utique : *om. C*   17/54 ut¹ : *om. C*   17/54 puniat : punire *C*   17/54 ut²
om. C   17/55 imponat : imponere *C*   17/56 de fine : *om. C*   17/56 debetur *C* : debuit
R   17/57 ad : *om. C*   17/58 ut² : *om. C*

17/35 *Mt* 7.12. Cf. *Tb* 4.16; Decretum Grat. dictum Grat. ante D.1 c.1.   17/41 Vid. sup.
16/229–48.   17/44 Vid. sup. 17/25–7.   17/45–6 Decretum Grat. D.1 c.2.

from the rule of natural law – contained both in the law of Moses and in the gospel – that says, 'that which you do not want done to you, do not do to another.' And from this it is clear why prescription in bad faith was introduced by civil law. Nevertheless there remains doubt about why canon law differs from civil on prescription in bad faith.

It must be understood therefore that civil law from one perspective has introduced prescription in bad faith and from another permits it. If we look at it from the perspective of civil law's double objective, prescription was introduced to punish the negligent and limit quarrels. But if we look at it from the perspective of the prescriber, prescription is simply tolerated by civil law, for, as was shown earlier, from this perspective it is inequitable and unjust. But the civil law cannot introduce anything inequitable and unjust, for 'all law is so called because it is just,' as is clear in D.1 c.2. Therefore it follows that so far as it relates to the intention of the prescriber, prescription in bad faith has not been introduced but only tolerated by civil law, because even though civil law – and indeed any other law – cannot introduce anything inequitable and unjust, nevertheless it may occasionally tolerate something unjust and inequitable on account of something good or just that might thereby result, and it is this that the law intends. This is also the case in the proposition, for civil law permits prescription to proceed by bad faith and inequity in order to achieve the double objective of punishing negligence and limiting quarrels. It does so because the ultimate purpose of civil law is to preserve civil society, and punishment of the negligent and the limitation of quarrels particularly serve this end. Therefore it prefers to punish the negligent and limit quarrels than to correct or remove the inequity of the prescriber, because pursuing the equity of its double purpose contributes more to the preservation of civil society than correcting the inequity of the prescriber. From

genda. Ex quibus omnibus apparet immediate quare in prescripcione male
fidei ius canonicum a iure civili discordet; possumus enim de hoc assignare
quattuor raciones quia est.

Prima est quia ista duo iura sibi mutuo subveniunt, cum sint fundata
65 super eodem iure naturali; nam si unum eorum alteri non subveniret, sequeretur quod unum eorum in omnibus sufficeret et per consequens alterum superflueret. Contingit enim sepe quod ad unum et eundem effectum
unum eorum sine altero non sufficit ut, verbi gracia, in puniendo clericum
dignum morte: si habet ordines sacros, non sufficit ius civile sine canoni-
70 co, quia non potest ipsum degradare; nec eciam sufficit canonicum sine
civili quia iudex canonicus non potest ipsum occidere. Quapropter dicta
iura sibi mutuo subveniunt in dicto casu quia quodlibet eorum exequitur
illud quod ad ipsum pertinet, ita ergo suo modo est imaginandum in prescripcione male fidei, quia in ea est aliquid iustum et prosequendum et
75 aliquid iniustum et prohibendum. Nam instituere quod dicta prescripcio
currat propter negligencium punicionem et licium terminacionem, hoc est
iustum et prosequendum; instituere vero quod dicta prescripcio efficaciam habeat, non obstante male fidei prescripcione, est iniustum et prohibendum. Hec ergo duo cum non possint fieri per idem ius, oportet quod
80 sit aliud ius quod dictam prescripcionem propter illum duplicem finem
instituat et aliud ius quod eandem prescripcionem propter malam fidem
prescribentis prohibeat. Et isto modo dicta iura sibi mutuo subvenient,
nec erit contradiccio inter ea, sicut melius declaravi in questione quam determinavi de usuris, ubi ostendi quod unum ius non poterat obviare alteri
85 per contradiccionem sed per omissionem, quia illud quod omittebatur ab
uno sepe assumebatur ab altero, sicut utique nunc est in proposito. Nam
quod mala fides prescribentis debeat prescripcionem infringere, hoc a iure
civili obmictitur, quia ad ipsum non spectat eam propter dictam causam
infringere, et ideo non est contradiccio, cum ius civile dicit talem prescrip-
90 cionem esse equam et iustam, ac per consequens instituendam; ius vero

17/62 discordet *C* : discordat *R*   17/63 quia est : *om. C*   17/68 sufficit : sufficiat *C*
17/68 ut : *om. C*   17/68 verbi : exempli *C*   17/73 illud : id *C*   17/73 ergo : *om. C*
17/76 negligencium *C* : negligenciam *R*   17/79 cum *C* : *om. R*   17/79 ius : idcirco *add.*
R   17/80 aliud *C* : ad *R*   17/80 prescripcionem : *om. C*   17/82 subvenient : subveniunt
C   17/90–1 ius vero ... talem *C* : *om. R*

17/83–4 Vid. sup. 6/31–128.

these considerations, it is quite clear why canon law differs from civil on prescription in bad faith; and we can adduce four reasons for this.

The first is that the two laws are complementary because they are both founded on natural law. For if one of them did not complement the other, it would follow that it was self-sufficient and that the other was superfluous. For it often happens that, to achieve some end, one law is insufficient without the other, as, for example, in the punishment of a cleric by death: if he is in holy orders, civil law is insufficient without canon law because it cannot degrade him, and canon law insufficient without civil because an ecclesiastical judge cannot impose a death sentence. Thus, in this case the two laws are complementary, because each pursues what pertains to its sphere. And so we should conceive the matter of prescription in bad faith, for here there is something just to pursue and something unjust to prohibit. For to sanction prescription in order to punish the negligent and limit quarrels is just and something to be approved; to sanction its effects, notwithstanding the bad faith of the prescriber, is unjust and should be prohibited. Since these two purposes cannot be realized by a single law, it is fitting that there be one law that sanctions prescription in bad faith with a view to the double objective and another that prohibits it because of the bad faith of the prescriber. And thus the two laws are complementary, nor will there be any contradiction between them, as I explained more fully in the question I determined on usury, where I showed that one law could not oppose the other by contradiction but only by omission, for what is omitted by one is often assumed by the other, as is the case here in the proposition. For civil law omits that the bad faith of the prescriber should invalidate prescription, because such invalidation does not belong to civil law, and therefore there is no contradiction when civil law says that prescription is equitable and just, and consequently to be sanctioned. But canon law says that prescription in bad faith is inequitable and unjust, and

canonicum dicit talem prescripcionem esse inequam et iniustam ac per
consequens prohibendam, quia in sic dicendo non actendunt huiusmodi
iura ad eandem causam nec ad eundem finem. Vbi autem est contradiccio,
oportet quod accipiatur secundum idem et respectu eiusdem.

95   Ex istis autem omnibus possumus formare unam talem racionem ad
propositum: illud quod est prohibendum a iure civili omitti, debet a iure
canonico assumi, quia ostensum est quod dicta iura sibi mutuo subveniunt. Sed prescripcio male fidei est prohibenda quia iniqua et iniusta ex
parte prescribentis, et tamen eius prohibicio a iure civili obmictitur, ergo
100   ipsius prohibicio debet assumi a iure canonico ac per consequens in dicto
casu unum ius discordabit ab altero, nec tamen propter hec talis discordia
erit contradiccio, ut superius est ostensum, quia non accipitur secundum
idem nec respectu eiusdem.

Secunda racio ad idem est talis: illud ius quod sequitur legem evange-
105   licam discordat ab illo quod non sequitur illam; ius autem canonicum
sequitur legem evangelicam et ei subalternatur, et quia lex evangelica discordat a iure civili, etiam ius canonicum discordabit ab illo. Quod autem
lex evangelica discordet a iure civili in rectificando actum interiorem patet
Matthei V, ubi dicitur 'omnis qui viderit mulierem ad concupiscendum
110   eam, iam mechatus est eam in corde suo.' Ius autem civile nititur solum
ad rectificandum actum exteriorem qui est ad alterum, per quem possit
civilis societas impediri, ergo et ius canonicum debet in hoc discordare
seu pocius superhabundare a iure civili, quia debet niti ad rectificandum
eciam actum interiorem, per quem possit a dicto deviari, ac per consequens
115   debet prescripcionem male fidei penitus prohibere, per quam actus interior obliquatur. Ex quo ulterius relinquitur quod in dicto casu a iure civili
racionabiliter discordabit.

Tercia racio ad idem est talis: illa iura debent in prescripcione male fidei

---

17/92 in sic dicendo : *om. C*   17/92–3 huiusmodi iura *C* : *om. R*   17/93 est : aliqua *add.*
C   17/94 respectu *C* : *om. R*   17/95 istis : quibus *C*   17/95 autem : *om. C*   17/96 omitti *C* : omittitur *R*   17/99 prescribentis : prohibentis *C*   17/102–3 quia ... eiusdem *C* : *om.*
R   17/104 est talis : *om. C*   17/105 discordat ... illam *C* : *om. R*   17/106 et² *C* : *om. R*
17/107–8 etiam ... civili *C* : *om. per hom. R*   17/108 interiorem : sicut *add. R* : *om. C*
17/110 eam² : *om. C*   17/110 autem : iam vero *C*   17/116 obliquatur : obliquat *C*
17/118 Tercia racio : Tertio *C*   17/118 est talis : sic *C*

17/102 Vid. sup. 6/137–47.   17/109–10 *Mt* 5.28.

consequently to be prohibited, because in so speaking it does not look to the same cause or end. But where there is a real contradiction, it is necessary that the contradiction refer to the same cause or purpose.

From these arguments, we can formulate the following consolidated argument with respect to the proposition. When something that should be prohibited is omitted by civil law, it must be assumed by canon law, because the two laws are complementary. Now prescription in bad faith ought to be prohibited because it is inequitable and unjust on the part of the prescriber; nevertheless civil law omits to prohibit it, therefore the prohibition must be assumed by canon law, and consequently, in this case, they are in disagreement with one another; but this disagreement is not contradiction, as was shown above.

The second reason is as follows: a law that follows the law of the gospel disagrees with a law that does not. Now canon law follows the law of the gospel and is subordinate to it. The law of the gospel disagrees with civil law because it corrects internal acts, as is clear at Matthew 5.28: 'everyone who looks at a woman lustfully has already committed adultery with her in his heart.' Civil law strives only to correct external acts against others that could injure civil society, therefore canon law rightly disagrees with it in this respect – or rather exceeds it – since it is founded on the correction of internal acts, which draws it away from civil law, and consequently canon law must completely prohibit prescription in bad faith, which involves a deformed internal act. From this it follows, moreover, that, in this case, canon law will disagree with civil law for good reason.

The third reason is as follows: two laws must disagree on prescription

necessario discordare quorum unum intendit conservare iusticiam propter
120   terminare litigia, alterum vero e converso intendit terminare litigia propter conservare iusticiam. Sed ius civile et canonicum ita se habent, quia
ius civile intendit conservare iusticiam propter terminare litigia, nam suus
finis principalis est conservare civilem societatem, que conservari non potest nisi litigia terminentur; ius autem canonicum e converso intendit ter-
125   minare litigia propter conservare iusticiam, quia suus finis principalis est
ordinare in Deum, ut legem evangelicam assequatur, qui quidem ordo in
Deum non habetur nisi iusticia conservetur, ut per eam actus interior, quo
ordinamur in Deum, reguletur, et hinc est quod una regula iuris canonici,
que habetur *extra de regulis iuris*, dicit quod 'utilius scandalum nasci per-
130   mictitur quam veritas relinquatur.' Quapropter relinquitur quod dicta duo
iura debuerint in prescripcione male fidei discordare, nam ius civile eo ipso
quod principaliter intendit terminare litigia, debuit instituere prescripcionem male fidei inducendam, quia quamvis in ea iusticia ad plenum non
servetur, tamen per eam ad plenum litigia terminantur; ius vero canoni-
135   cum e converso, nam quia intendit principaliter iusticiam conservare et in
Deum ordinare, idcirco merito debuit instituere prescripcionem male fidei
prohibendam, quia quamvis per eam ad plenum litigia terminentur, tamen
in ea ad plenum iusticia non servatur et per consequens a Deo deviatur et
ille finis tollitur, qui a dicto iure principaliter intenditur.
140   Quarta racio ad idem est talis: illa iura que ita se habent quod unum
eorum ita intendit de foro liti-|R222r-gii quod tamen finaliter remictit ad
forum consciencie, alterum vero sistit solum in foro litigii, non possunt
in prescripcione male fidei concordare, quia dicta prescripcio secundum
forum consciencie est dampnanda, secundum vero forum litigii inducen-
145   da. Ius vero canonicum et civile ita se habent quod ius civile sistit in foro
litigii, ius autem canonicum ita intendit de foro litigii quod cum finaliter
remictit ad forum consciencie, ut patet *extra de penitenciis et remissionibus*

17/119 propter : *om. C*   17/120 terminare : terminareque *C*   17/120 intendit : tendit *C*   17/123 que *C* : qua *R*   17/124 e converso : e contrario *C*   17/134 tamen :
ad eam *add. et exp. R*   17/135 e converso : e contrario *C*   17/136 Deum *C* : dicto
R   17/136 merito : necessario *C*   17/140 ad idem : *om. C*   17/142 possunt *C* : posunt
R   17/146 ius : *om. C*   17/146 autem : vero *C*   17/146 ita … cum : *om. C*   17/147 extra : *om. C*

17/129–30 X 5.41.3.   17/147–8 X 5.38.12.

in bad faith when one of them seeks to preserve justice in order to limit quarrels, and the other, by contrast, seeks to limit quarrels in order to preserve justice. Now civil and canon law have precisely this relationship, for civil law seeks to preserve justice in order to limit quarrels, since its principal objective is to preserve civil society, which cannot be preserved unless quarrels are limited. By contrast, canon law seeks to limit quarrels in order to preserve justice, since its principal objective is to direct us to God in order that it might conform to the law of the gospel. This guidance back to God is impossible unless justice is preserved so that it may regulate interior acts, by which we are directed to God, and hence there is a rule of canon law, which is found at X 5.41.3, that says 'it is better to permit a scandal than to relinquish the truth.' Therefore it follows that the two laws ought to disagree on prescription in bad faith, for inasmuch as civil law principally seeks to restrict lawsuits, it should sanction the introduction of prescription in bad faith because, even though this does not fully preserve justice, it nevertheless fully serves to restrict lawsuits. By contrast, because canon law principally seeks to preserve justice and direct us to God, it rightly sanctions the prohibition of prescription in bad faith because, even though this serves well to restrict lawsuits, it nevertheless does not fully preserve justice, and consequently departs from God and destroys the end which canon law principally seeks.

The fourth reason is as follows: laws that are such that one in the final analysis subordinates the court of law to the court of conscience and the other takes its stand in the court of law alone cannot agree on prescription in bad faith, because it must be condemned in the court of conscience but approved by the court of law. Now canon and civil law are two such laws, because civil law takes its stand in the court of law, but canon law, in the final analysis, subordinates the court of law to the court of conscience, as is clear in X 5.38.12. Therefore they must necessarily disagree on pre-

c. *Omnis utriusque sexus*, ergo necessario debuerint in prescripcione male
fidei discordare, quamvis talis discordia non sit contradiccio, ut superius
150   est ostensum, quia non est respectu eiusdem cause vel eiusdem finis.

Et ita patet quid nunc dicendum quantum ad istum articulum: quod
prescripcio iuris canonici est alia et debuit esse alia a prescripcione iuris
civilis. Et de hoc sunt assignate quattuor cause quas recolligendo in summa
dicemus quod prima est quia unum alteri subvenit, et quod unum dimicit,
155   alterum assumit. Secunda est quia ius canonicum in fine principaliter in-
tento cum evangelio convenit; ius vero civile de tali fine se non intromictit.
Tercia est quia ius civile conservare iusticiam propter terminare litigia intendit, ius vero canonicum totum contrarium facit, quia conservacionem
iusticie terminacionem licium proponit. Quarta est quia ius civile in solo
160   foro contencioso consistit; ius vero canonicum de foro contencioso ad
forum consciencie remictit. Et hoc sufficit quantum ad istum articulum.
Restat videre quarto.

\<18\> \<Articulus quartus\>

Quartus articulus, in quo probatur quod in prescripcione acquiritur dominium naturale et directum, alio tamen et alio modo, contra duas oppi-
niones iuristarum.
5   Vtrum in prescripcione acquiratur dominium. Ad evidenciam ergo
istius articuli est intelligendum quod quantum ad prescripcionem male
fidei que currit spacio XXX annorum, non videtur esse aliqua discordia
inter doctores iuris, nam omnes concorditer dicunt quod in ea non acquiritur dominium sed sola excepcio, quia si in ea acquiritur dominium, tunc
10   non solum fuisset inducta in odium negligencium sed eciam in favorem
mala fide possidencium, cuius contrarium apparet XVI q. III *Placuit* I.

17/148 debuerint : debebunt *C*   17/149 discordia : discordantia *C*   17/149–50 ut …
ostensum : ut dictum est *C*   17/151 nunc : *om. C*   17/151 quid : sit *add. C*   17/153 Et
de … cause : de quo quatuor assignavimus rationes *C*   17/154 dicemus : dicimus *C*
17/156 de : in *C*   17/159 terminacionem : terminationi *C*   17/162 Restat videre quarto :
om. C   18/2–4 Quartus … iuristarum : *om. C*   18/2 in prescripcione *C* : prescripcio
R   18/5 in : de *add. et exp. R*   18/5 ergo : *om. C*   18/7 non : num *C*   18/9 acquiritur :
acquiretur *C*   18/11 III : in *C*   18/11 Placuit : Placinti *C*

17/149–50 Vid. sup. 17/64–94.   18/11 Decretum Grat. C.16 q.3 c.8.

scription in bad faith, although such disagreement is not contradiction, as has been shown above, because they do not look to the same cause or purpose.

And thus it is clear what should be said with respect to this article, namely, that canon law prescription is – and ought to be – different from civil law prescription. Four reasons have been given for this, which, by way of summary, we can express as follows. First, that the two laws are complementary and that what one rejects, the other assumes. Second, that canon law principally seeks conformity with the gospel as its end, but civil law assumes no such end. Third, that civil law seeks to preserve justice in order to limit lawsuits, but canon law does just the opposite, since it places the preservation of justice before the limitation of lawsuits. Fourth, that civil law subsists purely in the law courts, but canon law appeals from the law court to the court of conscience. And this will suffice so far as this article is concerned. Let us now consider the fourth article.

18. Article 4

The fourth article, in which it is proven, against two opinions of the jurists, that prescription confers natural and absolute ownership, but in two different ways.

Is ownership acquired in prescription? For the clarification of this article it is necessary to understand that there does not appear to be any disagreement among the doctors of law with respect to prescription in bad faith that runs for a period of thirty years, for they all maintain that ownership is not thereby acquired, but only a defence, for otherwise prescription in bad faith would not only punish the negligent but favour those who possess in bad faith, as is clear at C.16 q.3 c.8. But regarding pre-

De prescripcione autem bone fidei videntur quamplures ad invicem discordare, namque quidam de antiquis doctoribus in iure dicunt quod in
prescripcione bone fidei que currit spacio X annorum contra absentem seu
15   eciam spacio XX annorum seu XXX aut XL contra presentem acquiritur
dominium utile et non dominium directum, quia probant per illum testum
qui habetur C. *de prescripcione XXX vel XL annorum* l. *Si quis empcionis*
in principio et secundo responso, ff. *de iure.* l. *Si duo* § *Iulianus.* Ibi enim
dicitur quod prescripcio habet utilem actionem in rem et habet excepcio-
20   nem contra dominum; si autem prescribens habet excepcionem contra dominum, ergo dominus contra quem fuit prescriptum habebat actionem,
quia excepcio non habet locum nisi ubi est possibilis actio; est enim excepcio actionis exclusio, ut patet ff. *de excepcione* l. II. Si autem dominus
contra quem prescriptum habet actionem, non potest habere nisi directam,
25   quia actionem utilem habet prescribens racione utilis dominii, et duo non
possunt esse simul domini in solidum uno respectu, ut patet ff. *commo.,* l.
Si ut certo § *Si duobus vehiculum.* Si ergo actio directa ac per consequens
dominium directum remansit apud illum contra quem est prescriptum,
relinquitur quod ipse prescribens acquisiverit per prescripcionem solam
30   actionem utilem et per consequens solum dominium utile. Et hanc opinionem sequuntur quamplures moderni doctores in iure.

Hec autem opinio videtur michi dubia et non racionabilis propter tria.
Primo quia homo non esset dominus rerum exteriorum nisi pro quanto
possunt venire in suum usum et utilitatem secundum ipsius arbitrium et

---

18/12 quamplures *C* : quod plures *R*   18/15 aut : seu *C*   18/16 probant *C* : probat *R*
18/16 testum *pro* textum *R* : textum *C*   18/17 C. : cap. *C*   18/17 vel : aut *C*   18/17 Si
quis empcionis : Si quis est praescriptionis *C*   18/18 et secundo responso : et 11 et 12 leg.
C   18/18 responso : l. *add. R*   18/19 prescripcio *C* : prescripcionem *R*   18/19 rem :
re *C*   18/20 dominum : dominium *C*   18/21 habebat : habet *C*   18/22–4 quia excepcio
... actionem : *om. per hom. C*   18/24 potest : autem *add. C*   18/24 directam : directum
C   18/25 habet *V* : patet *R* : perdit *C*   18/27 certo *scripsi* : certe *RC*   18/27 § *scripsi* :
est *R*   18/27 Si duobus vehiculum : *om. C*   18/32 racionabilis propter tria : rationabiliter
proposita *C*   18/33 pro quanto : per quantum *C*   18/34 possunt *C* : posito *R*   18/34 secundum *C* : *om. R*   18/34 ipsius : *om. C*

18/17–18 C. 7.39.8.   18/18 Dig. 12.2.13.1.   18/23 Dig. 44.2.1.   18/26–7 Dig. 13.6.5.15.
18/31 Cf. Gl. ord. ad C. 7.39.8, *Casus,* et vv. *Exceptionem, Actionem, Vti,* et *Possessor*
(ed. cit. cols. 1885–8); gl. ord. ad Dig. 12.2.13.1, v. *Praescriptionem* et v. *Actionem* (ed. cit.
cols. 1245–6); Gottofredo da Trani, *Summa,* X. 2.26 *de praescriptionibus,* n.6 (ed. cit. p.
234–235a); Hostiensis, *Summa aurea,* ad X 2.26, *de praescriptione rerum immobilium,* n.6
(ed. cit. fol. 119ra).

scription in good faith, there seem to be many disagreements, for certain ancient doctors of law say that prescription in good faith that lies for a period of ten years against an absent owner, or even for a period of twenty, thirty, or forty years against an owner who is present, confers useful but not absolute ownership, as may be proved by the texts at C. 7.39.8 near the beginning and in the second response, and at Dig. 12.2.13.2, where it is said that prescription confers useful ownership and a defence against the owner. But if the prescriber has a defence against the owner, then the owner against whom the prescription lies has an action, because a defence does not exist without a potential action; for a defence may be defined as the exclusion of an action, as is clear at Dig. 44.2.1. Now if an owner who has been prescribed has an action, it can only be an action for absolute ownership, because the prescriber has an action by reason of useful ownership, and two people cannot be owners of the same thing in the same respect, as is clear at Dig. 13.6.5.15. Therefore if an action for absolute ownership and absolute ownership itself remain with him who has been prescribed, it follows that the prescriber has acquired only an action for useful ownership. Several modern doctors of law adhere to this opinion.

This opinion seems to me doubtful and unreasonable on three grounds. First, because a man is not the owner of external things unless he can enjoy their use and benefit at will and choice, and therefore we see that things

35   voluntatem, et ideo videmus quod ille res que numquam possunt venire
      in usum et utilitatem hominis secundum ipsius arbitrium numquam pos-
      sunt cadere sub eius dominio, sicut patet de corporibus celestibus. Nunc
      ergo aliquis homo est dominus alicuius rei quando illam rem potest as-
      sumere vel suum usum et utilitatem assumere; propter quod eciam vide-
40   mus ulterius quod si alique res sunt apte nate cadere sub usu et utilitate
      hominis, et tamen numquam compertum est quod venerunt in usum et
      in utilitatem alicuius ex hoc ipso ab ipsa lege determinantur esse nullius
      et naturali racione conceduntur et subiciuntur dominio primi occupantis,
      ut patet ff. *de acquirendo rerum dominio* l. I § *Quod enim nullius.* Hoc
45   autem ideo videtur contingere, quia dominium quod habet homo in exte-
      rioribus rebus provenit ex earum usu et utilitate. Constat autem quod ille
      contra quem processit prescripcio bone fidei nullo modo potest assumere
      rem prescriptam in suum usum et utilitatem, ergo nullo modo dominus ac
      per consequens non remansit apud eum dominium directum, ut dicebat
50   prefata opinio.
         Secundo patet hoc idem quia videmus quod prescribens aliquam rem
      bona fide potest transferre dominium directum ipsius ad quemdam alium,
      utpote si vendat rem illam alicui domino et postea recipiat eam in feudum
      ab eo, dicetur transtulisse dictam rem in illum dominum quantum ad di-
55   rectum dominium et eam sibi reassumpsisse quantum ad dominium utile.
      Constat autem quod unusquisque homo tale dominium de re quacumque
      apud alium transfert quam apud se habet, ut patet ff. *de acquirendo rerum
      dominio* l. *Tradicio.* Si ergo prescribens tale dominium transferre potuit,
      videtur quod ipsum apud se habuerit ac per consequens quod dictum tale
60   dominium per prescripcionem acquisierit.
         Tercio patet hoc idem quia videmus quod ille qui solum dominium utile
      habet, non habet dominium totale, et ideo exhibet quid domino directo,
      utpote vel partem utilitatis vel homagium vel quidquid tale, per quod da-

---

18/41 compertum est : actum sit *C*   18/41 venerunt : veniant *C*   18/42 nullius : univer-
sales *C*   18/43 naturali : universali *C*   18/44 Quod enim nullius : Quod II universalius *C*   18/47 processit : procedit *C*   18/48 dominus : dominium *C*   18/54 dominum : dominium *C*   18/55 reassumpsisse : resumpsisse *C*   18/55 utile : universale
C   18/57 quam *C* : qua *R* : se *add. R* : vere *add. C*   18/58 tale : *om. C*   18/62 habet[1] *C* :
om. R   18/62 quid : aliquid *C*   18/63 quidquid : quidquam *C*

18/44 Dig. 41.1.3.pr.   18/49–50 Vid. sup. 18/12–31.   18/57–8 Dig. 41.1.31.

that cannot be enjoyed at the will and choice of someone cannot fall under his ownership, as is clear in the case of the heavenly bodies. Therefore, a man is owner of something when he can appropriate the thing or its use and benefit. For this reason, moreover, we see that if certain things have been created apt to serve the use and benefit of man, but it can be shown that they have never served the use and benefit of anyone, the law itself decrees that they are the property of no one, and by natural reason they are conceded to and subject to the ownership of the first occupant, as is clear at Dig. 41.1.3.pr. Now this seems to occur because the ownership which a man has in exterior things proceeds from their use and benefit. It follows, then, that since he against whom prescription in good faith lies cannot in any way assume the use and benefit of the prescribed thing, he is in no sense owner, and consequently does not retain absolute ownership of it, as the aforesaid opinion nevertheless declares.

Second, the same is clear because we see that one who prescribes something in good faith can transfer absolute ownership to someone else. For example, if he sells the thing to some lord and afterwards receives it from him as a fief, he is said to have transferred the thing to the lord so far as absolute ownership is concerned and reassumed it so far as useful ownership is concerned. Now it follows that a man can only transfer to another ownership of a thing that he possesses, as is clear at Dig. 41.1.31. Therefore if a prescriber can transfer absolute ownership, it appears that he possesses it, and consequently that he acquired absolute ownership through prescription.

Third, the same is clear because we see that he who enjoys only useful ownership does not enjoy complete ownership, and therefore he offers something to the absolute owner; for example, a portion of the benefit he

tur intelligi quod ipse non est dominus directus sed ille cui fit ista exhibicio
65   vel recognicio, ac per consequens eo ipso quod ille qui habet solum utile dominium recognoscit alium dominum, videtur ipse non habere totale
dominium. Si ergo prescribens bona fide acquisivisset per prescripcionem
solum dominium utile, non haberet totale dominium sed necessario recog-
nosceret alium dominium, utpote illum contra quem prescripsisset, quod
70   patet evidenter esse falsum.

Ad racionem vero istius opinionis potest responderi quod ille contra
quem processit prescripcio non habet actionem directam sed actionem
innanem, quia illa actio est inanis quam excludit inopia debitoris, ut patet *extra de spo.*, *Olim nobis*. Vel possumus dicere quod ille contra quem
75   processit prescripcio, quamvis habeat actionem antequam probetur contra
eum prescripcio, cum autem contra eum probata fuerit nullam habet penitus actionem. Propter que omnia videtur quod ista opinio non possit
racionabiliter sustineri.
Et ideo est alia opinio quorundam aliorum doctorum in iure dicencium
80   quod in prescripcione acquiratur non solum dominium utile sed eciam
dominium directum, quod probant per testum plurium legum in quibus
habetur quod prescribens spacio XXX annorum efficitur dominus. Si autem per prescripcionem acquireretur solum dominium utile, non diceretur
prescribens simpliciter effici dominus sed diceretur effici dominus cum
85   quadam determinacione adiuncta et diminuente.
Confirmatur autem hoc idem per tres raciones precipue. Prima est quia
fortior est possessio in rebus inmobilibus que acquiruntur per prescripcio-
nem quam in rebus mobilibus que ac- |^R222v –quiruntur per usucapionem;
sed per usucapionem acquiritur non solum dominium utile sed eciam di-
90   rectum, ergo multo magis debet hec eadem acquiri per prescripcionem.

18/65 eo ipso : ex hoc *C*   18/69 utpote : puta *C*   18/70 evidenter : *om. C*   18/71 re-
sponderi *C* : respondere *R*   18/73 inopia *scripsi*; *cf.* X 2.13.16 : depis *R* : depositum
C   18/74 de spo. : de ipso *C*   18/76 cum : contra *add. R*   18/76 cum ... fuerit
C : *om. R*   18/79 quorundam ... in iure : *om. C*   18/81 testum *pro* textum *R* : testi-
monium *C*   18/85 adiuncta *C* : adiunta *R*   18/87 que *C* : qui *R*   18/88 que *C* : qui
R   18/89 per : *marg. R*   18/89 eciam : *om. C*   18/90 hec eadem : hic idem *C*

18/74 X 2.13.16 (*recte* de restitutione spoliatorum).   18/81 Cf. Gl. ord. ad C. 2.3.20, v. *Et
usucapionibus* (ed. cit. col. 341).

derives from his useful ownership or homage or some such thing. In this way, he makes clear that he is not the absolute owner, but rather that the one to whom he grants the offering or recognition is the absolute owner. Consequently, by the very fact that he who possesses only useful ownership acknowledges another owner, he does not appear to enjoy complete ownership. If, therefore, a prescriber in good faith acquired only useful ownership through prescription, he would not possess complete ownership, but would necessarily recognize another owner – for example, him against whom he prescribed – which is patently false.

To the logic of the above argument, then, we may respond that one against whom prescription lies does not have a direct but rather a void action, for an action that the helplessness of the debtor excludes is void, as is clear at X 2.13.16. Or we can say that although one against whom prescription lies has an action before it is completed, he has none whatsoever after. For these reasons, it seems the opinion cannot reasonably be sustained.

But there is another opinion held by certain doctors of law who say that prescription confers not only useful but also absolute ownership, and they prove this by means of many laws in which it is held that one who prescribes for a period of thirty years is rendered owner. For if prescription conferred only useful ownership, it would not be said that the prescriber is rendered the owner, but rather owner with certain limiting qualifications.

This is confirmed by three arguments in particular. The first is that possession of immoveables obtained by prescription is stronger than the possession of moveables obtained by usucapion. But usucapion confers both useful and absolute ownership, therefore much more should prescription confer both useful and absolute ownership of things acquired in this way.

Secunda racio ad idem est quia si per prescripcionem non acquireretur dominium directum, iam videretur quod dominium directum esset inprescriptibile, quod patet esse falsum, nam videmus quod si pheudatarius vel emphiteuta seu superficiarius intervertent possessionem et possideant isto
95   modo spacio XXX vel XL annorum prescribent dominium; quod si dicatur eos non prescribere, sequitur quod cursus tanti temporis apud eos nichil operatur, quod omnino est inconveniens, nam et iura personalia, de quibus minus videtur quia sint ossibus nostris infixa prescribuntur cum spacio XXX annorum, ut patet ff. *pro socio* l. IIII et *de peculio* l. *Quis ergo*
100   *casus* et C. *de prescripcione XXX vel XL annorum* l. *Sicut.*

Tercia racio ad idem est quia ille qui tanto tempore tacuit presumitur consentire, ut ff. *de verb. sign.* l. *Alienacionis verbo.* Constat autem quod per consensum transfertur utile dominium et directum, ut *Inst. de rerum di.* § *Per tradicionem,* ac per consequens videtur quod tempore prescrip-
105   cionis acquiratur utrunque dominium, scilicet tam utile quam directum.

Hec autem opinio non videtur omnino racionabilis propter duo. Primo quia videtur ponere quod in prescripcione acquiratur necessario dominium directum quemadmodum et in usucapione, cuius contrarium evidenter apparet; nam videmus quod posset aliquis prescribere contra pheudatarium
110   non prescribendo contra dominium pheudi, in quo casu acquireretur per prescripcionem solum dominium utile et non dominium directum. Ulterius secundo non videtur hec opinio racionabilis quia non convenienter distinguit inter dominium directum et dominium utile, accipit enim directum et utile quasi duo dominia distincta, cuius oppositum statim ostende-
115   tur. Et quantum ad istam partem videtur prima oppinio defecisse sicut et ista; propter que omnia videtur esse aliter procedendum in isto articulo.

18/91 ad *V* : quod *R*   18/91 ad … quia : *om. C*   18/94 intervertent : inter veterat *C*   18/97 operatur *C* : opereretur *R*   18/97 personalia : praecriptionis *C*   18/98 minus : *om. C*   18/98 quia : quod *C* : cum *V*   18/98 prescribuntur : praescribunt *C*   18/99 l. IIII : 54 *C*   18/99 de peculio *V* : de pro octavo *R* : de pro .8. *C*   18/99 l.² : Si *add. RC*   18/100 C. *V* : § *RC*   18/101 Tercia … quia : Tertio sic *C*   18/103 Inst. : iustum *C*   18/104 § : C. *C*   18/104 tempore : per tempus *C*   18/105 utrunque *V* : utrum *R* : *om. C*   18/105 scilicet : videlicet *C*   18/106 omnino : *om. CV*   18/109 pheudatarium : praebendatarium *C*   18/111 dominium² : *om. CV*   18/111 directum : et econverso *add. V*

18/99–100 Dig. 17.2.3; 15.1.16(17); C. 7.39.3.   18/102 Dig. 50.16.28.   18/103–4 Inst. 2.1.40.

The second argument is that if absolute ownership were not obtained by prescription, it would appear that absolute ownership is imprescriptible, which is clearly false, for we see that if a tenant or a lease-holder or an occupant gains possession and then possesses in this way for a period of thirty or forty years, he will obtain ownership by prescription. If it is said that he does not so prescribe, it follows that the lapse of so much time has no effect in these cases, which is completely inconsistent, for personal rights that are less obvious because they inhere in our very bones are prescribed within a period of thirty years, as is clear at Dig. 17.2.3, 15.1.16 and C. 7.39.3.

The third reason is that he who remains silent for such a long time is presumed to consent, as at Dig. 50.16.28. But it follows that useful and absolute ownership are transferred by consent, as at *Institutes* 2.1.40, and consequently it appears that both forms of ownership, namely useful and absolute, are obtained through the time that elapses in prescription.

But this argument does not appear entirely reasonable for two reasons. First, because it seems to assume that absolute ownership is obtained in prescription in the same way that it is in usucapion, though the opposite is clearly true. For we see that someone can prescribe against a tenant without prescribing against the fief, and in this case he acquires only useful, not absolute, ownership. Second, this argument appears unreasonable because it does not adequately distinguish between useful and absolute ownership, for it takes them to be two distinct forms of ownership, though the opposite is the case, as I shall presently show. So far as this part of the question is concerned, it appears that this opinion is as flawed as the first, and so it seems best to proceed differently.

Sciendum ergo quod dominium directum et dominium utile quandoque distinguuntur sicut duo diversa dominia, quandoque vero sicut duo
diversi modi habendi idem dominium; debemus namque ymaginare quod
120   utile et directum quandoque capiunt distinctionem penes alium et alium
modum habendi. Primum patet, videmus enim quod alio modo utitur re
pheudata ipse pheudatarius et alio modo dominus ipse pheudi, nam pheudatarius utitur re pheudata capiendo de ea fructum per culturam et laborem; ille vero qui est dominus pheudi utitur eadem re capiendo de ea
125   fructum sine omni cultura et labore; et ita suo modo dicendum est de em-
phiteota et principaliter domino. In tali ergo casu dominium directum et
utile distinguuntur penes alium et alium modum utendi; quandoque vero
distinguuntur penes alium et alium modum habendi, sive penes alium et
alium modum acquirendi idem dominium. Habemus namque supponere
130   quod acquisicio dominii est a iure gencium, ut habetur ff. *de iusticia et
iure* l. *Ex hoc iure.* Ius autem gencium soli homini competit ad differen-
tiam iuris naturalis, quod omnibus animalibus est commune, ut habetur ibi
di. I. Sed ius naturale competit insuper omnibus hominibus, quia omnes
gentes eo utuntur, ut patet in decretis di. I *Ius gencium.* Quapropter non
135   videtur quod ius gencium sit aliud quam racio naturalis que sic est homini propria quod cum omnibus hominibus est collata, que quidem racio
naturalis est quasi quedam lex tacita, ut patet ff. *de bonis dampnatorum* l.
Cum racio. Est, inquam, lex tacita quia in corde hominis divinitus et naturaliter scripta, etsi mandato pretoris exterius promulgata; huius ergo legis
140   et huius iuris naturalis equitati oportet quod omnis dominii acquisicio innititur. Contingit autem quandoque quod acquisicio dominii in aliqua re
innititur equitati iuris naturalis directe, quandoque vero indirecte, verbi
gracia, de utroque. Si enim occupemus aliquam rem penitus delictam vel
que numquam extitit alicuius dominii, acquisicio dominii in illa re directe
145   concordat et innititur equitati iuris naturalis, ut patet per illam legem al-

---

18/121 quod : dominium *add. C*   18/122 dominus *CV* : possessor *R*   18/122 ipse :
om. C   18/123 ea *C* : eo *R*   18/133 naturale : utile *C*   18/134 ut : patet *add. et exp.*
R   18/137 bonis dampnatorum : bono ius depravatorum *C*   18/138–9 naturaliter :
universaliter *C*   18/139 pretoris : ulterius *add. et exp. R* : sit *add. C*   18/139 exterius :
ulterius *C*   18/142 innititur : innitatur *CV*   18/143 occupemus : occupamus *C*

18/130–1 Dig. 1.1.5.   18/132–3 Decretum Grat. D.1.   18/134 Decretum Grat. D.1
c.7.   18/137–8 Dig. 48.20.7.

It must be known, therefore, that absolute and useful ownership are sometimes distinguished as if they were two distinct forms of ownership, and sometimes as if they were two distinct modes of enjoying the same ownership. We should imagine, then, that useful and absolute ownership sometimes derive their distinction from two distinct ways of possessing. This is clear because we sometimes see that a tenant uses a fief in one way and the owner of the fief in another, for the tenant uses enfeoffed property by deriving fruits from it by his cultivation and labour; the owner uses a fief by deriving fruits from it without labour and cultivation. The same could be said of a lease-holder and principal owner. In this case, then, absolute and useful ownership are distinguished by two distinct ways of possessing. But sometimes they are distinguished by two distinct ways of owning and two distinct ways of acquiring ownership. Now we must presume that acquisition of ownership belongs to the law of nations, as is held at Dig. 1.1.5. The law of nations pertains only to man, in contradistinction to natural law, which is common to all living things, as is held at D.1. But natural law pertains above all to all men, because all nations adhere to it, as is clear in the decrees at D.1 c.7. Therefore, it does not seem that the law of nations is anything other than natural reason, which is peculiar to man because it is agreed on by all men, and natural reason is a sort of tacit law, as is clear at Dig. 48.20.7. It is, I repeat, a tacit law written by God and nature in the human heart, even if it has been externally confirmed by the praetor's edict. It is, therefore, fitting that all acquisition of ownership is founded on the equity of this silent and natural law. But sometimes it happens that ownership of a thing is based directly on the equity of natural law, and sometimes indirectly. I shall provide an example of each. For if we should occupy property that has been completely abandoned or was never subject to ownership, acquisition of ownership in the thing agrees with and is directly based on natural equity, as is clear in the law we cited

legatam superius ff. *de acquirendo rerum dominio* l. *Quod enim nullius.*
Dicitur enim in illa lege quod illa res que nullius est naturali racione oc-
cupanti conceditur ac per consequens acquisicio dominii in illa re naturali
racioni directe innititur, quia nulla est regula iuris naturalis sive racionis
150   naturalis que huius dominii acquisicionem valeat obviare. Vlterius eciam
si acquiramus dominium in aliqua re per liberam tradicionem illius cuius
est illa res, tunc eciam acquisicio dominii in illa re concordat et innititur
equitati iuris naturalis directe, quia a nulla regula iuris naturalis discordat,
et hoc eciam potest haberi ff. *de acquirendo rerum dominio* l. *Qua racione*
155   § *Hec quoque.* In illo namque paragrapho dicitur quod ille 'res que tradicione nostre fiunt, iure gencium nobis acquiruntur,' cuius racio redditur
in sequenti paragrapho, ubi dicitur quod 'nihil est tam conveniens naturali
equitati quam voluntatem domini volentis rem suam in alium transferre
ratam haberi.'
160   Patet ergo ex istis duobus exemplis quomodo acquisicio dominii in
aliqua re quandoque innititur equitati iuris naturalis directe. Restat ergo
videre in aliquo alio exemplo quomodo in acquirendo dominium quandoque innitatur indirecte equitati iuris naturalis. Contingit enim quandoque
quod acquirimus dominium in aliqua re per exactionem illius rei a debi-
165   tore nostro nomine pene, quia iura civilia volunt quod illud quod exigitur
a debitore nomine pene lucro debet cedere creditoris, ut patet ff. *de solucionibus et liberacionibus* l. *Id quod pene.* Acquisicio ergo dominii isto
modo innititur et concordat equitati iuris naturalis, non quidem directe
sed indirecte, quod patet ex duobus. Primo quidem quia illud concordat
170   equitati iuris naturalis directe cui non invenitur aliqua iuris naturalis regula obviare. Nunc autem huic acquisicioni dominii obviat illa regula iuris
naturalis que superius fuit allegata in secundo articulo et habetur ff. *de re.*
iu. ubi dicitur quod iure nature equum est neminem cum alterius detri-

---

18/146 nullius : universalius *C*   18/148 ac *CV* : ad *R*   18/149 racioni : racionem *R*
18/150 valeat : valet *C*   18/155 Hec : Hoc *CV*   18/155 quoque : quandoque *C*
18/157 nihil est tam : nulla est causa *C*   18/157 conveniens *V* : inconveniens *RC*
18/158 quam : quae *C*   18/158 domini *CV* : dominii *R*   18/158 transferre *V* : transferri
RC   18/159 haberi : prohibeat *add. C*   18/160 quomodo : quod *C*   18/167 Id quod
pene : Id poene *C*   18/171 obviat *C* : obvi *R*

18/146 Dig. 41.1.3.pr.   18/154–9 Dig. 41.1.9.3.   18/166–7 Dig. 46.3.74.   18/172–3 Dig.
50.17.206(207).

earlier, namely, Dig. 41.1.3.pr., where it says that a thing that belongs to no one is granted by natural reason to the first occupant, and consequently that the acquisition of the ownership of such a thing is based directly on natural reason, for there is no rule of natural law or natural reason that could oppose such acquisition of ownership. Moreover, even if we obtain ownership of a thing by free delivery from him whose thing it is, acquisition of the ownership agrees with and is based directly on natural equity, since no rule of natural law opposes it, and this is held at Dig. 41.1.9.3, where it is said that 'those things which are delivered to us become ours under the law of nations,' and it goes on to provide the reason: 'nothing is so conformable to natural equity as that effect should be given to the wishes of an owner wanting to transfer his thing to someone else.'

It is clear from these two examples how acquisition of the ownership of a thing is sometimes based directly on natural equity. It remains, then, to see by another example how acquisition of ownership is sometimes based indirectly on natural equity. Now it happens that we sometimes acquire ownership of a thing by exacting it from a debtor as a penalty, for the civil laws decree that what is exacted from a debtor as a penalty should accede to the creditor, as is clear at Dig. 46.3.74. Acquisition of ownership in this way is based on and accords with natural law equity not directly, but rather indirectly, and this is clear for two reasons. First, because that which no rule of natural law opposes accords directly with natural law equity. But the rule of natural law cited above in the second article and found at Dig. 50.17.206 – where it says that 'by the law of nature it is fair that no one become richer by the loss and injury of another' – opposes the acquisition of ownership in this way, and consequently such acquisition departs from

mento et iniuria fieri locupletiorem, ac per consequens acquisicio domi-
175   nii isto modo deviat ab equitate iuris naturalis quia dicta regula ei obviat
evidenter; revocatur tamen ad eiusdem iuris naturalis equitatem per aliam
que dicit quod pro quolibet peccato debet pena infligi ut nullum malum
remaneat impunitum.

Ex quibus omnibus apparet quod acquisicio dominii in isto casu con-
180   cordat equitati iuris nature, non quidem totaliter, ac per consequens non
directe, quia non concordat dicte equitati quasi directe originem ab ea
trahendo, immo quasi indirecte ad eam redeundo. Secundo patet hoc idem
quia acquisicio illius dominii que totaliter et directe innititur equitati iuris
nature habet suam efficaciam et vigorem sine omni favore iuris legalis, ut
185   patet in acquisicione dominii sumpta primo modo; nam dato quod nullum
esset ius legale, adhuc primus modus acquirendi dominium haberet locum.
Secundus autem modus acquirendi dominium, qui imme- |^{R223r} -diate est
dictus, non habet efficaciam vel vigorem nisi supposito favore iuris legalis, ac per consequens non innititur equitati iuris naturalis directe sed per
190   quandam reductionem indirectam, quam reductionem facit ius legale quia
ad ipsum spectat naturalis iuris regulas concordare, ut potest patere ex hiis
que dicta fuerunt supra in secundo articulo, et ideo talis modus acquirendi
dominium locum non haberet si ius legale non esset.

Apparet ergo ex omnibus hiis quod omnis acquisicio dominii innititur
195   iuri gencium sive iuri naturali, ita tamen quod sunt duo modi acquirendi
dominium, quorum unus innititur et concordat iuri naturali directe, alter
vero indirecte quemadmodum superius est expressum. Intelligendum tamen quod quamvis sint duo modi acquirendi dominium, illud tamen dominium quod acquiritur per utrumque modum non est aliud et aliud sed
200   unum et idem nam, quia dominium rei ordinatur ad usum eius, idcirco ubi
est tantum usus rei et unus modus utendi, ibi videtur esse tantum unum

---

18/176 aliam : regulam *add. C*   18/177 que dicit : dicentem *C*   18/182 redeundo : rece-
dendo *C*   18/184 sine : cum *C*   18/186 haberet : haberetur *C* : habet *V*   18/186 locum
V : *om. RC*   18/187 qui : est *add. R*   18/187–8 est dictus : esse dominum *C*   18/189 innititur : innitur *C*

natural law equity, because this rule is clearly contradicted. Nevertheless, acquisition of this kind also appeals to natural law equity, which says that a penalty should be imposed for every sin so that no wickedness goes unpunished.

From these considerations, it is clear that acquisition of ownership in this way is in agreement with natural law equity, but not entirely, and, consequently, not directly, for it does not correspond to natural equity as an immediate source, but indirectly because it can ultimately be traced back to it. Second, the same is clear because acquisition of ownership that is completely and directly based on natural equity has efficacy and force without the aid of positive law, as is clear in the example of the acquisition of ownership in the first way, for even if no positive law sanctioned it, it would still have force. But the second way of acquiring ownership just mentioned has no efficacy or force except by virtue of positive law, and consequently it is not based directly on natural equity, but may be traced back to it indirectly. This tracing-back is accomplished via positive law, because it is a characteristic of positive law that it corresponds to natural law rules, as is clear from the things said above in the second article, and therefore this second way of acquiring ownership would not exist if it were not sanctioned by positive law.

From all of this it is clear that all ownership is based on the law of nations or natural law, but in such a way that ownership may be acquired in two ways, one based upon and corresponding directly to natural law, the other indirectly in the way just explained. Nevertheless, it must be understood that although there are two ways of acquiring ownership, ownership acquired by one route is not different from the other, but rather one and the same, for ownership of a thing is directed towards its use; therefore when the use and way of using is the same, the ownership seems to be the

dominium. Et quia est idem usus rei et idem modus utendi quem habet ille qui acquirit eam per dominium directum a iure naturali directe exortum et ille qui eam acquirit per dominium utile ad ius naturale indirecte reduc-
205   tum, idcirco relinquitur quod per ambos prefatos modos sit unum tantum dominium acquisitum.

Et ita patet illud quod superius dicebatur, scilicet quod dominium direc-tum et dominium utile quandoque distinguntur penes alium et alium mo-dum utendi et tunc faciunt duo parcialia et distincta dominia, quandoque
210   vero penes alium et alium modum utendi vel acquirendi et tunc sunt unum tantum dominium possibile acquiri per prefatos duos modos.

Intelligendum insuper quod ex hiis que dicta sunt possumus colligere quod dominium directum non sic distinguitur ab utili quasi ipsum non sit utile sed quia applicat utilitatem rei cuius sit dominus alio modo quam
215   faciat illud dominium quod est tantum utile et ideo ubi dominium direc-tum et utile distinguntur solum penes alium et alium modum acquirendi, ibi tota utilitas que erat apud dominum directum debet transferri ad do-minum utilem, quia illud idem dominium quod habuit dominus directus habet postea dominus utilis, quamvis alio modo, quia ipsum alio modo
220   acquisivit, ut superius patuit.

Sciendum ulterius quod ex processu superius habito possumus collige-re duplicem racionem quare dominium directum dicatur ossibus nostris infixum et a nobis inseparabile, ut habetur ff. *pro socio* l. III et *de peculio* l. *Quis ergo casus.* Vna siquidem racio est quia tale dominium directe in-
225   nititur iuri naturali sive racioni naturali, ut patet ex dictis. Racio autem naturalis est cordi nostro infixa et a nobis inseparabilis, quasi quedam lex immobilis, ut ait Augustinus II *Confessionum* sic innuens: 'lex,' inquit, 'scripta est in cordibus hominum quod nec ulla quidem delet iniquitas.' Dominium ergo directum, quia innititur illi iuri quod nobis est infixum

---

18/210 vero : distinguuntur *add. C*   18/214 sit^2 *C* : huius *R*   18/217 dominum[1] : *corr. e* dominium *R*   18/218 quod *C* : vero *R*   18/223 peculio *C* : peculo *R*   18/224 l. : Si *add. RC*   18/225 sive : seu *C*   18/226 et *CV* : ut *R*   18/227 II : 3 *C*   18/227 innuens *V* : inconveniens *R* : *om. C*   18/229 est : illi iuri *add. et exp. R*

18/207 Vid. sup. 18/117–59.   18/220 Vid. sup. 18/194–206.   18/223-4 Dig. 17.2.3; 15.1.16(17) (*recte* Quis ergo casus).   18/227–8 Augustine, *Confessionum libri tredecim* 2.4, in CSEL 33, ed. P. Knöll (Vienna, 1896), p. 35.

same. Now because he who acquires a thing by way of absolute owner-ship that springs directly from natural law and he who acquires it by way of useful ownership that can be traced back to natural law indirectly use it in the same way, it follows that the same ownership is obtained in either way.

And thus what was said earlier is clear, namely, that absolute and useful ownership are sometimes distinguished by different modes of use, when they represent two partial or distinct forms of ownership, sometimes by different modes of use and acquisition, when the same potential owner-ship is obtained in both ways.

It must be understood, moreover, that from what has been said we may conclude that absolute ownership is distinguished from useful ownership not because it is not useful, but because it applies the utility of the thing owned differently from ownership which is only useful, and therefore when absolute and useful ownership are distinguished only on the basis of different modes of acquisition, the entire benefit that the absolute owner possessed should be transferred to the useful owner, because the same ownership the absolute owner possessed is now possessed by the useful owner, although in a different way, because he acquired it in a different way, as was made clear above.

Further, it must be known that from the above analysis we can conclude that there is a twofold reason why absolute ownership may be said to inhere in our very bones and to be inseparable from us, as is held at Dig. 17.2.3 and 15.1.16. One reason is that such absolute ownership is based directly on natural law and natural reason, as is clear from what was said. But natural reason is so inscribed on our hearts that it is inseparable from us, like an immoveable law, as Augustine says in book 2 of the *Confessions*: 'a law has been written in the hearts of men that no wickedness erases.' Absolute ownership, then, because it is based upon a law that is inscribed

230 et a nobis inseparabile, est etiam ossibus nostris infixum. Secunda racio
est quia ius naturale est forcius et efficacius quam sit ius legale et naturalis
racio forcior et efficacior quam sit humana voluntas, omne ergo illud quod
est nobis unitum naturali iure et naturali racione non potest a nobis separari iure legali et humana voluntate. Dominium autem directum est nobis
235 unitum naturali iure et naturali racione, ergo non poterit a nobis separari
per ius legale aut per humanam voluntatem, ac per consequens racionabiliter dicetur ossibus nostris infixum et a nobis inseparabile.
   Hiis ergo omnibus declaratis, possumus faciliter descendere ad illud
quod principaliter est quesitum in isto articulo. Nam cum queritur utrum
240 in prescripcione acquiratur dominium, in fine dicendum itaque quod in
ea et per eam acquiritur dominium utile et directum, et alio modo tantum dominium utile et non directum. Nam si accipiamus dominium utile
et directum prout distinguitur penes alium et alium modum utendi tanquam duo dominia parcialia, sic unum eorum non separatur ab alio; nam
245 si unum istorum acquireretur sine alio sequeretur quod ipse prescribens
non acquireret per prescripcionem totale dominium, immo magis dominium parciale, ac per consequens non haberet totalem usum in re prescripta nec totalem utilitatem de ea perciperet, ymo una pars usus et utilitatis
remaneret apud illum contra quem prescripcio processisset, quod patet
250 esse falsum. Possemus ergo ex istis dictis formare unam talem racionem
ad propositum: per illud acquirimus dominium utile et directum primo
modo per quod habemus totalem usum et utilitatem de re prescripta. Sed
per prescripcionem acquirimus totalem utilitatem et usum, ergo per eam
acquirimus utrumque dominium. Maior videtur esse nota quia directum et
255 utile accepta primo modo non distinguuntur nisi penes divisionem usus et
utilitatis rei super quam cadunt, et ideo ubi usus et utilitas rei non dividi-
tur sed manet integraliter apud unum sine omni distinctione, ille, inquam,
habet de illa re utrumque dominium sive totale dominium. Minor eciam
de se apparet quia quando prescribimus usum et utilitatem rei prescripte,
260 cum nemine dividimus, quod non est propter aliud nisi quia per eam ac-

18/230 est ... infixum *C* : *om. RV*   18/232 racio : est *add. C*   18/235 poterit : potest
C   18/237 dicetur : dicitur *C*   18/240 in fine : *om. CV*   18/240 itaque : *om. C*
18/241 et² : etiam *add. C*   18/243 distinguitur : distinguuntur *C*   18/244 ab alio *C* : *om.
R*   18/246 immo : *corr. ex* primo *R*   18/248 pereciperet *C* : percipet *R*   18/249 proces-
sisset : processit *C*   18/250 ergo : *om. C*   18/250 istis : quibus *C*   18/250 unam : *om.
C*   18/252–3 Sed ... usum *C* : *om. R*   18/259 quando : cum *R*

in us and inseparable from us, also inheres in our bones. A second reason is that natural law is stronger and more efficacious than positive law, and natural reason stronger and more efficacious than the human will. Therefore, anything bound to us by natural law and natural reason cannot be detached by positive law and human will. Absolute ownership inheres in us by natural law and natural reason, therefore it cannot be detached from us by positive law and human will; and consequently it may be said with reason that it inheres in our bones and is inseparable from us.

With these matters clarified, we can now more easily return to the principal question of this article. When it is asked, then, whether prescription confers ownership, in the end it must be said that prescription confers useful and absolute ownership and, in a different way, simply useful and non-absolute ownership. For if we understand useful and absolute ownership as distinguished by different modes of using, as if they were two incomplete forms of ownership, then the one is inseparable from the other. For if one were acquired without the other, it would follow that the prescriber did not acquire complete ownership by prescription, but rather incomplete ownership, and consequently he would not enjoy the complete use of the thing prescribed, nor could he receive its full benefit; indeed, part of the use and part of the benefit would remain with him against whom prescription lay, which is clearly false. Therefore, on the basis of what has been said, we could formulate an argument with regard to the proposition as follows: we acquire useful and absolute ownership through that by which we possess the complete use and benefit of the thing prescribed. Now we acquire complete benefit and use through prescription, therefore we acquire both forms of ownership through it. The major premiss seems clear, because absolute and useful ownership understood in the first way are not distinguished except with regard to the use and benefit of the thing to which they pertain, and therefore when the use and utility of a thing are not distinguished but lodge entirely with one person without distinction, he, I say, enjoys ownership of the thing in both senses, or complete own-

quirimus totalem usum et utilitatem, ac per consequens totale dominium.

Si vero accipiamus utile et directum secundo modo, scilicet prout distinguuntur penes alium et alium modum acquirendi, sic dicendum quod
in prescipcione acquiritur tantum dominium utile et non directum, nam
265   quamvis per eam acquireretur totale dominium, ut iam patuit, illud tamen dominium acquiritur per eam non modo directo sed modo indirecto,
quod potest probari una tali racione: illud dominium acquiritur indirecte
quod ab equitate iuris nature non directe exoritur, tamen ad illam equitatem indirecte reducitur. Sed dominium acquisitum in prescripcione non
270   oritur ab equitate iuris nature directe; reducitur tamen ad eam indirecte,
ergo dictum dominium non erit directum sed indirectum, quia non directe
sed indirecte acquisitum. Maior patet ex hiis que dicta sunt immediate in
isto articulo. Minor eciam potest patere ex hiis que dicta fuerunt supra in
secundo articulo; nam quamvis prescripcio non sit contra ius nature, ut
275   patuit in dicto articulo, non tamen sic directe concordat iuri nature quod a
nulla regula iuris nature discordare videatur, nam saltem videtur discordare ab illa regula que dicit quod nullus debet locupletari cum detrimento alterius. Quapropter non debemus dicere quod a iure nature directe oriatur
sed ad dictum ius indirecte revocetur, ac per consequens non acquiretur
280   per eam directum dominium sed tantum utile et indirectum.

Occurrit autem contra ista dicta una dubitacio, quia si ideo in prescripcione non acquiritur dominium directum quia non directe a iure naturali
exoritur sed indirecte ad ipsum reducitur, videtur quod pari racione nec
in usucapione acquiratur directum dominium, nam sicut prescripcio non
285   videtur a iure naturali directe oriri sed indirecte ad ipsum reduci, ita etiam

---

18/263 sic : sicut *C*   18/263 dicendum : est *add. C*   18/264 tantum *C* : tamen *R*
18/271 dictum : *om. C*   18/272 acquisitum : acquiritur *C*   18/272 immediate : superius *C*   18/273 potest : *om. C*   18/273   patere : patet *C*   18/273 fuerunt : sunt
C   18/273 supra : *om. C*   18/275 in dicto articulo : *om. C*   18/276 nam : quando quidem *C*   18/277 debet : compl *add. et del. R*   18/279 revocetur *C* : revocatur *R*

18/265 Vid. sup. 18/238–61.   18/274 Vid. sup. 16/282–91.

ership. The minor premiss is self-evident, because when we prescribe the use and benefit of a prescribed thing, assuming we share it with no one, we do so to acquire its complete use and benefit, and consequently complete ownership.

But if we understand useful and absolute ownership in the second way, namely, as distinguished by different modes of acquisition, it must be said that prescription confers only useful and not absolute ownership, for even though it confers complete ownership, as has already been established, it confers it not by a direct but by an indirect route. This can be proven by a single argument: ownership that does not arise directly from natural equity is acquired indirectly, although it may be traced back to natural equity indirectly. Now ownership acquired by prescription does not arise directly from natural equity, although it may be traced back to it indirectly; therefore, such ownership is not direct but indirect because it is not acquired directly but indirectly. The major premiss is clear from what has just been said in this article. The minor premiss is also clear from the things said above in the second article. For even though prescription is not contrary to the law of nature, as is clear in the second article, nevertheless it does not so completely accord with it that it does not appear to depart from any rule of the law of nature, for it seems to depart at least from the rule that says that no one should be enriched to the detriment of another. Therefore we should not say that prescription arises directly from the law of nature, but rather may be traced back to it indirectly, and consequently that absolute ownership is not acquired by it, but only useful and indirect ownership.

But a doubt arises that seems to contradict this conclusion, for if prescription does not confer absolute ownership because it does not arise directly from natural law but is only traceable back to it indirectly, it seems, by the same token, that usucapion does not confer absolute ownership. For just as prescription does not seem to arise directly from natural law

et usucapio, ac per consequens utrobique acquiretur tantum dominium utile et non directum, quod patet esse falsum, quia saltem in usucapione acquiritur | ^{R223v} dominium directum.

Ad istam ergo dubitacionem possum dupliciter respondere, uno modo
290   dicendo quod in usucapione acquiritur dominium directum prout directum distinguitur ab utili penes alium modum utendi et ideo quantum ad hoc non erit differencia in acquisicione dominii inter prescripcionem et usucapionem, quia utrobique acquiratur directum dominium isto modo. Alio modo possum respondere dicendo quod in usucapione acquiritur di-
295   rectum dominium non solum quantum ad modum utendi sed eciam quantum ad modum habendi et acquirendi; et quantum ad hoc erit differencia in acquisicione dominii inter prescripcionem et usucapionem, quia in prescripcione acquiretur directum dominium solum uno modo; in usucapione autem secundum duos modos superius pretaxatos, ac per consequens
300   simpliciter possumus dicere quod in usucapione acquiratur dominium directum, quamvis non possimus hoc dicere in prescripcione. Nec obuiat instancia que fuit facta, quia magis innititur equitati iuris naturalis quam faciat ipsa prescripcio racione materie circa quam habet fieri. Fit enim usucapio in rebus mobilibus, que quidem res mobiles, quando negliguntur
305   ultra quam debent, videntur penitus derelinqui, quia per hoc redduntur omnino derelicte tamquam inepte ad humanum usum et ideo usucapere tales res mobiles nil aliud est quam acquirere dominium super res omnino delictas; acquisicio autem dominii super res omnino derelictas directe innititur equitati iuris nature, ut patet ff. *pro derelicto* l. I *Si res.* Non po-
310   test autem hoc dici de prescripcione quia prescripcio fit solum in rebus immobilibus, que quidem res immobiles quantumlibet negligantur non possunt haberi pro derelictis quia per hoc non redduntur inepte ad usum humanum et ideo acquisicio dominii super eas non ita innititur equitati iuris nature sicut acquisicio dominii super res mobiles que usucapiuntur.
315   Patet ergo ex omnibus istis quid sit dicendum quantum ad istum articulum, nam dicendum est quod in prescripcione bone fidei uno modo

---

18/289–90 Ad istam ... dicendo : Ad hoc dupliciter respondetur primo dicendo *C*
18/298 acquiretur : acquiritur *C*   18/303 prescripcio *C* : prescripcione *R*   18/306 derelicte *C* : derelinqui *R*   18/306 tamquam *C* : *om. R*   18/307 super : supra *C*   18/308 super : supra *C*   18/310 prescripcione : que *add. R* : *om. C*

18/309 Dig. 41.7(8).1.

but is only traceable back to it indirectly, so also usucapion, and consequently both confer only useful and indirect ownership, which is clearly false, because at least usucapion confers absolute ownership.

I can respond to this doubt in two ways. First, I can say that usucapion confers absolute ownership in the sense that direct is distinguished from useful ownership with respect to the mode of use, and therefore in this regard there is no difference between the acquisition of ownership in prescription and in usucapion, because each confers absolute ownership in this mode. Second, I can respond by saying that usucapion confers absolute ownership not only with respect to the mode of use but also with respect to the mode of possession and acquisition. In this respect, there will be a difference between the acquisition of ownership by prescription and by usucapion, because prescription confers absolute ownership only in one mode, but usucapion in the two modes enumerated above, and consequently we could simply say that usucapion confers absolute ownership, although we cannot say this of prescription. Nor does the point made earlier present an obstacle, because usucapion is more based on natural equity than prescription by reason of the things whose ownership is in question. For usucapion applies to moveables which, when neglected beyond a certain point, appear completely abandoned, and for this reason utterly unsuited to human use. Therefore to usucapt such things is nothing other than to obtain ownership of completely abandoned things. But to acquire ownership of completely abandoned things is directly based on natural equity, as is clear at Dig. 41.7(8).1. But this cannot be said of prescription, because prescription applies only to immoveables, which, however neglected, cannot be considered abandoned, since they are not thus rendered unsuited to human use. Therefore to acquire ownership of them is not based on natural equity in the way that the ownership of usucapted moveables is.

From all that has been said, therefore, it is clear what should be said with respect to this article, namely, that in one way prescription in good faith

acquiritur dominium directum et utile et alio modo tantum utile et non directum. Restat ergo videre quinto.

<19> <Articulus quintus>

Quintus articulus, in quo ostenditur quod prescribens mala fide equipollet furi vel raptori quantum ad actum intencionis et consciencie.

Vtrum prescribens mala fide debeat censeri cum raptore vel cum fure
5 sive in qua alia specie peccati sit locandus.

Ad huius ergo quesiti evidenciam est primo attendendum que differencia sit inter furtum et rapinam et usuram. Sciendum ergo quod prefata tria se habent per ordinem, quia furtum se habet in plus quam rapina et rapina in plus quam usura. Potest eciam accipi furtum duobus modis: uno modo
10 prout nomine furti intelligitur omnis illicita usurpacio rei aliene, ut habetur XIIII q. V *Penale*, et isto modo in plus se habet furtum quam rapina quia eciam in rapina commictitur illicita usurpacio rei aliene, propter quod accipiens furtum isto modo omnis rapina est furtum, sed non convertitur quia potest accipi furtum alio modo prout dicit usurpacionem rei aliene
15 non solum illicitam sed occultam, secundum quem modum furtum non est rapina nec eciam rapina est furtum, quia licet in rapina fiat usurpacio rei aliene, illa tamen usurpacio rei aliene non est occulta, sicut in furto, immo est publica et violenta. Ex quo apparet immediate quod furtum primo modo acceptum se habet in plus quam rapina et est ea comunius, quia
20 secundum istum modum accipiendi racio furti se extendit ad rapinam et non e converso; propter quod bene dicebatur quod omnis rapina est furtum accipiendo ipsum eo modo; non tamen convertitur et sic dictum est de furto in comparacione ad rapinam.

Ita potest dici suo modo de rapina in comparacione ad usuram. Potest
25 enim accipi rapina duobus modis: uno modo prout nomine rapine importatur usurpacio rei aliene illicita et manifesta et isto modo racio rapine extendit se eciam ad usuram, et per consequens habet se in plus quam

---

18/317 et[2] : *om. C*   18/317 tantum : dominium *add. C*   19/2–3 Quintus … consciencie : *om. C*   19/3 et *scripsi* : *om. R*   19/5 sive : seu *C*   19/6 ergo : *om. C*   19/7 quod *C* : *om. R*   19/12 eciam : et tunc *C*   19/15 occultam : a *add. et del. R*   19/17 aliene[2] : illa tamn usurpacio *add. per ditt. R*   19/19 plus : pluribus *C*   19/21 converso : contra *C*   19/22 convertitur : convertuntur *C*   19/22 sic : sicut *C*   19/27 eciam : *om. C*

19/11 Decretum Grat. C.14 q.5 c.13.

confers absolute and useful ownership, and in another way only useful and indirect ownership. Let us now turn to the fifth article.

19. Article 5

The fifth article, in which it is shown that a prescriber in bad faith is equiv-alent to a thief or robber so far as intention and conscience are concerned.

Should a prescriber in bad faith be classified with the thief or robber, or classified with some other species of sinner?

For the clarification of this question we must first consider the difference between theft, robbery, and usury. It must be understood, therefore, that these three are arranged in an order, for theft is more comprehensive than robbery, and robbery more comprehensive than usury. Theft can be understood in two senses. In one sense, the word 'theft' means any illicit usurpation of another's property, as is held at C.14 q.5 c.13. In this sense, theft is more comprehensive than robbery, for robbery involves the illicit usurpation of another's property, so in this sense every robbery is a theft. But the reverse is not true, for theft can be understood in a different sense as not only the illicit but also the secret usurpation of another's property, and in this sense theft is not robbery nor robbery theft, for even though robbery involves the usurpation of another's property, such usurpation is not secret, as it is in theft, but public and violent. From this, it is quite clear that theft understood in the first sense is more comprehensive than robbery and has more in common with it, for understood in that sense the logic of theft extends to robbery, but not vice versa. For this reason, it was well said that every robbery is a theft understood in the first sense; but the reverse is not true, as has been said of theft by comparison to robbery.

And the same can be said of robbery in comparison with usury, for robbery can be understood in two senses. In one sense, the word 'robbery' means the illicit and manifest usurpation of another's property, and in this sense the logic of robbery includes usury, and consequently is more

racio usure, secundum quem modum videtur loqui de rapina Ambrosius in libro *de bono mortis* et habetur XIIII q. IIII, ubi dicitur quod 'si quis usuram accipit, rapinam facit,' in usura namque fit usurpacio rei aliene illicita et manifesta. Alio vero modo potest accipi rapina prout nomine ipsius importatur usurpacio rei aliene non solum illicita et manifesta sed eciam violenta, secundum quem modum racio rapine non se extendit ad usuram, nam quamvis usurpacio rei aliene que fit in usura sit illicita et manifesta quemadmodum in rapina, non tamen est simpliciter violenta sicut in rapina, quia quando dicta usurpacio fit per rapinam ita est violenta quod nullo modo voluntaria ex parte illius a quo aliquid subtrahitur vel rapitur; nam tunc proprie aliquid rapitur cum per violenciam capitur vel subripitur, idem enim est rapere quod vi aliquid rapere vel subripere. Vsurpacio autem rei aliene que fit per usuram non simpliciter est voluntaria ex parte illius a quo aliquid subtrahitur per usuram, quia ad hoc ut habeat mutuum ultra et consentit aliquid a se subtrahi per usuram quamvis suus consensus sit coactus et extortus, quia non consentit tamquam volens libere exhibere sed consentit coacte tamquam cavens mutuo carere. Et ideo dicta usurpacio per usuram facta videtur habere voluntatem mixtam, quia nec penitus voluntaria nec penitus involuntaria, sed habet aliquid de voluntario nec penitus ex eo quod est ibi consensus et aliquid de involuntario ex eo quod dictus consensus non est liber sed coactus et extortus, propter quod non potest dici simpliciter et penitus violenta sicut usurpacio facta per rapinam, de qua dicebatur supra, quod erat simpliciter et penitus violenta. Ex quibus omnibus apparet quomodo racio rapine se extendit ad usuram et quomodo distinguitur ab ea.

Apparet eciam ulterius ex hiis que sunt dicta in isto articulo quomodo differant prefata tria, scilicet furtum, rapina, et usura, et quot sunt de racione cuiuslibet eorum, nam si bene consideremus queque dicta sunt de racione furti, sunt duo, scilicet quod per ipsum usurpetur res, et hoc est primum; secundum est quod dicta usurpacio sit occulta. Per primum au-

---

19/29 IIII *V* : III *RC*   19/35 violenta *C* : violenti *R*   19/38–9 subripitur : *corr. e* subrapitur *R*   19/39 enim *C* : in *R*   19/41 habeat : habeatur *C*   19/42 ultra : ultro *C*   19/42 et : *om. C*   19/42 suus : eius *C*   19/46–7 nec ... eo : poenes id *C*   19/49 penitus : *om. C*   19/50 et penitus : *om. C*   19/53 ex hiis ... articulo : *om. C*   19/55 queque : quae *C*   19/56–7 hoc est ... est : *om. C*   19/57 sit *C* : ut *R*

19/28–30 Ambrose, *De bono mortis* (ed. cit. p. 752); quoted in Decretum Grat. C.14 q.4 c.10.

comprehensive than usury. Ambrose appears to speak of robbery in this sense in his book *On Death as a Good*, quoted at C.14 q.4 c.10, where he says that 'if anyone accepts usury, he commits robbery,' for usury involves the illicit and manifest usurpation of another's property. But robbery can be understood in another sense to mean not only the illicit and manifest but also the violent usurpation of another's property, and in this sense the logic of robbery does not extend to usury, for even though usury involves the illicit and manifest usurpation of another's property, as in robbery, it is not straightforwardly violent, as in robbery. In robbery, the usurpation is violent in such a way that there is no doubt that the thing is taken or robbed from an unwilling victim, for properly speaking something is robbed when it is seized or snatched with violence, and therefore to rob is to seize or snatch with force. But the usurpation of another's property in usury is not straightforwardly violent, because, for the sake of obtaining a loan, the borrower agrees that something additional be taken from him as usury, although his consent is coerced and extorted, since he does not consent as one who offers willingly but rather constrained by fear of going without the loan. Therefore, usurious usurpation seems to involve a mixed consent that it is not entirely voluntary or involuntary: it is voluntary because the consent, however imperfect, is real, and involuntary because this consent is coerced and extorted, and for this reason usurious usurpation cannot be said to be straightforwardly and completely violent as is the usurpation of robbery, of which we spoke earlier, which is straightforwardly and completely violent. From this it is clear how the logic of robbery extends to usury and how it is distinguished from it.

Moreover, it is clear from what has been said so far how the three – namely, theft, robbery, and usury – differ and how to define the distinctive characteristics of each. For on consideration, the distinctive characteristics of theft are two, namely, that it involves usurpation of another's property, and this is the first, and the second is that the usurpation is secret. The

tem istorum duorum racio furti extenditur ad rapinam; per secundum vero distinguitur ab ea.

60　De racione autem rapine sunt tria. Primum est quod per ipsam usurpetur res aliena, et per hoc collocatur sub furto. Secundum est quod dicta usurpacio sit manifesta, et per hoc rapina distinguitur a furto et extenditur ad usuram. Tercium de racione rapine est quod illa usurpacio sit penitus violenta, et per istud tercium distinguitur ab usura, ut patuit.

65　De racione autem usure sunt eciam tria. Primum est quod per ipsam usurpetur res aliena. Secundum est quod dicta usurpacio sit manifesta, et per ista duo collocatur racio usure sub rapina, quemadmodum rapina sub furto, et ideo ita possumus dicere quod usura est quedam rapina quemadmodum quod rapina est quoddam furtum. Tercium vero de racione | R224r

70　usure est quod illa usurpacio fiat per consensum coactum et extortum racione mutui, ac per consequens nec penitus voluntaria nec penitus violenta, et per istud tercium distinguitur a rapina, ut superius fuit dictum.

Visis autem hiis omnibus, possumus facilius respondere ad illud quod in isto articulo est quesitum; nam cum queritur utrum prescribens mala fide

75　debeat censeri cum fure vel cum raptore vel in aliqua alia specie peccati locandus, statim apparet quod volendo proprie loqui nec cum fure nec eciam cum raptore locandus est, quia peccatum furis vel raptoris consistit principaliter in rei aliene usurpacione, ut potest patere ex dictis, et non in rei aliene detencione. Nam dato quod fur vel raptor in ipso actu usurpa-

80　cionis deprehendantur, furis vel raptoris nomine censebuntur, et utrumque eorum tamquam fur a iudice punietur, non obstante quod in re aliena habuerunt solum actum indebite usurpacionis et nullum actum indebiti usus et detencionis. Peccatum ergo furti vel rapine consistit totaliter, vel saltem principaliter, in rei aliene usurpacione; usus autem rei magis concurrit ibi

85　ut circumstancia aggrauans peccatum quam ut racio principalis, et ideo videmus quod quanto tempore maiori res aliena ab eis detinetur tanto plus a legibus puniuntur.

19/60 est : *om. C*   19/62 hoc : propter *add. R*   19/62 rapina *scripsi* : rapinam *R* : *om. C*
19/63 de racione rapine : vero *C*   19/64 istud tercium : hoc *C*   19/68 ideo ita : sic *C*
19/71 nec[1] : non sit *C*   19/71 penitus[2] : *om. C*   19/72 istud tercium : hoc *C*   19/72 superius : supra *C*   19/73 autem : *om. C*   19/73 facilius : facile *C*   19/75 cum[2] :
om. C   19/76 volendo : loquendo *C*   19/76 loqui : *om. C*   19/77 locandus est *C* :
om. R   19/78 potest patere : patet *C*   19/79 vel : et *C*   19/82 indebiti *C* : indebite
R   19/84 usurpacione *C* : detencione *R*   19/84 usus autem rei *C* : *om. R*   19/85 quam ...
principalis *C* : *om. R*

first extends the logic of theft to robbery; the second distinguishes the two.

Robbery has three distinctive characteristics. The first is that it involves the usurpation of another's property, and this allows it to be classified as theft. The second is that the usurpation is manifest, and this distinguishes it from theft and extends it to usury. The third characteristic is that robbery is entirely violent, and this distinguishes it from usury, as is clear.

Usury also has three distinctive characteristics. The first is that it involves the usurpation of another's property. The second is that the usurpation is manifest, and these two allow it to be classified as robbery, just as robbery was classified as theft, and so we can say that usury is a kind of robbery in the way that robbery is a kind of theft. But the third characteristic of usury is that the usurpation is accomplished by consent, albeit coerced and extorted for the sake of the loan, and consequently the consent is neither completely voluntary nor involuntary; and this third characteristic distinguishes usury from robbery, as was said earlier.

In the light of these points, we are in a position to respond to the question posed at the beginning of the article, for when it is asked whether a prescriber in bad faith should be classified with the thief or robber or with some other species of sinner, it is immediately clear that, properly speaking, he cannot be classified with the thief or the robber because the sin of the thief or robber consists primarily in the usurpation of another's property, as is clear from what has been said, and not in its detention. For if a thief or robber is apprehended in the very act of usurpation, he will be labelled a thief or robber and punished by a judge as a thief, notwithstanding that the property of another was subject only to an act of illicit usurpation and not an act of illicit use and detention. The sin, therefore, of theft or robbery consists entirely, or at least primarily, in the usurpation of another's property; the use of the thing represents only a circumstance aggravating the sin, and therefore we see that the longer the thief detains the property of another the more severely he is punished by the law.

Quapropter apparet immediate quod prescribens mala fide non potest proprie et directe censeri cum fure vel cum raptore, quia peccatum ipsius
90 totaliter vel saltem principaliter in rei aliene detencione consistit. Nam dato quod a principio possessionis bonam fidem haberet, si tamen postea ante tempus prescripcionis mala fides adveniat, possessor et prescriptor male fidei est censendus, nec eius prescripcio curret secundum iura canonica, quamvis currat secundum civilia, ut patuit supra in tercio articulo.
95 Illud ergo quod est solum circumstancia aggravans peccatum in fure et raptore, scilicet, rei aliene detencio, ipsa quidem est peccatum constituens in male fidei possessione et prescripcione.

Ex quo eciam apparet ulterius quod non debet per leges pena infligi prescribentibus mala fide quemadmodum furibus et raptoribus. Nam ideo le-
100 ges furibus et raptoribus penam infligunt quia eorum peccatum non solum inficit conscienciam sed eciam ledit rem publicam, ad cuius conservacionem totus conatus legum insistit. Si enim fures et raptores non punirentur, civilis societas passim totaliter tolleretur, quia pauci vel nulli possent rem suam pacifice possidere. Peccatum autem possidencium et prescriben-
105 cium mala fide, quamvis conscienciam inficiat, rem tamen publicam non commaculat, quia nullius hominis pax ex hoc racionabiliter turbari debet contra illum qui prescripsit, quia perdicio sue rei magis debet ascribi suo proprio defectui, ex eo quod rem suam repetere neglexit, quam defectui et peccato ipsius possidentis vel prescribentis qui mala fide possedit vel
110 mala fide prescripsit. Et ideo patet quod pro tali peccato non debet a legibus pena infligi, immo debet divine providencie puniendum relinqui, quia et multa sunt talia peccata que lex humana dimittit et divine providencie punienda relinquit, tenente beato Augustino in primo *de libero arbitrio*, ubi sic ait: 'lex ista, que regendis civitatibus fertur, multa concedit atque
115 impunita relinquit, que per divinam providenciam vindicantur.'

19/91 principio : patrono *C*   19/91 bonam : veram *C*   19/94 quamvis : quamvis *add. per ditt. R*   19/99 ideo : *om. C*   19/100 furibus et raptoribus : istis *C*   19/102 conatus *C* : cognatus *R*   19/107 ascribi : attribui *C*   19/109 possedit : possidet *C*   19/110 patet *C* : *om. R*   19/111 puniendum : puniendus *C*   19/113 tenente beato Augustino : secundum beatum Augustinum *C*

19/94 Vid. sup. 17/4–162.   19/113–15 Augustine, *De libero arbitrio* 1.40 (ed. cit. p. 13).

Thus it is quite clear that a prescriber in bad faith cannot be properly and simply classified with the thief or the robber, because his sin consists entirely, or at least primarily, in the detention of another's property. For granted that possession at the outset was in good faith, if afterwards, before the period of prescription is complete, bad faith should intervene, he will be condemned as both a possessor and a prescriber in bad faith, nor will his prescription run under canon law, though it will under civil, as is clear above in the third article. Therefore, what is simply a circumstance aggravating the sin in the case of the thief or robber, namely, the detention of another's property, is the constitutive sin in possession and prescription in bad faith.

Furthermore, it is also clear that the penalty the law imposes on prescribers in bad faith should not be the same as the penalty it imposes on thieves and robbers. For the law imposes a penalty on thieves and robbers not only because their sin corrupts the conscience but also because it harms the commonwealth, whose preservation is the whole objective of the law. For if thieves and robbers were not punished, civil society everywhere would be utterly destroyed, because few or none could enjoy their property in peace. But the sin of possessors and prescribers in bad faith, although it corrupts the conscience, does not pollute the commonwealth, because no man's peace is disturbed by the prescriber. Indeed, the negligent owner's loss of his property should be put down to his own fault in neglecting to recover it rather than to the fault and sin of the possessor or prescriber who possesses or prescribes in bad faith. And so it is clear that the law should impose no penalty on this sin, but rather leave punishment to divine providence; for there are many such sins that human law ignores and leaves to divine providence, as the blessed Augustine holds in book 1 of *On Free Will*, where he says that 'it seems to me that the law that is enacted to govern the people rightly tolerates things that divine providence redresses.'

Intelligendum tamen ulterius quod quamvis mala fide possidens vel prescribens non possit proprie et directe censeri cum fure et raptore, interpretative tamen et inductive potest, et debet censeri cum utroque quia etsi
rem publicam non ledit quemadmodum fur vel raptor, suam tamen con-
120   scienciam coram Deo non minus inficit, nam veraciter est fur vel raptor
quantum ad interiorem affectum, quamvis non sit quantum ad exteriorem
actum, et iuxta istum sensum videtur loqui quoddam decretum, quod habetur XIIII q. V: 'si quid,' inquit, 'invenisti et non reddidisti, rapuisti.' Ille
enim qui invenit rem alienam et eam non reddit, quamvis non sit raptor
125   directe et proprie quantum ad actum exteriorem, quia rem alienam non
videtur per violenciam usupare, est tamen raptor interpretative et indirecte quantum ad actum interiorem, quia rem alienam ad modum raptoris
sibi appetit vendicare, et ideo coram Deo ita habet infectam conscienciam
sicut raptor, quia Deus magis ad affectum respicit quam ad actum. Et hoc
130   est quod dicitur in eodem decreto ibidem: 'qui alienum,' inquit, 'negat, si
posset eciam tolleret. Deus enim cor interrogat, non manum.' Concludo
ergo quantum ad id quod in isto articulo principaliter est quesitum quod
prescribens mala fide, quamvis proprie et directe non possit locari in eadem specie peccati cum fure et raptore, interpretative tamen et indirecte
135   potest et debet in eadem specie peccati cum eis locari.

Et ex hoc apparet immediate quod prescribens mala fide quantum ad
peccatum consciencie equipollet furi et raptori, ac per consequens indiget
purgare et rectificare suam conscienciam quemadmodum fur vel raptor.
Sed fur vel raptor non possunt suam conscienciam purgare et rectifica-
140   re nisi per restitucionem, quia 'non dimittitur peccatum nisi restituatur
ablatum,' ut patuit supra per Augustinum, ergo eodem modo prescribens
mala fide ne possit suam conscienciam purgare et rectificare nisi per restitucionem.

Ex hoc apparet ulterius immediate responsio ad principalem questio-

---

19/118 inductive *C* : inducere *R* : indirecte *V*   19/120 inficit *C* : efficit *R*   19/120 vel :
et *C*   19/123 non *C* : si *R*   19/123 reddidisti *C* : reddisti *R*   19/131 interrogat *scripsi* : interroga *R* : intuetur *C*   19/132 quantum ... quesitum : *om. C*   19/133 et : *om.
C*   19/138 quemadmodum : sicut *C*   19/138 vel : et *C*   19/139 vel : et *C*   19/142 ne
possit : non potest *C*   19/144 hoc : his *C*   19/144 ulterius immediate : etiam *C*

19/123 Decretum Grat. C.14 q.5 c.6.   19/130–1 Decretum Grat. C.14 q.5 c.6.   19/140–
1 Decretum Grat. C.14 q.6 c.1; VI *de reg. iur.* 4, *Peccatum*; vid. sup. 11/122–3, 235–9.

Nevertheless, it should be understood that although the possessor or prescriber in bad faith cannot be properly or simply classified with the thief or robber, he can and should be so classified implicitly or indirectly, because even if he does not harm the commonwealth as the thief or robber does, he pollutes his conscience in the sight of God no less than they, for in truth he is a thief or robber by interior disposition, though not by an external act, and this is what the decree found at C.14 q.5 c.6 seems to mean when it says, 'if you have found something and have not returned it, you have stolen it.' For although he who finds another's property and does not return it is not properly and simply a robber by external act – because he does not appear to usurp another's property by violence – he is nevertheless implicitly and indirectly a robber by interior disposition, because he seeks to appropriate another's property in the manner of a robber, and so in the sight of God he corrupts his conscience as the robber does, because God looks more to the disposition than the act. And this is what is said in the same decree: 'Let him bear this, if he can, who denies another's possession. For God questions the heart, not the hand.' With respect to the principal question of this article, I conclude that although a prescriber in bad faith cannot be properly and simply classified in the same species as the thief or robber, nevertheless he can be so classified implicitly and indirectly.

From this it is quite clear that so far as sin of the conscience is concerned, a prescriber in bad faith is equivalent to a thief or a robber, and consequently he must cleanse and correct his conscience as would the thief or robber. Now a thief or a robber can only cleanse and correct his conscience by restitution, because 'sin is not remitted, unless the stolen good is returned,' as is clear above in Augustine. Therefore, by the same token, a prescriber in bad faith cannot cleanse and correct his conscience except by restitution.

From this, furthermore, the response to the principal question is clear,

145　nem, nam si prescribens mala fide tenetur ad restitucionem quemadmo-
　　dum fur vel raptor, ut nunc est ostensum, relinquitur necessario quod sicut
　　fur et raptor non potest tenere vel defendere furtum vel rapinam contra
　　illum cui furatus est vel cui rapuit sine peccato, ita eciam nec ipse prescri-
　　bens mala fide poterit tenere vel defendere rem prescriptam sine peccato
150　contra illum cuius fuit res illa prescripta.

　　Ad argumenta autem in contrarium modo patebit in fine sequentis
　　articuli.

　　Et ita patet quid sit dicendum quantum ad istum articulum. Restat ergo
　　videre sexto.

<20> <Articulus sextus>

　　Sextus articulus, in quo ostenditur quod mala fides adveniens prescripcio-
　　ne completa eam frangit, contra communem opinionem iuristarum.

　　Vtrum mala fides adveniens prescripcione completa tollat prescripcio-
　5　nem et utrum obliget prescribentem ad restitucionem secundum iura cano-
　　nica quemadmodum mala fides preveniens. Ad hoc ergo satis communiter
　　respondent iuriste quod non propter tria. Primo quia si compleatur pre-
　　scripcio bona fide durante tutus videtur reddi prescribens, non solum se-
　　cundum ius civile sed eciam secundum canonicum, ut potest haberi *extra*
10　*de prescripcionibus*, c. *De quarta* et c. *Ad aures*, et XIII q. III c. I et III et c.
　　Dilectio. Posset ergo ex istis dictis ita formari racio: ad illius restitucionem
　　non tenetur prescribens, ad quod restituendum nullo iure cogitur et ad
　　ipsum retinendum utroque iure tutus redditur; sed ad restituendam rem
　　prescriptam bona fide durante, non obstante quod mala fides adveniat,
15　nullo | [R224v] iure cogitur et ad ipsam retinendam utroque iure tutus reddi-
　　tur, ergo ipsam restituere non tenetur.

　　Secundo probatur hoc idem: quia si compleatur prescripcio bona fide

---

19/146 nunc : modo *C*　19/148 cui[2] : *om. C*　19/151 modo *C* : vero *R*　19/153 ita :
sic *C*　19/153 quantum … articulum : in hoc articulo *C*　20/2–3 Sextus … iuristarum :
om. C　20/5 utrum : *om. C*　20/6 quemadmodum : facit *add. C*　20/6 ergo satis : *om.*
C　20/11 ita : talis *C*　20/17 hoc idem : *om. C*

20/7 Cf. Hostiensis, *Summa aurea*, ad X 2.26 *de praescriptione rerum immobilium*, n.3 (ed.
cit. fol. 116ra–b).　20/9–11 X 2.26.4, 6; Decretum Grat. C.16 q.3 c.1, 3, 7.

for if, as we have just shown, a prescriber in bad faith is obliged to make restitution in the way a thief or robber is, it necessarily follows that just as a thief or robber cannot retain or protect a stolen or robbed thing against its owner without sin, neither can the prescriber in bad faith retain or protect without sin the thing prescribed against the real owner.

The arguments to the contrary will be noted at the end of the next article.

And so it is clear what should be said with respect to this article. Let us now turn to the sixth article.

20. Article 6

The sixth article, in which it is shown that bad faith emerging after prescription is complete breaks it, contrary to the opinion of the jurists.

Does bad faith emerging after prescription is complete break it and does it oblige the prescriber to make restitution in accordance with canon law like the prescriber in bad faith discussed above? To this, the jurists commonly respond that he is not, for three reasons. First, because if good faith endures until prescription is complete the prescriber seems secure against an action for restitution, not only according to civil but also according to canon law, as is maintained at X 2.26.4 and 6, and at C.16 q.3 c.1, 3, and 7. From these texts, an argument could be framed to the effect that a prescriber is not obliged to restore something that no law requires him to restore and that both laws render him secure in the retention of. Now the restitution of a thing prescribed in good faith, notwithstanding the emergence of bad faith afterwards, is not required by any law, and both laws render the prescriber secure in his retention of it, therefore he is not obliged to restore it.

Second, the same point is proven thus: when prescription in good faith

durante, iam factum est meum quod erat alienum utriusque iuris auctoritate, non obstante quacumque mala fide postea superveniente. Hoc ergo
20 supposito, potest ita formari secunda racio: nullus tenetur ad restituendum illud quod quandoque fuit alienum et iam factum est suum; sed res prescripta, que quandoque fuit aliena, iam facta est sua utriusque iuris auctoritate, ergo non obstante quacumque mala fide superveniente, non tenetur ad eam restituendam.

25 Tercio probatur hoc idem: quia nullus tenetur restituere illud quod possidet iuste et bene; sed ipse prescribens possidet rem prescriptam iuste et bene, non obstante mala fide superveniente, ergo non tenetur eam restituere. Maior est nota. Minor probatur: quia illud quod habetur de iure possidetur iuste et bene, ac per consequens iam non est alienum, ut patet
30 XIIII q. IIII *Quid dicam*. Ipse autem prescribens habet et possidet rem prescriptam de iure, ergo iuste et bene, et ita non videtur possidere rem alienam sed suam, ac per consequens nec teneri ad restitucionem.

Istis tamen non obstantibus, teneo contrariam viam. Dico ergo quod si compleatur prescripcio bona fide durante et postea superveniat mala
35 fides, tenetur prescribens in foro consciencie ad restituendum rem quam prescripserat, quod probo tripliciter.
Primo sic: prescripcio et temporis determinacio in prescripcione non habet efficaciam nisi procedat secundum iuris eam statuentis intencionem. Sed illa prescripcio cui supervenit mala fides non procedit nec currit iux-
40 ta iuris eam statuentis intencionem, ergo nullam habet efficaciam, et per consequens non potest liberare prescribentem a restitucione. Maior potest esse nota ex ipsa descripcione superius posita in primo articulo. Minorem probo: quia intencio iuris statuentis prescripcionem bone fidei est ut dicta prescripcio cum suo tempore statuto ita currat quod nullam efficaciam in

20/20 potest … racio : sic argumentatur *C*   20/21 iam : est *add. et exp. R*   20/22 iam : vero *add. C*   20/22 facta *C* : factam *R*   20/25 probatur hoc idem : ad idem sic *C* 20/25 quia : *om. C*   20/30 IIII *scripsi* : III *RC*   20/33 Istis : His *C*   20/33 teneo : teneo *add. et exp. R*   20/33 viam : et *add. C*   20/33 ergo : *om. C*   20/34 superveniat *C* : superveniet *R*   20/43 prescripcionem *C* : prescripcionis *R*   20/44 cum : in *C*

20/29–30 Decretum Grat. C.14 q.4 c.11   20/42 Vid. sup. 15/97–149.

is complete, what was once another's property has been made mine by the authority of both laws, notwithstanding any bad faith that emerges after the fact. On this assumption, a second argument could be framed to the effect that no one is obliged to restore something that was once the property of another but has become his. Now a prescribed thing, which was once the property of another, has become the property of the prescriber by the authority of both laws, therefore he is not obliged to restore it, notwithstanding any emergent bad faith.

Third, the same point is proven thus: no one is obliged to restore something he possesses justly and honourably. But the prescriber possesses the prescribed thing justly and honourably, notwithstanding emergent bad faith, therefore he is not obliged to restore it. The major premiss is clear. The minor premiss is proven thus: that which is held by law is possessed justly and honourably, and consequently it is no longer another's property, as is clear at C.14 q.4 c.11. Now a prescriber holds and possesses the prescribed thing by law, therefore justly and honourably, and so he does not appear to possess the property of another, but rather his own, and consequently he is not obliged to make restitution.

Notwithstanding these arguments, I maintain the opposite. I say, then, that if prescription in good faith has run its course and bad faith emerges after the fact, the prescriber is obliged in the forum of conscience to restore the thing he prescribed. I shall prove this in three ways.

First thus: prescription and the time limit in prescription have no efficacy unless they proceed in accordance with the intention of the law that sanctions them. But prescription followed by emergent bad faith does not proceed or run in accordance with the intention of the law that sanctions it, therefore it has no efficacy, and consequently it cannot free the prescriber from the obligation to make restitution. The major premiss is clear from the definition included above in the first article. I prove the minor premiss thus: the intention of the law that sanctions prescription in

45   favore male fidei habeat. Totum tamen contrarium erit in proposito, nam
si ponatur quod completa prescripcione mala fides adveniat et tamen ea
non obstante prescripcio currat, statim sequitur quod mala fides superue-
niens per dictam prescripcionem fuerit favorata, et quod ita sit apparet;
constat namque quod mala fides in possessore facit eum de iure conscien-
50   cie cadere a sua possessione; si ergo mala fides prescripcioni superveniens
non facit prescribentem cadere a possessione rei prescripte, hoc non potest
esse propter aliud nisi quia per dictam prescripcionem recepit favorem,
cuius contrarium ius intendebat.

Secundo probo hoc idem sic: illud ius quod innititur alicui fundamento
55   a quo suam efficaciam trahitur non potest manere suo fundamento cessante. Sed prescripcio bone fidei est quoddam ius quod quidem innititur tanquam fundamento ipsi bone fidei, a qua trahit suam efficaciam acquirendi
dominium, per quam differt a male fidei prescripcione; ergo cessante dicto
fundamento, debet cessare dicta prescripcio. Istud autem fundamentum
60   cessat postquam advenit mala fides, ergo et prescipcio secundum suam efficaciam debet cessare. Nec valet si dicatur quod prescripcio innititur bone
fidei pro illo tempore quo complet suum cursum sed postquam iam suum
cursum compleuit, non indiget ulterius tali fundamento racione sui sed
racione sui effectus, utpote racione acquisicionis dominii, quia videmus
65   quod in prescripcione male fidei dominium non acquiritur, ut dictum fuit
supra in quarto articulo. Dominium autem acquisitum indiget in iure bone
fidei non solum in tempore sue acquisicionis sed eciam pro toto tempore
sue duracionis; nam sicut acquisicio dominii est de iure gencium ita eciam
et sua duracio, ac per consequens utrumque eorum, scilicet dominii dura-
70   cio debet concordare naturali iuri et naturali racioni directe vel indirecte.
Vbi autem ponitur mala fides, neutrum eorum potest concordare naturali
racioni directe vel indirecte quia naturalis racio semper requirit conscienciam rectam. Quapropter dico quod non solum acquisicio dominii que fit
in prescripcione sed ipsius conservacio et duracio que post prescripcionem

---

20/45 favore : favorem *C*   20/48 favorata : procurata *C*   20/52 per : totam *add. et del.*
R   20/54 probo ... sic : ad idem sic *C*   20/56 quidem *C* : quidam *R*   20/58 quam : quod
C   20/60 postquam : postea quam *C*   20/60 advenit : advenerit *C*   20/60 et : etiam *C*

20/65–6 Vid. sup. 18/5–11.

good faith is that prescription and its time limit run in such a way that they provide no benefit to bad faith. But it is quite the opposite in the proposed question, for if it is assumed that bad faith emerges after prescription is complete and that nevertheless the prescription holds, it directly follows that emergent bad faith benefits from prescription. And that this is so is evident, for it is the case that bad faith in a possessor causes him, by the law of conscience, to lose possession; if, therefore, emergent bad faith does not cause a prescriber to lose possession of a prescribed thing, this can only be because it benefits from prescription, the opposite of which is the intention of the law.

Second, I prove this point thus: a law which is based on a foundation from which it takes its efficacy cannot subsist when its foundation has been removed. Now prescription in good faith is such a law based on the foundation of good faith, from which it draws its efficacy to acquire ownership and by which it differs from prescription in bad faith. When this foundation has been removed, the prescription ceases to subsist. Now the foundation is removed when bad faith emerges, therefore the efficacy of prescription ought to cease. Nor does it help to argue that prescription is based on good faith for the time needed to run its course and that afterwards, when it has run its course, it no longer needs such a foundation, not in its own terms, but in terms of its effect, say, the acquisition of ownership, because we see that prescription in bad faith does not confer ownership, as was said earlier in the fourth article. But acquired ownership requires good faith not only during the period of its acquisition, but also for the entire period of its duration; for just as acquisition of ownership derives from the law of nations, so too does its duration, and consequently duration of ownership must agree directly or indirectly with natural law and natural reason. But when we assume bad faith, neither acquisition nor duration can accord directly or indirectly with natural reason, because natural reason always demands an upright conscience. Therefore, I say that not only does the acquisition of ownership accomplished by prescrip-

75   permanet indiget bona fide si naturali iuri et racioni debeat concordare; statim ergo cum post prescripcionem advenit mala fides, dominium, quod prius videbatur acquisitum a naturali iure et racione incipit discordare, et per consequens tenetur prescribens tanquam non dominus in foro consciencie ad restitucionem.

80   Tercio probo hoc idem sic: suppono namque quod fides erronea debet mutari et corrigi per fidem veram, quia semper veritas est correctiva erroris. Hoc ergo supposito, arguo sic: sicut fides erronea mutatur et corrigitur per fidem veram, ita et illud quod secutum est ad talem fidem erroneam debet per eamdem fidem veram corrigi et mutari. Sed si mala fides adveniat

85   post prescripcionem, fides adveniens erit fides vera; fides vero precedens erit fides erronea et ideo fides precedens mutabitur et corrigetur per fidem sequentem. Pari ergo racione et illud quod secutum est ad talem fidem erroneam, scilicet prescripcio et acquisicio dominii, mutabitur et corrigetur per dictam fidem veram advenientem, ac per consequens illud quod

90   videbatur prescriptum mutabitur in non prescriptum, et id quod videbatur ipsius prescribentis non amplius videbitur ipsius esse, et ita tenebitur ad restitucionem in foro consciencie.

    Raciones autem contrarie opinionis non videntur michi concludere et ideo respondebo ad eas per ordinem.

95   Ad primam dico quod si mala fides post prescripcionem adveniat, non cogitur prescribens ab aliquo iure positivo in foro contencioso ut restituat; cogitur tamen a iure divino et a iure naturali in foro consciencie, et ideo duo iura positiva, quamvis reddant eum tutum in foro litigii coram iudice, non tamen in foro consciencie coram Deo.

100   Occurrit tamen hic unum dubium, nam dicebatur supra in tercio articulo quod ius canonicum ita intendit de foro litigii quod tamen finaliter remictit ad forum consciencie, ac per consequens videtur quod possit reddere tutum ipsum prescribentem quantum ad utrumque forum. Ad hoc

---

20/75 permanet *C* : *om. R*   20/75 concordare *C* : cordare *R*   20/77 prius : enim *add. et exp. R*   20/80 probo ... sic : ad idem *C*   20/80 suppono *C* : supono *R*   20/82 Hoc ergo : Quo *C*   20/102 quod possit : *om. C*   20/102 possit : re *add. et exp. R*

20/100–1 Vid. sup. 17/140–61.

tion but also its preservation and duration after prescription require good faith if it is to accord with natural law and natural reason. Therefore, when bad faith emerges after prescription, what earlier seemed to have been acquired by natural law and reason immediately begins to depart from them, and consequently the prescriber is obliged in the forum of conscience to make restitution.

Third, I prove this point thus: I assume that mistaken faith should be changed and corrected by true faith. Assuming this, I argue as follows: just as mistaken faith should be corrected by true faith, that which leads to mistaken faith should be corrected and changed by the true. But if bad faith should emerge after prescription, then the emergent faith would be true, and the earlier faith would be mistaken, and therefore the earlier faith will be changed and corrected by what follows. By the same logic, then, that which leads to the mistaken faith, namely prescription and acquisition of ownership, will be changed and corrected by the emergent faith, and consequently that which appeared to have been prescribed will be changed into something not prescribed, and that which seemed to belong to the prescriber will no longer be his, and thus he is obliged to make restitution in the forum of conscience.

The arguments for the contrary opinion do not seem to me conclusive and so I shall respond to them in order.

To the first argument I say that if bad faith should emerge after prescription, the prescriber is not obliged in the forum of conscience by any positive law to make restitution; he is, however, obliged in the forum of conscience by divine and natural law. Therefore, although the two laws render him secure in a court of law before a judge, they do not in the forum of conscience in the presence of God.

Nevertheless, a question arises in this connection, for it was said earlier in the third article that canon law subordinates the court of law to the court of conscience, and consequently it seems that it could render the prescriber secure in both fora. The response to this argument is that canon

ergo dicendum quod ius canonicum potest hominem reddere tutum in
105   utroque foro non universaliter quantum ad omnes actus et eventus, sed
solum quantum ad illos qui contingunt, ut in pluribus, ita quod semper
possint ad utrumque forum deduci, scilicet ad forum litigii et ad forum
consciencie; et ideo si sint aliqui tuti eventus non possibiles dedu- | R225r
–ci ad forum litigii propter quamcumque causam, illos relinquit ius cano-
110   nicum sentenciandos in foro consciencie ipsi Deo. Talis autem est casus
quem habemus in proposito, nam quod mala fides completa prescripcione
adveniat, hoc est rarissimum nec est possibile deduci ad forum litigii, quia
nimis esset difficile et quandoque forte impossibile post tanti temporis
cursum malam fidem probari, et ideo talis casus merito relinquitur soli
115   Deo sentencianti et consciencie accusanti et testificanti.

Ad secundam vero racionem alterius opinionis dicendum quod nisi prescripcio sit completa ante adventum male fidei, res prescripta efficitur mea
auctoritate utriusque iuris, siquidem in foro consciencie et in foro litigii,
quia non compellor ab aliquo iure positivo eam restituere. Possum eciam
120   ulterius dicere quod res illa prescripta efficitur mea secundum iuris paten-
tem promulgacionem et non secundum iuris latentem intencionem, nam
talis est intencio iuris latens, scilicet ut taliter legum statuta observentur
quod tamen a consciencia non discordent.

Per hoc eciam apparet quid sit dicendum ad terciam racionem, ille
125   namque qui possidet rem prescriptam, non obstante mala fide superveniente, ipse quidem possidet de iure et iuste et bene quantum ad iuris intencionem latentem. Item possumus dicere quod possidet de iure et iuste
et bene in foro litigii, non autem in foro consciencie. Possumus eciam dare
aliam solucionem dicendo quod talis res prescripta, ubi supervenit mala
130   fides, quamvis possideatur iuste et bene de iure civili et canonico, non tamen de iure naturali et divino, et hoc sufficit ad obligandum eum in foro
consciencie ad restitucionem.

Ex hiis autem que dicta sunt potest patere quid sit dicendum ad argumentum principale questionis, quia si Ticius rem Sempronii mala fide pre-

---

20/104 ergo : *om. C*   20/107 ad forum[1 et 2] : *om. C*   20/113 nimis : multum
C   20/113 quandoque : *om. C*   20/114 probari : probare C   20/117 efficitur : m
add. et exp. R   20/118 foro[1] : canonico *add. C*   20/118 et C : sed R   20/119 eam : ea
C   20/121 latentem : *e* latencionem *corr. R*   20/122 taliter : totaliter C   20/129 solucionem : responsionem C   20/130–1 civili … iure C : *om. per hom. R*   20/133 que dicta
sunt : *om. C*   20/134 principale : in principio C   20/134 Ticius : quis C

law cannot render a man secure in both fora universally with regard to all acts and consequences, but only with regard to those which are such that they can be referred to either forum, namely, to the courts or to the forum of conscience. Therefore, if some consequences cannot be referred to the law courts for whatever reason, canon law leaves them to be adjudicated in the forum of conscience by God himself. But such is the case in the question, for the emergence of bad faith after prescription has been completed is extremely rare and impossible to refer to a court, because it is exceedingly difficult, sometimes impossible, after the lapse of so much time to prove bad faith, and therefore it rightly leaves such cases to the sentence of God, and to the accusation and witness of the conscience.

The response to the second argument in support of the opposing opinion is that unless prescription is completed before the emergence of bad faith, the prescribed thing is made mine by the authority of both laws, that is, in the forum of conscience and in the courts, because I cannot be compelled by any positive law to restore it. But I can also say further that the prescribed thing is made mine by the public promulgation of the law, not by its hidden intention, for the hidden intention of the law is that the decrees of the law be observed, not that they violate the conscience.

From this it is also clear what should be said in response to the third argument, that he who possesses a prescribed thing, notwithstanding emergent bad faith, possesses it by right, and justly and honourably according to the hidden intention of the law. Again, we can say that he possesses it by right, and justly and honourably in a court of law but not in the forum of conscience. We can also offer a different solution by saying that although the prescribed thing is possessed justly and honourably by civil and canon law, once bad faith emerges, it is not so possessed by natural and divine law, and this is sufficient to compel him to make restitution in the forum of conscience.

From the things which have been said, it is possible to spell out how we should respond to the principal question. If Titius prescribes the property

135   scribat non poterit eam tenere vel defendere sine peccato. Ad probacionem
vero cum dicitur quod id quod sit iure prescripcionis sit sine peccato, dico
quod verum est ex ea parte ex qua prescripcio non habet adnexum peccatum. Nunc autem prescripcio male fidei ex parte prescribentis habet adnexum peccatum nec tamen propter hoc sequitur quod ius civile prestet
140   favorem alicui peccato, quia non induxit eam in favorem illius qui mala
fide prescribit sed in punicionem illius qui rem suam repetere negligit, et
ideo dicebatur supra in tercio articulo istius questionis quod prescripcio
male fidei in quantum se tenet in parte prescribentis est a iure civile solum
permissa et non inducta; in quantum vero se tenet ex parte negligentis est
145   ab eodem iure non solum permissa sed eciam inducta. Et ita patet quid sit
dicendum quantum ad istum articulum et quantum ad totam questionem
principalem.

Expliciunt questiones de usura et prescripcione disputate et determinate
Parisius a fratre Gerardo de Senis, in sacra scriptura magistro, fratrum he-
150   remitarum ordinis sancti Augustini.

20/148 Expliciunt : Explicatae sunt *C*   20/149 Parisius : Parisiis *C*

20/143 Vid. sup. 17/38–63.

of Sempronius in bad faith, he cannot retain or protect it without sin. By way of proof, when it is said that something which is had by right of prescription is without sin, I say that this is true inasmuch as prescription is not conjoined with sin. Now prescription in bad faith is conjoined with sin on the part of the prescriber, but it does not follow from this that civil law shows favour to sin, because it did not introduce prescription for the benefit of the prescriber in bad faith, but to punish him who neglects to recover his property. Therefore it was said above in the third article of the question that prescription in bad faith is simply permitted by civil law with respect to the prescriber, not introduced in his favour; with regard to the negligent it is both permitted and introduced. And thus it is clear what should be said with respect to the article and to the entire principal question.

Here end the questions on usury and prescription disputed and determined at Paris by Brother Gerard of Siena, master of sacred scripture, of the hermit brothers of the order of Saint Augustine.

Bibliography

Manuscripts

L: Leipzig, Universitätsbibliothek, 894
R: Rome, Biblioteca Angelica, 625
W: Vienna, Österreichische Nationalbibliothek, Vindob. 4151

Printed Primary Sources

Ambrose. *De bono mortis*. Corpus Scriptorum Ecclesiasticorum Latinorum 32. Ed. Karl Schenkl. 2 vols. Prague and Vienna: F. Tempsky, 1896–7.

Aristotle. *Ethica Nichomachea (Ethica Nichomachea: translatio Roberti Grosseteste Lincolniensis sive Liber ethicorum recensio pura)*. Ed. René-Antoine Gauthier. Aristoteles Latinus 26.1–3, fasc. 4. Leiden: Brill, 1973.

– *Politica, Libri I–II.11: Translatio imperfecta interprete Guillelmo de Moerbeka(?)*. Ed. Pierre Michaud-Quantin. Aristoteles Latinus 29.1. Bruges and Paris: Desclée de Brouwer, 1961.

– *Politics*. Trans. Benjamin Jowett. In *The Basic Works of Aristotle*. ed. Richard McKeon, 1113–1316. New York: Random House, 1941.

Augustine. *De civitate Dei*. Corpus Scriptorum Ecclesiasticorum Latinorum 40. Ed. Emanuel Hoffmann. Vienna: F. Tempsky, 1900.

– *Confessionum libri tredecim*. Corpus Scriptorum Ecclesiasticorum Latinorum 33. Ed. Pius Knöll. Vienna: F. Tempsky, 1896.

– *De libero arbitrio libri tres*. Corpus Scriptorum Ecclesiasticorum Latinorum 74. Ed. William McAllen Green. Vienna: F. Tempsky, 1956.

Avitus. *Alcimi Ecdicii Aviti Viennensis episcopi opera quae supersunt*. Ed. Rudolf Peiper. Monumenta Germaniae Historica, Auctores antiquissimi 6.2. Berlin: Weidmann, 1883.

Biblia sacra cum glossa ordinaria. 6 vols. Paris, 1590.

Bonaventure. *Collationes de decem praeceptis. Opera omnia.* Vol. 5. Quaracchi: Ex typographia Collegii S. Bonaventurae, 1891.

– *Commentaria in quatuor libros sententiarum. Opera omnia.* Vol. 3. Quaracchi: Ex typographia Collegii S. Bonaventurae, 1887.

Corpus iuris canonici. Ed. Emil Friedberg. 2 vols. Leipzig, 1879; repr. Graz: Akademische Druck und Verlaganstalt, 1959.

Corpus iuris civilis. Ed. Theodor Mommsen et al. 3 vols. Berlin: Weidmann, 1915–28.

Corpus iuris civilis Iustinianei cum commentariis Accursii. 6 vols. Lyons, 1627; repr. Frankfurt-am-Main: Vico Verlag, 2006.

Decretales Gregorii IX pontificis [cum glossis]. Lyons, 1559.

Decretum divi Gratiani [una cum glossis]. Lyons, 1560.

Dante Alighieri. *The Divine Comedy.* Trans. and comm. Charles S. Singleton. Bollingen Series 80. 6 vols. Princeton: Princeton University Press, 1970.

– *The Divine Comedy.* Trans. Dorothy L. Sayers. 3 vols. Harmondsworth: Penguin, 1949–62.

Denifle, Heinrich, Emile Châtelain, et al., eds. *Chartularium Universitatis Parisiensis.* 4 vols. Paris: Delalain, 1889–97.

Digest of Justinian. Ed. and trans. Alan Watson et al. 4 vols. Philadelphia: University of Pennsylvania Press, 1985.

Dino of Mugello. *Commentaria in regulas iuris.* Venice, 1570.

Francis (Jorge Mario Borgoglio). *Apostolic Exhortation 'Evangelii Gaudium'* (24 November 2013). Vatican City: Vatican Press, 2013.

– *Encyclical Letter 'Laudato si'* (24 May 2015). Vatican City: Vatican Press, 2015.

Gerard of Siena. *Tractatus de usuris et de praescriptionibus.* Ed. Angelo Vancio. Cesena, 1630.

Giles of Rome. *Quodlibeta.* Louvain, 1646; repr. Frankfurt am Main: Minerva, 1966.

Giovanni d'Andrea (Iohannes Andreae). *In sextum Decretalium commentaria et in titulum de regulis iuris novella commentaria.* Venice, 1581; repr. Turin: Bottega D'Erasmo, 1963.

Gottofredo da Trani. *Summa super titulis Decretalium.* Lyons, 1519; repr. Darmstadt: Scientia Verlag Aalen, 1968.

Gregory the Great. *Moralia in Iob.* In Corpus Christianorum Series Latina 143B. Ed. M. Adriaen. Turnhout: Brepols, 1985.

Guido de Baisio. *Rosarium.* Lyons, 1549; repr. Frankfurt am Main: Vico Verlag, 2008.

Hamesse, Jacqueline, ed. *Les Auctoritates Aristotelis: un florilège médiéval: étude historique et édition critique.* Louvain: Publications universitaires, 1974.

Hostiensis (Henricus de Segusio). *Summa aurea*. Lyons, 1537; repr. Frankfurt am Main: Vico Verlag, 2009.

Innocent IV (Sinibaldo dei Fieschi). *In quinque libros Decretalium commentaria.* Venice, 1570; repr. Frankfurt-am-Main: Vico Verlag, 2008.

Mann, Thomas. *Buddenbrooks*. Trans. H.T. Lowe-Porter. New York: Random House, 1924.

Papias. *Elementarium doctrinae erudimentum*. Venice, 1491.

Plato. *The Collected Dialogues of Plato*. Ed. Edith Hamilton and Huntington Cairns. Bollingen Series 71. Princeton: Princeton University Press, 1961.

Pseudo-Augustine. *Sermo* 221. Patrologiae cursus, Series Latina 29. Paris: J.-P. Migne, 1865.

Raymond of Penyafort. *Summa de poenitentia et matrimonio cum glossis Ioannis de Friburgo* (*recte* Guillelmi Redonensis). Rome, 1603; repr. Farnborough: Gregg Press, 1967.

Sextus decretalium liber [cum glossis]. Lyons, 1559.

Thomas Aquinas. *Opera omnia*. Vol. 9: *Secunda secundae Summae Theologiae*. Rome: S.C. Propaganda Fide, 1897.

– *Opera omnia*. Vol. 47: *Sententia libri Ethicorum*. Rome: Ad Sanctae Sabinae, 1969.

– *Opera omnia*. Vol. 48: *Sententia libri Politicorum*. Rome: Ad Sanctae Sabinae, 1971.

Walther, Hans, ed. *Proverbia sententiaeque Latinitatis Medii Aevi: Lateinische Sprichwörter und Sentenzen des Mittelalters in alphabetischer Anordnung.* 9 vols. Göttingen: Vandenhoeck und Ruprecht, 1963–86.

William of Auxerre. *Summa aurea*. Ed. Jean Ribaillier. Spicilegium Bonaventurianum 18B. 2 vols. Paris: CNRS; and Rome: Editiones Collegii S. Bonaventurae ad Claras Aquas, 1986.

Secondary Sources Cited

Armstrong, Lawrin. 'Law, Ethics and Economy: Gerard of Siena and Giovanni d'Andrea on Usury.' In *Money, Markets and Trade in Late Medieval Europe: Essays in Honour of John H.A. Munro*, Later Medieval Europe 1, ed. Lawrin Armstrong, Ivana Elbl, and Martin Elbl, 41–58. Leiden and Boston: Brill, 2007.

– *Usury and Public Debt in Early Renaissance Florence: Lorenzo Ridolfi on the 'Monte Comune.'* Texts and Studies 144. Toronto: Pontifical Institute of Mediaeval Studies, 2003.

– 'Usury, Conscience, and Public Debt: Angelo Corbinelli's Testament of 1419.' In *A Renaissance of Conflicts: Visions and Revisions of Law and Society in Italy*

and Spain, ed. John A. Marino and Thomas Kuehn, 173–240. Toronto: Centre for Reformation and Renaissance Studies, 2004.

Arrighi, Giovanni. *Adam Smith in Beijing: Lineages of the Twenty-First Century.* London: Verso, 2007.

– *The Long Twentieth Century: Money, Power, and the Origins of Our Times.* London: Verso, 1994.

Aston, T.H., and C.H.E. Philpin, eds. *The Brenner Debate: Agrarian Class Structure and Economic Development in Pre-Industrial Europe.* Cambridge: Cambridge University Press, 1985

Barile, Nicola. 'Credito, usura, prestito a interesse.' *Reti Medievali Rivista*, Italia, 11 June 2010. Available at: http://www.rmojs.unina.it/index.php/rm/article/view/urn%3Anbn%3Ait%3Aunina-3044.

– 'Il dibattito sul prestito a interesse negli ultimi trent'anni fra probabilisti e rigoristi: Un bilancio storiografico.' *Nuova rivista storica* 92.3 (December 2008): 835–74.

Böckenförde, Ernst-Wolfgang. 'Woran der Kapitalismus krankt.' *Suddeutsche Zeitung*, 24 April 2009.

Bourdieu, Pierre. *Acts of Resistance: Against the New Myths of Our Time.* Trans. Richard Nice. Oxford: Polity Press, 1998.

– *La misère du monde.* Paris: Seuil, 1998.

Braudel, Fernand. *Civilization and Capitalism, 15th to 18th Century.* Trans. Siân Reynolds. 3 vols. New York: Harper and Row, 1981–4.

Buckland, William. *A Textbook of Roman Law from Augustus to Justinian.* Cambridge: Cambridge University Press, 1921.

The Cambridge History of Capitalism. Vol. 1: *The Rise of Capitalism: From Ancient Origins to 1848.* Ed. Larry Neal and Jeffrey G. Williamson. Cambridge: Cambridge University Press, 2014.

Ceccarelli, Giovanni. '"Whatever" Economics: Economic Thought in *Quodlibeta*.' In *Theological Quodlibeta in the Middle Ages*, vol. 1: *The Thirteemth Century*, ed. Christopher Schabel, 475–505. Leiden and Boston: Brill, 2006.

Chang, Ha-Joon. *Economics: The User's Guide.* London: Penguin Books, 2014.

Chesnais, François. *Les dettes illégitimes: Quand les banques font main basse sur les politiques publiques.* Paris: Éditions Raisons d'Agir, 2011.

Courtenay, William J. 'The Instructional Programme of the Mendicant Convents at Paris in the Early Fourteenth Century.' In *The Medieval Church: Universities, Heresy, and the Religious Life. Essays on Honour of Gordon Leff*, ed. Peter Biller and Barrie Dobson, 77–92. Woodbridge: Boydell Press, 1999.

– 'The Sentences Commentary of Gerard of Siena, O.E.S.A.: Manuscripts and Questions.' *Augustiniana* 59 (2009): 247–300.

Crouch, Colin. *The Strange Non-Death of Neoliberalism*. Cambridge and Malden, MA: Polity Press, 2011.

Dale, Gareth. *Karl Polanyi: The Limits of the Market*. Cambridge: Polity Press, 2010.

Davis, James. *Medieval Market Morality: Life, Law and Ethics in the English Marketplace, 1200–1500*. Cambridge: Cambridge University Press, 2012.

Derbes, Anne, and Mark Sandona. *The Usurer's Heart: Giotto, Enrico Scrovegni, and the Arena Chapel in Padua*. University Park: Pennsylvania State University Press, 2008.

Derolez, Albert. *The Palaeography of Gothic Manuscript Books from the Twelfth to the Early Sixteenth Century*. Cambridge and New York: Cambridge University Press, 2003.

Duménil, Gérard, and Dominique Lévy. *The Crisis of Neoliberalism*. Cambridge, MA, and London: Harvard University Press, 2011.

Fontaine, Laurence. *The Moral Economy: Poverty, Credit, and Trust in Early Modern Europe*. Cambridge: Cambridge University Press, 2014.

Glorieux, Palémon. *La littérature quodlibétique*. Vol. 2. Paris: J. Vrin, 1935.

Graeber, David. *Debt: The First 5000 Years*. New York: Melville House, 2011.

Hamesse, Jacqueline. 'Theological *Quaestiones Quodlibetales.*' In *Theological Quodlibeta in the Middle Ages*, vol. 1: *The Thirteenth Century*, ed. Christopher Schabel, 17–48. Leiden and Boston: Brill, 2006.

Harcourt, Bernard E. *The Illusion of Free Markets: Punishment and the Myth of Natural Order*. Cambridge, MA, and London: Harvard University Press, 2011.

Harding, Jeremy. 'Islam and the Armies of Mammon.' *London Review of Books* 31 no. 9 (2009): 19–22.

– 'The Money That Prays.' *London Review of Books* 31 no. 8 (2009): 6–10.

Harvey, David. *A Brief History of Neoliberalism*. Oxford and New York: Oxford University Press, 2005.

– *The Limits to Capital*. London and New York: Verso, 2006.

– *Seventeen Contradictions and the End of Capitalism*. Oxford and New York: Oxford University Press, 2014.

Helssig, Rudolf. *Katalog der lateinischen und deutschen Handschriften der Universitäts-Bibliothek zu Leipzig*. Vol. 3: *Die juristischen Handschriften*. Leipzig: O. Harrassowitz, 1905.

Kerridge, Eric. *Usury, Interest, and the Reformation*. Aldershot: Variorum, 2002.

Kirshner, Julius. 'Reading Bernardino's Sermon on the Public Debt.' In *Atti del simposio internazionale cateriniano-bernardiniano: Siena, 17–20 aprile 1980*, ed. Domenico Maffei and Paolo Nardi, 547–622. Siena: Accademia senese degli intronati, 1982.

Klein, Naomi. *This Changes Everything: Capitalism vs. the Climate*. Toronto: Knopf, 2014.

Krugman, Paul. *End This Depression Now*. New York and London: Norton, 2012.

Kuehn, Thomas. 'Conflicting Conceptions of Property in Quattrocento Florence: A Dispute over Ownership in 1425–26.' In *Law, Family, and Women: Toward a Legal Anthropology of Renaissance Italy*, ed. Thomas Kuehn, 101–26. Chicago and London: University of Chicago Press, 1991.

Kunkel, Benjamin. *Utopia or Bust: A Guide to the Present Crisis*. London and New York: Verso, 2014.

Langholm, Odd. *The Aristotelian Analysis of Usury*. Bergen, Oslo, Stavanger, and Tromsø: Universitetsforlaget, 1984.

– *Economics in the Medieval Schools: Wealth, Exchange, Value, Money and Usury According to the Paris Theological Tradition, 1200–1350*. Studien und Texte zur Geistesgeschichte des Mittelalters 29. Leiden, New York, and Cologne: Brill, 1992.

– *The Legacy of Scholasticism in Economic Thought: Antecedents of Choice and Power*. Cambridge: Cambridge University Press, 1998.

– 'The Medieval Schoolmen (1200–1400).' In *Ancient and Medieval Economic Ideas and Concepts of Justice*, ed. S.T. Lowry and B. Gordon, 439–501. Leiden, New York, and Cologne: Brill, 1998.

Lazzarato, Maurizio. *The Making of Indebted Man: An Essay on the Neoliberal Condition*. Trans. Joshua David Jordan. Semiotext(e) Intervention Series 13. Los Angeles: Semiotext(e), 2012.

Le Goff, Jacques. *Your Money or Your Life: Economy and Religion in the Middle Ages*. Trans. Patricia Ranum. New Haven and London: Yale University Press, 1988.

Marx, Karl. *Capital: A Critique of Political Economy, Volume 1*. Trans. Ben Fowkes. Harmondsworth: Penguin, 1976.

– *Capital: A Critique of Political Economy, Volume 3*. Trans. David Fernbach. Harmondsworth: Penguin, 1981.

– *Critique of the Gotha Programme*. In *Karl Marx–Frederick Engels Collected Works*, vol. 24: *Marx and Engels 1874–1883*, 75–99. London: Lawrence and Wishart, 1989.

– *Das Kapital: Kritik der politischen Ökonomie, Dritter Band*. Karl Marx–Friedrich Engels Werke 25. Berlin: Dietz Verlag, 1973.

McLaughlin, T.P. 'The Teaching of the Canonists on Usury (XII, XIII and XIV Centuries).' *Mediaeval Studies* 1 (1939): 81–147; 2 (1940): 1–22.

Mirowski, Philip. *Never Let a Serious Crisis Go to Waste: How Neoliberalism Survived the Financial Meltdown*. London and New York: Verso, 2013.

Narducci, Enrico. *Catalogus codicum manuscriptorum praeter graecos et orientales in Bibliotheca Angelica*. Vol. 1. Rome: L. Cecchini, 1893.

Nicholas, Barry. *An Introduction to Roman Law*. Oxford: Clarendon, 1962.

Noonan, John T., Jr. *The Scholastic Analysis of Usury*. Cambridge, MA: Harvard University Press, 1957.

Polanyi, Karl. *The Great Transformation: The Political and Economic Origins of Our Time*. Boston: Beacon Press, 2001.

Pavone, Claudio. *A Civil War: A History of the Italian Resistance*. Trans. Peter Levy. London: Verso, 2013.

Piketty, Thomas. *Capital in the Twenty-First Century*. Trans. Arthur Goldhammer. Cambridge, MA, and London: Belknap Press of the Harvard University Press, 2014.

Reinert, Erik S. *How Rich Countries Got Rich and Why Poor Countries Stay Poor*. London: Constable and Robinson, 2007.

Robbins, Lionel. *An Essay on the Nature and Significance of Economic Science*. 2nd ed. London: Macmillan, 1935.

Robinson, Jonathan. *William of Ockham's Early Theory of Property Rights in Context*. Studies in Medieval and Reformation Traditions 166. Leiden and Boston: Brill, 2012.

Rubin, Jeff. *The End of Growth*. Toronto: Random House, 2012.

Sandel, Michael J. *What Money Can't Buy: The Moral Limits of Markets*. New York: Farrar, Strauss and Giroux, 2012.

Schabel, Christopher, and William J. Courtenay. 'Augustinian *Quodlibeta* after Giles of Rome.' In *Theological Quodlibeta in the Middle Ages*, vol. 2: *The Fourteenth Century*, ed. Christopher Schabel, 545–68. Leiden and Boston: Brill, 2007.

Schulte, Johann Friedrich von. *Die Geschichte der Quellen und Literatur des canonischen Rechts*. 3 vols. Stuttgart: F. Enke, 1875–80; repr. Graz: Akademische Druck- und Verlagsanstalt, 1956.

Schüssler, Rudolf. 'Business Morality at the Dawn of Modernity: The Cases of Angelo Corbinelli and Cosimo de' Medici.' In *Between Creativity and Norm-Making: Tensions in the Early Modern Era*, ed. Sigrid Muller and Cornelia Schweiger, 131–47. Studies in Medieval and Reformation Traditions 165. Leiden: Brill, 2013.

Spicciani, Amleto. *Capitale e interesse tra mercatura e povertà nei teologi e canonisti dei secoli XIII–XV*. Rome: Jouvence, 1990.

Streeck, Wolfgang. *Buying Time: The Delayed Crisis of Democratic Capitalism*. Trans. Patrick Camiller. London and New York: Verso, 2014.

– 'Markets and Peoples.' *New Left Review* 73 (January–February 2012): 63–71.

– 'Markets versus Voters?' *New Left Review* 71 (September–October 2011): 5–29.

Tabulae codicum manu scriptorum praeter graecos et orientales in Bibliotheca Palatina Vindobonensi asservatorum. Vol. 3: *Cod. 3501–Cod. 5000.* Vienna: Academia Caesarea Vindobonensis, 1869; repr. Graz: Akademische Druck und Verlaganstalt, 1965.

Tawney, Richard Henry. *Religion and the Rise of Capitalism.* London: J. Murray, 1936.

Thompson, E.P. 'The Moral Economy of the English Crowd in the Eighteenth Century.' In *Customs in Common,* ed. E.P. Thompson, 185–258. New York: New Press, 1993.

Tierney, Brian. *Liberty and Law: The Idea of Permissive Natural Law, 1100–1800.* Studies in Medieval and Early Canon Law 12. Washington, DC: Catholic University of America, 2014.

Todeschini, Giacomo. *Richezza francescana. Dalla povertá volontaria alla societá di mercato.* Bologna: Il Mulino, 2004.

Weber, Max. *The Protestant Ethic and the 'Spirit' of Capitalism and Other Writings.* Trans. Peter Baehr and Gordon C. Wells. Harmondsworth: Penguin, 2002.

Winters, Jeffrey A. *Oligarchy.* Cambridge and New York: Cambridge University Press, 2011.

Zumkeller, Adolar. 'Die Augustinerschule des Mittelalters: Vertreter und philosophisch-theologische Lehre.' *Analecta Augustiniana* 27 (1964): 167–262.

– *Manuskripte von Werken der Autoren des Augustiner-Eremitenordens in mitteleuropäischen Bibliotheken.* Cassiciacum 20. Würzburg: Augustinus-Verlag, 1966.

Index of Citations

1. Canon Law

2. Roman Law

3. Scripture

4. Classical, Patristic, and Scholastic

General Index

Toronto Studies in Medieval Law

General Editor:
LAWRIN ARMSTRONG

Editorial Board
PÉTER CARDINAL ERDŐ
JULIUS KIRSHNER
SUSANNE LEPSIUS
GIOVANNI ROSSI

1. *The Politics of Law in Late Medieval and Renaissance Italy*, edited by Lawrin Armstrong and Julius Kirshner
2. *Marriage, Dowry, and Citizenship in Late Medieval and Renaissance Italy,* Julius Kirshner
3. *The Idea of a Moral Economy: Gerard of Siena on Usury, Restitution, and Prescription,* Lawrin Armstrong

Milton Keynes UK
Ingram Content Group UK Ltd.
UKHW030701021124
450385UK00002B/36/J